Prince John Magruder

Prince John Magruder

His Life and Campaigns

Paul D. Casdorph

John Wiley & Sons, Inc.
New York • Chichester • Brisbane • Toronto • Singapore • Weinheim

Copyright © 1996 by Paul D. Casdorph

Published by John Wiley & Sons, Inc.

Library of Congress Cataloging-in-Publication Data

Casdorph, Paul D.
    Prince John Magruder : his life and campaigns / Paul D. Casdorph.
        p.   cm.
    Includes bibliographical references (p.) and index.
    ISBN 0-471-15941-7 (cloth : alk. paper)
    1. Magruder, John Bankhead, 1807–1871.   2. Generals—Confederate
States of America—Biography.   3. Confederate States of America.
Army—Biography.   4. Magruder, John Bankhead, 1807–1871—Friends and
associates.   5. United States—History—Civil War, 1861–1865—
Artillery operations, Confederate.   6. Texas—History—Civil War,
1861–1865.   I. Title.
E467.1.M36C37   1996
973.7'42—dc20
                                                          96-16598

Printed in the United States of America

10 9 8 7 6 5 4 3 2 1

To my wife

Contents

Preface

WHILE WORKING ON AN EARLIER BOOK in which I sought published studies of leading Confederate fighting men, I discovered to my dismay that no full-length treatment—old or new—existed for Major General John Bankhead Magruder. Except for several academic theses available in university libraries and a number of articles dealing with various phases of his career, he has simply escaped the attention of Civil War biographers. My interest having been piqued, I embarked upon a research/writing odyssey that took me to the massive University of Texas library, the North Carolina State Archives (with its beautiful, larger-than-life portrait of Queen Elizabeth II hanging inside the front entrance), and a number of repositories in Richmond, as well as several other libraries. In piecing together the life and military legacy of Prince John Magruder, I have written and received upwards of 1,000 letters of inquiry in my search for materials; and more than a few of these quests developed into sub-adventures in their own right—the stuff of scholarly fulfillment. The effort to verify Magruder's law license alone could almost become the basis for a separate book.

Who was John Bankhead Magruder? Why was he always known as Prince John?

Although he was married and had children, an unorthodox—even colorful—approach to life and what was surely an addiction to alcohol earned him the enduring sobriquet. Those traits, coupled with a fondness for loud clothing and a carousing spirit, caused many, including his own wife, to shy away from him. Virginia-born in 1807, a

West Point graduate of the class of 1830, he served in the federal army for more than thirty years before the outbreak of the American Civil War. With duty tours in such disparate locations as the Carolina coast, Florida during the Seminole Wars, the New York and Maine frontiers, Fort McHenry, Washington, D.C., San Diego, Fort Clark (Texas), Baton Rouge, and Fort Leavenworth, Magruder came into contact with many, if not most, of the major political and military personages of the mid-nineteenth century. In 1847 he not only associated with General Winfield Scott as he paraded through the cafés of Mexico City after the American victory, but also introduced a young lieutenant—the future Stonewall Jackson—to the concept of fast-moving deployment of versatile artillery batteries. Magruder's list of notable acquaintances started as early as 1826, when he was the classmate of a young writer named Edgar Allan Poe at the University of Virginia; and he managed to have dinner with Thomas Jefferson while enrolled at the Charlottesville school. At West Point from 1826 to 1830, he was a contemporary of future Confederate leaders Jefferson Davis, Robert E. Lee, and Joseph E. Johnston, among others. Interspersed with his duties in the peacetime army, Magruder began a budding, albeit stunted, legal career after getting himself admitted to the bar in North Carolina and California.

The 1850s found Magruder an outspoken exponent of "light artillery" companies designed to provide improved mobility on the battlefield; although others, spearheaded by George B. McClellan, led official delegations to study gunnery developments in Europe, Prince John's persistent advocacy of battlefield mobility, as well as his tenure as commandant of the school of practice at Fort Leavenworth, prepared more than a few officers, north and south, for roles as master artillerists through the bloodletting of 1861–1865. Magruder's contributions to a rapidly maneuverable artillery have been overlooked by many modern historians; and his two European excursions, including a side tour of the Crimea—especially the second, in 1860–1861, at the direction of President James Buchanan, to examine overseas military modifications—did much to fashion his own thinking. When war finally came in the spring of 1861, Magruder, serving as commander of the Washington garrison, was personally known to Abraham Lincoln as well as several members of the cabinet; but his obligations as Lincoln's bodyguard did not keep him from rushing to his beloved Virginia upon the first Southern call to arms.

Following a spectacular display of audacity and initiative in the opening engagements of the war, Magruder, in part because of his drinking, soon ran afoul of the rigid standards of military and personal demeanor expected by first Joseph E. Johnston and then Robert E. Lee. Although President Davis placed him in charge of the Trans-Mississippi West, he was removed from that vital post without serving a single day; yet service followed as commander of the district of Texas, New Mexico, and Arizona, which actually meant that he was the Confederate officer appointed to defend the Texas coast after November 1862, because a manpower-strapped government in Richmond did not possess sufficient forces to contest the Far West. Once removed from his eastern taskmasters, Magruder quickly came into his own as he roused the Texans to a heroic defense of that remote corner of the Confederacy. Except for a brief stint as Confederate commander in Arkansas, he remained in Texas until the final Confederate collapse of April–June 1865. After Magruder fought and won the Battle of Galveston on New Year's Day 1863, Yankee forces, save for a few pinpricks along the coast and in the lower Rio Grande Valley, made no meaningful excursions into the Lone Star State; Prince John had saved Texas from the wholesale ravages visited upon other parts of Dixie by her Northern avengers.

Upon surrendering what was left of Confederate forces still under arms in 1865, although naval units still flew the Stars and Bars, Magruder made his way to Mexico, where he served briefly in the government of Emperor Maximilian; Prince John even arranged an escape plot for the doomed ruler as his Mexican enemies closed in for the kill, but when it went awry he made his way first to Cuba and then to the United States, in late 1866. Although he faced an uncertain future without funds for his personal support, Magruder retained his contacts with men of prominence including Lee, Beauregard, Simon Bolivar Buckner, and others. A lack of money did not prevent extensive travel across the United States throughout his last days; before settling in a Houston hotel, supported by a former aide, he undertook a much-publicized speaking tour in which he expressed his undying admiration for Maximilian and his attempts to impose an orderly government upon the Mexican people.

When a lonely, solitary death came in February 1871, Magruder was best remembered for his intrepid victories on the peninsula of Virginia and for his successful defense of Texas during the last days of the great struggle; and he never wavered in his devotion to the Confederacy and its commanders who led the Southern experiment in self-government. He was also remembered for his showmanship and his ornate uniforms, and for the raucous lifestyle that found disfavor among many of his associates. Others, however, were attracted to his ostentatious outbursts, which were undoubtedly a defense mechanism to cover some perceived flaw in his makeup. Throughout this endeavor to portray a Confederate extraordinaire, I have sought to strike a balance between his unfortunate private life and his considerable soldierly abilities.

Certainly one of the pleasures associated with writing is the opportunity to thank librarians and others who helped in the many ways necessary to produce a scholarly book. First, I would like to express my gratitude to my wife, Patricia Barker Casdorph, who not only found time to type and comment upon the manuscript, but also proved an amiable traveling companion as I visited archival collections around the country. Toni Leighty, secretary to the history faculty at West Virginia State College, lightened my burdens by copying all manner of Civil War materials. A former student of mine, Sherry L. Hodges, proved invaluable by ferreting a number of Magruder items from the National Archives. My longtime colleague, Professor Tim C. Alderman, assisted my research in an important manner. In addition to the countless librarians who responded to my pleas for help, Diana Haberfield, Shonnette Koontz, Kim Suiter, and Carol Machusak of the WVSC library went out of their way to respond to my incessant calls for library loans. And Elizabeth Scobell and Ron Wiley granted more special privileges than any library patron has a right to expect.

Professor Ervin L. Jordan of the Alderman Library at the University of Virginia not only provided me with manuscript items, but also shared his own unparalleled research into black Confederates; Sanford E. Lehmberg of the University of Minnesota once more came to my rescue by helping me track down Magruder's Scottish antecedents. Without the careful assistance of Alan D. Aimone and Suzanne Christoff of the U.S. Military Academy library, I would have been hard put to sort out Prince John's years on the Hudson. Another colleague who helped immeasurably was Lynda Crist, editor of the Jefferson Davis Papers, who shared the extensive collection of Confederate materials at Rice University, Houston, and thereby made my work much easier. John L. Slonaker and his staff at the U.S. Army Military History Institute, Carlisle Barracks, Pennsylvania, demonstrated how a government repository should help the researcher without erecting roadblocks for the uninitiated. Donaly E. Brice of the Texas State Library found numerous Magruder letters for me in the Official Records of Governors Francis R. Lubbock and Pendleton Murrah. I am indebted to Robert S. Conte, historian at the Greenbrier, for helping with an obscure photograph of Magruder and Robert E. Lee, and to my editor, Hana Lane, for her enthusiastic support throughout the project.

Two gentlemen must be thanked in a special way for their generous forebearance: William H. Richter, archivist at the Center for the Study of American History, University of Texas, helped me unearth Magruder materials buried in other manuscript collections at that marvelous repository of Americana; and most of all, I must express my appreciation to Stuart Frazer of Old Dominion University, whose keen expertise and wide-ranging familiarity with electronic access systems enabled me to find all manner of things at unsuspected locales; without his faithful attention the making of this book would have taken much longer.

1

Youth

WHEN JOHN BANKHEAD MAGRUDER, commander of the Department of Texas, New Mexico, and Arizona, stepped aboard the federal steamer *Fort Jackson* in Galveston harbor on June 2, 1865, with his boss, E. Kirby Smith, in charge of the Trans-Mississippi, and surrendered the last Confederate forces still in the field, another Southern officer observed: "He was every inch Prince John Magruder—as brave and skillful a soldier as any, but broken hearted."[1]

Although he was a major general in the Confederate army from October 1861, Magruder was never a top commander in the Southern cause; he was a fellow well met, a bon vivant and raconteur with a reputation for hard driving and the good life. Parties and conviviality followed him through his nearly forty years in the U.S. and Confederate armies. Even in Maximilian's Mexico, where he stayed briefly during 1865–1866, Magruder was remembered for his grandiose entertainments. Everywhere he served, in peacetime or war, he remained a purveyor of joviality and comradeship, and besides his impeccable manners, he always dressed in the very latest fashion. "General Magruder was a remarkably handsome man and very vain in his personal appearance," commented the *New York Herald* upon his death, in February 1871. "He was the aristocrat of aristocrats in the old army, but, notwithstanding his *hauteur,* was social and cordial to a degree."[2]

Many who knew and fought with him through the Mexican conflict and the Civil War shared the *Herald*'s assessment. "Magruder was a wonderful man," said an unidentified correspondent for the *San Antonio Light*:

> He stood six feet four inches in height, and had a form that the men envied and the women adored. His nerves were all iron. Foreign travel and comprehensive culture had given him a zest that was always crisp and sparkling. . . . He could fight all day and dance all night. In the morning a glass of brandy and a good cigar renewed his strength and caused the cup of his youth to run over with the precious wine of health and good spirits.

Despite an early marriage to a Baltimore belle, with whom he had three children, Magruder and his wife decided to live apart except for brief interludes. Yet, continues the *Light*, "he loved magnificent uniforms, magnificent horses, magnificent riders, and magnificent women. Gifted and graceful in conversation, he was a pet in the boudoir and a logician in the barracks."

Magruder always dressed to the hilt whether entertaining in the peacetime army, making his rounds of Civil War ramparts, or parading his troopers across a nearly vacant Kansas prairie. Besides a propensity for hard drinking, he had an "unfortunate lisp" that contributed to a lack of trust in him among the Confederate high command. At one of his "trademark banquets" in Richmond during the Civil War, Magruder encountered an uncomfortable but very hungry enlisted man; in order to break the ice, he inquired, "Well, thir, what are you doing here, thir?"

The man replied that he had come for dinner.

"Well, thir, and do you know with whom you propose to dine?" Magruder inquired sardonically.

"No, and don't give a damn either," the soldier shot back, adding, "I used to be particular in such matters, but it don't make a damn of difference now."

The unexpected response delighted Magruder. "Your impudenth ith thublime, thir," he laughed. "Keep your theat, thir."

Despite his shortcomings, Magruder always possessed the knack of "mixing the sting of the bee with the honey of the clover."[3]

As he served at various posts around the country, he became known as Prince John Magruder; but an unfortunate fondness for drink also plagued his career and in turn thwarted his climb through the federal ranks. Magruder remained a captain from the Mexican War until he resigned in 1861 to join the Confederacy, although he earned the rank of brevet lieutenant colonel for his exploits on the road into Mexico City during 1847. Afterwards he was "Colonel Magruder," but his drinking persisted, especially in California, where he was stationed for the 1850–1853 period. "Magruder is drunk," Major Samuel Heintzelman, his fellow officer at San Diego, wrote in his diary on February 8, 1852; nor was he swayed by the "Soldiers' Temperance Movement" that swept the ranks in the decade or so following the Mexican conflict. Magruder, a correspondent in the *Army and Navy Journal* relates, once announced his intention to become a teetotaler in just twenty-three days: " 'Well!' exclaimed J. B. M., with a lisp, 'I now take twenty-three eyeopenerth and cocktailth before breakfath; I am going to leave off one every morning, and on the twenty-third morning I will have taken my lath drink.' " His good intentions aside, the correspondent continues: "The story shall not be spoiled by any historical, or biographical doubts as to the results." Magruder may have wished to abstain, but he was never able to do so completely. The imbibing became part and parcel of his lusty persona.

Magruder's reputation for high living and showmanship may have commenced at an earlier time, perhaps as early as his brief stopover in Corpus Christi upon the outbreak of the Mexican War. But his exchange with several British officers on leave from their Canadian regiments during the Aroostook controversy of 1838–1840 culminated in an oft-repeated story. Although it has several variations, the tale involved his extravagantly set table while on field duty in the North. "We do not wish to be inquisitive, but we have been so impressed with your magnificence, that we are constrained to believe that American officers must be paid enormously. What is your monthly pay?"

Magruder replied with a jaunty air, "Damned if I know."

He then turned to his valet and inquired, "Jim, what is my monthly pay?"

The faithful servant could not bring himself to verify Magruder's sixty-dollar-per-month income.[4]

His innate flamboyancy and a measure of fighting tenacity allowed Magruder to gain some initial success in the early Virginia campaigns. At Yorktown during April 1862, he met McClellan's army head-on and, according to Edward Porter Alexander, General James Longstreet's artilleryman, Magruder "actually bluffed [the Yankees] from making any serious attack upon him, by marching his men around and showing them successively at different places, making them appear much more numerous than they really were." Yet Magruder remained an officer of contradiction throughout the war. While some thought him a steady soldier, others found him lacking at critical junctures. "General Magruder was a man of singular versatility," pronounced Richard Taylor, son of President Zachary Taylor and himself one of the last Confederates to give up the fight. "Of a boiling, headlong courage, he was too excitable for high command." When he arrived in the Trans-Mississippi during the fall of 1862, on the other hand, one contemporary labeled him "the gay, dashing Magruder . . . just the kind of man who suited Texas." And the end of Civil War hostilities did not weaken his unbreakable spirit; in both Mexico and the United States after 1865, he became known for his rollicking escapades.[5]

Whatever his faults, or the contributions to Confederate arms that fixed his place in the American saga, Magruder sprang from a fighting tradition. His ancestors were the unfortunate MacGregors of the Scottish Highlands who incurred the wrath of James VI shortly before he claimed the English throne upon the death of Elizabeth I. "In 1590 certain of the 'wicked clan Gregor,' continuing in 'blood, slaughters, her scips [heavy drinking], reifs [plunder], and stouths [theft accompanied by violence],' had murdered the king's forester in Glenartney, and then, according to the accepted account, cut the man's head off and carried it to their young chief in Balquidder." Although the privy council issued writs of "fire and sword," the Gregors escaped immediate censure. But some years later, in the early months of 1603, the clan again challenged the royal authority. This time, continues one scholar, "the MacGregors took part in a raid upon the Leimox when the Colquhouns of Luss were defeated with great slaughter—at Glenfruin and much spoil carried away." His patience exhausted, James declared all who bore arms at Glenfruin outlaws, proscribed the name MacGregor, and ordered their chieftain hanged. He further decreed "that no member of the clan might carry any weapon other than a pointless knife for his meat, and that not more than four of them might meet together at any time for any purpose."[6]

Some MacGregors subsequently embraced the name McGruder or Magruder, and by the mid-seventeenth century at least one of the clan had rejoined the Royalist cause of James's grandson Charles II. When the future king rallied his Scottish subjects against Oliver Cromwell and the Commonwealth upon his father's 1649 execution at Whitehall, one Alexander Magruder fought under the royalist banner. The Lord Protector, unable to abide royalist opposition to his Puritan regime, got up a new army to crush his Highland antagonists; following the great encounter at Dunbar during September 1650, Charles and his beaten followers fled to the royalist stronghold at Worcester, in northwest England. But Cromwell was not far behind to defeat the Scots anew, which forced Charles to flee in disguise and hide himself in an ancient oak—hence the "Royal Oak." These culminating battles of the English Civil War resulted in the heavy deportation of Royalists by the Roundheads.[7]

John Bankhead Magruder's direct ancestor Alexander Magruder was among the deportees who made his way to Maryland, where he became the progenitor of the American branch of the family. To the great amusement of Prince John Magruder, cattle rustling and a general rowdiness by this kinsman was long remembered across the Highlands; during one of his European jaunts, as he told the story, he inquired of some country man if he had ever heard of the Magruders. "The man said, 'Oh yes, he had seen one hung for cattle lifting.'" Magruder, his own account continues, "made no further inquiry."[8]

Although Montgomery County, Maryland, was home to the Magruders, no marriage records were kept before 1798, which makes it difficult to ascertain details of Magruder's lineage; according to one family genealogist, five generations separated the first Maryland Magruder from Prince John: "John Bankhead Magruder was the son of Thomas Magruder and Elizabeth Bankhead; grandson of George Fraser Magruder and Eleanor Bowie; great-grandson of William Magruder and Mary Fraser; great-great-grandson of Samuel Magruder and Sarah Beall; great-great-great-grandson of Alexander Magruder." Young Thomas Magruder followed other family members southward into the Old Dominion, where he married Elizabeth Bankhead, a native of Port Royal in Caroline County. It is unclear when the marriage took place because nuptials were not registered prior to 1822—later than the practice was instituted in Maryland—but the newlyweds soon settled at a country village near Port Royal, where John Bank-head Magruder was born in May 1807.[9]

Thomas Magruder not only started a family but also established himself as an attorney; "he engaged in the practice of law, in the circuit of which Caroline County formed a part," reads an 1862 account, "sustaining a high reputation among those illustrious lawyers of that day, whose legal lore and forensic abilities adorn the history of the Virginia bar."

Perhaps the boy's defect of speech caused the father to steer him toward another profession. The family apparently fell on hard times, which prompted the early preparation of the son for a military career designed to lighten its financial burden and to ensure the lad's future. If we can believe an 1821 letter by Congressman Robert S. Garnett endorsing Magruder's admission to West Point, his "father [was] a highly respectable lawyer, but in consequence of having ten children he [was] unable to support them." Still, the family must have enjoyed a certain gentility and social standing. William Nelson Pendleton, another Caroline youth and Magruder's roommate at West Point, writes in his own memoirs: "The gentleman farmers—the Pendletons, Taylors, Turners, Corbins, Hoomeses, Magruders, Dickersons and many others—resided on large estates and were noted for their profuse living and lavish hospitality.[10]

John's mother, Elizabeth Bankhead, was descended from old Virginia stock that apparently migrated into the state from Maryland; one branch of her family in Albemarle County became "noted millers." Like the Magruders they had served in the military from the first days of the country, and also in the Virginia legislature. The early literature says little about Elizabeth Bankhead other than that she was a native of Caroline County; although Congressman Garnett's letter suggests that she was the mother of ten children, other scholarship puts the number at eight—five girls and three boys. John Bankhead Magruder was her fifth child. Her brother, James Bankhead, however, not only enjoyed an enviable army career but also exerted considerable influence upon her son. Already a captain in 1808—but not a West Point man—James Bankhead rose to the rank of brevet brigadier general before his death in 1856; besides service in the War of 1812 and the Mexican conflict, he spent much of his early duty as adjutant to General Edmund P. Gaines; Bankhead's reputation as a respected artillery officer probably aided his nephew's admission to the military academy and his subsequent career in that branch.[11]

Magruder's young years were spent at a small hamlet named Villeboro or Ville Boro (the spelling varies), a few miles west of Port Royal; it was situated on the main road leading north from Richmond toward the federal capital at Washington. Taverns or public houses positioned at five- or six-mile intervals along the entire roadway not only attracted the famous but also served as centers of social intercourse. "Especially on Saturday afternoons the people assembled to engage in scientific, literary or political discussion, or to indulge in horse racing, wrestling, target practice, shooting-matches and other amusements," writes a local historian. A precocious youngster like Magruder unquestionably joined the good times, but no doubt "the muster of the county militia near these old public houses and where they held their barbecues" also caught his imagination. Originally known as Tad's Tavern, Villeboro was the first Caroline County stopover for travelers from the north; it was six miles south of the Spotsylvania County line.

Magruder's youth was surrounded by tales of notable Virginians who were also Caroline men. William Clark, best known for his surveying expedition to the Pacific northwest with Meriwether Lewis a few years before Magruder's birth, had been born in the county in 1770; although Clark was taken to Kentucky while a boy, local storytellers relished accounts of the famous enterprise around tavern hearths when the explorer gained renewed fame as governor of Mississippi Territory and as Indian agent at St. Louis; "Caroline's most distinguished son," Edmund Pendleton, had passed away in 1803, but his legacy of public service lived on in his nephew and adopted son, the spirited John Taylor of Caroline. Unlike his Federalist sire, Taylor pursued his place in Democratic circles as the premier defender of Virginia and her state's-rights traditions; both in the United States Senate and outside of it, John Taylor trod the political stage like a giant during his young neighbor's formative years. Whether Taylor's uncompromising opposition to the federal experiment influenced the future Confederate is unknown, but he may have witnessed events surrounding an 1813 petition by Port Royal residents not only to incorporate the town but also "to employ a public officer." A charter was necessary, said the townspeople, "because the increase of free negroes and mulattos in said town causeth sundry inconveniences, among these being that many hogs owned by these persons run at large, making conditions unsanitary." And three years later, as Magruder prepared for West Point at a local academy, a troublesome epidemic swept through the district around Villeboro and Port Royal, leaving dozens dead, although there is no indication that the nine-year-old boy suffered any ill effects.[12]

A puzzling controversy has swirled through the literature about the date and place of Magruder's birth, since the widely distributed *Dictionary of American Biography* found it to be August 15, 1810, in Winchester, Virginia. Earlier sources proffer identical statistics: A miniature booklet, *A Short History of General J. B. Magruder*, printed in 1888 and inserted into packs of Duke's cigarettes, plainly suggests August 15, 1810, in Winchester, and a 1913 article by his kinswoman Mae Samuella Magruder Wynne repeats the error. No less a historian than Douglas Southall Freeman offers the same time and place. Even the carefully edited *Biographical Directory of the Confederacy*, which appeared in 1977, also reports August 1810 and Winchester, as does a 1982 article about Magruder and the Peninsula campaign, published in a popular Civil War magazine. One of Magruder's scholarly biographers posits that the proximity of Front Royal to Winchester has induced subsequent writers to confuse the place with Port Royal in Caroline County.[13]

An 1863 work, published immediately after the Civil War victories in Texas at Galveston and Sabine Pass, says Magruder was born "at Port Royal, Caroline County, Va., in the year 1808." Paul B. Barringer's 1904 history of the University of Virginia puts it at "August 15, 1807, in Caroline County, Virginia." And the 1821 letter by Congressman R. S. Garnett seconding his candidacy for West Point calls him "a youth of about fourteen years of age," which supports the year 1807. Garnett also puts "Villeboro," Caroline County, as the place of birth. An 1871 obituary in the *New York Herald* reports: "He was born in Virginia in the year 1810," while the *New York Times* says "he was born at Port Royal, Carolina [sic] County, Va."; in Texas, where he died on February 18, 1871, in a Houston hotel, one obituary reads, "Gen. Magruder was born at Port Royal, Va., in 1808, and was only 22 years of age, when he graduated at West Point." Since he did finish in the class of 1830, the 1807 date again seems feasible. Finally,

Magruder's matriculation card at West Point, signed by him, lists his age as nineteen years, two months, upon his July 1, 1826, admission to the academy, which suggests May 1807 as the date of birth; the West Point document plainly lists his home as "Vielleboro, Virginia." Had he been born in August 1810, Magruder would have entered the military school at fifteen years and eleven months, an undeniably young age for cadet status.[14]

There can be no doubt about the place of birth: it was Caroline County and not Winchester, located in the Shenandoah Valley, more than 100 miles to the northwest; further, Magruder's West Point files confirm 1807 as the year of his birth, and that Thomas Magruder was his guardian.

Congressman Garnett's comment about the father's economic status aside, the family fortunes must have improved, because the youth was able to enter the Rappahannock Academy in preparation for West Point; presumably the family discovered sufficient funds to educate his brother Allan as well, who later became a newspaper editor in Charlottesville. Rappahannock Academy, situated in Caroline County a few miles south of Moss Neck, plantation home of the Corbin family, where Stonewall Jackson spent the winter of 1862–1863, had been formed in 1810, when Magruder was a mere toddler; it functioned as an adjunct to the Episcopal Mount Church in St. Mary's Parish until the Civil War era. The Mount Church predated the Revolution, although the date of its formation is unknown; it was "one of the largest and most beautiful churches in Virginia in that day, and contained a fine organ imported from England, an unusual thing for that time," notes a local historian. "After the Revolutionary War, with the social, political and religious revolution which followed it, Mount Church fell into disuse and was afterward appropriated by the State and given over to school purposes, becoming the Rappahannock Academy."

The place must have attracted a rowdy element as well as would-be scholars; two years after its creation, school trustees petitioned the Virginia assembly "for an Act to punish adults for selling intoxicants to the students." Even though little is known about Magruder's tenure at the school, he must have used his time wisely to gather "a tolerable knowledge after the ordinary branches of an English education." And, continues Garnett's recommendation, the boy made "some progress in Latin, French, and geography" under the tutelage of "Mr. French," the academy's principal. Magruder, who remained an incessant conversationalist throughout his life, surely laid the groundwork for his well-known proficiency in several foreign languages while there. It was an area of study he pursued at the University of Virginia, West Point, and abroad. "He studied French in Paris, Italian in Rome and Spanish in the Halls of Montezuma," writes an unknown Texas admirer.[15]

Although it remains unclear when Magruder left the academy or how he occupied his time after Garnett's letter, he was in Charlottesville for the initial session of the University of Virginia; Thomas Jefferson's great contribution to American higher education had been on the drafting board for several years, and following the necessary appropriations by the general assembly, he had hoped to see the first group of students admitted on February 1, 1825. Unforeseen difficulties, however, including the recruitment of several professors from England, delayed the opening session until March 7, when Magruder joined 123 other registrants at Charlottesville. His matriculation record in the university archives adds more fuel to the controversy over his birth; the eighteen-year-old put down March 1, 1807, as the date and listed his home post office as "Caroline Co." His age and upbringing fitted him for participation in a class of privileged youths "reared under a system tending to nourish in them unusual independence of character in spite of their immaturity." But Magruder, who remained fixed upon a military career as the path to economic independence, differed from his fellows, many of them sons of plantation gentry who looked forward to inherited property and place in the antebellum South; only two members of the freshman class were from beyond the South, and indeed only twelve listed a home address outside Virginia.[16]

At the startup session beginning on March 7, 1825, Magruder only enrolled for mathematics study under Professor Hewitt Key. He seemingly knew some math from his days at Rappahannock, because, notes a university chronicler, "no student was to be admitted to the School of Mathematics who was not 'adept in all of the branches of numerical arithmetic.' " Since he stayed at the university for two terms, Magruder presumably worked his way through two parts of the mathematics curriculum, even though Jefferson had organized the discipline into four classes. His study encompassed "the theory of designating numbers, the scales of notation, the derivation of several arithmetical rules, and the first problems of algebra, analyzed without the use of numbers to show the advantage of employing numbers." When he returned for the second session on February 1, 1826, Magruder "began the study of geometry, and also of general trigonometry in its broadest applications." That was followed by exposure to spherical trigonometry and the drawing of maps. Key, who taught Magruder his mathematics, was one of several professors recruited from Oxford by Francis Walker Gilmer to staff the new university. "Versed in every branch of mathematics," Key remained at the school until March 1827, when he returned to England and a position at the University of London; the author of several Latin grammars before his death in 1875, Key was described by Burwell Stark, one of Magruder's classmates, as "a faithful and competent teacher." Key had been accompanied to Virginia by his wife, which persuaded Stark to comment that the six-foot professor "who possessed a handsome face" was seldom seen at Charlottesville social functions.[17]

When the first class entered the university, Thomas Jefferson developed the practice of asking the boys to dine at Monticello; before his death on July 4, 1826, "it was his custom to invite about a dozen pupils at one time, till all had visited him two or three times." Magruder was certainly among those summoned to the ex-president's table, and, continues Stark, "his hospitality and sociability made us free in his company, and endeared him to all of our hearts." Magruder's fellow student makes it clear that Jefferson was highly visible around the university campus during 1825 and 1826: "As an instance of the high estimation in which the students held him, when they saw that he would pass on a certain side of our grounds, they would go out of their way in order to receive his recognition and most courteous bow." Besides frequent contact with the former president, other social activities abounded, including dancing lessons "with the faculty's consent within the precincts"; apparently the lads were obliged to pay for their own instruction, yet it seems inconceivable that a youth of Magruder's voracious appetites would have missed the fun. Students, however, "were barred from cotillions which the teacher gave at intervals in Charlottesville."[18]

Pleased though he was with the new university, Jefferson was upset on the night of October 1, 1825, when a brief rebellion erupted on campus; the upheaval commenced after a bottle "filled with a foul liquid" was thrown through the window of Professor George Long. A seething resentment that had been brewing over "the foreign professors" came to a climax when practically the entire student body reacted. Things got out of hand when two other professors, John T. Emmet and George Tucker, were thumped around while attempting to confront the riled-up youths.

Although Magruder was not a participant in the attack, he was a bystander and he probably cheered on his comrades; university records indicate that he was handed a reprimand for signing a remonstrance against the Englishmen along with sixty-five others. Several students were expelled over the incident, and Jefferson branded the demonstration "one of the most painful events in my life."[19]

During the second session, Magruder registered not only for additional mathematics under Hewitt, but also for "Ancient Languages" with George Long, the same Professor Long involved in the fall upheaval. And he found himself in the company of others destined for a place on the national stage, including a melancholy youth named Edgar Allan Poe, before he began his career as a poet and an expositor of the macabre. Philip St. George Cocke was a classmate who, like Poe, followed Magruder to West Point; Cocke, who enjoyed a checkered military career and became a writer on agricultural policy in the old South, took his own life as a Confederate officer in the first days of the Civil War. Another university student was William Ballard Preston, later secretary of the navy in Zachary Taylor's cabinet; Preston also served in the convention that took Virginia out of the Union, and as a senator from the Old Dominion to the Confederate congress.[20]

Magruder's association with such men of prominence as Thomas Jefferson, and with his energetic classmates at the university about to make their mark, commenced a pattern that continued throughout his life—that of being on the periphery of significant events. An exuberant nature, however, coupled with a propensity for trouble that started with his shadowy role in the Charlottesville riots of 1825, continued into cadet days at West Point and his lackluster career in the old army; it prompted many of these very men to view him with a jaundiced eye. His tenure at the University of Virginia may have enlarged his academic horizons, but it also saw the beginnings of a reputation that hounded him throughout the Civil War and beyond.

In spite of his previous troubles with Long, Magruder obviously used his time to advantage with the onetime fellow at Trinity College, Oxford. Perhaps Long's close association with Magruder's mathematics professor, Hewitt Key, induced him to accept the young scholar in his classes. "In the beginning, the rule was adopted that no student should be admitted to the School of Ancient Languages unless in the professor's judgment, he was qualified to read the Latin and Greek classics of the advanced grades," writes a university chronicler; "it will be recalled that Jefferson opposed any portion of a professor's time being taken up with 'drilling a primary class.' " Yet Bruce's massive history of the university suggests that the stringent requirements were relaxed for the ill-prepared student. The bachelor Long, whom Burwell Stark labels "a sociable fellow" often seen at off-campus festivities, had been recruited from England "despite not knowing any Hebrew"; like Key and the others, he amassed a string of scholarly publications before and after his 1827 return to Europe. But Magruder's studies with Long and Key came to an abrupt halt in the spring of 1826, when he failed to complete his second session: "Left [here] for West Point," reads a terse entry on his university record card.[21]

Magruder had known for several months before his departure from Charlottesville that he had been appointed to the military academy. Although Congressman Garnett had written on his behalf in February 1821, his entry into the soldier's life did not come until four years afterward. "I have the honor to acknowledge the receipt of your letter of the 27th February appointing me conditionally a Cadet in the service of the U. States and in conformity to the instructions therein I thereby accept the same," he wrote to the secretary of war on March 11, 1825. The beautifully preserved letter in the archive at West Point to John C. Calhoun was posted "Near Ville Boro." Since the opening term at the university commenced on March 7—four days before the formal response from his father's home—the inference is clear that the eighteen-year-old scholar sped to Charlottesville in time to be a late registrant for the 1825 term. Throughout his career in the United States and Confederate armies, Magruder invariably signed his correspondence as J. Bankhead, but the 1825 letter is signed John B., and an attached memo reads, "Accepts Appd of Cadet for 1826."

The entrance examination that every plebe was required to undergo "was framed primarily to test the applicant's knowledge of mathematics and his command of the English language," writes a West Point historian. "Recognized standards" [a few years after Magruder] required that the cadet write "a fairly legible hand, and that he perform with facility and accuracy various operations of the ground rules of arithmetic, including the problems of reduction—of simple and compound proportion—and vulgar and decimal fractions." Prospective cadets all over the country enrolled in schools and academies or engaged a private tutor for the ordeal that would determine their futures. Magruder not only chose mathematical and foreign language studies at the University of Virginia, but also postponed his journey to the Hudson for another year.[22]

Antebellum cadets normally arrived a month or so before the entrance examinations to prepare themselves. Magruder's fellow cadet from Caroline County, William Nelson Pendleton, who became one of his barracks mates, left an account of his route northward from Virginia. In the days before railroads, extended travel across country could be a torturous affair; Pendleton spent an entire week on the journey. Although more than a few men stopped to visit the "fleshpots" of New York City, Pendleton, says his daughter, who edited his *Memoirs,* went by "stage to the Potomac, up that river by steamboat to Washington, on to Baltimore by stage, and across the Chesapeake by boat to Frenchtown. From there to New Castle, Delaware, where he again took the stage. A steamboat carried him up the Delaware to Trenton. Jersey was crossed by stage and canal to Amboy, from which point steamboats ran daily to New York, a city of less than two hundred thousand inhabitants." Then it was up the Hudson by steamboat, and there is every reason to think that Magruder traveled the same or a similar path from Villeboro. For a youth who had not ventured farther than the seventy miles to Charlottesville along the well-worn roadways of the Old Dominion, the trek to West Point surely became a passage to manhood in itself.[23]

Magruder unquestionably stayed in private lodgings until his successful completion of the qualifying exams during mid-June 1826, when he was handed a barracks assignment with three other plebes, all of whom were destined to enter Confederate service. First there was Pendleton, who rose to high place in the Episcopal Church after teaching mathematics at the military academy until 1833, and later at several colleges before he entered the ministry. At the onset of the Civil War he not only became Robert E. Lee's chief of artillery, but also fought at Magruder's side during the campaign to save Richmond in 1862; Pendleton made his home in Lexington, Virginia, after the war, where he served as pastor of Latimer Parish Church and officiated at the funerals of both Lee and Stonewall Jackson. A Maryland boy named Lloyd J. Beall also shared quarters with Magruder; later he bucked the pro-Unionist stance of the Old Line State and served in the Confederate Navy as a colonel of marines following a long career in the federal army. William Cruger Heyward, the fourth roommate, although from New York, also served in the Confederate Army until his death, in September 1863, while Magruder struggled to defend the Texas coast from the onslaughts of Nathaniel P. Banks.[24]

Magruder and his messmates were confronted with a no-nonsense regimen of hard work and close attention to detail; even before the start of the academic term, entering cadets were "hustled off by upperclassmen to 'help' erect tents on the plain." Everyday life in search of military precision often became monotonous and routine, but primarily it was demanding and Spartan in its simplicity. "The barracks rooms were small, and we are hot in summer and cold in winter. Cadet furniture was primitive. At night narrow mattresses were spread upon the floor; room space was too restricted for the luxury of beds," wrote one former cadet. Running water and bathtubs did not exist, and the cadet mess was apparently bountiful and wholesome, although more than one man complained about "a super-supply of black molasses, and too great a ration of bread and potatoes at the expense of too little meat." Magruder, like all entering fourth classmen, was subjected to a strenuous round of exercise and drills; at West Point, classes of cadets are designated in reverse, with freshmen, or first-year men, constituting the fourth class and seniors the first class. As the future officer advanced toward graduation, his life became somewhat easier, but every plebe underwent "daily infantry drill on the plain" as well as intermittent artillery practice. And, to make his days more disagreeable, he was faced with near-constant hazing by upperclassmen.[25]

Although the first cadets arrived during the 1801–1802 academic year, the academy's early years were marked by uncertainty and indecision about the proper education for army officers in a free republic; the entire place changed in 1817, nine years before Magruder's admission, when Captain Sylvanus Thayer entered the superintendent's office. A former West Point man himself and a graduate of Dartmouth as well as a veteran of the War of 1812, Thayer remained on the Hudson until 1833; he had no sooner taken charge than he moved to end the old laxity in cadet discipline by creating a model for measuring each man's progress. "Under his rule, candidates reported before June 25, in time for the summer encampment, and at that time only," writes Stephen Ambrose. "He set up two formal examinations, one in January and one in June, at which time all cadets were tested; only after the June examination could any cadet graduate, and then the whole of the First, or senior, class would go into the army. Or at least those who passed would."

Thayer is best known at the school for his system of ranking every cadet from the day he entered until his graduation. The new scheme under which Magruder found himself was designed to eliminate "subjective feelings, while it took into account nearly everything a cadet did for four years, both in and out of the classroom. . . . It was the most complete and impersonal system imaginable," continues Professor Ambrose. "Every cadet was graded on every activity, in the classroom and on the drill field in a positive manner, and in every other way negatively. In his subjects, the cadet received marks ranging from 3.0 for perfect to 0.0 for complete failure; the more points he had the higher he stood. But no matter how brilliant he was, his rank could be low if his behavior was poor, because Thayer set up a system of demerits for each infraction of the regulations, and the demerits lowered a cadet's standing." John Bankhead Magruder would learn Thayer's system soon enough; by the end of his first term, in June 1827, he had been debited seventy-nine black marks, which put him 114th out of 202 cadets.[26]

When he joined Pendleton, Beall, and Heyward for the 1826–1827 academic term, Magruder encountered a veritable galaxy of future Confederate leaders and officers. First and foremost was his fellow Virginian, Robert E. Lee—reared in Alexandria, forty-five miles north of Caroline County—who had come to West Point the year before, in 1825; unlike Magruder, the man destined to lead the Confederate armies went through the entire curriculum without earning a single demerit. That almost-unheard-of performance, which signified great self-control, led to Lee's second-place finish in the class of 1829. In 1862, when Magruder missed his chance during the Seven Days, if Lee did not precipitate his move to the Trans-Mississippi, he certainly did nothing to thwart Jefferson Davis's decision to remove him from the Virginia campaigns. Another cadet, Joseph Eggleston Johnston, a classmate of Lee, was fated to downgrade Magruder's maneuvers to keep McClellan from advancing on Richmond in June 1862; proud and obstinate, Johnston engaged in a well-known bout of fisticuffs with Jefferson Davis, who had entered the academy with the class of 1824; Johnston would later spar with the future Confederate president over a supposed slight at not being designated number one in the Confederate officer corps, but Magruder, who associated and studied with Lee, Johnston, and Davis at West Point, remained true to Davis until the last muster roll in June 1865.[27]

Although most Confederate officers were younger and sprang from later classes at the academy, Magruder found others from the South during his four years at the school, including Theophilus Hunter Holmes; a member of the class of 1829, Holmes also observed Magruder at close quarters, and when he was sent to Texas in 1862, the North Carolinian was his superior for several months before E. Kirby Smith (class of 1845) took command of the Confederate Trans-Mississippi. Albert Taylor Bledsoe was another southerner in the class ahead of Magruder; the Kentucky-born Bledsoe resigned from the old army in 1832 to become professor of mathematics at the University of Mississippi and a writer of books on religion. In 1854, Bledsoe beat out Stonewall Jackson for the chair in mathematics at the University of Virginia, where he remained until the onset of the Civil War, when he became a bureau chief in the Confederate War Department.[28]

Lucius B. Northrop, a South Carolina cadet, one year behind Magruder, likewise served in the federal army until 1861, when he joined the Confederacy as commissary general of her armies. A Missouri lad, a member of Magruder's own class, Meriwether Lewis Clark was a future Confederate who fought under Sterling Price and Braxton

Bragg in the West during 1861–1865. The son of William Clark of Lewis and Clark fame, and a Caroline County man, cadet Clark surely reminded Magruder of home and family. Eighty-three men entered the class of 1826, only forty-two of whom survived the rigors of cadet life to graduate in June 1830; eleven of the eighty-three were Virginians, although only Magruder and Pendleton stayed the full four years.[29]

Several Northern soldiers of prominence during the Civil War were also present, including John G. Barnard, Erasmus D. Keyes, and Philip St. George Cooke, the future father-in-law of Jeb Stuart. Magruder, however, found himself more at home with his Southern companions as he made acquaintances that would have a profound impact upon his later career as a Confederate major general; and the question remains whether the Southern cadets studied the text by William Rawle, *A View of the Constitution of the United States*, with its espousal of an individual state's right to secede from the Union. The controversy surrounding Rawle stems from a diary recollection by Samuel P. Heintzelman, who graduated in the class of 1826, just as Magruder was entering the academy; it has spawned a persistent debate among Civil War historians, although some contend that the book had been discarded from the required reading list by the late 1820s. Whether or not Magruder—an ardent secessionist during 1860–1861—was concerned about constitutional intricacies during his cadet experience, it is clear that he had already become something of a showman and dandy before his graduation. "My old friend and classmate John B. Magruder, was perhaps the most elegant and *distingué* cadet at the academy in those days, and I do not believe West Point has ever had his equal," wrote an unidentified correspondent in the *Army and Navy Journal*. "He was a first-rate soldier, of fine appearance and very strict when on duty as 'officer of the day,' never failing to report the slightest violation of the regulations, even though the delinquent was his most intimate friend and room-mate." And, he added: "This trait in his character I have reason to know from personal experience. John was for the corps the arbiter of things elegant, the glass of fashion."[30]

Although Magruder kept his demerit tally comparatively low during his fourth term, drinking was already becoming a problem for him; visits to Benny Havens's place, a nearby saloon, and even imbibing in the barracks increased as the years progressed until his senior year, when he approached Thayer's 200-demerit limit for expulsion. As he went about his initial studies, he was nearly expelled during December 1826–January 1827 for his role in a notable drinking escapade. Thayer had long attempted to quell a West Point tradition that called for illicit partying before reveille on Christmas morning. Yet Jefferson Davis and another cadet were commissioned to fetch liquor and eggs from Havens's—about two miles from the academy. Following a hurried, clandestine adventure, the potables were smuggled onto the second floor of North Barracks, which set the stage for the memorable "Eggnog Riots" of 1826. "Very early the next morning, perhaps as early as 1 A.M., the mixing and drinking began," finds a Davis biographer. "Around 4 A.M., with the party in full swing, the ever-vigilant Captain [Ethan Allen] Hitchcock heard a lot of walking in the halls of the barracks and decided to investigate. . . . Stepping inside [room number 5], he found some thirteen cadets including [Robert] Sevier and Davis' roommate Walter B. Guion." Hitchcock, who was one of Magruder's instructors, ordered all present, including Magruder, to return to their own lodgings.

> Then he looked around the room and asked that some trunks be opened, no doubt expecting to find the liquor there. Just as he was doing so, Jefferson Davis came running into the room and did not see the Captain. . . . Davis ran up to the fireplace, and anxiously announced, "Boys, put away that grog. Captain Hitchcock is coming in."[31]

Instead of dispersing as ordered, the occupants of the room started a small-scale riot "in which they used clubs and other weapons to drive the officers out of the barracks or into their own quarters." At a formal court-martial that opened in mid-January, Cadet Samuel K. Cobb testified under oath that Magruder and a number of others, including Jefferson Davis, were in his room on that fateful Christmas morning and that "spiritous liquor" was being consumed. "I was informed afterwards that the liquor was put in cadet [David M.] Farrelly's trunk, when Captain Hitchcock came to the room," Cobb avowed. "After Capt. Hitchcock came in—he ordered the visitors to their rooms." There can be no mistake that Magruder was on hand at the start, but had followed Hitchcock's instruction to depart before Davis blundered into the party calling for everyone to hide the liquor.

Still the affair was enough to cement a bond—at least on Magruder's part—with the future Confederate president that persisted to the end of their lives.

Magruder and Davis escaped court-martial and expulsion even though thirty-nine others did not; both managed to convince school authorities that they had obeyed orders and returned to their rooms as the mayhem unfolded. Also, no one could be found to swear that either had been drinking. "I have ever regretted my error and regarded it as one of the greatest personal misfortunes of my life," wrote Benjamin G. Humphreys, a Mississippi youth expelled over the incident. The expulsion edicts were approved by President John Quincy Adams—and, continued Humphreys, who managed to prove that he had not been intoxicated during the riot: "This was perhaps an error on my part as most of the boys found *guilty* were reinstated expressly because they were drunk." Whether "drunk" or not, Magruder avoided a crippling reprimand as he had done at Charlottesville the previous year.[32]

The incessant demands of cadet life may well have contributed to the drinking and grandiose behavior of a high-spirited boy of nineteen years like Prince John, although that appellation was not attached to him until later. His zestfulness aside, Magruder managed a thirteenth-place finish in mathematics among sixty-three members of his class that completed the fourth term in June 1827; his mathematical studies, which continued into 1827–1828, when he stood twelfth out of fifty-five cadets, were completed under the tutelage of Charles Davies and Lieutenant Edward C. Ross. Although both were brought to the school by Thayer to upgrade instruction, Davies, whom the students called "Old Tush" because of protruding upper teeth, in time became the best-known mathematician in the country. He was also nicknamed "Rush" or "Tush-Rush," owing to an abundance of nervous energy that spilled over into his lectures. Ross, on the other hand, reportedly "effected long whiskers which he pulled constantly in the classroom, while chewing tobacco as he talked." Later, as professor of mathematics at Ohio's Kenyon College, he helped school future president Rutherford B. Hayes.

These and other math instructors at the academy helped make it the premier engineering school in the nation, if not the world. Magruder's wise choice to pursue similar studies at Shenandoah Academy and the University of Virginia prepared him for the rigors of West Point. His French studies, also commenced at Shenandoah, turned out equally well during his first two years. In Thayer's scheme, an educated soldier meant the cadet possessed a familiarity with French military tomes; the boys were required to study French, notes historian Ambrose: "If they could speak the language, fine, but it was not necessary. What they did need was an ability to read their texts." Claudius Berard, another of Thayer's recruits, and a former instructor at Dickinson College in Pennsylvania, was Magruder's French professor. He gained considerable proficiency in the language, finishing twelfth in 1826–1827 and 1827–1828 among his classmates. Berard regularly demanded that his charges read *Gil Blas* by the eighteenth-century novelist René Lesage, and Voltaire's *Charles XII*, as well as his own textbooks.[33]

According to Pendleton and the official list of demerits in the academy archive, Magruder was often in trouble for his music making. "Magruder, like Pendleton, was something of a musician, playing on the flute, and the two enjoyed their music so much that their room was not infrequently reported for 'music in study-hours,' " records Pendleton's daughter. "Cadet Beall, finding he must share the demerits, determined to take part in the fun, and took to playing the fiddle on his own account." Except for the absences on drinking soirées during his first term, the majority of Magruder's demerits were for minor infractions of academy regulations. A sampling of the "Register of Delinquencies" reveals penalties for failure to have his hair cut at a specific time, remaining in bed after reveille, and being late for mess and formation—in addition to "flute and violin playing" on several occasions. Although demerits and their influence on class standing were important to the individual cadet, Leonidas Polk was moved to write his father: "Five years after graduation will obliterate the fact of an individual's standing here or there, or if it is recollected, it will be said perhaps, that he obtained it for having a knack at small things, great plodding and the like." After his initial seventy-nine demerits in 1825–1827, Magruder's tally fell to thirty at the end of his third term; during 1828–1829 they rose to sixty-seven, and to a whopping 196 for his graduation year.[34]

At the conclusion of his third class, in June 1828, Magruder, despite his thirty black marks, stood thirteen in his class and sixty-eighth among a total corps of 207 cadets; he had improved his position by forty-six slots to make it the best performance of his West Point career; in addition to his work in mathematics and French, the "Register of Merit" shows him as eighteenth among his classmates in drawing. Magruder also started his climb to military command during the year by serving as third corporal of Second Company throughout June–December 1827, and he advanced to second corporal of Third Company for the following spring. He was again bonded with Jefferson Davis, who graduated in June 1828 when he joined a "Hose Company" with fifteen others: "In the case of fire, Cadets Davis and Magruder will repair to the fire plug," reads the official appointment document. "They will see a hose properly attached to the same, and regulate the supply of water."

Magruder did his firefighting with "a small hand fire engine" and a squad commanded by Lieutenant John H. Winder, who was later placed in charge of Union prisoners of war east of the Mississippi, which included the infamous Confederate compound at Andersonville, Georgia. Winder, who finished in the class of 1820 and returned to West Point in November 1827 following a stint in the First Artillery, also served as Magruder's drill instructor for the 1827–1828 term. When Winder assumed an unorthodox stance at his first field exercise and shouted, "If the file-closers don't do their duty, I'll arrest them, by G–d," near pandemonium convulsed Magruder and his companions on the parade ground. And the outcry only increased "the commotion, for we were unaccustomed to swearing on parade, the different companies hallooing and shouting as they marched off," writes the ubiquitous unidentified correspondent in the *Army and Navy Journal*. "The demonstration of the cadets soon brought the Lieutenant's heels together, who folded his arms across his bosom, and crossed the sword across his chest." Winder had earlier come to attention with his feet apart, in violation of established practice; it was this gesture that had excited his charges, who expected an unbending routine.[35]

Although Winder left West Point in 1828 for other duties, Magruder continued his drills and classroom studies under other instructors. Unfortunately, his courses for 1828–1829 are not available in the academy archive, but he certainly continued to work his way through Thayer's curriculum, which was designed to mold the competent soldier/engineer: French, drawing, infantry and artillery tactics, ethics, history, chemistry, physics, mathematics, and more. The classical languages were not included, nor were they an entrance requirement, which is surprising in view of their heavy importance at nearly all colleges in the country; the emphasis throughout was placed upon mathematics and engineering; otherwise, one wag said, the academy would turn out philosophers instead of soldiers.

Third-year cadets were required to sit through Professor Jared Mansfield's course in "natural philosophy," which is what physics was called at that time; Mansfield, who argued constantly with Thayer and the secretary of war over school policy, remained until 1829, when he was replaced by Edward H. Courtenay, later professor of mathematics at the University of Virginia. It was Mansfield who exposed Magruder to such topics as "statics, dynamics, hydrostatics, hydrodynamics, hydraulics, pneumatics, machinery, optics, and even astronomy, thanks to a crude telescope." The study was demanding, and by June 1829 Magruder's original class of sixty-three had fallen to forty-five through unrelenting attrition, and three more left before completion of their first term. Robert E. Lee, Joseph E. Johnston, Theophilus H. Holmes—all his future commanders in the Confederate service—graduated in June 1829; and at the term's conclusion Magruder "stood 109th of 209 members of the Corps of Cadets for the year." In spite of his sixty-plus demerits, he rose in the cadet command structure as sergeant of First Company for the entire season.[36]

When Magruder advanced to captain of First Company for the 1829–1830 school year, the stage was set for a serious confrontation with Augustus Allen, "Baron Allen," a cadet from Mississippi. A fracas between the two started when Magruder summoned Allen, a private in the corps, to "close-up"; Allen took it as a personal affront to be singled out by name on the parade ground. Allen's eagerness for redress was followed by a formal challenge, which Magruder readily accepted. "The meeting took place, the preliminaries were all settled, and the word was about to be given, when [Pendleton] stepped in between the hostile parties, insisting that the matter had gone far enough and protesting against further proceedings," their roommate Beall recalled later. Pendleton, who acted as Magruder's second in the affair, was able to soothe ruffled tempers so that "the matter was adjusted, and relations amicably restored." Into that world of proud, even hotheaded young men came Magruder's acquaintance from the University of Virginia, Edgar Allan Poe, for the academic year, following a stint in the regular army. Although the two were not intimates, Poe no doubt drilled under Magruder's command. The military life, however, offered no allure for the future writer, who departed after a single term to avoid court-martial because of his misconduct. Yet Poe managed to publish a slender volume of poetry while on the Hudson.[37]

Magruder, meanwhile, completed his senior year and graduated fifteenth out of forty-two remaining cadets in his class of 1830. David B. Douglass, who stayed on the faculty until 1833, served as his professor of engineering; he was in turn succeeded by the legendary Dennis Hart Mahan, father of the renowned naval historian of a later era, Alfred Thayer Mahan. While Magruder finished seventeenth in his engineering class, Douglass made use of "Colonel Guy de Vernon's textbook on 'the science of war and fortifications,' " which drew upon the writings of Baron Antoine-Henri de Jomini. Bonaparte had been dead but eight years in 1829, and Magruder, like other soldiers of his generation, was given a heavy regimen of Napoleonic strategy as interpreted by Jomini, a Swiss banker who wrote the classic *Précis de l'Art de le Guerre* (*The Art of War*), after serving on the staffs of Marshal Ney and Napoleon himself. Jomini defined the good commander as the general capable of "high moral and physical courage which takes no account of danger." Whether Magruder assimilated the critical message or not, he certainly displayed great physical courage in Mexico and on the peninsula of Virginia during the summer of 1862, although he failed to act decisively at the supreme moment in his military career.[38]

Although Magruder finished fifteenth in the class of 1830, he kept himself in the upper half throughout his last year at the Point; besides his seventeenth-place standing in engineering, he attained an identical ranking in two other courses: Rhetoric and Moral Philosophy, and Artillery. Had he not accumulated such a list of demerits his graduation place would have been higher among his fellows. At year's end, Thayer relaxed his rigid discipline long enough for Magruder to find an outlet for his inherent showmanship; "the corps was allowed by the Superintendent to give a Fancy Ball," records Benjamin S. Ewell, class of 1832, brother of Richard Stoddert Ewell, and himself a later president of the College of William and Mary. The "elite of New York" made the trip to West Point for the soirée, which found Magruder in the midst of the elaborately costumed affair. Prince John had already become the "polished and popular society man."[39]

When Magruder walked across the reviewing stand to receive his diploma and commission into the infantry, he automatically entered a select group of finely trained young men destined to lead two great armies in a disastrous civil war, although he could hardly have known what lay ahead on that June day. Early-nineteenth-century America was a rural land where only the well-to-do upper classes could secure the benefits of higher learning—and Magruder, like his compeers, now owned perhaps the best education available on this side of the Atlantic. It is undeniable that some of them carried negative assessments of his soldierly abilities, and his shenanigans had insulted their puritanical sensibilities, but the camaraderie of the place ensured a bond that not even disunion could destroy. "So well did they know their opponents that they could anticipate each other in a way few military leaders have been able to divine their enemies' actions," finds historian Gerard A. Patterson. Confederate general George Pickett, who graduated in the class of 1846, labeled it "this entente cordiale between us old fellows." John Bankhead Magruder thus became one of 306 West Pointers to enter the Confederate military. A thirty-year stint in the federal army followed his graduation, but his academy credentials in time assured him of a position among the officer corps of both armies.[40]

2

Lieutenant Magruder

W HEN TWENTY-TWO-YEAR-OLD John Bankhead Magruder graduated from the military academy, he faced a stagnated career in a small
peacetime army, with little prospect of quick promotion; at best, his
immediate future was one of monotonous duty at isolated army installations, although he plotted from the beginning to secure more de-
sirable postings when he was not pestering headquarters with
requests for leaves of absence to rejoin his new wife in the Baltimore
social swirl. Since his low class standings precluded assignment in the
engineers—this was reserved for high-achieving cadets—Magruder
had to content himself with a short-lived stint as second lieutenant in
the Seventh Infantry.

Even though he finagled a transfer to the artillery within thirteen
months after leaving West Point, without serving a day of active duty
with the infantry, the promotions and recognition did not come. Six
years elapsed before his 1836 promotion to first lieutenant, and an additional eight before his elevation to captain. And he was not the only
officer to feel the disappointment associated with a moribund army.
Even Robert E. Lee, who graduated second in the class of 1828—two
years before Magruder—had not attained general rank at the outbreak of the Civil War. After he had spent sixteen years at a succession of minor assignments, the Mexican conflict of 1846–1848 and a
major expansion of the army finally brought him advancement; promotion to brevet major came in 1847, and to brevet lieutenant colonel
a few months later, for his initiative at the Battle of Chapultepec. But
he was still a captain on the eve of secession. Throughout the pre–Civil

War era, his raucous lifestyle and widely known, often drunken escapades did not help his reputation throughout the officer corps.

Magruder did not go on active duty for more than a year after receiving his commission. In a July 1831 letter to Roger B. Taney, acting secretary of war in Andrew Jackson's cabinet, he asked for a transfer to the "Topographical Bureau." He wrote, Magruder said, to present his side of a difficulty with General Alexander Macomb, who objected to the fact that he had not joined his regiment.

> I beg most respectively to remark in reference to the first objection that the furlough in question commenced the first of July 1830 at which time I graduated at the military academy without having received a furlough for four years. That during the first six months my health went so bad as to frequently render me [incapacitated for] long periods unable to rise from my bed.

The remainder of his absence resulted from an understanding with the Baltimore financier George Winchester that he would work on construction of the Baltimore & Susquehanna Railroad, extending north from the city at the same moment the Baltimore & Ohio was pushing toward its Ohio River terminus. Magruder reminded Taney that he had the support of his brother George Magruder, Virginia congressman Andrew Stevenson, then speaker of the House of Representatives as well as a railroad speculator, and former secretary of war John H. Eaton, to work on Winchester's project.[1]

Although Macomb thwarted Magruder's transfer to the topographical service, other West Pointers and army engineers were readily assigned to construction duty with the nation's infant railroads, one of the best known being Major George Whistler, father of the renowned painter. In an era of initial railroad building, army officers with their West Point educations were about the only practicing engineers available; and dozens were assigned to private companies, including that of Winchester, a staunch Federalist beaten in the same jail melee that resulted in the near death of Lighthorse Harry Lee during the War of 1812. But Magruder was unsuccessful, in spite of family and political efforts to obtain his transfer from the Seventh Infantry. After complaining about his poor health, Magruder continued:

> Regarding the second objection I can only say there are now on topographical duty many officers who have never joined their regi-

ments—lieutenants who have been detailed on that service as soon as they graduated, and whose situations are similar to mine in every respect. They have the advantage of putting into practice the theoretical of engineering which they have acquired at the military academy and thereby qualify themselves to undertake at any time a work of that kind if their services be so requested after joining their regiments. I beg leave to ask why this advantage should not be allowed me . . . when I have the promise of the late Secretary of War that I should be ordered on it as soon as details were applied for by the Topographical Bureau.

Magruder's cries for relief notwithstanding, Taney and Macomb—then commanding general—denied his request and ordered him to active duty.[2]

Although ill during his yearlong furlough, Magruder may have been less than honest in his explanation for not joining his regiment; his May 18, 1831, marriage to Henrietta Von Kapff, heiress to a sizable Baltimore fortune, suggests a lengthy, energetic courtship throughout late 1830 and early 1831. His bride was the third of seven children born to Bernard J. Von Kapff and Hester H. Didier of Baltimore; Von Kapff, a native of the German duchy of Lippe-Detmold, not only served as consul at Baltimore, but also founded "Von Kapff & Anspach (later Von Kapff & Brune), one of the largest wholesale and tobacco importing businesses in the city." That the Von Kapffs were active in Baltimore society was readily apparent and surely led to Magruder's entrée into the family. Henrietta's younger brother Frederick married Anne Donnell Smith, granddaughter of Robert Smith, secretary of state under James Madison and attorney general in Andrew Jackson's second administration; the Smiths, one source says, "were intimately associated with the social life of Baltimore." Although Bernard Von Kapff died in 1828 before his daughter's marriage to Magruder in the Protestant Episcopal Church, Magruder was readily accepted into the Von Kapff clan.[3]

By all accounts, the new Mrs. John Bankhead Magruder was a charming, dutiful wife. Three children were born to the union in rapid order: Isabell (1833), Kate (1835), and Henry R. (1838)—the latter two never married. Magruder, however, "appeared to have only two objects in view—one to make a great show and the other to have a good time in society," writes an 1880 correspondent identified only as "Ebbett." And his heavy drinking, coupled with the high life, led to a crumpled marriage; in an oft-recorded scenario, Ebbett relates an incident shortly after the marriage that "created great amusement in the Army." While assigned to recruiting detail in Baltimore and living at Barnum's Hotel, Magruder returned home after a night on the town; unable to reach his quarters, he fell asleep among several mail bags in the post office then located in the hotel basement.

> After a while the stage coach for the mail and passengers for Washington arrived, and the driver finding the way bill ready and waiting for him, with one passenger noted on it, concluded John must be the man. He tried to wake him up, but as he could not arouse him he picked him up bodily and put him into the stage and started for Washington where he arrived the next morning.

Still unable to awaken his passenger, the stage driver placed him on a Washington bench and proceeded with his own duties; totally lost and disoriented, Magruder finally awoke long enough to visit a nearby tavern "for an eye-opener." Then, after eating breakfast, Magruder walked outside and "saw the old capitol and the two rows of Lombardy poplars which then lined Pennsylvania Avenue. . . ." A chance encounter with an army pal soon set him aright, and an embarrassed lieutenant made his way home. This widely reported excursion and similar alcoholic bouts led to a marital breakdown and Mrs. Magruder's eventual move to Italy with the children—after paying her husband's debts—where she spent the remainder of her life except for occasional visits with her husband. "His wife was very weak, but a good woman, and in love with him to an uncommon degree," writes Robert E. Lee's kinsman John Fitzgerald Lee. "But he managed to alienate her devoted attachment, to make her separate from him & leave him to the irregular life which was anything but happy or respectable." Magruder last saw his wife in 1866 when she and the younger children visited him in Mexico while he served Maximilian's regime. Many people, both in and out of the army, did not even know that he was married.[4]

In the year after leaving the military academy, Magruder employed one stratagem after the other to secure a better army assignment, despite Macomb's insistence that he join his infantry regiment; his July 1831 letter to Taney in fact may have been influenced by the graduation of his friend Albert Miller Lea in the class of 1831. Lea, who later served as secretary of war in Millard Fillmore's cabinet and enjoyed a distinguished engineering career in his native Tennessee as well as in Texas, apparently gave Magruder his place in the First Artillery following his own entry into the topographical service. Several directories have Magruder at Fortress Monroe, situated on the peninsula of Virginia at Hampton Roads, but he is not listed in the post returns; nor did he serve in the three companies from the First Artillery that left the fort in August 1831 to police the area around New Jerusalem—present-day Courtland, Virginia—following the famed slave rebellion led by Nat Turner. His friend Robert E. Lee, however, who left West Point two years before Magruder, was at Fortress Monroe during the brutal insurrection that not only took the lives of nearly sixty whites but also spread an awesome panic through the tidewater counties of Virginia and the Carolinas.[5]

Fears of servile uprisings also took several companies of the First Artillery to New Bern and Beaufort, North Carolina, during late 1831–1832; the slave populations of both Craven (New Bern) and Carteret (Beaufort) counties had increased dramatically in the decades after 1800. Located about 150 miles south of New Jerusalem, both communities were mightily agitated by the Nat Turner episode, although numbers of slaves from the region had been transported by their masters to the new cotton-producing areas along the Gulf Coast. Yet, "slaves enough remained to alarm whites whose anxieties, heightened by the antislavery movement, proved ready to lend credence to suspicions of conspiracy and rebellion," writes a local historian. In an attempt to calm a tense situation, troops were hurried south from Fortress Monroe, although they were recalled within a few weeks when the local population quieted. As his First Artillery companions tramped through the tidewater, however, Magruder and his bride of eighteen months were enjoying an extended furlough at his parents' home in Caroline County, far removed from the panic-stricken areas further south. Once more he had escaped an onerous assignment by appealing to Washington for a leave of absence because of health reasons.[6]

When he reported for duty in October 1832, Magruder secured a berth at historic Fort McHenry, near the Von Kapffs, and afterward as recruiting officer in Baltimore proper. Situated "at the tip of a narrow peninsula between the North, West, and Ferry branches of Maryland's Patapsco River," McHenry was near the gathering places of Baltimore society that attracted the young lieutenant and his wife. After its glory days during the Revolution and War of 1812, the old installation had fallen into disrepair throughout the 1820s. In the autumn of 1833—following Magruder's arrival—Lieutenant Henry Thompson, nephew of General Charles Gratiot, army chief of engineers, undertook supervision of numerous "repairs and new fortifications" that extended over several years. But Magruder no sooner took up his new post than he was off on a jaunt to the fashionable White Sulphur Springs in Greenbrier County, Virginia. One of several spas in mountainous western Virginia thought to possess medicinal qualities, White Sulphur attracted a well-to-do clientele, and continues to do so to the present day.

The venerated Bishop Francis Asbury, thought by many to be the father of American Methodism, branded the spas "seats of sin" because the holidaymakers were "gay and idle." An 1838 visitor to White Sulphur encountered a world that Magruder would have appreciated: "When we arrived at the springs, the company were going to dinner, and all the walks and avenues leading from the different cabins were streaming with lovely forms. A band of music was playing gaily in the portico of the dining hall; and the whole face of things had the look of enchantment." People visited the spas during the 1830s for the partying and good times—to see and be seen—but Magruder was also concerned about his wife, who awaited the birth of their first child. "On account of the very delicate condition of Mrs. Magruder's health," the adjutant general wrote to White Sulphur, his request for extended leave was granted while he remained in western Virginia; it is unclear whether his eldest daughter Isabell arrived during the stay or after the return to Baltimore.[7]

Magruder's tenure in Baltimore ended abruptly in February 1835 with an order to join the First Artillery at Fort Macon, on the North Carolina coast; a careful perusal of the monthly post returns reveals that he had a sporadic career over the next six months or so; and the inference is clear that he was politicking for a return to the Baltimore-Washington area at the first opportunity. Macon was a relatively new installation that had been constructed since 1828, although earlier posts had stood near its location at Bogue Point in Beaufort harbor;

when Magruder reported for duty in February 1835, the pentagon-shaped facility had been manned by his regiment since December 1834. Unfortunately, writes its chronicler, it was "never able to practice artillery drills for the fort remained unarmed." Magruder stayed at the post until July 22, when he took a leave of absence followed by a transfer to Fort Johnston, also in North Carolina. Fort Macon, although new, was never a popular posting because, as Magruder's superior, Reynolds N. Kirby, told one correspondent, "This is a miserable country and presents no objects to induce one voluntarily to remain in it." Sleeping quarters for men and officers were reportedly damp, which did not contribute to its desirability. Shortly after Magruder left, the place was left ungarrisoned, "except for an ordnance sergeant," when elements of the First Artillery were ordered to Florida.[8]

Magruder is first mentioned in the rolls of Fort Johnston for August 1835; and his new berth enabled him to escape—at least for the moment—duty in the Seminole wars, which were then heating up. It was ninety miles down the coast from Beaufort at the entrance to the Cape Fear River near Wilmington. Although military fortifications for the region had been discussed since colonial times, Johnston was not completed until 1816, "with a battery of eight mounted twenty-four-pound cannon, a brick building for the officers, a block house, a guard house, a hospital, and a range of buildings for the enlisted men." Magruder's commanding officer was Justin Dimmick, a Connecticut native and West Pointer, who went on to a distinguished career in Florida and Mexico; also serving at the fort was First Lieutenant John H. Winder, who, unlike Dimmick, not only joined the Confederacy but had been Prince John's drillmaster at West Point. Magruder was not present during September, and a terse entry in the official returns says he was on leave until September 3; he never returned to Fort Johnston, which, along with nearby Fort Caswell, was abandoned in February 1836; nor is he mentioned among the commissioned officers that accompanied "fifty-one N.O. officers, musicians, artificers & privates [who] left on 3 Feb 1836 aboard the steam boat John Storey" for the Florida wars.[9]

When Magruder left Fort Macon, he traveled to Wilmington by way of the North Carolina state capital at Raleigh; following an examination "before two or more judges of the supreme court," reported a city newspaper, "Lieut. John B. Magruder, of the U.S. army" was admitted to the practice of law in the state's county courts. The statutes say only that would-be attorneys were required to appear in front of the high court for examination, but the inference is clear that Magruder had used his yearlong furlough from his regiment to acquire some knowledge of the law. He avoided the stipulation that prospective lawyers reside in the state for one year by "producing for said judges, a testimonial from the chief magistrate of such state or county [of previous residence], or from some other competent authority, that he is of an exceptional moral character." Although the record is silent about his sponsor, he received his license to practice after payment of an enrollment fee; Magruder was also required "in open court before the judges thereof [to] take the oath prescribed for attorneys, and also the oaths of allegiance to this State, and to support the constitution of the United States, prescribed for all public officers." Only then, the law stated, could he practice upon his "good behavior." His brief tenure at Fort Johnston precluded a stint before the North Carolina bar, but fifteen years later he used his license to open a law office in San Diego, where he was posted following the Mexican War.[10]

With his legal career on hold and his First Artillery comrades headed for some rough campaigning in the Everglades, Magruder sped to Washington, where he pleaded with the adjutant general for another leave; the request was granted, along with an assignment to Fort Washington, on the Potomac. If he could not relocate at Baltimore, he got the next best thing, which placed him in commuting distance of his wife as well as his own family. Fort Washington, originally known as Fort Warburton, named for an early manor house in the region where George Washington once signaled with flags from Mount Vernon, beyond the river, had been designed by Washington himself in 1795. First constructed to guard the new capital, the fort proved worthless during the British invasion of 1814; Charles L'Enfant, "the famed military designer," completely rebuilt the place following the War of 1812, but, writes its historian, "Fort Washington was allowed, as most fortifications throughout the United States, to go to rack and ruin for want of proper care of its armaments and entrenchments; until 1850 it was a mere military post having one or two companies of artillery." Although units of the First Artillery under Colonel Miles

Mason had been there for several months, Magruder was placed in temporary charge upon his arrival in late 1835; and he was immediately confronted with a number of personal dilemmas that led to the discharge of at least one enlisted man and the post surgeon—one Dr. Stinnecke—in unrelated matters. His first independent command was clearly one of short duration, because, reads a note in the post returns, "Lt. J. B. Magruder relinquished command on 6 November 1835." He remained several weeks, however, before his transfer to a desk job in Washington.[11]

About the time Magruder left Fort Washington, an episode known as the Dade Massacre, on December 28, 1835, in the faraway swamps of Florida inflamed the so-called Second Seminole War. Trouble between the Florida Indians and white men ever encroaching upon their territory intensified following Andrew Jackson's election to the presidency in 1828. Jackson's 1813–1814 campaign through the Southwest "had broken forever the military power of the southern Indians," and the old Indian fighter remained convinced that transportation of natives to the virgin lands west of the Mississippi—principally Oklahoma—was the proper course. His famous encounter with Chief Justice John Marshall over Indian removal served to fix the presidential resolve. In order to conform, a group of Seminole chieftains met with Jackson's representative, James Gadsden, at Payne's Landing on the Oklawaha River during 1832 and agreed to relocate in the west. The Payne's Landing pact, much heralded by white Floridians because it freed the state from "the savages," was followed by a second treaty signed at Fort Gibson. Under the 1833 accord, four hereditary caciques—Jumper, John Blunt, Charley Emathla, and Holahta—signed a document that committed every Indian in Florida to join the western exodus within three years.[12]

Far from being a homogeneous people, the Florida tribesmen were not racially unified, nor were they agreed upon a common approach to incursions by the white man. "Tribes of Muskhogean stock had made their home in Florida for upward of a century, all of them identified with Alabama or Georgia Creeks," notes a historian of the period. "Some were known as Seminoles, some as Mikasukis, others as Apalaches, still others as Tallahassees. Antedating these [peoples] in Florida were the so-called Spanish Indians: the Calusas, supposedly of Choctaw origin; and the Tequestas, whom tradition says came to continental America from the nearby Bahama Islands." Many rank-and-file Indians—primarily Seminoles—not only repudiated the Fort Gibson accord and the four chiefs, but also summoned a new leader, the legendary Osceola. Described as "a fierce young warrior," Osceola soon took up the tomahawk and rifle against his persecutors. His mother, an Alabama Creek, had been married to a white man named Powell, although conflicting reports dispute whether Powell was Osceola's father. Osceola unquestionably had white blood in his veins, but, driven from Alabama with his mother following Andrew Jackson's invasion, he nursed an unremitting hatred of everything white. "Contemporaries said that he was a little below common height, elegantly formed, with small feet and that he displayed great skill in all physical games," writes a Seminole scholar. "One observer recorded that a continuous smile played over his face, particularly when shaking hands with the officers." When Jackson learned that Osceola and his warriors had no intention of honoring the Treaty of Fort Gibson, which the president regarded as sacrosanct, a force under General David L. Clinch was sent to enforce compliance. When Clinch dispatched an expedition into the interior under brevet major Francis Langhorn Dade, it was ambushed with the resultant death of one hundred and ten officers and enlisted men.[13]

A military buildup commenced immediately after the Dade slaughter, in which Osceola himself was slightly wounded. Units of the First Artillery reached Florida as early as January 1836—several of them from Fort Johnston, Magruder's old post before he secured his place at Fort Washington. At least three commanders besides Clinch had been in charge of Florida operations before Magruder's coming in November 1837: Winfield Scott, Edmund P. Gaines, and finally Thomas S. Jesup. Although Scott and Gaines made little headway against Osceola because of violent personal clashes, Magruder's comrades from the First Artillery were in the thick of it from the moment of their arrival in Florida. Captain Dimmick, post commander at Fort Johnston during Magruder's stay, led a May 1836 foray against the Seminoles near St. Augustine; the move came after Winfield Scott ordered several artillery companies mounted "to patrol and scour the frontiers and settlements east of the St. Johns [River]." Dimmick was sent "to follow up an Indian trail, and near Matanzas overtook a small party of Indians, killing three and wounding several, with a loss of one private killed and three wounded." Company D, Magruder's old charge in North Carolina, had done the fighting a few miles down the coast from St. Augustine; eight companies of the First Artillery remained active in pursuing the Seminoles through their hummocks and swampy retreats during the autumn of 1836.[14]

Portions of the regiment had been on duty in Alabama, but "when the Creek War came to a sudden close in the fall of 1836, Gen. Jesup transferred Company I with his other regular troops to Tampa Bay to form part of the army of Florida." And, continues a regimental historian, "the entire regiment was then for the first time in Florida, but was woefully deficient in numbers both of officers and men. No discharged soldier would re-enlist, and the recruits became sick within a short time after joining." The war office issued special order No. 69 to not only summon all regimental officers to Florida but also to bring the First up to full strength; and Magruder was told to comply. While his fellows were suffering the trials of camp life among the swamps, he fired off an October 18 appeal to the adjutant general, accompanied by a surgeon's certificate requesting a leave of absence from the campaign that was rapidly becoming the nation's costliest Indian war. In fact he received a reply endorsed by Macomb himself: "Although you may not be able as stated, to perform the active duty of the field, yet as your services may be usefully employed in the commissary and quartermaster's Departments at St. Augustine, Tampa Bay, or lighten the desks at other stations in Florida, the general-in-chief does not deem it prudent to release you from the operation of Order No. 69." A followup directive, however, dated November 9, acknowledged a new medical report by the secretary of war, and extended his leave until December 31, after which he was required to join the regiment.[15]

At his own request, Magruder had been assigned to drafting-topographical duty at the termination of his leave. Throughout, he suffered from a persistent bronchial/lung disorder that caused him greater difficulty through the 1840s upon his return north from Florida. As matters developed, the climate must have helped his condition, because he took an active part in the ensuing campaigns. After some months at the Topographical Bureau, five years following his first attempt to join that branch, he was told to rejoin the First Artillery, and by November he was making his way southward aboard the *South Carolina*. With stopovers at Norfolk and Charleston, South Carolina, he reached the Florida coast in time to participate in the concentration of forces at Mosquito Lagoon—near the present-day Kennedy Space Center—as part of a renewed offensive against the Seminoles. As Magruder approached the rendezvous, Jesup performed an act of outright treachery and duplicity by clamping Osceola in irons when he came to parley with the army on October 27. Although the renowned chief was transported to Fort Moultrie in South Carolina, "where he died a few months later," the backbone of Seminole resistance had been broken before Magruder reached the fighting.[16]

Following Osceola's removal from the struggle, other chieftains remained in the field, most notably Sam Jones, a.k.a. Apiaka, in the Okeechobee region of south Florida. Jesup, who had taken over the campaign from territorial governor Richard K. Call, "had a fully developed plan of campaigning for the winter of 1837–1838 that would push the Seminoles further into the peninsula and leave the north Florida frontier relatively free of the Indian danger." The scheme sent armies against the foe on four fronts: General Joseph M. Hernandez moved southward from St. Augustine "to scour" the country east of the St. Johns River, which flows north and parallel to the Atlantic for more than 150 miles. When Magruder arrived at Smyrna in late November, he was attached to this command. Colonel Zachary Taylor marched inland from Tampa Bay to strike the area north of Lake Okeechobee; others in the master plan included Persifor F. Smith, dispatched eastward from Charlotte Harbor, and Abraham Eustis, who moved down the Gulf coast of western Florida. Lieutenant Levi M. Powell, of the navy, who got himself overrun during the campaign, was ordered to the Jupiter Inlet–New River area to map the southeastern coast. Little campaigning had occurred through the summer of 1837, so Jesup was obliged to replenish his force during October–November. When the army marched—with the First Artillery taking a prominent role—Jesup had the largest force ever employed during the conflict: 4,636 men from the regular army, and 170 marines.[17]

Jacob Rhett Motte, an army surgeon attached to the First Artillery, has penned a detailed, if somewhat wordy, account of the campaign under Hernandez from late 1837 until the regiment's departure to the north in August 1838. After his movement from St. Augustine, Hernandez paused at Smyrna, he relates, for a general organization of his forces; at daylight on November 29, Magruder's company and two others, under William W. Mackall and William H. French, were ordered to move down Mosquito Lagoon toward Cape Canaveral; the narrow, shallow lagoon, an inlet from the Atlantic, extends several miles to a spot known as the haulover—"so-called from its being a strip of land nearly a mile wide, which separated the Lagoon from Indian River, over which the Indians were accustomed to drag their canoes from one water to the other." Although the movement was headed by a naval lieutenant, Motte continues, "Lt. Magruder as commander of the force, and myself as Fleet Surgeon accompanied the commodore in the 'Flagship,' which was a small sloop or sailing vessel. The troops followed in ten to a dozen Mackinaw boats that had been prepared one day earlier under Magruder's direction." Once ashore at the haulover, Magruder's bivouac rested several days to await the arrival of Hernandez, moving down an interior road with the rest of his units. "The scenery was anything but prepossessing; nothing visible but the dried and tangled limbs of the dead mangrove trees, which had been killed by a frost during the severe winter of 1835; nothing green not even a blade of grass met the eye to enliven the view," Motte continues. Great flocks of sea birds swarmed in every direction.

Magruder and his compeers stayed at the haulover until December 30, when Jesup and Hernandez renewed the offensive; at Christmas, "we revelled upon gopher soup and whiskey toddy, which were the chief luxuries that graced our board," the doctor relates. "By the bye; as regarded *gopher soup*, no epicure in the world but would smack his lips could he get a taste of this rare dish known only in Florida; and the whiskey toddy was highly relished also, to judge by the quantity that we stowed away, though its chief recommendation was the fact of it being the only liquor that was attainable at Camp Haulover." Magruder must have been in the midst of the Yule festivities, and his bronchial difficulties must have abated, because Dr. Motte has him joining in the musical renditions that engulfed the encampment: "McGruder[18] also occasionally contributed his mite on the [guitar] and his voice was not disagreeable, and always in tune for 'Ouoi Liset est cp vous.'" He had great versatility, his companion says, though a number of owls often hooted along with the merrymakers. By December 31, Magruder and his fellow revelers had moved to Indian River Inlet, at the tip of Hutchinson Island, where they helped with the construction of Fort Pierce near the St. Lucie River.[19]

Meanwhile, Zachary Taylor, Magruder's future commander in the Mexican War, on his march from Tampa Bay had fought the largest engagement of the war against Sam Jones and 400 warriors on Christmas Day, in something called the Battle of Lake Okeechobee; "Taylor lost 26 men, with another 112 wounded, while Indian casualties were 11 and 14 respectively, but because the Seminoles withdrew to the lake and then faded into the countryside, his assault was declared a major victory," declares a recent historian. The Sam Jones–Taylor imbroglio took place a few miles southwest of Fort Pierce, where Magruder awaited Jesup's next move. Then, on January 16, the young lieutenant saw the results of Indian warfare up close when Lieutenant Powell and his naval contingent straggled into Fort Pierce from a tragic fight near Jupiter Inlet in which two soldiers, two sailors, and a naval surgeon had been killed and fifteen wounded. Magruder looked on as Dr. Motte and his helpers ministered to what remained of Powell's company, in which every officer had been wounded. The next morning, January 17, Jesup gave the word to march south in search of Powell's tormentors.[20]

Contact was made on January 23–25 in the Battle of Lockahatchee (or Loxahatchee) following a march through country described by Motte as

> one unbroken extent of water and morass; a very little land; much saw-palmetto; and more snakes, mosquitoes, and other venomous "*critters*" than one can shake a stick at. Nothing, however, can be imagined more lovely and picturesque than the thousand little isolated spots, scattered in all directions over the surface of this immense sheet of water, which seemed like a placid inland sea shining under a bright sun.

For a man of Magruder's sensibilities, south Florida was not the ideal locale for campaigning of any kind; nor was he directly involved in the fighting under Jesup, "in which the government troops suffered heavier casualties than the Indian forces they defeated." The fight in which Jesup himself was wounded took place north of the Jupiter River, not far from Taylor's triumph at Lake Okeechobee. Although Magruder was not on the field, he was assigned by Jesup and Pierce to oversee the unloading of several transports laden with supplies for the advancing columns. Jesup's ability to win at Lockahatchee resulted in considerable measure from Magruder's diligence as "assistant quartermaster" in getting the supplies in place by running his own boat "through surf and swarms of sharks."[21]

Next, Jesup tramped farther south along the eastern fringe of the Everglades. While Magruder's precise movements cannot be verified with certainty, he surely marched with Hernandez's command to Fort Lauderdale. William L. Haskin, historian of the First Artillery, proclaims it "the disgust of all" that the regiment remained on station following the victories of Taylor and Jesup. Treacherous sawgrass literally cut the shoes off men as they marched, and horses were useless in the half water, half earth of the region. "After all, Florida is certainly the poorest country two people ever quarreled for. The climate in the first place is objectionable; for even in winter, while persons further north are freezing, we were melting in heat," Dr. Motte records. "In the next place, the larger portion of Florida is a poor, sandy country in the north; and in the southern portions nearly all wet prairies and swamp; and in the south even the Indians said they could not live a month without suffering, and in summer not at all."

Magruder's uncle, Colonel James Bankhead, led an expedition of 400 men from Fort Lauderdale into the Everglades during late March that terminated in another questionable engagement with the Seminoles; in what became the last offensive action of the campaign, the Indians simply took refuge in the ever-present sawgrass, which "afforded them complete concealment that pursuit would be useless." Finally the First Artillery was transferred from the region in April for duty against the Cherokees along the North Carolina–Tennessee border; but after a month or so of inactivity the regiment was sent to northern New York. Although Magruder was ensconced at his new bivouac in Plattsburg by the autumn of 1838, the Florida wars dragged on for several years, until the government simply gave up and left the Indians unmolested in their swampy haunts. Nor was he pleased with his time among the Seminoles in that pristine era before the advent of modern amenities; in 1844, six years after he left, Magruder complained to the adjutant general in Washington that his tenure in Florida merited a promotion to brevet captain.[22]

Seven years elapsed between Magruder's arrival on the Canadian frontier and the outbreak of war with Mexico, which finally brought him a measure of recognition. It was a period of frustrating garrison duty along the cold northern reaches of the country—an abrupt change from the steamy lowlands of south Florida. Although he was Prince John once more, with a growing reputation for grand living, as evidenced by the encounter with his British counterparts over his lavish mess, Magruder experienced several disappointments. His long-sought promotion to captain eluded him, his marriage fell apart, and he was forced to combat a debilitating lung ailment during 1842–1844. But it was a seeming inability to manage his accounts that caused trouble with the high command. The departure of Mrs. Magruder for Europe with the three children left him not only short of money but also dependent upon his own meager pay. Endless money shortfalls—with both his personal and army lists—plagued him at posts in New York and Maine.

Some months after his assignment to command Company B in upstate New York, Magruder was obliged to contact the "Bank of the Metropolis" in Washington, seeking relief from a $160 note; the issue was resolved after he designated one J. M. Carlisle to use "rents" from his Washington property to settle the debt. In May 1841, as he recruited in Boston, Magruder got into a dispute with army auditors over his handling of company funds at Plattsburg. But when he asked to visit Washington to adjudicate any discrepancies, he was ordered to stay put; although he wanted to proceed toward his Baltimore home, the "third auditor" told him to pay up from Fort Independence in Boston Harbor, where he was quartered. More difficulties ensued after he took charge of his company at Houlton, Maine; at least two letters followed him to Corpus Christi during 1846, where he served with Zachary Taylor's Army of Occupation. He was not only required to show why "post funds" were used for Company B expenditures, but he was instructed in March that transfers of that nature were "disapproved." This poor handling of his company funds cast Magruder in a consistently poor light with army brass, and doubtless contributed to his slow promotions.[23]

The First Artillery—followed by Magruder in September 1838—was rushed to the frontier from North Carolina in response to trouble along the U.S.-Canadian border; in an early outpouring of Manifest Destiny, Americans living in upstate New York felt an obligation to help a number of Canadian dissidents, led by William Lyon Mackenzie, bring an end to British domination of the colony. "The insurgents found it easy to recruit men and supplies at Buffalo, Rochester, Montpelier, and ten or a dozen other places along the frontier," writes a prominent historian. "They also established a base on Navy Island, a Canadian possession in the Niagara River not far above the falls." The revolutionaries, emboldened by support of their Yankee allies, created a provisional government and opened a series of attacks against the colonial authorities. Events reached fever pitch on December 29, 1837, when a band of Canadian militia crossed into United States territory and fired on the *Caroline*, a small American-owned steamboat used to run guns and supplies from New York to Navy Island. The vessel was not only destroyed and dispatched over the falls, but an American citizen was killed during the fray. A huge outcry of indignation swept the frontier as New Yorkers and others yelled for British blood.[24]

President Martin Van Buren, the "Little Magician," adopted a strict neutrality, to the considerable chagrin of hotheads south of the border who wanted to intervene in the Canadian upheaval; his proclamation of nonintervention was followed in March 1838 by congressional authorization of $625,000 in defense monies and a sanction to employ force if necessary to prevent "new outrages." Although the difficulties did not subside for several months, the First Artillery moved into Plattsburg when a post was created on September 5, 1838. Magruder and thirty-three men under his command were present from the beginning of the encampment. Also present was Captain Francis Taylor, commanding Company K, the man who shortly introduced Stonewall Jackson to the artillery during the Mexican War. The Plattsburg installation had been established under the command of Justin Dimmick, Magruder's superior on the Carolina coast and in Florida, although he was shortly ordered across Lake Champlain to plant an army presence in northern Vermont. Subsequent base commanders included Enos Cutler, Giles Porter, Reynolds N. Kirby, and B. K. Pierce, who remained in charge until the regiment left during the spring of 1840.[25]

Although removed from the border flashpoint around Niagara and western New York, Magruder and his companions not only encountered the discomforts of camp life but also had to combat several incursions by "scatterbrained men" from the north; and the regular officers dispatched to the region took a dim view of any Americans who abetted the foreign insurgents. Van Buren's intentions notwithstanding, a lodge called The Hunters was organized in New York and Vermont to help the Canadians, to the disgust of the army; the brotherhood even seized and destroyed a British ship, the *Sir Robert Peel*, near Oswego, in retaliation for the *Caroline*. While Magruder went about his duties and continued his incessant pleas for leaves of absence, the Hunters launched several cross-border raids from Ogdensburg, New York, and from as far west as Detroit. Still, Magruder, a mere first lieutenant, commanding but one company—it had increased to thirty-six privates by March 1839 but dropped to twenty-four in November—soon found himself embroiled in tedious peacekeeping operations. In February 1838, only five or six months after his arrival in Plattsburg, he was back in Washington, although he was summoned to report to his commanding officer by March 1; and by April he was again reported "sick," with his leave extended through May 30. Since additional leave was granted during October 1839, he certainly spent inordinate amounts of time riding the well-established stage line connecting New York City and the Lake Champlain corridor.[26]

Magruder and his fellow officers lived in a Plattsburg hotel, since the encampment had been formed so quickly that no barracks were available for them. Writes Major Haskin:

> As winter came on, and heavy snows blocked up the country roads, which were none the best at any time, the guerrilla movements of the rebels in Canada and their sympathizers on our side increased in number and destruction. Burnings of houses, barns, etc., were frequent, and we were constantly on the move to arrest offenders of our neutrality obligations. Serving in snow storms and the intense cold of the region, the thermometer ranging a good part of the time

from zero, below to ten, fifteen, twenty-six degrees came hard on our men, who had been so long under the southern temperature of Florida, and whose uniform, the same as issued in Florida, was totally inadequate to the extreme northern climate.

Magruder, like the others, faced a set of stressful living conditions, although the hotel accommodations were more suitable than those of his men. The harsh conditions brought a desire for cooperation with their British counterparts beyond the border, who had been rushed to the opposing frontier from "the Coldstream Guards, one Battalion of the Grenadier Guards, the 7th Hussars, Queen's Own, the 1st Dragoon Guards, the 1st Royals, 73rd Highlanders, and other crack regiments." In a spirit of collegiality, a series of sporting events and "ice races" were initiated between the American and British troops. Prince John Magruder, "of course," acted as master of ceremonies for the contests over "one mile of swept ice" on frozen Lake Champlain. His great affability was already making him a favorite throughout the army, even if he could not impress the high command.[27]

While not on leave, Magruder served at Plattsburg through March 1840, when the First Artillery was ordered farther east to the United States border with New Brunswick; but he left the regiment temporarily for another stint at recruiting—this time in Boston. By late 1842 he had rejoined his messmates as commander of Company B at Hancock Barracks, located in Houlton, Maine. Although a truce arranged by Winfield Scott between American and British forces had been in effect since March 1839, he was nonetheless ordered to rejoin his unit. The First Artillery went to the Maine frontier in response to that picturesque episode known as the Aroostook War, in which no one was killed in spite of heated bombast by politicians on both sides of the Atlantic. The international impasse grew out of a lingering boundary disagreement that resulted from an imperfect wording of the 1783 treaty ending the Revolution. After the Missouri Compromise and the admission of Maine to the Union, the new state commenced issuing land titles along the Aroostook River in an area claimed by the British, who planned to build a military road through the region to connect Nova Scotia and the St. Lawrence. An arbitration pact hammered out by the Dutch, however, which London accepted, was rejected by the United States Senate.

After Canadian lumberjacks moved into the region during 1838–1839, Maine governor John Fairfield and his legislature sped militia companies to disperse the timbering camps, "and the Aroostook War was on." While Magruder remained at Plattsburg, Congress rammed through an authorization for the President "to call out 50,000 volunteers and voted $10 million for defense." But Van Buren, still the pacifist, rushed his ace troubleshooter, Winfield Scott, to the frontier before a warlike confrontation erupted with the British regulars arrayed beyond the border in New Brunswick. Although his truce of March 1839 averted war, units of the First Artillery were sent not only to Hancock Barracks but also to Forts Kent and Fairfield, farther north. When Magruder got to Houlton, the regiment—again faced with a torturous winter—had settled down to a garrison routine. The famed Webster-Ashburton Treaty of August 1842, settling the dispute—7,000 acres to Maine and 5,000 to Canada—as well as other differences with England, had already been inked in a Washington ceremony.[28]

Hancock Barracks, started in 1828 as part of preparations for war, was a well-established place when Prince John reported for duty. The bivouac "was in the style then favored by United States army engineers in other areas of the nation: a quadrangle of quarters and offices surrounded by a parade ground, the whole enclosed by a thick stockade," records a post chronicler. "It was constructed upon a rise east of Houlton village, on the north side of the Woodstock Road." And, observes a local historian, "the powder magazine was located some distance beyond the Northwest angle; the hospital was built back from the line of the other buildings, in the Southeast section of the enclosure; the quarters for the privates extended around two sides of the quadrangle; and the larger and more commodious houses for the officers and staff were built along the East side." Magruder's housing may have been comfortable, but the place, like Plattsburg, was unattractive to the army because of its disagreeable weather. "The allowance for wood in this climate, the degree of latitude being 46 deg. 13 min., is not equal to the quantity necessary for comfort during the severity of the winter," wrote Major N. S. Clark, an early post commander. "I deem it a duty therefore to recommend an allowance in favor of this post by one-half at least during the months of December, January, February, and March. This Post, with a single exception,

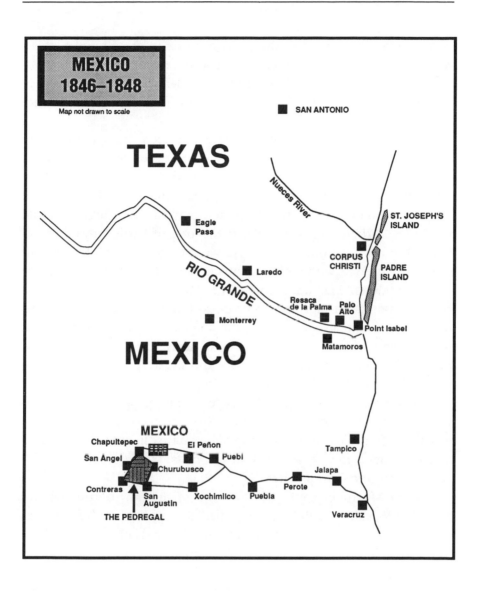

MEXICO
1846–1848

Map not drawn to scale

SAN ANTONIO

TEXAS

Nueces River

ST. JOSEPH'S
ISLAND

Eagle
Pass

CORPUS
CHRISTI

PADRE
ISLAND

RIO GRANDE

Laredo

Resaca
de la Palma

Palo
Alto

Monterrey

Point Isabel

Matamoros

MEXICO

MEXICO

Chapultepec

El Peñon

San Angel

Puebi

Tampico

Churubusco

Jalapa

Contreras

Perote

Xochimilco

Puebla

San
Augustin

THE PEDREGAL

Veracruz

is the most northern of all the Military posts in the United States."
Situated on the Meduxnekeag River, thirteen miles east of Woodstock, New Brunswick, where it joins the larger St. John, the place
was abandoned in August 1845, when the First Artillery and other
units headed south for the Mexican War.[29]

In January 1843, Magruder, feeling the keen disappointment of
having been passed over for promotion, attempted to transfer out of
his company into one of the "flying batteries." Traditional artillery
units, with their heavy, cumbersome guns, could do little more than
take a position on the battleground and pray that the fighting would
shift toward their emplacements. If the tide of battle flowed in another direction, the older units were virtually useless, while the light
or flying batteries, with their maneuverable limbers, were much more
effective. When Magruder learned that several light batteries were
being consolidated into new companies during the summer of 1842,
he set out to land a spot in one of them. The reorganizational scheme
was prompted by a reduction in overall army size following ratification of the Webster-Ashburton Treaty and the absence of any foreign
threat. Mostly enlisted men were cut from regimental rolls, while the
officer corps was kept intact, thereby reducing the opportunity for advancement. And, observes, Major Haskin, "each company of artillery
was thereafter to consist of one captain, two first lieutenants, one second lieutenant, four sergeants, four corporals, two artificers, two musicians, and forty-two privates."[30]

When Magruder applied to join one of the new outfits, he was
told that Washington did not recognize the right of "subalterns" to
transfer from one company to another on the basis of seniority. "The
rights of field officers with respect to duty and command are limited
to the Regiment in which they are commissioned. So are the rights of
subalterns and captains for duty and command restricted to the company in which their promotion may carry them and in which they are
mustered." And, in a fit of bureaucratic justification: "When any
changes or transfers of subalterns are made the arrangement is with
the requirements of the public service." Undeterred, Magruder continued his fight for promotion during his stay at Hancock Barracks
and later when he returned to Baltimore on sick leave.

By May 1845—three months before his move to Corpus Christi—
he had secured and filed recommendations with the adjutant general

from a number of prominent men: Virginia congressman and later United States senator R.M.T. Hunter, who was also Speaker of the House of Representatives; General Thomas Jesup; Commodore David D. Porter; John Tyler's secretary of war, William L. Wilkins; Major Justin Dimmick of the First Artillery; his uncle Colonel James Bankhead; and a number of lesser officials. Bankhead, who came to his support for a captaincy, must have overcome his earlier disapproval of Magruder's carousing. Although he was attached to the Second Artillery, Bankhead nonetheless kept a close watch on his nephew, and the two would serve together in Mexico.

> But John's dissipations, debts, and escapades of various sorts, wearied the patience of his uncle, who one day took to lecturing his nephew for his conduct. Grasping a pinch of snuff, the old Colonel commenced with: "John, why the devil can't you behave yourself? You are always in some damned scrape, and now these fellows are complaining that you won't pay their bills for champaign and cigars. Now there's your brother George . . . who is a quiet and well-behaved gentleman as ever lived; why is it that you are not like him."

Thus writes the ubiquitous Ebbett in his widely circulated biographical sketch.

"Well, uncle," said John, "George, you know—ah—followed your prethept. I thupothe, I—ah—followed your ekthample." The Colonel, who was very deaf, had John repeat his remark. Drawing his red bandanna across his upper lip to wipe off the snuff, he turned to old Major Payne, who was sitting near him, and said: "Payne, did you hear what that G—— —— rascal said?"[31]

All was apparently forgiven during 1844–1845 as Magruder sought his uncle's help; he had, after all, gotten no recognition since his March 1836 promotion to first lieutenant. Nor did he abandon the struggle. In January 1846, following his arrival in Texas, he enlisted the aid of General William Jenkins Worth to win the promotion. Worth, who had not attended West Point, had risen through the ranks after his 1813 commission during the War of 1812; the New York–born general had been superintendent of the academy during Magruder's fourth and third terms on the Hudson. Unlike Prince John, who received no promotion during the Seminole War, Worth had attained general's rank for his service in Florida.

"In the event of an increase of the military establishment which seems not unlikely, Lieutenant J. Bankhead Magruder desires to be remembered & measured as a candidate for promotion and it gives me pleasure to offer my humble testimony, ineffective as it may be, . . . to his mature qualifications," he had written to Secretary of War William L. Marcy. Worth, who said that he spoke with zeal, added: "M——— is now perhaps one of the oldest if not the oldest 1st, Lieut.s in the army and he is, by general agreement the most accomplished & soldierly man in the service by education, habits, & association. . . ." The letter was missent to New Orleans and did not reach Magruder's hand until April, as he served on the Rio Grande with Zachary Taylor, awaiting the opening shots of the Mexican War. When he rushed the missive to Washington on April 23, he headed his cover letter: "Army of Occupation, Camp opposite Matamoros." Magruder asked that Worth's recommendation—he called him a subaltern of merit—be laid before the secretary of war "immediately," after pointing out that he had served under Worth "for the past seven months." Although others, including Colonel B. K. Pierce, had also seconded his petitions, Magruder did not get the promotion before he left the United States; and, in Mexico, even with Worth's good words, the captaincy did not come until June 18, 1847, more than a year afterward.[32]

Meanwhile, Magruder had been posted to recruiting duty in New York following his stint at Hancock Barracks. In July 1844, as he struggled with Washington, he returned to Baltimore on leave. Something of his despondency can be gathered from a note in his own hand addressed to Lieutenant Joseph Hooker, then serving as regimental adjutant for the First Artillery. "The principal object of my leave of absence, which had been extended to the 22nd August, was to arrange with my brother-in-law, now in Europe certain important family matters, which have been postponed for a long time, in consequence of professional occupation on my part." But his brother-in-law had been detained, which induced Magruder to ask for another month's leave, because "my business cannot be accomplished in his absence." As he pleaded with Hooker, who later opposed him on the peninsula as a subcommander in McClellan's Army of the Potomac, he added a postscript: "Perhaps it is well to mention that I have not had more than fifty days leave of absence, altogether in the last ten years." Whatever occurred when his Von Kapff kinsman reached Baltimore, Mrs. Magruder, who had moved her residence to Rome, did not rejoin her husband until after the Civil War, although he made at least two trips to Europe in the interval.[33]

A few weeks after his requests to Hooker, Magruder visited private physicians in Baltimore complaining that his nagging respiratory ailment prevented a return to the Canadian frontier. Dr. M. R. Stewart concluded that remaining in a northern climate would "surely aggravate your disease," while Dr. William Power also examined him during the first weeks of September 1844. Power could discover no "organic attrition of the lungs," but, he added in a letter to Magruder, "The evidences of a chronic bronchitis is very palpable—diffused throughout both sides of your chest, but more intense at the summit of the right lung, where owing to the thickening of the mucus membrane lining the bronchial tubes and the viscid secretion from its surface the function of respiration is very improperly performed." He, too, advocated "a residence in a mild climate." When the adjutant general demanded another, official opinion, Magruder visited Dr. H. S. Stinnecke, who had remained on active duty and who reinforced the two other physicians; he even referred to Power as "a gentleman of considerable reputation for skill in determining the character of diseases of the chest from physical signs—perceptible only by means of the stethoscope." His onetime nemesis at Fort Washington thought continued service in Maine would be detrimental.[34]

The findings were duly laid before Winfield Scott, who penned a September 19 memo found in "Letters Received by the Adjutant General": "If the case be as the private physicians represent, Lieut. Magruder will be excused from returning to his post & may be employed in distributing recruits." Probably unaware of Scott's ruling, Magruder informed the adjutant general on September 23 that illness prevented his rejoining Company B; and, he added, "I have suffered a serious hemorrhage from the lungs" since forwarding the medical reports. Within three weeks, however, he had recovered sufficiently to leave Baltimore for his new assignment in New York. Although he had failed to secure his berth in a "temperate climate," he was pleased that he had avoided a return to Hancock Barracks. In December 1844 he was in Savannah, Georgia, at Oglethorpe Barracks, with twenty-four raw recruits that he "turned over to the post commander in good order."[35]

Magruder's stay in the balmy temperatures of the south was short-lived indeed; by August 1845 he had rejoined the First Artillery at Fort Independence in Boston Harbor, as the war clouds gathered along the Rio Grande in the far southwest. As he prepared to sail for the Texas coast, Magruder made a last appeal to join one of the light artillery companies by petitioning Washington for permission to merge his own Company B with Captain Francis Taylor's Company I, also assembling for the voyage southward. "I am instructed to inform you that the application having been disapproved both by the commander of Department (your Colonel) and General of Division, that the General-in-Chief cannot give his sanction to your request," the adjutant general responded on August 14. In the fifteen years since his graduation from West Point, Prince John Magruder was still a first lieutenant attached to a regular artillery company, with little prospect of immediate change in his spotty military career; and though he had managed to alienate his wife and was suffering a severe lung disorder that may have hinged on tuberculosis, Mexico would at last afford an opportunity to prove himself. The fiery anvil of battle on the roads once traveled by Cortés and the conquistadors not only brought fame with the flying batteries—he secured a transfer later—but also an opportunity to associate with some of army's most influential officers.[36]

3

A Box in the National Theater

FIRST LIEUTENANT JOHN BANKHEAD MAGRUDER, going about the country "distributing recruits" during the early months of 1845, was surely aware that trouble was brewing between the United States and Mexico over a proper boundary between the two nations. Texas, of course, was the sticking point, and when the Lone Star was admitted to statehood by a joint congressional resolution on February 27–28, the country found itself on the downward slope to war—a war that would pluck the thirty-nine-year-old Magruder from his obscurity. For the first time since January 1815 and the Battle of New Orleans, the United States officer corps would be summoned to fight a civilized nation; nearly every officer of any standing, Northern or Southern, in the American Civil War got his first taste of organized warfare in Mexico, Magruder included. The unprecedented army expansion required to defeat Generalissimo Antonio López de Santa Anna at the gates of Mexico City in September 1847 infused excitement into an otherwise stagnant service, and brought advancement to hundreds of officers who emerged from the Mexican conflict with new insignia and braid on their sleeves that gave them an increased prestige through the 1850s. Magruder was no exception—he returned to the United States a brevet lieutenant colonel of artillery.

Although Northern abolitionists decried Texas annexation as "the great slave plot," an attempt to expand the slaveholding South, President John Tyler had rammed it through in the aftermath of Polk's election to the White House in November 1844; deep-seated convictions, many of them transported from the Old World, had convinced

Anglo-Saxon North America that the Catholic Spaniard—to say nothing of the darker-skinned Mexican—was an impediment to American domination of the continent. And when their fellow Protestants beyond the Red River in Texas found themselves living under an alien regime, sentiment within the United States was overwhelmingly on the side of Sam Houston and his "Texicans" as they crushed Santa Anna at San Jacinto in April 1836. Now their kinsmen were no longer obliged to marry before a priest or suffer other prejudices, and, best of all, Texan independence meant they would someday join the federal Union. The United States government maintained an outward neutrality throughout the hostilities between the Republic of Texas and Mexico, 1836–1845; but the country at large sympathized with Anglo-Saxon Texas during an endless stream of cross-border confrontations. Manifest Destiny—the notion that North America was a sacred preserve for the white races—led inexorably to a struggle for mastery over the peoples below the Rio Grande. During the years of Texas independence, Americans "grew progressively more antagonistic toward Mexico as a nation," finds John Eisenhower. By the early months of 1845 war between the two countries had become inevitable.[1]

Mexico had never recognized Texas nationhood, officially regarding the place as a province in revolt; and when word reached Mexico City that the American Congress had adopted a joint resolution affixing Texas to the United States, Mexican rulers had no option but to react with vehemence against the hated "gringos." The immediate question was a new international boundary that Mexico said rested on the Nueces River, which flows into the Gulf of Mexico at Corpus Christi, while Texas and Washington put the frontier at the Rio Grande, 120 miles farther south. As both sides jockeyed for position in this vast no-man's-land of sand dunes, cactus, and prickly pears, the Mexican government broke off diplomatic relations on May 28; simultaneously, Secretary of War William L. Marcy, a key member of the new Polk administration, penned an ominous note to General Zachary Taylor, commanding U.S. troops at Fort Jesup on the Louisiana border with Texas:

> As soon as the Texas Congress shall give its consent to annexation, and a convention shall assemble and accept the terms offered in the resolution of Congress, Texas will be regarded by the executive

government here so far a part of the United States as to be entitled
. . . to defense and protection from foreign invasion and Indian incursions. The troops under your command will be placed in readiness to perform that duty.

Taylor's "Army of Observation" was shortly ordered nearer the
Rio Grande, and by July 31, three weeks after Texan ratification of
the annexation document, Old Rough and Ready had established
himself at Corpus Christi.[2]

Although Washington had not issued a declaration of war, Taylor
amassed a formidable military force over the next several weeks, em-
bracing more than half of the United States army. Lieutenant Magruder, his health having apparently improved, could no longer avoid
active service, and by late August he had resumed command of Company B, as the First Artillery assembled in New York for the voyage
south; the regiment, writes William Haskin, himself accompanying
the troops, "received orders to proceed to Texas, and in obedience
thereto embarked on the United States storeship *Lexington* at New
York together with three companies of the 2nd artillery, on the 1st
September, arriving at St. Joseph's Island on the 4th October, 1845."
Twenty-one miles long by five in width, St. Joseph's Island, nestled
between Matagorda and Mustang islands, is one of the low-lying
strips very near the Texas coast. Thirty miles or so north of Corpus
Christi, the island became a port of entry for great chunks of Taylor's
army. "The only wood is what . . . is called the Mesquite . . . that can
be used for no other purpose than fire wood, and is very poor for
that," observed George Gordon Meade, who passed through the island on September 18; "the water is obtained by digging holes in the
sand, and letting the water percolate into them, when it becomes
fresh enough to drink. Of course, the supply, both of wood and water, is limited, and the latter so brackish as to induce its moderate
use." But Ethan Allen Hitchcock, Magruder's old teacher at West
Point, found a different island when he passed through in late July:
"This morning (July 28) rode around the camp . . . , scattered for
three miles up and down the length of the island. We found good water and had fish and oysters to eat. . . ."[3]

Magruder and Company B remained on St. Joseph's until October 11, when he joined the hegira to Taylor's camps on the Nueces
(or "nuts" in Spanish, from the early conquistadors, who found giant

pecan trees growing along its banks upon their first arrival); like others before him, Magruder traveled by mackinaw boat down the inland bays to Corpus Christi. As he journeyed along the Texas coast, he had no notion that seventeen years later he would be called upon, as military commander of Confederate Texas, to defend this very place against many of his comrades. Magruder remained at Corpus Christi until March 1846, when he received marching orders for the Rio Grande. "I send back your horse from the camp of the second Dragoons—he has been fed, watered & curried by competent grooms & he has not been used for a longer period than half an hour," he told his friend Lieutenant James Duncan. Although Duncan was killed at the Battle of Monterrey in September 1847, Magruder assured him that he had a "Capital horse—that deserves to be taken care of." In order to relieve the monotony of camp, Magruder must have joined fellow officers on rides across the Texas prairies.

Although Magruder evidenced no great enthusiasm for the chase in his available correspondence, hunting was a high priority for the Corpus Christi encampment; "speaking of hunting, this country excels anything in the world (leaving out the Buffalo country), it is no uncommon thing to see herds of five and six hundred deer, twelve or fifteen miles from this place—vast herds of wild horses are also near here—Turkeys, Ducks, Geese, and Brants are very abundant—also Panthers, and the wild hog of Mexico are not uncommon," observes another of Magruder's friends, George T. Mason, killed a few weeks later near Fort Brown on the Rio Grande. It was just as well that young, hot-blooded officers with Taylor had outlets other than daily drill routines and preparations for the approaching combat. Mason told one correspondent about a fistfight between Captains Ker and Ransom: "Ransom had against him the additional charges of 'drunkenness on duty' and 'conduct unbecoming an officer and a gentleman' in riding through camp in a state of intoxication, and of introducing into the tent occupied by Stephens and himself a 'woman of known and noted bad character,' and 'drinking with her during the night,' and keeping there till 'forcibly removed by the guard.'" E. A. Hitchcock noted in his diary for the same period that arrival of the Second Dragoons at Corpus Christi had precipitated "several disgraceful brawls & quarrels, to say nothing of drunken frolics." The dragoons, Hitchcock continues, "have made themselves a public scandal. One captain has resigned to avoid trial . . . two others are on trial for fighting over a low woman."[4]

Although Magruder escaped charges of misconduct, he certainly experienced money problems at Corpus Christi and later when the army reached the Rio Grande at Fort Texas; besides repeated demands from army auditors that he settle his accounts from Plattsburg and Hancock Barracks, addressed to him in Texas, he was often short of funds while in the Southwest, indicating that he, too, had consorted with fellow officers on their soirees. General William F. Barry, a captain during the Mexican interlude, who went on to a Civil War career on the peninsula and served as William Tecumseh Sherman's chief of artillery through the Georgia campaigns of 1864, penned a telling vignette of Magruder's money woes in Texas: "Magruder was distinguished for the ease with which he spent money, and the difficulty he had in getting it," his account opens.

> He approached the sutler one day in June 1846, asking with his inimitable lisp: "Would you be so kind as to cash my pay accounts for September?" The sutler explained that he didn't have the money, but thought he could raise it for him, as it was only three months ahead. "Oh," said Magruder carelessly, "it's my pay accounts for September 1847, that I want to get cashed!"[5]

Magruder's reputation for high showmanship and entertaining—for being Prince John in New York and Maine—followed him to Corpus Christi. Shortly after his arrival, Taylor, Worth, and other commanders called upon him to oversee construction of an 800-seat theater and to manage its stage productions as a means of keeping "men out of the gambling dens set up by camp followers." Erected by the enlisted men, with scenery and backdrops painted by the officers, the place became an instant hit throughout the encampment. One theater had already been built in Corpus Christi proper, but "another one on a much larger scale is now being put up in the Dragoon Camp under the superintendence of John Magruder," his friend George Mason wrote in a December letter. "Where Magruder is to get his company I do not know."[6]

Fortunately, a young officer named James Longstreet, who became a member of his troupe, had answered Mason's query. "As there was no one outside the army except two rancheros within a hundred miles, our dramatic company was organized from the officers who took both male and female characters," Longstreet wrote in his Civil War memoirs. When sufficient funds were gathered, costumes were secured from New Orleans. And the young West Pointers, at first without female performers, unwittingly found themselves in the true Shakespearean tradition, as the Bard's original plays had only male casts. "The 'Moor of Venice' was chosen [as their first tragedy], Lieutenant Theodoric Porter to be the Moor, and Lieutenant U.S. Grant to be the daughter of Brabantio," Longstreet says. "But after rehearsal Porter protested that male heroines could not support the character nor give sentiment to the hero, so we sent over to New Orleans and secured Mrs. Hart. . . ." Not surprisingly, Grant remains silent about his fledgling acting career in his own reminiscence of the Mexican War. That a good time was had at Magruder's expense is readily abundant. Young George Meade spoke for the theatergoers in a January 1 letter from Corpus Christi: "You must know that since our arrival here they have built a theatre and imported a company of strolling actors, who murder tragedy, burlesque comedy, and render farce into buffoonery, in the most approved style."[7]

The playacting aside, Taylor ordered his 3,000-man army (estimates vary) to depart Corpus Christi on March 8 for the Rio Grande; although Mexico regarded this intrusion into disputed territory beyond the Nueces as an act of war, enemy troops were in no position to challenge the move. The trek through the live oaks and sand dunes of south Texas came to a halt on March 28, when Taylor's lead column reached the "wet weather road," along the north bank of the Rio Grande, that linked Matamoros and Point Isabel on the coast. Before his departure, Taylor had consolidated his artillery, including Company B, under the command of Lieutenant Colonel Thomas Childs; and Magruder's unit along with eleven other artillery companies was assigned to infantry duty under the overall control of W. J. Worth. The force departed over several days, and, notes Major Haskin, Worth and the artillery companies "led the way." Small bands of enemy raiders looked on from a safe distance as the army proceeded. Upon reaching the river, Meade found that "the one hundred and seventy miles between Corpus Christi and this point was the most miserable desert, without wood or water, that I ever saw described, and perfectly unfit for the habitation of man, except on the banks of a few little streams we crossed."[8]

When Taylor reached the roadway along the river, he divided his force—sending part to Point Isabel and the remainder westward to a spot opposite Matamoros; at the latter place a bivouac that included Magruder and Company B was quickly established and named Fort Texas. Attempts were initiated to contact Mexican units beyond the river, but General Francisco Mejia refused to receive Taylor's embassy; war had already commenced, said the enemy, as Magruder and his companions settled down to await the opening shots. Although army brass on both sides shunned negotiations in the aftermath of the march, "the habits of these people were curiously displayed," writes Ephraim Kirby Smith, a young officer with Taylor.

> Young women came down to the river side, disrobed without any hesitation, and plunged into the stream, regardless of the numerous spectators on either bank. Some of the young officers were in the water opposite them. The Mexican guards, were not, however, disposed to let them come much nearer than the middle of the river, so they returned after kissing the hands of the tawny damsels which was laughingly returned.

Whether Magruder joined in the pseudo-kissing is unknown, but he was very much a part of the Fort Texas interlude. While there, he secured Worth's letter of recommendation for his captaincy and dispatched it to Washington from "Camp opposite Matamoras [sic]." And, as he sought the promotion, his fellow West Pointer, the Kentucky-born Philip N. Barbour, noted in his diary for March 31, only three days after reaching the border: "Magruder was spoken to today by a person from the other side, saying that three of our men and a negro deserted to Matamoras [sic] last night, and that they would soon wish themselves anywhere else, for all was misery over there." Barbour does not say whether the deserters were lured into the Battalion San Patricio, a Mexican outfit composed of American deserters.[9]

Nearly constant skirmishing took place during April and May between the Americans and the forces of Mariano Arista, who had not only replaced Mejia in command at Matamoros, but had also constructed

Fort Paredes—named for the current Mexican president—to strengthen his own defenses. Both armies augmented themselves with men and supplies, which prompted Taylor to send cavalry probes to thwart enemy excursions north of the Rio Grande; on April 25 a mean confrontation took place a few miles from Matamoros, when a force of dragoons under Captain William Thornton found itself cut off and surrounded by 1,600 enemy horsemen. Sixty-three Americans were killed, wounded, or captured. After news of the debacle swept the camps like a tornado, Taylor hurried a post rider toward Washington with word that "the opening shots had been fired." When President James Knox Polk received confirmation of the Thornton affair on May 9, he quickly urged Congress to act in the name of Manifest Destiny and American honor. Following House (May 11) and Senate (May 12) passage of a war declaration, the presidential signature was affixed on May 13: "Whereas the Congress of the United States, by virtue of the constitutional authority vested in them, have declared by their act, bearing date this day, by the act of the Republic of Mexico, that a state of war exists between that government and the United States."[10]

Arista crossed the Rio Grande in force the night of May 7 to block the way from Point Isabel to Matamoros; and as he lay in wait, Taylor, by his own account, approached the Mexicans, who numbered 6,000, with only 2,300 men—mostly regulars with two eighteen-pounders and two light batteries. The first major engagement of the war took place at a water hole known locally as Palo Alto, surrounded by "an open prairie without brush of any kind." Although Taylor's lieutenants counseled against a confrontation before the enemy's superior numbers, he opened fire without awaiting word from Washington that war had been declared. At the first shots, Magruder was on the extreme left with the dismounted artillerymen under Childs. The issue was never in doubt as Taylor's superior artillery and Yankee prowess drove the enemy from the field, because the flying batteries, reads his report, constituted "the arm chiefly engaged, and . . . the excellent manner in which it was maneuvered and served." One can but speculate that Magruder, watching from the flank near the Rio Grande, also witnessed the great mobility and firepower of the light artillery and rehatched his drive to secure a place in its ranks. "The trend of the battle could be gauged almost at the outset," finds

Taylor's major biographer. "Slicing and chopping through the Mexican lines, the American shot opened great gaps in Arista's ranks, unnerving the Indian conscripts and paralyzing the dumbfounded Mexican officers, who had never witnessed such uncanny accuracy."

When Taylor sent his account of the fray to Washington, he listed his losses at "4 men killed, 3 officers and 39 men wounded, several of the latter mortally." Arista, hoping to recoup his losses, had ordered several charges late in the battle, and though one of Lieutenant W. H. Churchill's eighteen-pounders tore holes in their ranks, the Mexicans kept coming. The Americans—including the men under Childs—formed themselves into squares to meet the onslaught. Major Haskin, quoting from an unnamed participant, presents a graphic account of Magruder's part in the fight: "In Magruder's company, two men whilst at an order had the bayonets of their muskets cut off by cannon balls passing just over their shoulders and between their heads. He also had a man killed on his immediate right and left." Haskin also notes that troops in Company B exhibited courage and discipline as Mexican shot rained down on their squares. Following an order to open a return fire, the enemy retired from the field.

Magruder had had his first taste of organized warfare, and on the next morning (May 9) he was caught up in the battle at Resaca de la Parma. On the previous day, however, at Palo Alto, he had no doubt observed the general commanding when he appeared on the field in unadorned costume. "There he was, in a blue checkered gingham coat, blue trousers without any braid, a linen waistcoat and broad-brimmed straw hat. Neither his horse nor his saddle had any military ornament." Magruder was seemingly unimpressed by Taylor's lack of show, the loud hurrahs and admiring glances from the ranks notwithstanding, because he remained Prince John, clothed in the flashiest uniforms possible to the end of his military career.

The Resaca de la Parma imbroglio on May 9 took place at a ravine that crossed the road to Matamoros a few miles east of Palo Alto; Arista had thrown his enlarged army across the roadway "with thick chaparral, or thorny bushes on each side before it reached the ravine, a pond of water on either side where it crossed the ravine, constituting a defile," comments Haskin. It was another rout as the flying batteries under James Duncan, W. H. Churchill, and Randolph Ridgely sent the Mexicans reeling from the field. Magruder again watched from the sidelines with his dismounted companions under Childs. The enemy was "soon driven from his position, and pursued by the battalion of artillery and a light battery, to the river," Taylor put in his report. And, he added: "Our victory was complete."[11]

Following his initial battles along the Rio Grande—both of them in Texas—Taylor moved into Matamoros and commenced a reorganization of his troops before his descent on Monterrey, the chief trading and governmental center of northern Mexico. According to Taylor's General Orders Number 83, July 7, Company B along with four others was dissolved, with the enlisted men assigned to other units and the officers returned to the States for recruiting duty; Magruder is mentioned by name, although by June 3 he was already in New Orleans, where he had taken ship following the occupation of Matamoros, actively recruiting for his regiment. He was not located in a specific city, but was allowed to recruit also in New York and Baltimore as well as other points. By the second week in September he had worked his way to Baltimore, where he promptly sought a transfer to Company I, which was one of the flying batteries; although his request was turned down, he must have been busy at the recruiting desk because he hurried a September 15 communiqué to Washington asking if Germans who spoke no English could be enlisted in the army. Then, one week later, he was appointed to command at Fort McHenry when its commanding officer was ordered to Mexico.[12]

Magruder's letters to Washington indicate that he continued his recruiting activities while in charge at McHenry; but he was also fixed upon a return to Mexico when he asked that Company B be mounted for greater mobility once his request to join one of the flying batteries had been turned down. Momentous events in Washington, however, intervened to change Magruder's place in the artillery while he looked for new recruits and supervised the handful of regulars under his charge. President Polk, after conferring with Missouri senator Thomas Hart Benton, who had been a colonel during the War of 1812, decided that Mexico could never be crushed by Taylor's army at Monterrey and Buena Vista. Following several heated cabinet sessions through early November, with Benton in attendance at the president's request, it was resolved to launch an invasion by way of Veracruz; and the army would not only march on Mexico City from the coast, but a new general-in-chief would be named to spearhead the attack. Winfield Scott, Magruder's mentor on the New York and Maine frontiers, was accordingly given charge of the new invasion force on November 18; to reinforce the new schema Polk authorized a call-up of nine additional regiments.[13]

Magruder, meanwhile, learned that Captain J. R. Irwin of Company I had resigned from the army, and on September 13 he fired off a request to be granted Irwin's command. His plea was again rejected, and on November 16 he was told to assume command of Company B in New York City. While still in Baltimore with "a severe cold," Magruder tried a different tack; he asked that the transport consigned to carry him to Mexico "put into Tampa Bay to land this company of recruits most of whom have not even fired a fowling piece & to take on board Company I, 1st Artillery, composed of well drilled soldiers who must be of more service in Mexico." His persistence paid off when Scott, now making his headquarters in New York to oversee preparations for the Veracruz operations, ordered that Magruder be given the company when he reached Florida. The following day, November 28, a second directive to his uncle, Colonel James Bankhead, who was overseeing the debarkation of the Second Artillery at Fort Columbus, instructed him to send one of his own companies with Magruder and Company I not to Point Isabel—where reinforcements for Zachary Taylor were being assembled—but to Tampico. The Mexican port of Tampico, 250 miles up the coast from Veracruz, had been selected by Scott as his staging area; and Magruder, only one of thousands headed for the rendezvous, obviously enjoyed the favor of the commanding general himself.[14]

When Magruder reached Tampico on January 26, following a passage of several weeks via New Orleans, he had a pair of captain's bars firmly attached to his uniform; actually, he knew the promotion was in the offing before he left Baltimore, although, in their dispatches from Veracruz, Scott and others refer to him as Lieutenant Magruder. "In reference to your promotion as captain, Company I, I have to state that you were promoted on the 10th inst., to fill the vacancy of Captain J. R. Irwin," the adjutant general informed him on August 30. "But the senate not having gone into executive session . . . the promotion with others was not acted upon." George W. Cullum sets the date at June 18, 1846, which appears too early, and Haskin, his regimental chronicler, says the rank was effective from January 1, 1847;

the overdue promotion was unquestionably facilitated by Scott, who remained Magruder's champion; Robert Anderson, his fellow officer in Mexico, says flat out that Magruder's uncle "was an old friend and favorite of Scott's." That association was transferred to Prince John, and to the end of his days he spoke with great feeling about not only Scott but also others in Mexico who helped boost his career.[15]

Tampico was a "place much larger than I expected, and really quite delightful," writes George Meade, who reached the city two or three days before Magruder, following an overland march from Monterrey with General Robert Patterson. "There is a large foreign population of merchants, and in consequence the town has all such comforts as good restaurants, excellent shops, where anything can be purchased, and in fact as much of a place as New Orleans." The easy lifestyle and ready availability of women from every station fitted Magruder's tastes, although Meade reports one party with "some twenty-five or thirty ladies present . . . and the prettiest girl would not have been noticed in one of our ball rooms." Magruder's stay was taken up with preparations and training of his company for the move to Veracruz, as well as at least one treacherous assignment. When Colonel L. G. de Russey, onetime commandant at West Point, was overwhelmed by a superior force under the Mexican commander Martin Cos, while on a scouting jaunt several miles down the coast, Magruder was ordered to proceed with Company I and one other as a relief column. de Russey, however, managed to give his foes the slip by leaving burning candles in his tents and marching north under cover of darkness. Magruder had landed his men from a steamboat upon a nearby beach, which enabled de Russey to escape his would-be captors. Back in Tampico, amid the city's "luxurious cafes," he learned that uncle James Bankhead had been appointed military governor over the civilian population. Company I and the other artillery outfits remained encamped outside the city, where, according to George Brinton McClellan, "champagne dinners were the order of the day." Magruder's stay in the cultivated atmosphere of Tampico was temporary at best, and one month after his arrival on February 25 he was ordered to board a transport for Lobos Island.[16]

After naval officers assured him that a direct landing at Veracruz was not possible, Scott conceived an island-hopping strategy made famous in a future American war. Lobos, about forty miles south of Tampico and a considerable distance out in the Gulf of Mexico, was but another staging area for the army's voyage to the reef of Anton Lizardo, a few miles south of Veracruz itself. Company I finally reached the shoreline opposite Lizardo on March 9, eleven days after its departure from Tampico. The landings had been a major, if not the first, large-scale amphibious assault in modern warfare. "It was a stretch of open surf-beaten beach . . . about three miles to the southwest of Veracruz, beyond, or at, the extreme range of the most powerful guns of the fortress," writes A. H. Bill. "But there was no better place available, though its exposure to the prevailing storms of the season was demonstrated at once by a norther that made it necessary to postpone the landing for three days." Scott soon gave the go-ahead, and with British and French warships as onlookers, the men were towed ashore in "small surf boats" on March 9; by ten o'clock that night, 10,000 American troops had been landed on the Mexican shore. "There was no opposition save for a single futile shot from a gun that was found abandoned among the chaparral the next day." As night fell over the beachhead, several regimental bands could be heard blaring out patriotic airs: "Yankee Doodle," "Hail Columbia," "The Star-Spangled Banner."[17]

The dominating fortification of San Juan de Ulloa—situated on an offshore reef—and the formidable city walls ruled out any thought of a frontal attack, which led Scott to ring Veracruz with artillery on the landward side. Robert E. Lee, a high-profile member of Scott's engineering staff, was given the task of placing the American artillery pieces for maximum effect; Company I, now a part of Twiggs's division, found itself north of the city along with Company K, which contained a recent West Point graduate named Lieutenant Thomas Jonathan Jackson. In spite of persistent storms and fresh northers, Scott managed to strengthen his army, and then gave the order to open fire on March 22 as soon as the first guns were in place; but it was soon obvious that his light batteries could not reduce the castle or the city walls. Naval guns, including three thirty-two-pounders and several eight-inch shell guns, were quickly hauled from the fleet and mounted upon platforms designed and constructed under Lee's supervision. Lee was in frequent contact with Magruder, Jackson, and a host of young officers destined for illustrious Civil War careers as he rode the encircling lines of artillery, constantly positioning Scott's guns.18

As Magruder marched his company from the Veracruz beachhead, he was detached for skirmishing duty against squads of enemy cavalry blocking roads into the city. "An important mail which I had the honor to transmit to the head-quarters by Captain [Francis] Taylor, was taken last night by Captain Magruder, 1st artillery, who was in command of one of the supporting companies sent out yesterday morning to skirmish in front of my brigade," Twiggs put in his March 15 report to Scott. "The mail carrier was shot at, and is supposed to have been wounded. His horse, hat, and cloak were left on the ground and the mail along with the effects. Captain Magruder deserves praise for his zeal and good conduct in this affair." After his return to the States, Magruder entered into a lengthy correspondence with the adjutant general about the episode, and even requested that his role in the capture be toned down.

Magruder soon joined a number of other company commanders at Battery No. 4, initially composed of one twenty-four-pounder and two eight-inch siege howitzers, along with a complement of 250 troops. "The twenty-four pounder and one of the howitzers were placed in position at once, but the platform for the second howitzer, and one of the embrasures were not ready until about eight o'clock in the morning of the 25th," Haskin records. Magruder and the others kept up a brisk fire until late in the afternoon, when an order arrived to break off the bombardment; additional guns and replacement troops were brought forward, and Haskin continues: "Battery no. 4 was divided into two sections; one consisting of three twenty-four pounders, manned by Company I, and under the command of Captain Magruder, who was assisted by Lt. [Martin J.] Burke—the regimental adjutant—and Lt. [Henry] Coupee." None other than Haskin himself commanded the remaining guns in Battery No. 4, and he makes it clear that the enemy's return fire tore gaping holes in the American lines. Magruder attended the guns under his supervision over the next two days until the capitulation of March 27, after the Mexicans were unable to withstand the incessant pounding.[19]

Once entrenched at Veracruz, Scott could not tarry long before commencing his movement inland; wishing to avoid the dreaded *vomito* or yellow fever, along with crippling diseases common to the coastal lowlands, he ordered a forward movement for April 8, although the advance was delayed for several days. Scott also reorganized his meager force into two divisions during the Veracruz interlude: Magruder's champion William J. Worth had the first division, with Colonels John Garland and N. S. Clark as brigade commanders; David E. Twiggs, with Persifor Smith and Bennet Riley, had charge of the second division.

After an uneventful march across a vast expanse of "sand as far as the eye could see," the lead columns reached the Río del Plan, a small river flowing through a 500-foot canyon from the Sierra Madre into the larger Río de Chachalas and thence into the Gulf of Mexico. Here, sixty miles from the coast, Scott's troops encountered Santa Anna, newly returned to power following another interminable shift in Mexican politics. The Americans under Worth and Twiggs also saw for the first time two almost identical hills—Atalaya and Cerro Gordo—astride the roadway, as well as a fortified ridge near the precipitous Río del Plan, far below. "A battery was placed at the head of this stretch of highway, commanding it for a distance of more than half a mile," writes R. S. Henry. "Another battery was placed at the main Mexican camp, at the ranch of Cerro Gordo, half a mile to the west of this point. And dominating the whole position were the guns atop the 700-foot cone of Cerro Gordo itself."[20]

Scott not only halted to reconnoiter and evaluate Santa Anna's gun emplacements, but again called upon Captain Robert E. Lee to seek a pathway around the barriers before him. Although he was nearly captured in the venture, the future Confederate commander-in-chief found a way around the guns atop Atalaya. It was a difficult route at best; then-Lieutenant U. S. Grant wrote in his 1885 memoir of the war, "the artillery was let down the steep slopes by hand, the men engaged in attaching a strong rope to the rear axle and letting them down a piece at the time, while the men at the ropes kept their ground on top playing out gradually, while a few at the front directed the course of the piece." Over terrain the Mexicans considered impassable and on which Grant admits animals were useless, the American artillery was hauled into place undetected by the enemy. With the arrival of reinforcements under James Shields, an assault on Atalaya was set for April 17. The men under Twiggs, including Magruder

and Company I, with Colonel William S. Harney as brigade commander, swept over the crest, capturing guns and sending enemy soldiers reeling toward the National Highway. The hill was not only
taken, but the impetuous attackers, fired up and eager for combat,
even started up the steep sides of Cerro Gordo.

Insufficient manpower caused Scott to break off his forward rush
until the following day; "at about seven in the morning—before
Shields or Riley had reached the road beyond Cerro Gordo—Harney's
men charged," continues historian Henry. "Down Atalaya's slopes
they dashed across the intervening hollow, up the slopes of Cerro
Gordo, firing at will as they went." Mexican general Vasquez was
killed in the attack, in which Captain John Bankhead Magruder and
his light artillery were in the forefront of the action. Besides getting
his men and guns to the crest in quick order, Magruder gained a bit
of fame by seizing several enemy pieces and firing them at the fleeing Mexicans. "Captain Magruder's gallantry was conspicuously displayed on several occasions, and he rendered me efficient service,"
Harney put in his battle report. And Thomas Childs, his regimental
commander, was equally gracious: "Captain Magruder, in attempting
. . . to join me, with nine of his men passed gallantly through a shower
of bullets from the enemy's musketry." If that were not praise enough,
Scott and Twiggs both penned favorable—if short—tributes to his
daring in the Cerro Gordo fight.[21]

Magruder, clearly a fearless if not intrepid warrior at Cerro Gordo,
attracted more than a little notice throughout the army. His long fight
for promotion and transfer to the new service arm had rendered an
obvious dividend; Corporal George Ballentine, an English adventurer,
who joined Company I a few weeks later while the army paused at
Jalapa, notes that Magruder was a "dashing officer" already "distinguished for his skill in light artillery maneuvers." In an ironic twist,
however, his posturing at Atalaya and Cerro Gordo may have had a
greater impact upon twenty-three-year-old T. J. Jackson, who stood
transfixed as Magruder hurried his guns forward with Harney's column; Jackson then and there commenced a successful campaign to
join his idol, and not only fought under him to the very gates of Mexico City, but the knowledge and élan he gained in the rapid deployment of guns and men became the stuff of legend during the Civil
War. "I wanted to see active service, to be near the enemy and in the

fight; and when I heard that John Magruder had his battery, I bent all of my energies to be with him, for I knew if any fighting was to be done Magruder would be on hand," John Esten Cooke quoted Jackson in his 1866 biography of Stonewall, following interviews with several of his contemporaries. Cooke, a kinsman of the cavalryman Jeb Stuart, and invaluable chronicler of the Virginia campaigns of 1861–1865, states emphatically that Magruder did much to shape Jackson's military thinking.[22]

From Cerro Gordo—also known as El Telégrafo, from an ancient signal tower at its crest for communication between the capital and Veracruz—Magruder and Company I joined the army at Jalapa on April 19; the report of Colonel Childs indicates the First Artillery remained at this first principal place on the road to Mexico City until June 18, a period of two months. While Ballentine does not mention Magruder by name, he indicates "that foolish and tyrannical conduct by a number of young officers in the American service" induced several men to desert during the stay at Jalapa. "Out of the company to which I belonged ten deserted, more than an eighth of our entire company, which was not eighty at the time." Ballentine's account of his march with Magruder has some merit, but it should be consulted with caution because of glaring discrepancies with other contemporaries.

More than one third of the Mexican army had been destroyed or captured at Atalaya and Cerro Gordo, and Santa Anna, in no mood to dispute the Yankee advance, retreated through Perote and Puebla to a more formidable position nearer the capital. Although the National Highway lay open, guerrilla bands and irregulars contested the passes through the Sierra Madre separating Cerro Gordo and Perote on the other side. A particularly nasty spot was the pass of La Hoya, where Childs ran into difficulty on June 20, two days out of Jalapa. His command included Magruder with "two 12-pounders and a mountain howitzer" as well as four companies of the Second Dragoons and a unit of Pennsylvania volunteers. "The Mexicans finding that the troops were advancing in a different direction from what they anticipated, precipitately left the mountain firing as they went," Childs writes in his official report. "The advance of the 2nd dragoons coming up drove the enemy in confusion from hill to hill for two and a half miles, they leaving seven or eight dead on the field." Ballentine, however, presents a more lively rendering: "The division was halted, and our guns being unlimbered and brought to bear upon them, we fired several shots, when we could see their white dresses gliding among the green trees, reminding us of a flock of scared wild fowl."[23]

After the skirmishing along the mountain passes—Childs set the enemy force at 600—Magruder reached Perote on June 21 without further mishap. Lead columns under Worth had, without meeting resistance, captured the massive castle near the town before his arrival. Although Santa Anna did not defend this gateway to Puebla and the allure of central Mexico that had captivated the conquistadors three centuries before, Robert E. Lee, also present with Scott's staff, took time to describe it for his wife: "The castle or fort of Perote is one of the best finished that I have ever seen—very strong, with high thick walls, bastioned front, and deep, wide ditch." If Lee considered its construction defective in spite of its massiveness, not every American soldier shared his enthusiasm for architectural beauties in the region as the army advanced through enemy territory. With their stout swaggers and Yankee dollars in their pockets, many a trooper "watched the inviting glances of any Indio or Mozo maiden." Then, continues a Scott biographer: "There would be many blond babies born in central Mexico in the early months of 1848."[24]

Magruder remained two days at Perote before his departure to Puebla, situated "about seventy-five miles from the valley of Mexico." Upon reaching La Puebla de los Angeles, the young officers under Scott encountered a city steeped in Roman Catholic tradition with numerous priests and nuns walking on its avenues. Now promoted brevet major for "Gallant and Meritorious conduct in the Battle of Cerro Gordo," Magruder and his fellows found a world to their liking. "At the Tivoli and Paseo every afternoon sherbets were drunk, there was dancing on the lawns to the music of American regimental bands, and American officers vied with the native cavaliers in displaying their horsemanship before the assembled carriages," wrote A. H. Bill. "Young officers continued to write home, as they had been doing since the beginning of the war, that they had not seen a single pretty Mexican woman. But others appear to have been less hard to please." Promiscuity and its attendant diseases were prevalent throughout the ranks at Puebla and afterward, during the occupation of the capital.

While the army remained encamped until early August, thousands of fresh troops flooded into the town, including Tom Jackson, who arrived with a force under General George Cadwalader; his transfer papers completed at last, the future Stonewall was assigned to Magruder's company and immediately made its commissary officer, to the young lieutenant's considerable disappointment. And as the army swelled to more than 14,000 men at Puebla, Scott totally reorganized his command structure before the advance toward Mexico City.

> Colonel Harney led his Cavalry Brigade . . . the four divisions of infantry were led by Twiggs, Worth, Pillow, and Quitman, and included four regiments of artillery, the Rifles, and the Voltiguers, and twelve other regiments of Regular infantry, the New York, South Carolina and Pennsylvania regiments and a battalion of Marines—this last is the reason why the Marines, who as usual, were an infinitesimal portion of the whole force, were able to build up the delusion that they had fought "from the Halls of Montezuma to the shores of Tripoli"; that they had carried the burden of Uncle Sam's warfare.

Magruder's company was attached to Pillow's division for the final push into the Mexican heartland. Gideon J. Pillow, a onetime law partner of President Polk who had strong ties to the White House, not only spoke favorably about Magruder's fighting in the battles before Mexico City, but also became instrumental in securing an additional promotion for him. The pleasures of Puebla—another American theater had even been established, although Magruder does not appear to have been a part of its troupe—came to an abrupt halt when General Franklin Pierce marched into town on August 6 with an additional 3,000 troops. Scott, feeling that his army was ready at last, gave the order to advance on the morrow.[25]

Events and battles unfolded with stark rapidity over the next six weeks until the army battered its way into the enemy capital, although the Duke of Wellington proclaimed Scott "lost" when he descended into the great central valley of Mexico without a support column. He had no soldiers to leave behind, except for a small force to guard the sick and wounded interned at Puebla. Fortunately, Magruder's own reports, which have been reproduced in congressional documents, supplemented by the writings of George Ballentine, Stonewall Jackson, and others, present a detailed summary of his part in the capture of Mexico City. Following the departure of Pillow's division on August 8, the army met no opposition until it reached Ayotla, within a few miles of the easternmost entrance into the capital by the San Lazaro *garita*. Mexico City, positioned in the midst of a great depression in the center of the country, is shielded from the east by a series of lakes running north to south: Zumpango, San Cristóbal, Texcuco, Xochimilco, and Chalco. Nearly impassable swamps and marshes fan out from the lakes so that the only avenues into the city were a number of causeways—some of them built by the Aztecs. Each causeway was in turn guarded by a *garita* or customs/ military station occupied by one or two soldiers in more peaceful times.

As the National Highway nears Chalco, the most southeasterly of the lakes, it divides into a northern and southern branch; a short way beyond the road juncture near Ayotla, on the northern branch or direct route through San Lazaro, is El Peñon. Here, atop its 300-foot lava peak, Santa Anna had placed thirty pieces, effectively blocking the eastern approaches. Scott called a halt on August 12 to order forward reconnoitering parties under Lee to survey the El Peñon defenses. When word came back that the San Lazaro pathway was not feasible, other advance teams were dispatched under P. G. T. Beauregard to search the roads south and west of Lake Chalco. After a hurried staff conference during the night of August 13–14, Scott resolved to proceed by the southern routes along the shores of Chalco and Xochimilco—to attack the capital from the west, thereby avoiding the fortifications of El Peñon. By the seventeenth, his advance units had established his headquarters at the village of San Augustin, located near the eastern shore of Lake Xochimilco on the great road leading south from Mexico City. When Scott sent a dispatch to Washington confirming his whereabouts, he told the president that he was nine miles from the capital.[26]

Santa Anna had shifted his army to meet the Yankee threat; but his general, Valencia, advanced south of the capital to an elevation opposite the villages Padierna and Contreras, in disobedience of the generalissimo's order to concentrate nearer the city. The roads leading south divided at a place called Churubusco because of an immense lava field known as the Pedregal. Before they rejoined at San Augustin, where Scott had ensconced himself, the western branch passed through the villages of Coyoacán, San Angel, and Contreras, while the more direct eastern branch transversed San Antonio and Coapa. A forward movement was out of the question with Valencia on his left flank, and Scott again sent Lee to find a route through the lava beds that could be used to attack the enemy at Contreras and Padierna. Pillow, also commanding Twiggs's division, with Magruder and Company I in the van, was handed the task of attacking across the Pedregal, which one officer said "was exceedingly difficult even in daytime for infantry and utterly impassable of artillery, cavalry, or single horsemen." But Lee's reconnaissance found a pathway that enabled the movement of Magruder's guns and other infantry units, although it was "not much more than a mule-track." When Magruder filed his own report two or three days later, he revealed that his light batteries had been "carried by hand up the steep acclivity" to Valencia's lines in front of Contreras. An assault was ordered for 5:00 A.M., August 19, and Ballentine confirms that "we had some difficulty with our battery, having to get a regiment of infantry with drag ropes to assist us in bringing up our guns and caissons."[27]

Valencia had arrayed his "heavy guns" along a plateau at the western limit of the Pedregal, and Magruder, still spearheading Pillow's assault force, had to wait until 2:00 A.M. before his batteries could open on the enemy entrenchments. He said afterward that the Mexicans had thwarted his move to the front by placing lava chunks across his path, but once through the obstacles, his guns were directed into place by Robert E. Lee, who had a firm grasp of the terrain between the army and Valencia. Shortly after Company I opened fire, Lieutenant J. P. Johnstone, a nephew of Joseph E. Johnston, who was present in Mexico, "fell mortally wounded by an eighteen pound ball." "In a few moments," Magruder's report continues, "Lieutenant Jackson, commanding the 2nd section of the battery, who had opened fire on the enemy's works from the right, hearing our own fire still farther in front, advanced in handsome style, and being assigned by me to the post so gallantly filled by Lieutenant Johnstone, kept up the fire with great briskness and effect." Although Magruder's guns kept pounding the Mexicans until ordered to cease around 11:00 P.M., it was clear from the inception that the light artillery was no match for the bigger guns of the enemy. Yet it served a useful purpose throughout the raging fight on August 19; the guns attracted Valencia's attention while Scott's infantry concentrated on the Mexican right and moved under cover of darkness toward the village of San Geronimo—a few hundred yards north of Contreras.[28]

> During the whole of the night of the 19th, my command was at work, and after the capture of the fort the next morning, I supplied the place of the broken carriage by one of the captured 6 pounder carriages, and bringing the disabled pieces and caissons, arrived, in fighting condition, at the head-quarters of General Twiggs, at 8 o'clock, p.m. on the 20th, after forty hours of interrupted labor.

So Magruder wrote in his official report. Although his own and Jackson's guns operated against the enemy's ramparts throughout the nineteenth, his continued diligence during the night paid handsome dividends on the morning. "All our corps, including Magruder's and [Franklin D.] Callender's light batteries, not only maintained the exposed positions early gained, but all attempted charges against them," none other than Winfield Scott penned afterward. When the Contreras fight reopened on August 20, the American infantry overran Valencia's entrenchments in a startling seventeen minutes after the first man moved forward. Prince John's guns covered the advance, but he was a key player in Scott's victory because of his contributions the day before with his bombardment of the Mexican flank. "It was, on a small scale," Robert Selph Henry persuasively argues, "much the sort of role which Captain Magruder would play fifteen years later when he was left in command of the lightly held Confederate lines east of Richmond to make a demonstration while Captain Lee swung out to the flank to open the battles of the Seven Days."

Following the rout of August 20, Valencia started a headlong rush to join Santa Anna at the Churubusco River, which flows through canalized banks into Lake Xochimilco within sight of the capital ramparts. Both wings of Scott's army, with Worth's division leading the way, converged to once more crush the Mexicans during the afternoon as Magruder, with the future Stonewall at his side, made his return trip across the Pedregal toward the village of San Antonio on the road from Scott's headquarters to Churubusco. Contreras earned Magruder and Jackson numerous accolades; General Franklin Pierce, who passed near Magruder's guns late in the day, said that Company I "suffered greatly from the enemy's vastly superior weight of metal," but that Prince John had unhesitatingly come to his aid at a critical moment. Despite the near-constant exposure to Valencia's return fire, Magruder's losses had been surprisingly light: "One officer killed [Johnstone], one sergeant, and three privates . . . wounded, (two very severely), one private missing, supposed to be wounded, and ten horses killed or wounded."[29]

The dual triumphs at Contreras and Churubusco goaded Santa Anna, ever the wily tactician, to arrange another armistice—the Truce of Tacubaya—on the pretext that he wanted to open peace negotiations with Nicholas P. Trist, special envoy of President Polk, who was traveling with Scott's entourage. In reality, he pounced on the lull to reinforce his positions south of the city. As the two armies lay in wait, Winfield Scott made a momentous decision himself: He would proceed not along the Piedad causeways—there were two of them—but farther west, through the San Cosme and San Belén *garitas*. Finally, on September 8, after two weeks of pondering his moves, he ordered Worth to assault El Molino Del Rey—the Mill of the King—on the mistaken notion that the facility was being used to recast churchbells into cannon; moreover, the building had been heavily fortified with infantry, cavalry, and converging gun emplacements. William J. Worth directed the entire operation against the estimated 12,000 to 14,000 Mexicans holding the place with an attacking force of 3,200 men.

The heavy fighting notwithstanding, it was all over within two hours of the opening shots "at 3 o'clock on the morning of September 8"; but Magruder was not part of Worth's initial strike force. "On the 8th instant, at daylight, I was directed by Major General Pillow to move rapidly from the hacienda, near Mixcoac, through Tacubaya, to support if necessary, Major General Worth's division then fiercely engaged with the enemy near Chapultepec," he observes in his report of September 18, after the final surrender. "This order was complied with; and I arrived on the field in time to witness the defeat of the enemy, with great loss on both sides, and to assist in driving off a large body of cavalry, which threatened our left flank and rear." A troop of horsemen had been posted on the northwestern edge of the foundry buildings to fall upon the approaching Yankees, but they had shown little disposition to join the fray. They were scattered, Magruder says, "by a few well directed shots from the section under the immediate command of Lieutenant Jackson." Worth estimated enemy losses at

2,000 as the Americans threaded their way toward the city gates; he had taken 3,000 prisoners and three guns, with a loss of "117 killed, 653 wounded, eighteen missing—total casualties of almost one fourth of the command engaged." More profoundly, young officers like James Longstreet and, indeed, Magruder, who watched the carnage that inevitably flowed from an attack upon entrenched troops, would become hesitant to order common soldiers into similar situations during 1861–1865.[30]

Five days elapsed between the victory at El Molino del Rey and the storming of Chapultepec; and Magruder, who made his bivouac at Mixcoac following the action of September 8, penned a detailed account of his movements in the interval. When Pillow's division moved forward to the village of Piedad, east of Chapultepec and two miles south of the San Belén *garita,* he placed Jackson's battery "out in front nearer the enemy lines." Magruder moved his company headquarters to Piedad on the tenth, and spent the entire day and evening constructing a new road northward that would better conceal his guns from Santa Anna's horsemen. "Before daylight, on the morning of the 11th, the section was placed in its new position, perfectly screened by rows of Maguay [*sic*] (Ogava Grande), from the enemy's view," Magruder records. "At 4 o'clock in the afternoon, on the 11th, the Mexican cavalry began to move by its left flank, from its entrenchments; and having crossed the road in front, to the number of about five hundred, I opened fire upon them, across the field, with the twelve-pound howitzer, charged with spherical case shot—having trailed the six-pounder, loaded with round shot, down the straight road, to give them a ricochet fire as they returned." Magruder told headquarters that he had been unable to determine exact enemy losses, although he insisted they were "considerable." By September 12, Scott's heavy guns opened upon the fortress of Chapultepec, and although Company I was in line from four in the morning, Magruder took no part in the bombardment preparatory to the assault of the thirteenth. "During this day (the 12th), the battery was employed in watching a cloud of cavalry, which appeared again on our left and rear, and in preventing their approach towards Chapultepec, to molest the operations of the heavy artillery, then playing on the work." When the late-evening order arrived for the army to invest Chapultepec, Magruder split his two batteries; while his orderly sergeant took one section to guard against enemy movements from the rear, Jackson moved forward with the other.[31]

The symbolic fortress of Chapultepec was separated from El Molino del Rey by an ancient cypress grove within two miles of the capital. It was "an isolated mound of rock, one hundred and fifty feet high, surmounted by a large building constituting the castle; a solid wall enclosed the building and grounds." Santa Anna, of course, had turned it into a fortified position, with heavy artillery and mines guarding the western approaches. It was also Scott's last obstacle on the road to victory. Since 1833, Chapultepec had served as the Mexican equivalent of West Point, and even today animosities linger from the deaths of its youthful defenders.[32]

Although Robert E. Lee and P. G. T. Beauregard counseled a southern advance on the city, Scott said no—the army would attack Chapultepec and strike from the west across the San Cosme and San Belén causeways. When the bombardment of September 12 accomplished little, he ordered a forward movement for the following day; Worth was on the extreme north or left, supported by Pillow, with Quitman moving to the southern gates of the city as a diversionary maneuver. "On the morning of the 13th, I was directed by Major General Pillow," Magruder records, "to place the latter section, under the command of Lieutenant Jackson, at the opposite angle—that is on the left flank of Chapultepec—and at a given period to open fire from the right section, under my immediate command, upon the enemy entrenchments and covers, both as a signal for the general action to commence, and to brush away the enemy's skirmishers, in order to facilitate the advance of our own and the storming parties." When Jackson moved his battery forward, he fell under the command of William B. Trousdale, who ordered him to the northwest corner of the fortress, where he quickly came under the fire of a superior battery.

"As I rode up to this section, I was dismounted by a grape shot but without material injury, and succeeded in finding Lieutenant Jackson, whose section, however, was so situated, as to render it more unsafe to return than to remain where it was." But Jackson, in a heroic moment, heaved one of his guns over an intervening ditch and, with the help of his gunnery sergeant, managed to keep the Mexicans at bay; after he regained his equilibrium and following a battlefield conference with Worth, Magruder rushed to Jackson's side with a fresh battery. Together, Magruder and Jackson stymied enemy efforts to stem the American onslaught against the northwestern slope of Chapultepec; he afterwards reported his losses at one killed, eight wounded, and eleven missing. Following capture of the fortress, Magruder, twice wounded, was breveted lieutenant colonel and Jackson major for "gallant" conduct. Although a chastened Santa Anna later gathered a fresh army to strike unsuccessfully at Scott's garrison at Puebla as well as at a supply column moving along the National Highway from Veracruz, the fall of Chapultepec ended the war with Mexico.[33]

It had taken Magruder seventeen years to make captain, following his graduation from West Point, and now, as he marched into the City of the Aztecs with Scott's victorious army, he was the toast of the command as a brevet lieutenant colonel. Though he remained in Mexico City a few short weeks before his departure for the United States in November 1847, he was actively engaged in the occupation from the beginning. While basking in his new glory, he was one day riding down "the long street of Iturbide" with Scott and several others "when a white puff of smoke curled out from an open window." The bullet, which severely maimed another in the party, was clearly intended for Scott, who turned to Magruder at the instant and asked, according to an unsigned source, "How long will it take you to batter down the house?" "An hour by the watch, General," was the reply. "Then open fire at point-blank range and leave not one stone upon another," Scott ordered. The tale is somewhat fanciful at best, but there is no question that Magruder lost no time in becoming part of the headquarters clique.[34]

When the famed Aztec Club was organized on October 13 (although it may have met earlier), Magruder was named second vice president; the group was formed to maintain "a club-house for the entertainment of its members and guests while in the city." The prestigious body, which exists to this day for descendants of the original members, not only held frequent meetings, but also attracted practically every officer in Scott's army. Alexander Watkins Terrell, another expatriate who joined Magruder in Mexico following the Confederate collapse, recites an 1865 conversation while in the National Theater:

While waiting for the curtain to rise, I heard Magruder sigh profoundly, and observed that contrary to his habits, he seemed sad and
depressed. On asking the cause, he directed my attention to a box
on the right occupied by the beautiful young wife of Marshal
Bazaine. "That," he said, "was my box while we occupied the city
in 1847, and on the stage you will see when the curtain rises, the
Aztec Club served its banquets."

"The Aztec Club was the creation of Magruder," Terrell continues, and it was probably at one of its functions that he had an alter-
cation with General Franklin Pierce. Witnesses confirm that Prince
John "slapped the face" of Pierce during a card game; and though
Jackson—who never attended the Aztec soirées—was sent with a
challenge to the future president, no duel was fought. Five years later,
during the 1852 presidential canvass, Magruder, then posted in California, released a formal letter "showing the best feeling" for his old
comrade. He was not a man to carry grudges.[35]

In early November, Magruder sent a surgeon's certificate to Washington verifying that his former health problems had returned; Haskin
says that all four light batteries, including Company I, remained in
Mexico City until the Treaty of Guadalupe-Hidalgo was approved on
March 10, 1848, although Magruder had already returned to the
United States. He was in Washington by mid-January, though his
brother George, in Philadelphia, had learned from others that he was
ill upon leaving Veracruz, and asked Washington for more information. Mrs. Magruder had arrived from Europe with the children, and
following a reunion in Baltimore, he asked for command at Fort
McHenry. Instead he was put on recruiting duty after the adjutant
general informed him: "Learning in conversation with you, some days
since that you were suffering under a serious disability, for the recov-
ery of which, rest and repose were indispensable, I should fear that
you are not able to attend to the active and constant duties which de-
volve upon the Commanding Officer of Fort McHenry." When the
last American trooper left Mexico City on June 12, Magruder had
been at home a good six months, and despite his laurels, he was once
more attempting to secure a favorable posting near his Baltimore
home.[36]

4

"John Was Always Magnificent"

THIRTEEN YEARS WITHOUT PROMOTION stretched between Magruder's return from Mexico City as captain and brevet lieutenant colonel of artillery until his entry into the Confederate army. Although he served at such widely separated posts as Fort McHenry, San Diego Mission, Fort Yuma, Baton Rouge Barracks, San Antonio and Fort Clark (both in Texas), Fort Adams (Rhode Island), and Fort Leavenworth (Kansas), his carefully cultivated reputation followed him everywhere. As the convulsive debates over slavery and the struggle for sectional mastery drove the country toward civil war throughout the 1850s, Magruder made two trips to Europe and even visited the fighting fronts in the Crimean War. Every antebellum chronicler who mentions Prince John in any manner sees fit to comment on his social proclivities, and they are rarely complimentary. His actions in the Aztec Club and in the fashionable homes and meeting places of the Mexican capital became a topic of conversation throughout the army.

His penchant for flashy dress had prompted his fellow officer George H. Derby, who afterwards wrote under the pseudonym John Phoenix, or John Squibob, to propose a subject for debate at the Aztec Club: "Are Magruder's pants blue with red stripes or red with blue stripes?" Magruder became the butt of jokes in Mexico for wearing an adorned uniform "upon which the brilliant red facings exceeded even the generous limits of the regulations." The friendship with Derby was renewed during Prince John's 1850–1853 sojourn in California, where Derby wrote for several newspapers and helped with Magruder's West Coast partying. But Captain Edward C. Boynton, his fellow West Pointer of the class of 1841, and a comrade in Mexico, spoke for many if not most officers: "The impressions I had previously received in regard to this officer were strengthened, and his after career more than justified the unwillingness I had always manifested when solicited to become one of his followers," he said in 1879. "Magruder was a bad example for young men to follow." And, he continued, "Ambitious, unscrupulous, treacherous, and dissolute, he had one good quality at least—he was a dashing fearless soldier."[1]

Fearless or not, Magruder continued his campaign to secure a posting near his wife and children in the first part of 1848. "I have the honor to request that the Light Artillery Battery which I command be assigned to Fort McHenry if it can be done without injury or prejudice to the just expectations of others," he advised the adjutant general on August 1. Nor did he hide his reasons: "I have interests in Baltimore of great importance to me and I believe no other officer of the Light Artillery is similarly situated in respect to the post." If he could not command, Magruder added, he requested that Company I at least be posted to McHenry. If that were not possible, he asked to find a place at Carlisle Barracks, Pennsylvania, sixty-five miles north of Baltimore. Within a week he asked General I. B. Crane that Rufus Sledge and James Sanner, "two excellent artillery soldiers," be sent to his company at McHenry because of their adept "management and grooming of horses." Crane approved his request on September 16 for forty-two horses and four caissons to be delivered at Baltimore while Magruder remained at the home of his brother in Charlottesville. Although his orders did not arrive until later, Crane, a New Yorker who had served with Magruder in Mexico, and was now in command of the First Artillery, was already acting on his requests.[2]

Just back from the glories of Mexico and sporting a gold-studded sword bestowed by the Commonwealth of Virginia as well as his new rank, Magruder was anxious to hold his place in the light artillery. It had not only proved invaluable during the drive into Mexico City, but was also the premier army branch in its aftermath; it is unclear, however, if he received the horses and guns sanctioned by Crane. Although he did some recruiting in Baltimore and Charlottesville while waging his campaign to get command at Fort McHenry, he was handed a jolt in his plans to reorganize and retain his service arm. "On the 31st of August, 1848, the president made a new division of territory of the United States into military divisions and departments, and under his order Gen. [Winfield] Scott assigned the 1st Artillery . . . to department 3, which included the states of New York, New Jersey, Pennsylvania, Delaware, and Maryland," records William Haskin. Fort McHenry was in the jurisdiction of Magruder's regiment when Crane was designated to parcel out individual companies except two that were dispatched to the Oregon coast. Magruder got his berth at Baltimore, and then thunder struck on September 21! Company I was ordered dismounted.[3]

A versatile artillery arm was a thing close to Magruder's heart. As early as April 18 he had implored the adjutant general's office to approach Secretary of War William L. Marcy with an elaborate plan that he had formulated "for the inauguration of the Light Artillery into a Battalion." But when he got word that his beloved company had been dismounted, he made a personal call at the war office. Although his October 2 interview with Marcy was "abruptly terminated for lack of time," Magruder asked Adjutant General Roger A. Jones to reopen the dismount question with him.

In a lengthy letter the following day from Fort McHenry, he invoked cost effectiveness as well as duty and patriotism to keep his own and other light batteries intact. And Magruder reviewed their contributions in the Florida wars and in Mexico: "I did not succeed to it by the accident of promotion of a personal nature for I was scarcely known to the commanding General but as a Soldier, and that I commanded in the battles of Contreras, Piedad, Molino del Rey, Chapultepec and the Garita of San Cosme to the satisfaction of all my commanding officers." Now, he added, "painful circumstances were about to sever" him from his mounted unit. "My men are all clothed in the Light Artillery uniform, with sabres, and supplied with Guns, and Harnesses." All of that gear would have to be abandoned, he argued, and the company resupplied with "new muskets, Cartridge Boxes & Belts." Since he doubted the government would realize any savings for "at least a year or two," Magruder pleaded that Company I remain mounted until Congress had time to make new appropriations.[4]

Marcy, who served throughout James K. Polk's administration, remained unresponsive to Magruder's urging; after being told on

October 5 and 26 that the unit would not be mounted, Magruder undertook a different ploy with the secretary, a former senator from New York and afterwards secretary of state in the cabinet of Franklin Pierce. On December 5 he asked that the company be combined with a mounted unit in the Second Artillery; but Marcy pointedly "declined to make any order on the subject." Company I had been dismounted since September 30, and Magruder might well have known that sympathetic congressmen wanted to help. The last session of the Thirtieth Congress mandated that four companies "be organized and equipped as Light Artillery" before it disbanded in March 1849. Each company was allotted "four pieces and forty-four horses." The *Niles Register* confirmed that Magruder and Company I were among the designated new outfits, which also may have been his first mention in a national newspaper.[5]

Magruder, however, had little opportunity to savor his rejuvenated company because he received orders directing him and Company I to California before he had time to secure the necessary mounts; and he once more started a campaign to avoid the transfer. Although he was told to prepare for immediate departure for San Francisco via Cape Horn, Magruder's company did not sail for another two months. On December 7 he was given permission to turn the company over to his first lieutenant and then proceed via Panama "so as to arrive in San Francisco two months ahead of your company, and in time to make and superintend the preparations for its reception and accommodation." Magruder promptly got into a hassle with Washington over pay for his men until he was told on January 7, 1850, to proceed at once even though the company would not be paid before embarkation. When additional delays ensued, the adjutant general issued a stinging rebuke: "It is now more than two months since you received orders to prepare your Company for distant Service, with instructions to send it to California without unnecessary delay." Furthermore, the men had been paid on January 5, "and yet remained on shore." Instructions, Washington asserted, "have been sent to the Commanding Officer at Fort McHenry to inspect [the company], as well as the Transport with Orders to direct the departure of Troops for California, without further delay, unless there be some sufficient reason to justify their longer detention." Magruder was reminded anew that his orders required him to be in San Francisco ahead of his men.[6]

His dalliance may have had a personal motive, as Magruder and his wife—who sailed for Europe with the three children when he left Baltimore—commenced an on-again, off-again relationship that continued until his death, over thirty years later. They had occasional contact, but the usual husband-wife relationship appears to have vanished when Prince John took up his duties on the West Coast. And there is no question that he was very much a part of Baltimore society during the interlude at Fort McHenry. "Visiting a brother officer one day he told his friend who inquired the cause that he had just left the company of a well known Baltimore belle who during the visit looked intently at him for a moment or two and then exclaimed— 'Colonel Magruder! I know you are a slandered man, common belief is that you wear a wig and dye your mustache, I can now assert that this is not true,'" Benjamin S. Ewell recalled later. "Hence the Colonels [sic] good humor for he did both!" Magruder, according to Ewell, "was fond of ladies and by his polished manners and courtliness made himself a favorite." But other correspondence between McHenry and Washington proved fruitless; he was even informed that he was no longer in command as he had turned over Company I to his first lieutenant on November 23 and that it was past time for him to proceed. Shortly after his men sailed via the Horn, Magruder struck out in compliance with earlier orders, although as late as May 1851, when his brother Allan made inquiries from Charlottesville, he was told, "I have to inform you that Bvt. Lt. Col. Magruder's Company is one of those dismounted. The length of time it will serve in California is of course uncertain."[7]

An excellent study by Robert S. Milota indicates that Magruder reached San Diego on April 19, 1850, aboard the steamer *Panama;* his men, however, did not land in San Francisco until August 10, after a grueling voyage, which afforded him time to travel northward for their arrival. Once he had secured the necessary provisions, Magruder and his company arrived at San Diego on August 25, this time aboard the transport *Monterey.* And he was once more Prince John: He advised Major Samuel P. Heintzelman that he intended to remain on the beach with his men until he departed for the barracks at Mission San

Diego, and, Milota's account continues, "Magruder and his men began their stay in the spirit of fun, for the next day Heintzelman records [in his diary]: 'Col. Magruder is having a nice time with his men. They are getting drunk.' "[8]

Now forty-three years old, Captain Magruder would remain in San Diego, with numerous side trips to San Francisco and Los Angeles, for the next three years; but he did not assume command at Mission San Diego until 1851, when the army presence in the area was divided between the mission and other military installations near the city. The Spanish had been in the San Diego region since the sixteenth century, when Father Marcos de Niza came overland in 1539, seeking the mythical Seven Cities of Cíbola; other conquistadors followed, building missions in the quest to Christianize the Indian peoples of Alta California. American occupation commenced in 1846 during the Mexican War with the coming of Captain Samuel Francis du Pont aboard the USS *Cyane* on June 29. Then followed John C. Frémont and Philip Kearny until Lieutenant Colonel Philip Cooke arrived in January 1847 with the famed Mormon Battalion and made his headquarters at a Franciscan church—the Mission of San Diego de Alcala, six miles northeast of the motley collection of buildings around the harbor at San Diego.

De Alcala, located a few hundred yards north of present-day Interstate 8, had been erected in 1769. Cooke found the place abandoned, except for a single priest, before he moved north toward San Luis Rey and San Juan Capistrano. The mission, which reverted to church control in 1862, flourished under Magruder's rebuilding and supervision: "The buildings which are adobe, are not extensive, but in good preservation. They possess more an Oriental appearance than any similar establishment," noted John Russell Bartlett when he visited San Diego in 1852. "The place is celebrated also for a flourishing orchard of olive trees, which still remain yielding a great abundance of olives the excellence of which we had the opportunity of tasting on our homeward journey." Bartlett, who headed the surveying party to fix the new international boundary following the Treaty of Guadalupe-Hidalgo, was not only lavishly entertained by Magruder but he also heaped praise on him for keeping the mission "in good repair."[9]

The fun-loving Magruder, moreover, did not live with Company I amid the religious atmosphere of the mission, but rented a house with several companions in New Town San Diego. While his men made do with questionable quarters until refurbishing work could be completed, he shared a home "at Market and State Streets" with fellow officers George Stoneman, Adam J. Slemmer, and Francis E. Patterson. They were Northern boys destined for general rank during the Civil War, and all but Patterson, who saw hard combat in Mexico with McCulloch's Texas Rangers, were West Point graduates. Contemporary reports abound of Magruder's carousing as he set about accumulating a good deal of real estate. Shortly after his first arrival, says a local historian, "he was given a dozen lots because of his charm," by developers in the New Town section of the city. And before his return to Baltimore in 1853, he had invested in additional properties, including one called Rancho Jamacha, as well as plots in San Juan Capistrano and elsewhere. Some of his holdings were owned and/or leased with Eugene Pendleton, "a relative by marriage," who paid taxes on his real estate long after Magruder left for other postings. At the time of his death, in 1871, his estate listed California properties in excess of $3,000 at probate.[10]

Mission San Diego existed primarily as a supply depot for Fort Yuma, situated inland on the Colorado River, which afforded Magruder ample time to engage in several social and business ventures while on the coast. Besides his property acquisitions, he actually found time to own and operate a saloon in Los Angeles, a city he visited frequently while on leaves of absence. With an acquaintance from the Mexican War, Samuel Drummer, and borrowed funds, Magruder became a partner in the El Dorado, located on Main Street; when in Los Angeles, he reportedly lived upstairs in the newly constructed building that, ironically, later became the city's first Methodist church. The establishment, complete with an imported billiards table, enjoyed a rousing success, but when it began to fail after a year or so, Magruder withdrew from the enterprise. Although the partners had wanted to operate a "respectable saloon for the gentility," the El Dorado was one more place in a sea of "gaming, drinking, and whoring." And, continues a Los Angeles chronicler of the period, "monte banks, cockfights and liquor shops are seen in all directions, and the only question that is asked is whether a man had been successful at monte." Interspersed with his command duties around San Diego, he even started up a cattle-grazing operation with several others on some of his recently acquired lands. That venture failed too, and before he left in the summer of 1853, Magruder was made president of a proposed San Diego–based railroad, the Atlantic & Pacific, organized to connect both coasts, with San Diego as its western terminus because it would "always be free of snow." It was another of his commercial failures. Yet he retained his position with the A&P as well as his numerous holdings upon his return to the East, which suggests that he intended to settle in California at a later time.[11]

Although he led his men in "a Grand Procession across the Plaza" to mark San Diego's July 4, 1851, celebration, complete with booming cannon, Magruder had barely arrived at his new post before finding himself in hot water with Washington.

> Sometime in the month of April last an anonymous letter was received from California, charging Bvt. Lt. Col. Magruder, commanding Light Company I, 1st Artillery, Stationed at San Diego with using the men and horses of the Company for his own purposes. This letter was immediately sent to Bvt. Major General [Persifor F.] Smith, but as he had departed for California before its receipt, the General in Chief desires that you will give this matter your attention.

So reads a July 9 missive from the adjutant general to General Ethan Allen Hitchcock, commanding at Benicia, California. Hitchcock, who had encountered Magruder at West Point during the "Eggnog Riots," passed over the accusation, but the following year Magruder's mismanagement at Mission San Diego was again called into question when Secretary of War Charles M. Conrad issued a directive for him "to turnover to the Quarter Master most convenient" proceeds from the sale of cattle owned by the army. More difficulty followed when he was "accidently" paid twice in the same month and was obliged to reimburse the paymaster when he failed to do so upon his own account. In June 1852, however, he apparently satisfied Colonel George McCall, an inspector general dispatched from Washington, that all was well. After examining the army depot in San Diego, McCall moved on to the mission. The officers, McCall found, were performing in an able manner, and the enlisted men were "obedient and very attentive to personal appearance—the non-commissioned officers in particular perform their duties with promptitude in a very good state of discipline."[12]

In November 1851 the army depot and Mission San Diego had been officially separated, with Magruder given an independent command. Almost immediately, records Heintzelman, he left "to enjoy the fleshpots of Los Angeles," but soon became embroiled in his only military action while on the West Coast. Upon learning that the Cahuilla clan was gathering at Los Coyotes, about fifty miles northeast of San Diego, Magruder returned to his command on December 8. The tribes around San Diego and Los Angeles had been restive for some months for a variety of reasons, among which was a breakup or secularization of the Spanish mission system, which had disrupted their accustomed living patterns. Passions boiled with the influx of Anglos following the gold strikes of 1848 farther north; a veritable tidal wave into Alta California by way of the Gila River and across the Colorado at present-day Yuma, Arizona, caused the border Indians to resist the newcomers. Antonio Garra and his father of the same name, educated in the missions, not only became the leaders, but their wrath exploded when the sheriff of San Diego, Agostin Haraszthy, a genuine Hungarian count, decided to collect taxes on Indian lands and cattle.

Although the younger Garra was taken into custody in early December, Heintzelman, acting on orders from Hitchcock, took the offensive against other Indians causing trouble. On December 17, Magruder joined him at Santa Isabel, fifty miles or so from Mission San Diego, where preparations were finalized to strike at Los Coyotes. Magruder, who commanded about fifty men, marched directly "from Santa Isabel across the mountains to Los Coyotes Canyon. Captain Heintzelman, with a force of forty-six men, left on a circuitous route so as to enter the canyon by way of the desert," writes campaign historian Phillips. As it turned out, Heintzelman's contingent did all of the fighting when contact was made on the twentieth: "After moving about half a mile, the soldiers sighted a party of between thirty and forty Indians advancing to attack." A short and hot fight ensued, which the Indians nearly won and about which Heintzelman was forced to confess that his men had done badly. Afterwards Magruder was dispatched to round up several fleeing bands, but when caught, "the Indians, including women and children," were merely taken into custody without further bloodshed. The brief campaign not only ended the troubles around San Diego but also Magruder's direct involvement in the West Coast Indian wars.[13]

Following the Garra upheaval, Magruder and Company I returned to San Diego de Alcala while Heintzelman and his command marched eastward to contain the Indian bands around Fort Yuma and the lower Colorado River. Yuma had been established at the famed river crossing on the southern trail into California during late 1850; located "less than a mile below the mouth of the Gila," the place was "separated from San Diego by 160 miles of mountains and utterly barren desert." It not only became a nightmare to supply, but also a tedium for the troopers stationed there. Its only practical means of provision was by ship from San Diego around Baja California to the mouth of the Colorado, where freight was transferred to small river steamers. Magruder, though he visited Yuma on court-martial duty, became associated with it for several months following a notorious murder. "Men hated the isolation, the heat, and the boredom of the wattle-and-daub post perched on the hills above the humid, steaming lowlands of the river," writes historian Woodward. "Troopers began to desert. Two such men shot and killed Lt. Col. Louis S. Craig on June 6, 1852, near Alamo Mocho." When friendly Indians turned the assassins over to the army, Magruder was assigned to preside over their lengthy court-martial in San Diego.[14]

From July 29, when the trial opened, until the deserters' execution in February, which Magruder carried out with considerable pomp, he was never far from his duties as president of the court. Yet he chased a vigorous social life upon his return from the Los Coyotes melee, and several weeks before opening the court-martial, he became a charter member of the Pioneer Pacific Yacht Club—"the first yacht club on the Pacific Coast." A race or regatta was held on April 7, over a twenty-mile course in the harbor at San Diego. Magruder entered "a nine-ton sloop" dubbed the *Contreras* in recognition of the Mexican War battle that earned him the brevet rank of major. Although he did not win, he surely took part in the gala soirée that followed; and his partying nearly got him killed at Los Angeles later in the summer, when he started an argument with Dr. William Osborn, the town's druggist and postmaster. A heated confrontation developed at a banquet after Magruder proclaimed Andrew Jackson "the great-est man to ever trod shoe leather," over the objections of his adver-sary. According to writer George Derby, both men were Masons, which prompted the intervention of friends to avert real trouble. Oth-ers, however, had Magruder aiming his derringer at the face of Os-born—who had fired and missed—before calling out, "I'll spare you for the hangman," with a suitable oath, thereby ending the affray.[15]

As he sat in judgment of Craig's murderers, Magruder also main-tained a law office after receiving his California license dated Febru-ary 18, 1851. Drawing upon his experiences in North Carolina, he was approved by the State Supreme Court with the recommendation of Frederick Billings, and he began running advertisements soliciting clients in the *San Diego Herald* during March–September 1852. The extent of his lawyering is unclear, although his name appears in sev-eral San Diego deed books as trustee for various parcels of land. But he did get himself embroiled in the fall presidential canvass between Franklin Pierce and Winfield Scott; during the campaign, when Pierce was chided for his less than manly performances in Mexico, someone recalled the Pierce-Magruder set-to, which prompted Ma-gruder to give public support to his old comrade-in-arms. But the incident may well have spawned his troubles with the new adminis-tration, when his West Point chum Jefferson Davis—who served as secretary of war under Pierce—steadfastly refused his requests from the field.[16]

In August 1852, however, as he sat on the prolonged court-martial, his brother Allan opened a correspondence with Secretary of War Charles M. Conrad, seeking his return from the Coast. "I am in re-ceipt of a letter from my brother, Lt. Col. J. B. Magruder, now sta-tioned at San Diego, Cal, in which he apprises me of certain very urgent reasons which have impelled him to apply to the Dept. for a leave of absence of six months with permission at the [expiration] to apply for an extension of the leave." He wanted to join his family in Italy, owing to the grave illness of his seventeen-year-old daughter, Isabell. Mrs. Magruder, her brother-in-law continues,

> with the entire concurrence of her husband sailed for Europe and has for some two years sought to repair the shattered health of her daughter—having travelled on the Continent with her and spent the past winter in Sicily and Italy. By the last accounts Mrs. Magruder's

family consisting of a little Son & two daughters were in Rome where her invalid daughter had been confined by violent inflammation of the lungs and unable for three months to leave her room.

Allan Magruder trusted that his own and his brother's personal acquaintance with Conrad would not "affect the merits of the application," but he reminded Conrad that he was also known to Secretary of the Interior Archibald H. Stuart. Stuart, a kinsman of the future Confederate cavalryman, was likewise a friend of his brother in California, he added.[17]

Although Magruder did not leave San Diego for nearly a year, he launched another campaign to have Company I remounted in anticipation of his move. An April 24 request was rejected, and as late as June 1853, after the new administration had taken office, Jefferson Davis also denied a remount on the company's departure from California. Meanwhile, Conrad told his brother on September 11, 1852, that orders would be cut for the leave, with permission "to leave the U.S. and join his family in Europe." Lieutenant Thomas W. Sweeny, a fellow officer at San Diego, indicates in his own memoirs that official communiqués from Washington required more than one month. Since the leave had to be approved by the "Commander of the Pacific Division," Magruder did not receive authorization until late October 1852 at the earliest, when he was preoccupied with the trial. Later, following his return to Washington and Baltimore, when Jefferson Davis turned down his request for travel in Europe, he sought to explain his delay in accepting the leave. "In April or May 1852 I received information that my whole family were on the point of death in Naples with a "malignant Roman fever," he wrote on December 13, 1853. "They were in a foreign country without a protector and I thought of nothing but reaching them in the shortest time. When the leave of absence of six months reached my post, I was absent as President of a Court Martial beyond the desert at Fort Yuma and having been President of a court which sentenced the murderers of the late Colonel Craig to be hung, I could not properly leave the country until the President's decision became known—which was received and carried out by myself." He had not considered, Magruder added, that his delay while tending to his duties would negate the leave.[18]

Although he was relieved of his command at Mission San Diego in late March, he did not leave California until June 1853, and, reported the *New York Times*, he was detained at the Isthmus of Panama after his baggage became lost. Following a seventeen-day layover at Aspinwall—present-day Colón—he left Panama on July 20 aboard the *Steamship Georgia*, sailing into New York nine days later. Shortly after reaching the city, Magruder attended a "Grand Military Banquet" at the famed Astor House; and, noted the *San Diego Herald*, reprinting from a New York paper: "Colonel Magruder of the Army entered the room and was immediately called up. . . . He informed the company, of his just having arrived from California, and hardly free enough from salt water and sea legs to make a very interesting speech." But he found the energy to address the gallantry of the volunteer soldier while stressing the need for "education and unification" of the armed forces.

Some weeks later a lengthy letter appeared in the *New York Herald* that echoed these sentiments, although it was signed only by a "National Democrat." While no direct evidence exists that Magruder was the author, the *Herald* piece is remarkably similar to his subsequent arguments to Jefferson Davis, and the Pierce administration for an enhancement of the light artillery. Among other points, the "National Democrat" affirmed that he "had studied the growth of the English and French artillery; how inefficient they were and how efficient they have become and are now." When he was attempting to wangle a leave from Davis to visit his family, that became his precise point—that he needed to continue his study of European artillery developments. Whatever his difficulties with the Washington hierarchy over remounting his own company and restoring the light batteries to their once-proud position during the Mexican War, he arrived in typical Magruder fashion. "Colonel Magruder and servant," said one newspaper, disembarked from the *Georgia*.[19]

Magruder's torrent of criticizing efforts to curtail funding for the light batteries, and his incessant demands that his company be remounted, clearly struck a raw nerve in Washington; and he had no more success with the war office under Pierce and Davis than with previous administrations. Following the stay in New York and a brief stopover at Baltimore, he made his way to Washington during mid-

August, where he sought a personal interview with Jefferson Davis; but the new secretary of war and the president had departed on August 17 for an extended tour through New York and New England. "John Magruder seemed disappointed that after all of his patience you had given him the slip—but I listened with becoming fortitude to 'a thrice told tale,'" Archibald Campbell wrote to Davis on the twentieth. Campbell, West Point class of 1835, chief clerk in the War Department under Marcy, continued to serve throughout the Davis years and he surely shared Davis's assessment of his old friend from West Point. "He is still harping on Orders for Europe," Campbell continued. "I don't know but I should be content to see him . . . sent with orders to China." Robert J. Walker, on his way to the Orient on a diplomatic mission for Pierce and Campbell, facetiously suggested that Magruder accompany him. "I believe the war Dept. would save money by the operation—certainly time," he added.[20]

Although Campbell thought Magruder's visits relieved "the dullness & monotony consequent on your absence from the Dept," he was told to approach the *Richmond Enquirer* "on his own hook" to publicize his views. The Virginia newspaper did wage an 1853 crusade to preserve the artillery intact: "It is manifestly wrong, that in a time of profound peace the Artillery should be armed and made to serve as Infantry. Officers who have gone into the Artillery have generally done so because they desired that arm of service," read an October 8 editorial. "Many of them might have gone into the Infantry or Dragoons, where, owing to their different organization, the promotion is more rapid. But they have sacrificed the advantage of more rapid promotion, to their preference for the Artillery arm." The *Enquirer* issued a call to have both the light and heavy branches, as well as the regular schooling of officers and men, strengthened through increased appropriations. And Campbell confessed that Magruder's "celebrated letter has brought thus far very little fruit," a reference to his earlier pleas for expanded training and equipage of the light batteries.[21]

Magruder remained in Washington for several months, arguing for leave to go abroad and calling for improvements in his service arm. Quartermaster General Thomas S. Jesup had ordered him from California to settle several outstanding accounts from the Florida campaign, and he was obliged to tell Davis that all of his papers had been destroyed in a San Francisco fire. But his main focus remained to secure leave to join his family while he toured military emplacements, and in two lengthy letters he traced recent developments among European armies. There was not a country in the world, he said, that could not benefit from improvements in its artillery. "In connection with this subject I cannot but bring to the notice of the Hon., the Secretary of War, the fact that we are entirely without any system of Instruction or drill for a combination of Batteries—which combination must take place as soon as an army for war in our own country or Canada is organized." We require drills and preparation, he told Jefferson Davis. Before leaving California, Magruder proffered, he had given "President Taylor information, which I obtained from reliable sources, of several important improvements, which had been made in Europe, in the art of artillery particularly, in the construction and use of fuses, and shells, which had attained a degree of perfection, in the last few years, not known in our Army."[22]

Davis, however, referred his arguments to Colonel Henry Knox Craig, chief of army ordnance; Craig, who served in the federal army from 1812 until his retirement as brigadier general in 1863, meticulously answered the points advanced, without reaching any firm recommendations. After examining Magruder's contention that American officers needed to visit European countries for firsthand observations, Craig advised:

> As regards improvements in arms and munitions which are the results of actual experience in the field, our own limited experience in actual warfare makes us especially dependent . . . on what is done in the military services of other countries. We have availed ourselves of all such improvements as have come to our knowledge either from reports of our own officers, who have had the opportunity of observing the arms and munitions of other countries, or from foreign publications on military subjects, or from intelligent foreigners coming to this country.

All such findings, he assured Davis, had been incorporated into the United States Army. Although Craig advised that some contact might be useful, he thought it best for officers in charge of the various branches of the military to make their own decisions about departmental changes. Two days later Davis advised Magruder that "his suggestions could not be adopted at the present time."[23]

Magruder, hellbent on getting to Europe, called upon Maryland governor Enoch L. Howe to second his trip "for the purpose of getting military information," although Howe erroneously informed Davis that Magruder was a "native of this state." The next day, December 23, Davis sent a memo to the adjutant general authorizing him "to go beyond the seas" to visit his family "who are sick in Europe." The directive said nothing about the collection of military intelligence, but it did stipulate that he was subject to orders "issued by the Commanding general of the Army." By March 30, 1854, he had reached Paris, where he dispatched a letter to Davis requesting an extension of his leave "and an allowance to enable me to observe European armaments, especially in the Crimea." Although Davis denied the request on April 21, Magruder found a means to reach the fronts on his own.[24]

His unidentified biographer in the *San Antonio Light* says not only that he reached the battlefields but that "he astonished the French officers by sleeping at the front with the Chasseurs under fire." Yet he did not go with the blessing of Davis, who, more than a year later, appointed an official delegation to Europe and the Crimea, composed of George B. McClellan, Richard Delafield, and Alfred Mordecia. Magruder may not actually have been in the Crimea, as the French did not declare war on Russia until March 28—two days before his letter to Davis—although *corps d' armee* had sailed for Turkey earlier. Since French and English forces concentrated around Varna on the present Bulgarian coast, as well as around Odessa, also on the western Black Sea, he likely toured the French encampments in that area. "After bombarding Odessa in April [1854] there was very little activity until the time came to shepherd the armies across to the Crimea and stand guard outside Sevastopol." By that time Magruder was back in the United States. On his own account he had managed something of a coup, as the formal American commission was not allowed to inspect any French positions—but only those of the "English, Sardinian, and Turkish armies."[25]

When Magruder sailed for home during the summer, his wife and children accompanied him to Baltimore. Although Mrs. Magruder returned to Europe upon her husband's assignment to rejoin his company, his eldest daughter, Isabell, met a young physician named Dr. Riggin Buckler. A graduate of Harvard, Buckler soon followed the family to Italy, where the young couple was married in July 1856; upon his death in 1884, Buckler, who had tended the wounded on the battlefield at Antietam while his father-in-law made his way to command in Confederate Texas, was highly esteemed by his colleagues, who, in an obituary issued by the Medical and Chirurgical Faculty of Maryland, said, "Though not as much known outside this city, as his talents deserve, his loss will be very widely and deeply felt in this community," while another practitioner called him "essentially a medical man." Never strong after her 1852 bout with the "malignant Roman fever," Isabell Magruder Buckler died in July 1869 without children of her own. Magruder called on his ailing daughter at her Baltimore home upon his 1866 return from Maximilian's court; Riggin Buckler produced another family when he remarried following his wife's premature death at age thirty-six.[26]

When Magruder came home in the summer of 1855, he renewed the cry to have Company I remounted; and when Davis again rejected his pleading, he asked for a transfer into other units on at least two occasions. I. B. Crane, commanding officer of the First Artillery, even advised Davis during March 1855, "Some other company than the one under the command of Bvt. Lieut. Col. J. B. Magruder should be selected when another company is to be put on duty as a light battery." And, as he dallied in Washington and Baltimore, Adjutant General Samuel Cooper, who later held the same position with the Confederate army, demanded to know why he had not rejoined his command. By February 21, 1855, Cooper warned that he had been absent without leave since October, which prompted Davis to issue an "implicit instruction" for his travel to San Antonio.[27]

Following Magruder's departure from San Diego, Company I had been assigned to escort duty with the surveying party fixing the new boundary with Mexico; his men had moved eastward from Fort Yuma toward Fort Bliss at El Paso, Texas, at the same time he was begging for a transfer to Captain Francis Taylor's light battery. But Jefferson Davis said no, and by 1855 Magruder had no choice but to rejoin his men; although he had been ordered to El Paso earlier, he caught up with the company in New Mexico and, during November, brought the unit to San Antonio Barracks, where the army had established itself after the Mexican War. Little wonder that Davis's patience was wearing thin! Magruder fired off a December 8 letter to Washington from his "artillery camp near San Antonio," asking that the company be remounted. But he had little time to brood over the lack of horses, as orders arrived in early January for Company I to take up a new station at Fort Clark, 120 miles to the west, on the Texas frontier.[28]

Magruder arrived at the post in January 1856, and remained until November; situated near Brackettville on Las Moras Creek, a tributary of the Rio Grande, the fort was intended "to safeguard the San Antonio-El Paso travel route." When Magruder and Company I got there, several other units were already at the isolated post five or six days' travel from San Antonio. He spent much of his time arranging for scouting parties against hostile Indians along the Pecos–Rio Grande frontier. Dozens of invoices in the University of Texas archive spell out his agreements with various scouts: On April 24, 1856, he approved "$18 to William Barry for 9 days scouting for Indians." A quartermaster's invoice signed by "J. B. Magruder, Captain, Rifles," on June 24, reimbursed Severiano Poticio the sum of eight dollars "for four days Indian scouting at $2.00 per day." Earlier, Poticio had been given twenty-four dollars for his services as a guide from June 7 to June 18.

During September 1856, twelve troopers from Company I joined contingents of the First Infantry and Second Cavalry for a memorable campaign—although Magruder was not present—that plunged into remote country unaccustomed to army patrols. "The expedition was conducted with so much judgment and energy that, in the operations of a day, three parties of Indians were surprised between the Rio Grande and Rio Pecos near their junction," notes William Haskin. "Four of the Indians were killed and four wounded, their animals and other property taken or destroyed."[29]

Company I was permanently reduced to infantry status when Cooper wrote, on February 27, 1856, "The secretary of war instructs me to say that he has no recollection of having at any time informed you verbally that Company I, 1st Artillery, would be mounted as soon as the service of the escort to the Mexican Boundary Survey should have been completed." The continued rejection by Davis and the remoteness of the frontier, however, did not cramp his zeal for the good life. A man had to keep up appearances! Mrs. Lydia Spencer Lane, the wife of an officer who accompanied her husband on numerous trips from her Pennsylvania home to various posts in New Mexico, recalls a stopover with Magruder during the Fort Clark interlude: "The dinner was plain as could be, but it was served in courses and in grand style." And, Mrs. Lane added, "John was always magnificent."[30]

Evidence abounds that Magruder found ample opportunity to make the "five or six day" jaunt into San Antonio, and to involve himself in the presidential contest of 1856 that unfolded during his stay on the frontier. After he opened a correspondence with James Lyons, "an ardent secessionist" and leading member of the Virginia legislature who had arranged the Marquis de Lafayette's 1824 tour of the Old Dominion, he was invited to elaborate his thoughts on the burning issues of the day. What transpired affords the modern reader an intimate glance into Magruder's views on abolitionism and the projected secession of the South. In response to a plea from several Texas politicos, including Isaiah A. Paschal, a San Antonio lawyer with Unionist leanings, and Samuel A. Maverick, a Bexar County legislator who became a strong Southern man during the Civil War, Magruder prepared a small printing of his letters to Lyons, complete with his own introduction. Army officers, he suggested, were not interested in local politics, but were vitally concerned with national questions. "I may here state, what, after diligent enquiry, I believe to be a fact, . . . that among the thousand or twelve hundred officers of the Army, coming as they do from every congressional district in the Union, . . . there is not to be found a single abolitionist." Although his findings may have been suspect, Magruder was satisfied to publish his letters, he said, "if they bring a single vote to the side of Union, Security and Peace."[31]

Lyons, who called Magruder "a distinguished writer," had already forwarded some of his letters to the *Richmond Enquirer*. The success of the Northern abolitionists in November, Magruder argued, would surely lead to disunion; until 1856 he had consistently supported the Whigs, but now he favored the Democrats because the party of Henry Clay and Daniel Webster, he continued, had withdrawn from politics. And he could not embrace the new American party—which later nominated ex-president Fillmore—because of its attacks on Roman Catholicism which he labeled as "wrong in principle and madly impolitical." His first letter ignored the fledgling Republicans with their commitment to free-soil doctrines and the non-extension of slavery into the territories; yet he condemned abolitionism of every stripe. Magruder remained convinced that the "safety of the Republic rested in the great Democratic party of the nation."

A second letter, dated August 25, also posted from Fort Clark, heaped scorn upon those nativist Know-Nothings drifting into the American party. Written after the national conventions had selected their candidates and drafted platforms, this one took the G.O.P. to task, although he never uses the term Republican. "I cannot believe that the people anywhere, especially in my own state, honest, earnest, patriotic, intelligent Virginia, can be played upon by trading politicians, political schemers and jugglers, so successfully as to be induced to cast their votes, to strengthen the abolition candidate, Freemont [sic]." A vote for Fillmore, who sought to avoid the slavery question by demanding a preservation of the Union, Magruder reasoned, was a vote taken from James Buchanan, the Democratic standard-bearer. Although Buchanan won the nomination because he had been out of the country as minister to Great Britain during the upheavals in Kansas and therefore had said nothing about slavery, Magruder was ecstatic in his praise for the candidate. He had first encountered Buchanan at a London banquet hosted by Lord John Russell during his visit to Europe, and had been impressed with his statesmanlike qualities. Never one to miss an opportunity for name-dropping, Magruder told his readers that he became personally acquainted with John C. Breckinridge—Buchanan's running mate—during the latter's congressional career. Like Buchanan, Breckinridge was a man of "moral firmness" that he "commended to the hearts and voices of my countrymen."[32]

Magruder's third letter, dated September 18, posted from San Antonio and addressed to his Texas friends, was another condemnation of Frémont and "the abolitionists" as well as a strong plea for "Union-loving men" to support Buchanan and the Democrats. Exactly one month later, Company I, with Magruder in command, was ordered to Baton Rouge Arsenal, where he remained until after the election; his missives to Lyons and the Texans recited fears that his "native state" and Maryland might opt for Fillmore and the third-party Americans. As it turned out, Buchanan and Breckinridge carried the election, with Frémont and the Republicans—Magruder's "abolitionists"—

running a threatening second. The Democrats won handily in Virginia while Fillmore triumphed in but one state—Maryland.[33]

Magruder withdrew for the moment from active politics, although his brother Allan lost track of him for a few weeks. A December letter to Jefferson Davis asked where he might be, as Allan Magruder had noticed in the press that Company I was headed for Fortress Monroe and not Louisiana as previously announced. A military installation had been maintained at Baton Rouge since 1816 as an "ordnance depot to both conveniently supply troops within the city and the posts on the Red and Mississippi Rivers." Nearby stood the Baton Rouge or Pentagon Barracks, which housed upwards of a thousand troops; the combined posts were a major supply outlet for the Mexican War, and eventually became the largest ordnance depot in the South. Unlike his difficulties with Davis and the Pierce administration—his record as a Whig, coupled with his drinking, had not helped—Magruder used his time in Baton Rouge to ingratiate himself with the new regime in Washington. After seven and a half months on the Mississippi, he was ordered to Newport, Rhode Island, where he assumed command of historic Fort Adams.[34]

A few weeks after Buchanan's inauguration, Magruder's lot changed drastically when he was propelled into perhaps the country's most fashionable resort town after months on the California and Texas frontiers. He arrived with Company I in May 1857, and remained until the autumn of 1859. And there can be little doubt that he joined the "summer people" who flocked to Newport hotels such as the "Ocean House, which a New York journalist termed a 'huge yellow pagoda factory' and which became nationally known as a pleasure dome of those comparatively few Americans who could stop working in summertime." Since the 1780s, continues a town historian who wrote the above words, groups of South Carolinians and other well-to-do southerners had made the place their summer destination, and they were soon joined by nabobs from around the country; during the 1830s Newport had become established as a resort for the wealthy, and by the time of Magruder's arrival their pleasurable activities had evolved into a fixed routine.[35]

Magruder's sobriquet, "Prince John," some writers contend, derived from his willingness to join Newport society; nearly all Civil War chroniclers who mention him draw upon Douglas Southall Freeman's

1942 classic, *Lee's Lieutenants: A Study in Command,* to paint Magruder as "a bon vivant and obliging host" at Fort Adams. Freeman, in turn, paraphrases an 1884 memoir by Armistead L. Long, who later served under Magruder in Kansas. At Newport "he enjoyed a fine field for exercising his high social qualities and fondness for military display," Long observes. "His princely hospitality and the brilliant show-drills with which he entertained his visitors made Fort Adams one of the most attractive features of the most celebrated watering place in America." Although Mrs. Lane and many others had paid their compliments to his courtliness and colorful demeanor, Magruder came into his own at the new post, and he seized every opportunity to display himself as well as his company. At the July 4, 1858, festivities in Newport, comments a town newspaper: "The United States troops under Col. Magruder, came over to town, with their battery, and after parading through the streets went through their evolutions in firing, etc., near Mr. Wetmore's in South Touro Street." Children and adults, the paper added, "enjoyed themselves." Magruder availed himself of numerous leaves while in Rhode Island, but he also made it his business to be present at Newport's seasonal levees.[36]

Fort Adams, located immediately south of Newport on Brenton Point, had been a military facility since 1638, when William Brenton placed two cannon imported from England to safeguard the entrance into Narragansett Bay. Named for President John Adams, the modern fort was established in 1799 but nearly fell to ruin after the War of 1812. Following a congressional appropriation of $50,000, a major overhaul took place during 1824–1857 under the direction of Colonel Joseph C. Totten, afterwards engineer general of the army. Although Magruder took command within months of Totten's rebuilding, he was obviously displeased with his quarters. "In consequence of the dampness of the Casemates assigned to the use of the officers at Fort Adams, yourself and the Asst. Surgeon stationed at that post, may be permitted to reside in the town of Newport and receive commutation of quarters and fuel," reads a May 25, 1859, communiqué from Washington. Secretary of War John B. Floyd personally approved the new arrangement with compensations that placed Magruder in the midst of Newport's summer vacationers. And six weeks afterwards, as he prepared for his move to Kansas, he returned to Fort Adams long enough "to visit the city with the light battery" for the annual July Fourth parade.[37]

Although Company I did not leave Fort Adams until November 1, Magruder journeyed down to New York City several weeks ahead of his men; as early as May 16, 1859, an order from Washington told him to march the company overland to Fort Leavenworth, on the Kansas frontier. But as he tarried in New York, Floyd advised him to call upon Colonel D. D. Tompkins, quartermaster general in the city, about another path to his new post. As usual, he tried to avoid duty in the West—this time by asking to remain in New York "for the purpose of compiling and adopting to our service a system of Evaluation of the Line for two or more Light Batteries." Magruder may have had his faults, but he was still a professional soldier with a vital concern for the latest artillery developments at home and abroad. Though the Mexican War had ended a decade earlier, the glories of the light companies on the road into Mexico City lingered with him. In 1858, however, he waited too long. "The Secretary of War [instructs me] to inform you, in reply, that a work of the character indicated by you prepared by Major Robert Anderson, of the 1st Artillery, has been adopted by the War Department," the adjutant general's office advised him on November 5. The Kentucky-born Anderson, soon designated "the hero of Fort Sumter," was shortly ordered to the South Carolina post, where he became a key player in the opening rounds of the Civil War; as Magruder took up command at Fort Leavenworth, Washington dispatched a copy of Anderson's *Instruction for Field Artillery* for his perusal.[38]

When he first arrived at the Kansas fort, Magruder was placed in command of the regular garrison, although he afterwards assumed charge of the "Artillery School of Practice." Fort Leavenworth, established in 1828 by Colonel Henry H. Leavenworth, Third United States Infantry, was situated on the Missouri River about twenty-five miles upstream from Kansas City; "the post comprises an area of about nine square miles, being bounded: North and east by the Missouri River; south by the City of Leavenworth, and west by the town of Kickapoo. The general proportions of the tract have not changed materially since first defined," reads an 1884 description. "They extend north and south along the Missouri a little more than five miles, and westward inland for one-fourth to two miles; the western boundary conforming to the eastern line of the town of Kickapoo." Until 1846, Leavenworth had little value to the army except as an Indian garrison; the Mexican War and subsequent overland expeditions by Philip S. Kearney to Santa Fe, and Joseph H. Long to Oregon, understandably shot it to prominence. The Pathfinder, John C. Frémont, the abolitionist candidate detested by Magruder in 1856, began his several treks through the Southwest and California from the fort. But during the "border troubles and intestine wars of Territorial Kansas, the troops stationed at Fort Leavenworth played no important part." Fortunately, John Brown and his band of antislavery warriors had already left for the East by the time Magruder assumed command.[39]

Sprawling Leavenworth, with its attached school for beginning artillerists, was Magruder's most prestigious duty after thirty-three years in the army. And several officers destined to play a role on the Civil War stage, North and South, were there when he took charge on December 19, 1859, including Armistead L. Long, Arnold Elzey, William B. Taliaferro, and William F. Lee. All of them later rose to general rank in the Confederate army. Elzey fought at Stonewall Jackson's side throughout the Valley campaigns, while Taliaferro and "Rooney" Lee, second-oldest son of Robert E. Lee, campaigned with the Army of Northern Virginia during much of the war. Long also served with Jackson in the Shenandoah after a brief stint with Robert E. Lee in the mountains of western Virginia; after the Civil War he earned lasting fame as the blind biographer of Lee, and his 1886 work, *The Memoirs of Robert E. Lee*, quickly became a bedrock source for all subsequent writing about the great Confederate general. Another of Magruder's charges at the artillery school was Henry Jackson Hunt, an officer who learned his lessons well. It was Hunt who placed George B. McClellan's guns at Malvern Hill that drove Magruder and the rest of Lee's command from the field in July 1862; a year later Hunt put his artillery at George Meade's disposal at Gettysburg to nearly wreck the Army of Northern Virginia. John Bankhead Magruder may well deserve more attention than has been previously accorded him for his instruction in the employment of artillery and its tactics on the eve of civil conflict.[40]

Edwin Vose Sumner, who happened to be Armistead L. Long's father-in-law as well as commander of the Department of the West at

St. Louis, during Magruder's tour at Leavenworth, sided with Prince John after Long and another lieutenant lodged a protest against his conduct at the school. They objected, read the complaint, "respecting the detail of Officers of foot companies to serve with light batteries." Anxious to propagate his notion of light artillery effectiveness throughout the officer corps, Magruder made it his business to run his students through the proper manual. "The *tour of duty* with a battery for the purpose of instruction whether as *instructor on drill* or as *subaltern on drill and stake* duty lasts four days . . . and terminates with them, even though from some cause there should have been no drill." Although each "subaltern" was handed stake and drill duty every week, Floyd could find no "hardship or wrong to be addressed." Sumner, who went on to high command in the federal army, not only agreed with the secretary of war but also said Magruder "had performed his mission with intelligence and zeal."[41]

Magruder was riding a high at Fort Leavenworth, which led more than one contemporary to record his exploits as he put the student gunners through their paces. "The aesthetical and precise Bankhead Magruder . . . was a good showman or ringmaster. He instituted pageants for our edification, sham battles and such like," wrote A. F. Callahan in an 1883 memoir. "The artillery boomed o'er the prairies, and reverberated through the fastness much to our amusement." Still, it is easy speculation that the loading and reloading as well as the incessant maneuvering of his howitzers and caissons was making an impression on men like Elzey, Rooney Lee, and Henry J. Hunt. "Magruder brought with him the disposition which had characterized him at Newport," A. L. Long wrote. "Although in the West the brilliant show-drills and dress-parades were often only witnessed by a group of frontiersmen, or a squad of Indians from the plains, he appeared as well satisfied as on similar occasions at Newport, where the spectators were the gay crowd of a fashionable watering-place." A lavish dinner, "provided with all the taste of a connoisseur," invariably followed the grandiose exercises. Even Long, apparently recovered from his snit over being made to serve with the light batteries, was obliged to admit that Magruder's school at Leavenworth had "great value" for the future commanders.[42]

When not on the parade ground, Magruder was constantly seeking to upgrade his garrison as well as the artillery school, although at one point he was required to assign several troopers to hospital duty during a manpower shortage; and he was granted permission to buy additional horses for Company I. But he ran into trouble with a January 27 request for a band at Leavenworth. Floyd not only said no to Magruder's scheme to have musicians enliven his dress maneuvers, but also thwarted a plan to clothe his troopers in "straw hats and pantaloons." His shenanigans on the prairies brought a direct order from the war office to stop "drilling the batteries under your command under the French system." He must, said the adjutant general, follow the regimen prescribed in Anderson's manual. Then, as he went about his training and marching, a July 19 letter reached Leavenworth from his fellow Virginian John Pegram. It contains a hint that Magruder may have had a special friend during his wife's residence in Europe. Writing from his post in New Mexico, the future Confederate general not only thanked him for his recent hospitality, but also informed him about the death of a mutual friend. And then Pegram added a brief postscript: "With especial regards to [A. L.] Long and Madam Marie."[43]

One month before the cataclysmic election of November 1860, an October 11 missive, sent from Washington, arrived at Magruder's desk: "The Secretary of War directs that you report in person, at the War Department, without delay, for special duty." John B. Floyd, onetime governor of Virginia and another future Confederate whom some argue positioned the army to favor the South during the secession crisis, may have spurned Magruder's requests for trumpeters and showy uniforms, but he readily issued orders for him to visit Europe; and unlike his predecessors, he permitted Magruder to travel on an official mission to review foreign military developments—perhaps with an eye on the coming conflict between North and South. Actually, Magruder, who had been on leave since September, posted an October 10 letter to Floyd from Washington, giving his reasons for going abroad as the sectional controversy heated up: "As commandant of the largest school of practice in the West, that of the Light Artillery at Fort Leavenworth, where my command has been composed of Light Artillery, Foot Artillery, & Light Infantry, I have found great need for a system of Drill for instruction applicable at once to the combined movements of these different Arms of Service and that much inconvenience & loss of time are experienced in maneuvering them together." A new, improved method of communication between disparate units on the field was sorely needed, he petitioned the war office. Magruder had been "informed on reliable authority" that several European countries had devised methods that warranted study by an American officer who could adapt them to the needs of the U.S. army. A number of technical inventions overseas, including the "Broadman Fuze," had, he thought, changed the nature of artillery warfare: "The improvements are considered of great importance & we have them not—they are to be found in the Belgian & different German services—France in these particulars strange to say not having kept pace, with the countries above named." Additional developments in military bridging and portable pontoons for marching troops, Magruder said, also merited investigation.[44]

Without a moment's hesitation, Floyd summoned him "to repair to Fort Leavenworth, Kansas Territory, and turn over the public property in your charge to the officer next in command to yourself at that post, and then proceed to Europe to accomplish the objects indicated in your letter to the Adjutant General." Captain William Barry, who afterwards commanded the federal artillery at First Manassas, had been in temporary charge during Magruder's absence; and when he returned in compliance with Floyd's instruction, Captain Horace Brooks, another Union artillerist, took charge at Leavenworth. Magruder lost no time in returning east, where he was told "to remain in France so long as you may deem it advisable . . . and report especially upon the progress made by the French, in the construction of rifled cannon, breech loading or otherwise"; thereupon, he was to visit Prussia, Austria, Russia, Italy, and Belgium. Further instructions directed him to "return by the way of England" in order to review developments in Great Britain.[45]

Having reached Paris on November 24, Magruder indicated in a December 2 letter that he was departing immediately to witness "the Siege of Gaeta" by the Sardinian army. Although sickness delayed his Italian journey, he spent considerable time observing the French military: "The French officers still think their guns (rifled) superior to the Armstrong Gun & are still making daily experiments to improve their artillery." An English invention in 1855, the Armstrong cannon, with a range of 2,200 yards at five degrees elevation, was later imported in small numbers for use in the Confederate service. When

Magruder left his quarters at "No. 68 Rue Neuve des Mathurins" in January 1861 for Italy, following "a six weeks delay," his communications with Washington ended abruptly until his return to the United States in March. Mrs. Magruder, who would not see her husband until their 1866 reunion in Maximilian's Mexico, did not return to Baltimore, but remained in Italy with her two unmarried children.[46]

When he reached Washington on March 10, Magruder assumed command of Company I, which had been on garrison duty around the capital since January 29; and he was soon engulfed in the momentous events that had been unfolding during his European sojourn. Following the four-cornered election among John C. Breckinridge, Stephen A. Douglas, John Bell, and Abraham Lincoln in November 1860, which had resulted in a Republican sweep, South Carolina had withdrawn from the Union on December 20. With that "Black Republican Lincoln" in the White House, said the South Carolinians, they could no longer honor the federal compact. In rapid succession six southern states—Mississippi, Florida, Alabama, Georgia, Louisiana, and Texas—rammed through similar declarations that took them out of the Union and into the new government formed on February 4 at Montgomery, Alabama. With Jefferson Davis and Alexander H. Stephens as president and vice president, the Southern experiment in self-government not only commenced the seizure of federal property, including Fort Sumter in the harbor at Charleston, South Carolina, but also began preparations for the inevitable conflict with the North.[47]

Magruder found himself in the uncomfortable position of having to defend—even protect—the Republican-dominated regime in Washington as his beloved Virginia, the jewel of the Southland, pondered its relation to the new order in Montgomery. Although he remained at his post for the next forty-one days—from March 10 until his resignation from the army on April 20—Magruder watched the drama in Washington and in Richmond, where the Virginia Secession Convention had been in session from February 13; throughout the secession maelstrom, his focus remained with his Southern kinsmen, as evidenced by his encounter with Major John C. Pemberton in his Washington office. Pemberton, a Pennsylvanian married to a Virginia lady, was caught in a dilemma over a proper course of action as the country came apart. "He said to Colonel Magruder, 'What *shall* I do?'

reads Benjamin Ewell's account. In the style of Mr. Dick in *David Copperfield*, Magruder responded, "Why, have a drink." And, Ewell says, "this they did and soon after the second was taken Pemberton departed for Richmond."[48]

His jocularity aside, Magruder also observed the role played by his brothers Allan, who had moved from Charlottesville to a Washington law firm, and George, still on active duty with the navy. While the Virginia Convention went through its deliberations, Lincoln decided to confer with George W. Summers, a prominent Unionist from western Virginia who sat in the Richmond body; the president asked Allan Magruder to be his envoy to Summers, requesting that he come immediately to the White House. When he reached the convention, however, Summers, an aging gentleman preoccupied with his own affairs, refused the presidential summons, but sent another Virginian, Colonel John B. Baldwin, in his place. Baldwin thereupon accompanied Allan Magruder to Washington, and "after breakfasting and making his toilet at the house of Captain [George A.] Magruder," the two proceeded directly to Lincoln's office.

Although the April 3 interview ended in failure, John Bankhead Magruder, also a guest in his brother's home, was intimately linked to the ensuing scenario; Lincoln's hope of keeping a portion of Virginia loyal to the federal standard collapsed over events surrounding the resupply of Fort Sumter, which the Virginians opposed. When the opening salvos were fired at the South Carolina post on April 12, and the Virginia Convention responded by taking the Old Dominion out of the Union five days later, Prince John Magruder decided to tender his resignation from the federal service. Like his fellow Virginians, he had resolved to cast his lot with the Confederate endeavor.[49]

5

Big Bethel

MAGRUDER'S APRIL 20, 1861, LETTER to Colonel—later General—Charles F. Smith severed a thirty-five-year military career that began when he entered the 1826 class at West Point. As commander of the Washington garrison, Magruder told the new president from Illinois that he was honor-bound to follow his native Virginia into the Southern Confederacy. A few days before his official resignation, when a telegram from Virginia governor John Letcher reached Washington refusing a presidential demand to help put down the rebellion, Prince John had sat with Lincoln to discuss security matters around the capital.

Although Magruder had assured the president of his personal loyalty and protection as the country came apart, he used the session at the White House to explain his reasons for joining the Southern breakaway. Following Appomattox, Magruder gave his own version of the tête-à-tête with Lincoln in a number of national newspapers. His 1870 account, written from Galveston, Texas, was prompted by an outburst from Simon Cameron, who had been Lincoln's secretary of war preceding Edwin M. Stanton, but was then a United States senator from Pennsylvania, who castigated him by inference on the senate floor: "I remember that Capt. Somebody, who became a general in the rebel army, but had the command of a battery here, and he was going to start off not only with himself but with his battery, but somehow or other the battery did not get off." And when Kansas senator Samuel Pomeroy asked, "That was the captain who escorted the President to the White House?" Cameron offered a quick rejoinder:

"The same man. He escorted the President to the White House, and I heard him say to the President that he admired him, and was going to stand by him during the war." Not only Cameron and Pomeroy but other postwar Republicans across the North asked why "rebels" like Magruder had been allowed to escape into the Confederacy.

Upon learning of Cameron's diatribe, Magruder penned a letter recounting his farewell meeting with the president. In doing so, he has given us a first-rate rendering of his movements after learning that Virginia had left the Union. Cameron's remarks, Magruder says, constituted "one monstrous, malicious, reckless and infamous lie," because he had "never been with Mr. Lincoln in the presence of Mr. Cameron" in his life. He did confirm that he had encountered Cameron at the home of his brother, Commodore George A. Magruder, upon his return from Europe; Cameron, Magruder continues, during a private conversation, offered "to send me to Russia, there to remain, until the termination of the pending war." Less than a year later, when Cameron got into trouble over financial dealings at the war office, Lincoln decided to make Stanton his secretary of war, and named the Pennsylvanian his ambassador to the czars. Despite the later tiff with Cameron, Magruder told Lincoln in April 1861, as he joined the exodus to Richmond, that he "very much regretted secession," but that he would fight alongside "those among whom I was born and bred, my relations, and friends all of whom believe they are right." And he bent the presidential ear with a justification not only of his own decision but also of that of many Southern-born soldiers to leave the federal army: "I stated to him that I was a graduate of West Point, but that West Point was not a charity school; . . . that the Government had always recognized the right of officers to resign, . . . and that the obligations to which an officer subscribed were simply to obey the lawful orders of his superiors as long as he held the commission of the Government."

Lincoln "acquiesced in the propriety of these views," according to Magruder, who told him that as long as he held command of the Washington garrison, the president and his family had nothing to fear:

> "Yes," said he, "I know it, for you are an officer of the army and a Southern gentleman, and incapable of any but honorable conduct."
> I thanked him warmly and said: "Mr. President, if I do resign you will be the first to hear of it after my resignation is placed in the

hands of the adjutant, if I can reach you. I will remain at least twelve hours in Washington after my resignation." "Why," said he, with some surprise, "should you do that?" "Mr. President," I replied, "I wish to be gracefully off with the old love before I am with the new." "I am sorry to lose you," he said with great animation, "but if you must go, I'll help you to be gracefully off with the old love," meaning I supposed, that he would accept my resignation when the time came to offer it.[1]

Magruder crossed the Long Bridge into Alexandria and seceded Virginia at around 9:00 P.M. on the evening of his resignation; unable to call on Lincoln, he commenced his journey southward by "taking a hack" to the Potomac. "It was a bright moonlight night, and as I got out of the coach I found my own battery guarding the bridge. The men uncovered as I passed through them to see the Lieutenant in charge. I asked him if he would be kind enough to lower the draw-bridge for me, as I was all packed and was only three minutes behind time." Although the crossing was sealed at 9:00 P.M., Magruder persuaded the officer in charge to let him pass. "He touched his hat and answered courteously, 'Colonel, I will lower the draw-bridge, but would do it with greater pleasure if you were coming from Virginia instead of going to Virginia.'

"Taking off my hat to my old comrades, some of whom I commanded for thirty years, and with a sad heart I bade them farewell," Magruder continues. His theatrical exit accomplished, he spent April 21–23 in Alexandria, where he visited his old friend from Charlottesville and West Point, Philip St. George Cocke. Even before Virginia joined the new Confederacy on May 7, Robert E. Lee had been placed in command of the state's military forces as Governor John Letcher hurried to secure her borders against Yankee intrusion. Cocke, a West Point man, class of 1832, two years behind Magruder, had been placed in command of a troop opposite Washington, while Kenton Harper, Daniel Ruggles, and William B. Taliaferro, among others, were posted at various Virginia locations. Magruder not only called upon his old compeer from the federal army, but also secured a letter of recommendation to the Richmond authorities. "I congratulate you upon the acquisition of the services at this juncture of so valuable an officer," Cocke wrote on April 22 from his Alexandria headquarters. After recounting their days at the University of Virginia and West Point, and their several years together in the old army, he implored the governor to find Magruder a place suitable to "his rank and position." Prince John may have abandoned his "old love" with a doff of the hat, but he obviously had his eye on the future. Tragically, his friend Cocke, dubbed by one contemporary as "a naturally impetuous fellow," took his own life in December 1861 as Magruder held the keep opposite Fort Monroe.[2]

Magruder was not the only member of his family to join the Southern cause. His brother Allan followed him to Richmond, and when John Bankhead Magruder assumed his first real command on the lower peninsula, Allan served as his chief commissary officer. George A. Magruder Jr. shortly joined his uncle as aide-de-camp, during the Peninsula and Seven Days campaigns; he even followed Magruder to Texas in late 1862. Although there is no indication that sixty-one-year-old Commodore George A. Magruder embraced the Confederacy, he did tender his resignation from the navy on April 22, two days after his brother gave up the Washington army garrison. Actually, his commission as captain was the highest naval rank sanctioned until 1862, "but prior to that date a captain commanding, or having commanded, a squadron was given the courtesy title of commodore." Unlike his brother, George A. Magruder had difficulty leaving the federal service. "You are hereby detached from the Bureau of Ordnance and Hydrography," Lincoln's secretary of the navy, Gideon Welles, informed him one day after his resignation. A second letter, assuring the administration "that under no circumstances could I be induced to bear arms against the Constitution and Flag I love," brought a return letter from Welles, dated May 13: "By direction of the President your name has been stricken from the rolls of the navy."[3]

The two brothers and George junior, meanwhile, had made their way to Richmond, although the exact date of their arrival is open to question; but there can be no doubt that John Bankhead Magruder, armed with Cocke's letter, moved quickly to land a commission in first the military forces of Virginia and, subsequently, the Confederate army. The secession convention, which did not adjourn until May 1, was the center of activity as Robert E. Lee, appointed to command the state's military apparatus on April 23 with the rank of major general, directed military preparations in close cooperation with Governor Letcher and the Virginia Council on War, composed of Judge John J. Allen, Commodore Matthew Maury, and VMI superintendent Francis H. Smith. Lee quietly and effectively created a viable military force for the onslaught that was sure to come once Virginia voted to leave the Union, despite Letcher's earlier attempts to protect the state's frontiers. Raw recruits by the thousands had to be whipped into fighting units, and hundreds of officers appointed to train and lead them. Lee, who had known Magruder since their cadet days on the Hudson, played a key role in finding him a first command. The commanding general assigned him the immediate job of organizing artillery batteries around the capital as "Colonel, Virginia Volunteers."[4]

In addition to the recommendation from Cocke, Magruder explored other paths to advance his new career. On April 26, as he awaited the initial assignment from Lee, he addressed a lengthy letter to President Davis at Montgomery; he had, after all, known Davis since 1826, when he first entered West Point, had served with him in Mexico, and, during 1853–1857, when Davis had served as secretary of war under Franklin Pierce, they had exchanged considerable correspondence about Magruder's incessant pleas for army leave. "I have ascertained the precise plan for the occupation and defense of Washington," he informed Davis, and he gave the new Confederate president a close military briefing on how best to reduce the defenses of not only the Yankee capital but also of Baltimore. "If we do not act," he said, "the Federal troops will, as soon as they feel themselves secure in Washington—& the foot of the abolitionists will be firmly planted on the neck of Maryland." Although Virginia had not yet joined the Confederacy, Magruder was obviously courting Davis—he hoped for his "life and health," and he was not the only Virginia-born officer looking for preferment in the new Southern army once the Old Dominion opted to leave the Union. Thomas Jonathan Jackson engaged in a forceful campaign from the outset to enlist relatives and political acquaintances in his bid to climb the command ladder; and Joseph E. Johnston, soon to be Magruder's superior, hied himself to the Alabama office of Davis in search of a Confederate commission.[5]

By April 29—less than two weeks after his resignation from the federal service—Magruder sent his first dispatch to the war office from the "Richmond Baptist Seminary," with details of the new artillery units under his command. He was now caught up in a gigantic swirl that continued for four unrelenting years, because never for a moment was the new army and its government free from attack; and from the beginning, he was a prominent player in the effort to attain separate nationhood, even before Virginia joined the regime created at Montgomery during February 1861. Although most of his service would be spent on the remote Texas coast, Magruder found himself the man of the hour during the opening phases of the Civil War.

Before he assumed charge of the peninsula army a few weeks later, like other officers rushing to the new flag, he was busy with organizing and training the troops under his direction. "For the purpose of assisting in drilling these companies, I request that the cadets, of the highest classes be detached and ordered to report for temporary duty," reads his April 29 letter to the state's adjutant general, Robert S. Garnett. Professor Tom Jackson, also named colonel of Virginia volunteers, had marched his cadets from the Virginia Military Institute at Lexington into the capital at about the time Magruder arrived from Washington. Many of the boys had recently helped Jackson test a number of new Parrott guns purchased by the state; this, coupled with their regular training in artillery tactics, caused them to be pressed into service at Richmond. The secession convention even voted a monthly stipend of twenty dollars per month for the youthful drillmasters. Magruder's request was approved the following day by Joseph E. Johnston, erstwhile quartermaster general of the federal army and a man Prince John would encounter soon enough on the ramparts. When he asked for help from Jackson's cadets, he told Garnett that he had "no staff officers of any description"; and since he could not obtain sufficient harnesses and carriages for his artillery pieces, Magruder included a second request: "I would respectfully recommend that a pattern of artillery harnesses be sent to each of the considerable towns on the lines of the railroads where they can be manufactured."[6]

As he worked with his artillery recruits around Richmond, Magruder also learned a hard lesson about the Confederate war. There were never enough men and supplies to equip every field unit; everything from shoes to cannon and especially troops were lacking as the conflict dragged on. In the first days of war, experienced officers were needed at every juncture, and Lee issued a directive to the army on

May 8—one day after Virginia officially entered the Confederacy—which gave Magruder command of "Virginia forces in and about Richmond." Although other officers were rushed to the front, he was required to stay near the capital, overseeing his batteries. Magruder must have continued his requests for command, although Letcher and Lee were seemingly hesitant to put him in the field during the initial rush; but Lee issued another order on May 21, one month after he left Washington, that gave him real command: "Col. John B. Magruder of the Provisional Army of Virginia, is placed in command of the troops and military operations on the line to Hampton." With the help of units under D. H. Hill, Benjamin S. Ewell, B. S. Cary, T. P. August, and others, Magruder was directed to establish his headquarters at Yorktown and "take measures for the safety of the batteries at Jamestown Island and York River, and urge forward the construction of the defenses between College and Queen Creeks, in advance of Williamsburg."[7]

The historic peninsula of Virginia, formed by the York and James River estuaries, was the site of the Jamestown colony, where the first permanent Englishmen in the Americas had settled three hundred years earlier, as well as Williamsburg, the picturesque capital of colonial Virginia, and of the Yorktown battlefield, where George Washington had cornered Lord Cornwallis to end the American Revolution. In the spring of 1861 it had great strategic importance for both antagonists, because Fort Monroe sat on its easternmost tip in Elizabeth City County on the Chesapeake. Fort Monroe, situated at Old Point Comfort, where a military fortification of some kind had been functioning since colonial times, was still in Yankee hands and there it would remain throughout the Civil War; easily supplied by sea, the fort was both a thorn in the side of Confederate nationalism and a convenient staging platform for a federal thrust at Richmond. Because of its spectacular geography, the peninsula was destined to host a major struggle between North and South from the first days of civil strife until George Brinton McClellan's Army of the Potomac was forced to abandon it following the battle at Malvern Hill in July 1862. Although Magruder would not retain command on the peninsula until the end, he knew from the beginning that his task was to keep the federals at Fort Monroe from advancing toward the Confederate capital.

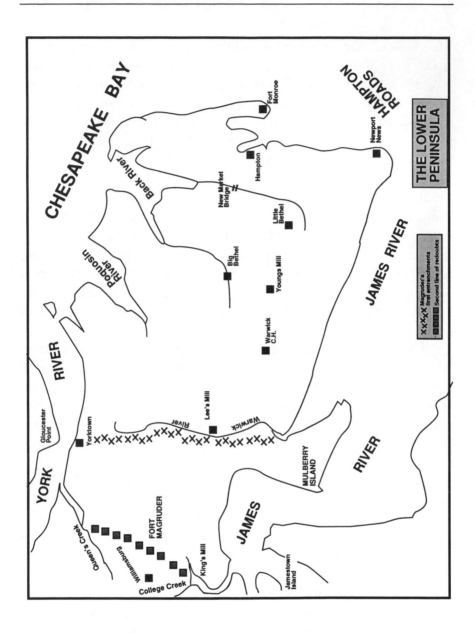

Two days after his appointment to command, Magruder was still in Richmond, but he was already making his military preparations. A letter to Colonel William B. Blair in the Confederate Commissary Service requested an advance shipment of rations for 2,500 troopers already posted on the peninsula; by May 24 he was heading down the York River aboard the steamer *Logan*, where he learned from locals that an equal number of federals were already posted around Fort Monroe; however, he lowered his estimate of enemy troop strength the following day, while at the same time beginning to demand additional reinforcements: "I shall need at least four companies of cavalry to operate against the advance of troops from Hampton, to cut off their parties, to harass them on the march, and to beat up their quarters at night." And once Magruder established his Yorktown headquarters, he began a daily correspondence with the war office in Richmond. Some writers have capitalized on his "Prince John" reputation from the old army to portray his war communiqués as flamboyant and theatrical; but a close reading of the dozens if not hundreds of letters dispatched by him during this phase of the war suggests otherwise. They demonstrate instead a straightforward treatment of military necessity. Yes, they contain persistent demands for more and more troops, but so did those of all Confederate commanders as the Yankee Goliath facing them increased in strength.[8]

William and Mary president Benjamin S. Ewell, who already commanded the Thirty-fourth Virginia Regiment at Williamsburg, says that construction of defensive works was under way when Magruder arrived on the scene; Robert E. Lee, Ewell asserts, had gone over the ground during an earlier visit to the region before he seconded a fortification scheme devised by Colonel Alfred M. Rives and Ewell himself. "General Magruder after he took command approved of them and ordered their completion but he did not originate them." And there can be no question that he was a "picturesque figure" as he directed construction of defenses across the peninsula: "He had a fondness for tinsel and tassels. With an irrepressible spirit of restless energy, instinctively susceptible of the charm of danger, full of health and physical force, it was evident that nature had made him a soldier." But, continues Baker P. Lee, who observed him closely during this period, "it was in the field, in full military array, well mounted, as he always was, with the fire of patriotic ambition and personal pride in his eye, that he was seen at his best."[9]

Lee's May 21 order directed him to build his fortifications along the narrow neck of land between College Creek, which empties into the James, and Queen's Creek, an inlet from the York; it was a spot where only the streets of Williamsburg provided a dry passage on the path from Hampton to Richmond. "The width of the peninsula varies greatly, its narrowest point being east of Williamsburg, where it is about seven miles." And, continues a historian of the region,

> a prominent feature is its abundance of swamps which make up from the rivers on either side, or from the creeks and estuaries emptying into them. These swamps are practically impassable, except at occasional points, where corduroyed roads or embankments of earth for mill ponds form a crossing. The region is so level that such an embankment will make a mill pond miles in length, while every cove or hollow that drains into it will become a swamp more difficult of passage than the pond itself, as it is at once too soft for the pedestrian and too solid for the boatman.

It was here in the watery lowlands of the Virginia peninsula that Magruder set to work on his batteries and redoubts. "Proceeding to fortify against assault, whether by land or water, or both combined, Magruder's works very soon showed that the eye of an entilligent [sic] engineer had carefully looked through the topographical surroundings and characteristics of the situation in all of its length and breadth." When Jefferson Davis arrived in Virginia to establish his capital, he found Magruder on the peninsula as well as Benjamin Huger at nearby Norfolk confidently "guarding the approach to Richmond from the seaboard."[10]

Magruder, by his own admission, moved his operations a bit closer to Fort Monroe:

> Deeming it of vital importance to hold, for a time Yorktown, on York River, and Mulberry Island on James River, and to keep the enemy in check by an intervening line, until the authorities might think proper to take such steps as should be deemed in the Peninsula, I felt so composed to dispose my feeble forces in such a manner as to accomplish these objects with the least risk possible.

Magruder's May 3, 1862, battle summary, written during the buildup for the Seven Days campaign, however, says that his "real line of defense was slightly in advance, at Harwood's and Young's Mills." Along the west bank of the tidal Warwick River, which originates a short way south of Yorktown and makes its way into the James east of Mulberry Point, amid "boggy and difficult streams and swamps," he put his engineers to work on a fortified line across the peninsula. His left flank, east of Yorktown, relied upon the swamps and ravines leading into the York at Wormley's Creek; gun emplacements beyond the York at Gloucester Point also strengthened the Yorktown defenses. Magruder's right, his report to Adjutant General Samuel Cooper continues, "was defended by the fortifications at the mouth of Warwick River, and at Mulberry Island Point, and the redoubts extending from the Warwick to James River." The heavily wooded center prompted him to boast afterward that 25,000 troops at his command could have held the line against all comers.[11]

As he worked at his defenses through the last days of May and early June, Magruder attracted his share of admirers and detractors. Daniel Harvey Hill, newly assigned to the peninsula, wrote his wife on the thirtieth: "Col. Magruder in command is always drunk and giving foolish and absurd orders. I think that in a few days the men will refuse to obey any order issued by him." Unfortunately, the press of work and the pending forward movement by Benjamin F. Butler's superior forces at Fort Monroe caused a naturally impetuous Magruder to imbibe more than he should have. In that pristine age before the widespread availability of tranquilizers and related substances to soothe tangled nerves, he fell back on the only available palliative.

Although Hill, a brother-in-law of Stonewall Jackson and a North Carolina mathematics professor in more peaceful times, kept his outward composure when reporting to his new superior, he was not bashful in criticizing Magruder's personal conduct. Hill, who had been elected colonel of the recently formed First Regiment of North Carolina Volunteers, was something of a cantankerous sort—his chief biographer calls him "Lee's Maverick General"—but he did good service in the soon-to-come struggle under Magruder's direction. Cadmus Wilcox, on the other hand, encountered a different commander when he arrived on the peninsula; the 1846 West Point graduate—

in the same class with Hill's brother-in-law and four years before Hill himself—had served with both soldiers as well as Magruder in Mexico. Around the Yorktown ramparts, Wilcox found "some who believed Magruder would ultimately command the army." Even the general commanding found his early work praiseworthy: "I take pleasure in expressing my gratification at the movements that you have made, and hope that you might be able to restrict the advance of the enemy and securely maintain your own position," Lee telegraphed from Richmond as Magruder prepared for his first engagement.[12]

That fight would also be the first "land battle" of the war, and Magruder worked speedily to get his personal staff in order. Besides D. H. Hill, who soon caused trouble despite their early rapport, another young officer destined to make his mark joined his official entourage. After his arrival at Yorktown on May 31, Magruder placed the Kentucky-born John Bell Hood in charge of his cavalry at Lee's expressed command. Not only was the young cavalryman told to establish a training camp for his horsemen, but he was also instructed to make a "judicious disposition of the pickets and vedettes." Hood's outriders were soon probing federal positions around Fort Monroe as well as nearby Hampton and Newport News, to the increasing displeasure of B. F. Butler. "I was only a First Lieutenant, and the companies of course were under the direction of captains; a question eventually arose in respect to my rank, and Magruder, unwilling to await action at Richmond, declared me Captain by his own order," Hood wrote in his postwar memoirs. "Subsequently discussion arose touching the date of commissions of Captains, and he at once, by the same process, declared me Major. This settled all matters pertaining to authority and I continued on outpost duty, covering Magruder's front." Although Hood did not receive his pay as captain until later, he remained on excellent terms with his commander until both soldiers were assigned elsewhere.[13]

But the surface amity between Magruder and D. H. Hill was shattered in a dispute over rank. A few days after he established "a special express" to Richmond, Magruder told the war office about the tiff: "There is some difference of opinion here as to the rank of Colonel Hill, of the North Carolina regiment, and myself," he informed General Garnett on June 2. "I think I rank him, but am of the impression that it is a subject of some feeling on his part. He has, however, obeyed my orders so far, and I presume will continue to do so." Yet Magruder considered Hill to be his second in command and regularly left him in charge of the Yorktown headquarters when "he galloped off to make an inspection or attend a dinner."[14]

From the beginning of his duty on the peninsula, Magruder was faced with hard military choices. With never enough men to garrison his redoubts along the Warwick, he informed Richmond that steamers and transports were steadily bringing fresh troops to Fort Monroe and the federal outposts beyond his lines. And B. S. Ewell sent the alarm to Lee on May 29: "I beg to call the attention of the Commanding General to the fact that the force now here is insufficient to repel a serious attack. If Yorktown, Jamestown, or the defenses below Williamsburg fall, the way will be open to Richmond." Additional troops and artillery were needed, Ewell pleaded. "Colonel Magruder is well convinced of this. So far as he has mentioned his opinions to me, his views coincide with mine." Ewell thought Magruder was right, although he later argued that a 25,000-man garrison would have made his positions impregnable. But Magruder's small force was powerless to check reinforcements from reaching Fort Monroe and to prevent their subsequent occupation of the surrounding countryside. "The women and children have been passing here [Yorktown] all day from Hampton," he informed Richmond on May 27. He had been obliged to abandon Hampton when Major J. B. Cary withdrew from the place "with about sixty-five men out of two hundred, which he had a day or two since—the remainder of his men being occupied attending the retreating families." Both Magruder and the Confederate high command suffered from insufficient naval power to seal the peninsula. As long as Fort Monroe was allowed to fly the old flag, a manpower-starved South would have difficulty securing Richmond's eastern flank.

Magruder was able to employ several hundred blacks from peninsula plantations to work at his entrenchments. While many did work on the Confederate battlements—to the disgust of Butler, an abolitionist politician from Massachusetts before the war—hundreds of others fled to the federal lines around Fort Monroe. "The negroes [sic] came pouring in day by day," Butler writes in his 1892 autobiography. "I found work for them to do, classified them and made a list of them so their identity might be fully assured, and appointed a 'commissioner of negro affairs' to take this business off my hands, for it was becoming onerous." Although Magruder could not stem this flow of Southern manpower from his grasp, it created a reverse refugee problem for the federals. When Butler asked Winfield Scott for instructions, the federal commander told him simply "to keep an accurate account of their work." Butler, too, was using peninsula slaves—whom he declared contrabands—to work on his own fortifications.[15]

If Butler and other federal commanders were enthusiastic about helping blacks toward freedom, Magruder could be equally magnanimous. "Not long after he went to Yorktown, a colored woman applied to me as commandant at Williamsburg for the release of her husband who had been impressed to work on the fortifications," wrote Ewell. "Her appeal was touchingly and well made," but she was advised to make the same appeal at Magruder's Yorktown headquarters, as Ewell had no authority to grant her request. "The result," Ewell adds, "was her return accompanied by her husband." When McClellan arrived to launch his campaign against the Yorktown defenses, his outriders scoured the peninsula countryside in search of food and lurking rebels, to the apprehension of the local citizenry. One distraught woman "who lost her pigs and chickens to the light-fingered Yankee cavalrymen encamped on her farm," relates Stephen Sears, "had taunting advice for her guests. Want to get to Yorktown, did they! 'General Magruder's thar an' he kin drink more whiskey en anny general you'uns got, but he won't be thar when you git thar . . .'" Apparently Magruder's reputation for hard drinking had preceded him.[16]

Colonel John Bankhead Magruder had been on the peninsula a total of eighteen days when the opening fight at Big Bethel took place about mid-distance between his lines on the Warwick and Fort Monroe. During that brief interval he managed to put an efficient personal staff in place; in addition to his brother, Allan, appointed major, as his commissary officer, and his nephew, George A. Magruder Jr., he enlisted several capable aides, including Isaac M. St. John, later commissary and brigadier general. For the vital post of adjutant he had several officers: Colonel (later Brigadier General) John M. Jones, Colonel George Crosby (who also reached general rank), and Captains Henry Bryan and Edward P. Turner. Magruder's engineering officer, Hugh T. Douglas, noted that Bryan fought beside Prince John at Big Bethel, and later, when Joseph E. Johnston took charge of the peninsula army, he remained with him through the fights at Williamsburg, Savage Station, and Malvern Hill. "I remember him so well. A gentleman of the Virginia school of the days that are dead; a gallant, enthusiastic and efficient soldier, beloved by those with whom he was associated," Douglas observed in 1909. "He was not physically strong but wiry and untiring, always doing his full duty." When Magruder was shunted to the Texas coast, Edward P. Turner was serving as his adjutant. Magruder's other difficulties notwithstanding, he was blessed with faithful associates who made his work of command much easier, and Turner, who became a Texas lawyer after the war, even provided him a place to lodge during his last tragic days.[17]

Even though it was a mere trifle—nothing more than a skirmish compared to later Civil War engagements—the inevitable clash between Magruder and Butler occurred on the morning of June 10. While he may not have fired the first shot, Magruder's posturing was surely a precipitating factor in the battle. "Half way down the peninsula he showed himself, 'giving the dare' to any and every Federal commander whose aspirations after early laurels might move him to advance upon the Confederate camp at Big Bethel." Throughout the first days of June, Magruder constantly surveyed his defenses accompanied "by a fine troop of cavalry inspecting his ramparts and encouraging his command." And he was ever the showman. "When Magruder's cavalcade at a full gallop inspected the thin lines of the Warwick, it was a sight for men and the gods," noted Moxley Sorrel, who arrived a bit later with reinforcements. "Of commanding form and loving display, he had assembled a numerous staff, all, like himself, in the most showy uniforms." Yet he was always the soldier. Hood was forward almost daily, probing the federal pickets, and a few days before the battle, D. H. Hill had been posted east of Yorktown near a crossroads church known locally as Big Bethel to distinguish it from a nearby black congregation called Little Bethel. "There was a point nine miles from the fort on the road leading from Hampton to Yorktown, which I learned the rebels intended to entrench and hold," Butler, who left a surprisingly detailed account of the affray, noted in his memoir of the war. "After the most careful and thorough preparation and a personal reconnaissance of the lay of the land by Major [Theodore] Winthrop, I came to the conclusion to attempt to take this post."[18]

"I did not return from Hampton last night till after 11 o'clock," Magruder informed the adjutant general on June 9: "From all I could learn, I am satisfied that Hampton is within a few days to be occupied as a military post by the Federal troops," he added from his bivouac at Winders, Virginia. In the same note from his temporary headquarters at Big Bethel, written one day earlier, Magruder not only complained about the scarcity of rations for his troopers but also reported substantial activity by Butler's forces: "Yesterday [June 7] I received a note from Colonel Hill, stating that a considerable body of Federal troops were advancing on his position." A circumspect Hill writes in his official battle report that he had moved from Yorktown to Big Bethel on specific orders from Magruder; he was accompanied by his North Carolina regiment as well as by four guns under Major George W. Randolph. But, J. W. Ratchford, one of Hill's aides, says, "It looked as if Magruder was only sending us down to the vicinity of the fort as a dare to General Benjamin F. Butler. He no doubt thought that we would have sense enough to get out of his way. I never heard of any order from Magruder instructing us how far to go, when we should turn back or whether or not we should capture the fortress, and I do not believe he gave any from what I heard Colonel Hill say and I was with him all the time."

Hill erected what fortifications he could, and when he received reports about "a marauding party" within a mile or so of his line, he hurried forward men and a single howitzer; a hot little fight took place near the "New Market Bridge," and, Hill continues, "reliable citizens reported that two cart loads and one buggy load of wounded were taken into Hampton. We had not a single man killed." At nightfall, Magruder himself arrived to assume personal command.[19]

Butler, meanwhile, had set his own forces in motion. Although both armies fought with amazing ineptitude, the federals under Ebenezer W. Pierce were engaged in a comedy of errors from the outset; Butler himself admits that everything was "utterly mismanaged." He had assigned two columns to the van—one to march from Camp Hamilton, near Fort Monroe, and the other from an encampment at Newport News, with his remaining force in the rear. All told, Butler sent about 2,500 bluecoats against 1,200 Confederates under Magruder and Hill. "When the troops got out four or five miles to the junction where the regiments were to meet, it being early dawn and the officers very scared, Colonel [John E.] Bendix mistook the colonel and staff of the other regiment for a body of cavalry, and fired upon them," Butler observes. "The fire was returned; and by that performance we not only lost more men than we lost in the battle, but also ended all chance for a surprise."

The early-morning shooting alerted Hill's North Carolinians to the approaching danger, although he had moved forward around three o'clock, but had returned to the Big Bethel entrenchments upon learning of Pierce's advance. The renewed assault against Hill's lines came at 9:00 A.M., and it was concentrated against his right and center. After several uncoordinated thrusts at Randolph's howitzers, Hill writes, all federal "organization was completely broken up." "There was no concert of action between Pierce's units," writes B. M. Hord, one of Hill's North Carolina boys. "A regiment would come up, fire a volley or two, mostly over our heads and precipitately fall back. . . . It seemed that their principal object was simply to get a sight or a shot at a Rebel, then fall back as quickly as possible." Magruder remained on the ramparts directing his men, and Hill says that when this phase of the fighting ended around ten o'clock, "we were now as secure as at the beginning and as yet had no man killed."[20]

Stymied on his left, Pierce and his attackers shifted their stabs to Magruder's positions nearer the York River swamps, while his commander remained at Fort Monroe; Butler says that it was proper for him to stay behind. Just as the earlier successes had been inspired by Magruder's decisive shift of troops at the critical moment, he now moved to bolster the Confederate left. When the Bethel Regiment—after this fight, the First North Carolina always carried that sobriquet—absorbed the new attack, he reacted immediately by ordering more companies into the fray, and, says D. H. Hill, "now began as cool a firing on our side as was ever witnessed." The assault might have worked, "but Brig. Gen. Pierce who commanded the expedition appears to have lost his presence of mind," telegraphed a *New York Times* correspondent; and the *Baltimore American* said most of the carnage was caused by Randolph's "rifled cannon." Butler, however, was exceptionally bitter about the later fighting: "From that time there did not seem to be a head more than a cabbage head to undertake anything, except it might be [Theodore] Winthrop." Confederate success was obvious when Hill reported to Richmond that Winthrop—shot dead when he jumped up on a log to observe Magruder's position—"was the only one of the enemy who exhibited even an approximation of courage the whole day."[21]

Finally, continues the *Times* account, "a council of colonels was held, and the order given to retreat, after the men had been exposed an hour and a half to a destructive fire." The southerners were "in high glee"—Hill's term—as the Yankees paraded toward the safety of Fort Monroe. "They seemed to enjoy it as much as boys do rabbit-shooting," he reported. A good part of the fighting had been done by two hundred or so cadets from a Charlotte, North Carolina, military academy who followed the Bethel Regiment onto the field. At least one participant attributes the checkmate of a New York Zouave regiment under Colonel Abram Duryée to the skill and training of the boys, some of whom were as young as sixteen years of age. "Thinking in after years of this Bethel fight, it reminded me more of a lot of boys fighting a bumblebee nest than a real battle," writes B. M. Hord. "One would rush up for the nest of bees a time or two with his switches, get stung, run back, and another would take his place." As the federals withdrew, Magruder reported only that he carried away the wounded "to farm houses in our rear" and ordered the burial of Butler's dead. Although Hood's cavalry chased the retreating enemy about five miles before his horsemen were halted by a destroyed bridge across Back River, the day had been a decided success for Magruder and his command. It may not have been a great victory, and it offered no crushing rout of the enemy, but it was a triumph, and the Confederate nation was quick to recognize her new hero.[22]

As with the Confederate success at First Manassas three weeks later, which left Irvin McDowell's army encamped inside of Virginia, Butler's bluecoats, though temporarily chastened, were still on the peninsula. Although Magruder's foes at Fort Monroe had not been hurled into the Chesapeake, he immediately dispatched his nephew, George junior, to Richmond with news of the engagement. Actually, he hurried two reports to headquarters on June 10; the first, addressed to Secretary of War L. P. Walker, was dispatched shortly after the fight ended: "I have the honor to inform you that we were attacked by about 3,500 troops of the Federal Army, with several pieces of heavy artillery, firing grape shot, this morning at 10 o'clock, and at 12½ routed them completely with considerable loss on their side." Magruder also reported that 1,200 of his 1,400-man force had engaged the enemy; his communiqué was not only carried to the capital by his nephew with a plea for reinforcements, but it also said that "Yorktown and Williamsburg have quite sufficient troops to defend them." The confident commander had the enemy on the run, although he was afraid of a counterattack against his exposed position beyond the Warwick, and therefore needed additional troops.

A longer, more detailed report later in the afternoon reiterated that the contest had lasted two and one half hours and had culminated in the death of one Confederate with a mere seven wounded; the dead soldier, Private Henry L. Wyatt, Company B, Hill's Bethel Regiment, according to Edward Porter Alexander, had volunteered "to go out & burn a house between the lines." Wyatt thus became the first Confederate to die in this, the first land battle of the war. Magruder, his report says, found ten dead federals on the field following Pierce's withdrawal; he had taken three prisoners. Unlike the carefully detailed reports of D. H. Hill, William D. Stuart of the Third Virginia Infantry, E. B. Montague of the Virginia Artillery Battalion, and others under his command, Magruder's summaries of June 10–12 were more general in scope. Although exuberant and upbeat, they say almost nothing about his role in the battle; mostly they are complimentary in the extreme about the gallantry of his men. D. H. Hill in particular, he says, "was worthy of his ancient glory"; and he felt the victory could be attributed to the "skill and gallantry" exhibited not only by Hill but also by the howitzer batteries under George W. Randolph, who, by the way, was a grandson of Thomas Jefferson.[23]

Magruder's triumph gained him the quick admiration of a new nation anxious for success. Although Joseph B. Carr, Second New York Infantry, who took part in the fight, thought Big Bethel "had no important result save as an encouragement to the Confederates," the Southern diarist Mary Chesnut terms it "Magruder's victory." "One poor young man found dead with a shot through his heart had a Bible in his pocket in which was written, 'Given to the defender of his country by the Bible Society,'" she records. "How *dare* they mix up the Bible with their own bad passions." And if Mrs. Chesnut had her own view of the federal intruders, Robert E. Lee, still chafing at his Richmond desk as military adviser to President Davis, was quick to telegraph his appreciation: "I take pleasure in expressing my gratification at the gallant conduct of the troops under your command and approbation of the dispositions made by you, resulting as they did, in the rout of the enemy," he told a jubilant Magruder. "I have referred your letter to the President of the Confederate states, that he might be fully informed of the operations so successfully conducted. . . ." Davis must have been impressed because, during an address to the Confederate congress in November, he termed Magruder's performance "a glorious victory."[24]

Southern newspapers were ecstatic in their praise, recounts Douglas Southall Freeman. "Avidly the south read how Magruder had met a flag of truce, seeking the body of a slain Federal officer, had granted the removal of the corpse, and, in parting, had shaken hands with a Lieutenant and had said solemnly, 'We part as friends, but on the field of battle we meet as enemies.' " Magruder told correspondents that Big Bethel equaled any of the battles in Mexico. While *The New York Times* labeled it "the unfortunate affair at Great Bethel," the *Baltimore Republican*, a pro-Southern journal, gave all of the credit to Magruder, "who planted his six pieces near the banks of the stream; four in the front rank, and the other two in the rear, on the hill side, with his riflemen and infantrymen in an unfinished ditch, and his cavalry thrown back as a reserve." The day belonged to Magruder, continued the *Republican*, after he "moved two of his front rank guns farther up the hill, so that he was enabled to rake the Federalists from three points with a crossfire."[25]

Even if the sector was short on hills, Magruder and his small command had singlehandedly blocked the Yankee march on Richmond by the Yorktown-Williamsburg route; an easy federal entry into Richmond would have been a near certainty had he not stood firm. Although Colonel Carr says "nothing of importance occurred on the peninsula" until April 1862—ten months later—when McClellan arrived at Fort Monroe with a larger, better-equipped army, Magruder was clearly the man of the hour in front of the Confederate capital. And he owed his success in part to the awesome firepower of the recently manufactured Parrott gun. Developed during the 1850s by Robert Parker Parrott of the West Point class of 1824, the cannon were distinctive on Civil War battlefields because of the bold steel band around the breech that gave the pieces great explosive power. Virginia on her own had purchased several of the guns after Professor Thomas Jackson tested a Parrott at the Virginia Military Institute by firing at tent flies set up on an adjacent hillock. Jackson even drafted a widely read analysis of the gun's effectiveness that no doubt reached Magruder at Fort Leavenworth. D. H. Hill, Jackson's brother-in-law, also witnessed the VMI tests, and used the guns to great effect on the peninsula, but, records Baker P. Lee, it was Magruder "who sighted by his own accurate eye" the first cannon fired at Big Bethel.[26]

Magruder entered quickly into a correspondence with Butler over the exchange of prisoners following the battle; when he learned that Butler had captured four Confederates—one trooper and three private citizens—he told the federal commander that he would act only in the case "of Private Carter," who had been one of his vedettes guarding against attack. Carter, moreover, had apparently fallen asleep while on picket duty and had been taken by Butler's advance guard. Although Butler did not consider the man a prisoner of war, he nonetheless agreed to his surrender: "He was asleep on his post, and he informs me that his three companions left in such haste that they neglected to wake him up, and, they being mounted and my men on foot, the race was not a difficult one." Not to be outdone and always protective of his men, although his letters to Butler were proper to a fault, Magruder informed his adversary: "With respect to the vedette Private Carter, I desire to inform you that when a picket of four is placed out for twenty-four hours, as in this case, at least one is permitted to sleep. This picket had orders to retreat before a large force of the enemy. Four men against five thousand constituted, however, such great odds, as to have justified the retreat of the picket even without orders." And with tongue in cheek, he added, "Had Private Carter been awake, perhaps a retreat would not have been necessary." The three civilians were likewise exchanged, but not before the two commanders traded barbs about "traitorous assassins" and stout men defending family and hearth from mean-spirited invaders.[27]

As Southern newspapers hung on every letter of the exchange between Magruder and Butler, Prince John received word of his promotion to brigadier general effective June 17, one week after Big

Bethel. As he worked to strengthen his defenses along the Yorktown line, he was elevated to major general on October 7, but the later promotion raised some criticism throughout the army and in civilian circles. "Ebbitt," his 1880 chronicler in the *Army and Navy Journal*, reports that an appreciative Magruder "abstained from drinking for a long time after he was made brigadier general, although some of the hardest knocks that the Federal forces ever received were from forces commanded by him." The drinking would return soon enough, but in the months following Big Bethel, Magruder moved quickly to implement Lee's instruction to entrench and fortify his lines. Lee, Davis, and the Richmond staff were under no illusions: A more substantial incursion from Fort Monroe would place Magruder's small army in a precarious position. "The advantage to the enemy of his possession of Yorktown will be sufficient to induce him to adopt every means to take it," Lee informed Magruder on October 16. "It is hoped that every precaution will be adopted to prevent its being carried by surprise." The admonition came in response to Magruder's call that he had but 5,500 effectives and that he required another 4,500 to firm up his position. Magruder also wanted an additional fifteen heavy guns, although cannon of every kind were in short supply throughout the Confederacy. Lee, however, replied that "there are no siege guns at present available for your post," but that additional troops would be hurried to him.[28]

Jefferson Davis praised Magruder's "arduous and exposed service on the Peninsula" in his hugely circulated account of the war, although he separated himself from Prince John during the summer of 1862. But that rift, which had roots extending back to their cadet days, developed over Magruder's conduct in the Seven Days battles; from the moment of Big Bethel until the next spring, when McClellan began his move on Richmond from Fort Monroe, Magruder worked on his lines with all available resources. This included erection and manning of a second group of redoubts about twelve miles east of Yorktown, at Williamsburg. The grandest of these works, dubbed Fort Magruder, "was constructed at a point a short distance beyond where the Lee's Mill and Yorktown roads united." Magruder, furthermore, not only asked for additional troops but also reported a near-constant reinforcement of Fort Monroe and adjacent installations by the federals.

Benjamin F. Butler relinquished command opposite Magruder on August 17, when he turned his troops over to Major General John E. Wool, a veteran of the Mexican War well known to Magruder and Lee. And the Yankee buildup grew steadily under Wool throughout the period from August 1861 to April 1862. Magruder, for instance, informed Richmond on September 11 that "four large steamers passed to Fort Monroe from Washington just before daylight this morning." Powerless to stem the flow of men and matériel, he could do little but press his calls for more troops to do what the Confederate navy could not. Although Lee and Assistant Adjutant General R. H. Chilton reassured him that supplies were on the way, it had become increasingly clear by late 1861 that the new government was already outmanned and outsupplied by the economically superior North. Undeterred by shortages of every kind, Magruder struggled through the fall and winter to strengthen his fortifications. Besides his gun emplacements at vital points along the Warwick, as well as several more at Gloucester Point north of the York, and those along the James River estuary, observes a campaign historian, he "kept the naturally boggy ground inundated by building dams at each of five fords across the river, which also served as water barriers at the crossings."[29]

Nor did Magruder adopt a purely defensive posture, but kept his outriders on the probe for every opportunity to swipe at the enemy. John Bell Hood, whom Magruder relied upon to foil the bluecoats with his cavalry, wrote:

> Soon after the affair at Big Bethel, it became the custom of the enemy to send out every few days scouting parties of infantry in the direction of our position at Yorktown. I determined to go at night into the swamp lying between the James and York River roads, remain quietly under cover, and, upon the advance of such a party, to move out upon its rear, and capture it if possible. In accordance with this plan, I concealed my troops in the swamp several nights, when finally a battalion of infantry came forth upon the James River Road.

Hood's pouncing on the unsuspecting federals produced "a great consternation and the enemy ran in all directions through the woods." Although Hood lost several troopers in the melee, Magruder was quick to recognize his intrepid cavalryman: "Too much praise cannot be bestowed on Major Hood and the cavalry generally for their untiring industry in efforts to meet the enemy, and for the energy with which they have discharged their harassing and unusually laborious duties." Whatever his other shortcomings, including his inherent showmanship and self-aggrandizement, Magruder was never mean toward his subordinates. Although he called it "a brilliant little affair," unlike his earlier confrontations with Butler, Magruder did not return several prisoners taken in the skirmish, but sent them to Richmond.[30]

Other fights occurred throughout late 1861, particularly in the vicinity of Hampton and Newport News; the latter place, located on a bluff overlooking Hampton Roads, where the Jamestown colonists had kept a lookout to bring the first news of Christopher Newport's supply ships from England—hence its name—remained firmly in federal hands. Magruder approached the town on August 7 with something over 4,000 men, but unable to draw out the bluecoat cavalry, he directed his attention toward Hampton. His men, however, soon learned that Butler intended to refortify the city as "he did not know what to do with the many negroes [sic] in his possession unless he possessed Hampton; they were still coming in rapidly; that as their masters had deserted their homes and slaves, he would consider the latter free, and would colonize them at Hampton, the home of most of their owners." When Magruder learned about the scheme from a captured issue of the New York Tribune that contained a copy of Butler's report to Secretary of War Cameron, he resolved upon immediate action. "Having known for some time past that Hampton was the harbor of runaway slaves and traitors, and being under the guns of Fort Monroe, it could not be held by us, even if taken, I was decidedly under the impression that it should have been destroyed before." Then, continues his August 9 communiqué to Richmond from his temporary headquarters at Big Bethel: "When I found from the above report of its extreme importance to the enemy, and that the town itself would lend great strength to whatever fortifications they might erect around it, I determined to burn it."

Actually, Magruder had decided to step up pressure along his front once he learned of the Confederate romp at Manassas on July 21; he feared, with some justification, that the federals might transfer their major operations to the peninsula. As early as July 30 he had cavalry units under Colonel Robert Johnston reconnoitering in the direction of Hampton and Newport News; Butler, still in charge at Fort Monroe, became alarmed at Magruder's show of force and ordered the torching of strategic sections of the town as he withdrew from the former place. Magruder says that "about one third of Hampton" had been burned when he arrived to complete the job. "A few minutes after midnight Gen. Magruder, with about 500 Confederates—some of them belonging in Hampton—entered the town, and immediately fired the buildings with torches," reported a *New York Times* correspondent. "A greater part of the five hundred houses were built of wood, and no rain having fallen lately, the strong south wind soon produced a terrible conflagration. There were perhaps twenty white people and double that number of negroes [*sic*] remaining in the town from inability to move, some of whose houses were fired without waking the inmates." Although the *Times* called it "a wanton act of cruelty to the resident Unionists, and moreover useless," Magruder did not crow in his official report; he devoted but few lines to the incident and used most of his lengthy report to call for better sanitary conditions among his troops, owing to an outbreak of sickness. He had given ample notice to the sick and infirm, he told his Richmond superiors; he had conferred "with the gentlemen at Hampton, many of whom are in the army under my command," and, he added, "they seemed to concur with me as to the propriety of this course." Magruder had also hoped to draw the enemy out from Newport News, but when Butler failed to take the bait, he returned to his encampment at Bethel, and later Yorktown.[31]

Magruder and his Army of the Peninsula fought other engagements at Young's Mill, October 4, and New Market Bridge, November 11, during late 1861; and despite D. H. Hill's carping about "silly orders," he successfully molded a smoothly functioning command. After a bit of rebelliousness by a battalion of Louisiana Zouaves, in which five officers resigned en masse, although Magruder called them "gallant fellows," the trouble subsided when Lieutenant Colonel George Coppens took charge with Lee's blessing. Magruder completely restructured his command into "two divisions" on November 10, commanded by Brigadier Generals Gabriel J. Rains and Lafayette McLaws. Rains, who had finished at West Point three years ahead of Magruder, first came to the peninsula as a member of D. H. Hill's command. When the army retreated toward Richmond under Joseph

E. Johnston, he gained a footnote in history as the first soldier "to use land mines and booby traps in warfare"; even as he held the keep at Yorktown, Rains had been busy with mines in the York and James rivers, designed to thwart the federal navy. McLaws, on the other hand, whom Magruder placed beyond the Warwick line at Young's Mill, soon transferred to Stonewall Jackson's command. Magruder's reorganizational scheme also demanded that "commanding officers of Regiments, Battalions and Separated Detachments send their reports to their respective Generals of Divisions."[32]

Just weeks after his arrival on the peninsula, Magruder had fought the opening land engagement of the Civil War, at least slowed his drinking, and become an effective general in control of his troops. One spinoff of his new status came in the form of numerous requests for advancement and sundry favors. In October he wrote to Governor John Letcher on behalf of Major E. B. Montague, among others, seeking promotions; and two weeks later, when Captain C. St. George Nolan, formerly of the U.S. Navy, applied for confirmation as major in the Confederate army, he heartily endorsed the request: ". . . to add from my own knowledge that your services on the Peninsula, constitute a just ground upon which, that rank could be bestowed upon you independently of your former rank elsewhere." In his own hand, not that of an adjutant, he again wrote to Letcher asking that Henry C. Cabell, who became his chief of artillery, be promoted to colonel, a recommendation subsequently approved by the Confederate Congress. Magruder obviously enjoyed considerable prestige in the new scheme during 1861–1862, though he would incur later difficulties. His letters to Davis, Lee, and Letcher demonstrated a stout self-confidence, yet his affinity for pomp and display bred an undercurrent of resentment through some wings of the officer corps. As for the contention that he attracted attention to himself and courted preferment by tooting his own horn, or that he achieved recognition by letting D. H. Hill, George Randolph, and others do his fighting for him, dozens of other officers in both armies did the same with regularity. Magruder did not shrink from the ramparts, but was present throughout the Big Bethel fighting. Not only did he place himself in harm's way when the test of steel arrived, he did what a commander is supposed to do—he commanded![33]

6

Up the Peninsula

ALTHOUGH CHANGES IN RICHMOND AND WASHINGTON soon undermined Magruder's place in the Confederate command structure, he worked steadily at his positions through January, February, and March 1862, despite a growing uncertainty that his redoubts and fortifications could withstand a major offensive from Fort Monroe. "I understand that my lines of defense are under discussion at Richmond," he wrote to Jefferson Davis on January 10. "I know I can expect from you the justice to postpone any decision until I can report at length. . . . I have taken not only the best but the only way of successfully defending this Peninsula with the means at my disposal, and this defense will be successful." And he assured the president that he was doing his best "to prepare for the emergency of a landing in this Peninsula or on the Rappahannock River, which I now think more probable, or for an attack on James River." These preparations, he added, would take time. As his fears increased about a possible thrust from Fort Monroe, Magruder became engaged in a running battle with Richmond over the use of local militia companies and the employment of slaves in his preparations. Finally he was granted permission to employ both if he did not exceed his authority.

"Genl. Magruder has caused all of the roads to be blockaded between our lines and Newport News, so that it is next thing to an impossibility for any one to get along much less an army," wrote Lieutenant Robert H. Miller, who served with a Louisiana volunteer regiment. "The state of inactivity we have been in has been very harassing to us but we have spent it profitably and our Reg. has done

137

more work than any two others on the Peninsula." There can be no question that Magruder impressed many segments of the army as he improved his defensive lines. Even Joseph E. Johnston, who superseded him on the Warwick, wrote in his postwar memoir that his "resolute and judicious course . . . was of incalculable value." In 1874, Johnston, somewhat hypocritically, as it turned out, admitted that it saved Richmond. North Carolina governor Henry T. Clark used Magruder's perceived success to argue that additional Tarheel troops were not needed by Richmond: "I make the suggestion on the ground that General Magruder has had every facility in men and good, skillful officers for seven months to fortify the Peninsula; that it has been successfully done; that his entrenchments, fortifications, and guns have been so successfully and extensively done that they can now be defended with half the men required some months ago. That the place will only allow a defensive warfare, and he is prepared for that, and he can now spare some of his force." Clark, unlike Johnston, who wanted to strip his state bare for the defense of Richmond, was fearful lest Yankee general Ambrose Burnside overrun the entire Carolina coast.[1]

By the beginning of March, Magruder found himself confronted by an increasingly hostile enemy. Only a week after the famed encounter between the ironclads *Monitor* and *Merrimac* in Hampton Roads, he informed Richmond that John E. Wool's troopers had driven in his pickets, and that without additional men he would be obliged to withdraw up the peninsula. Although Robert E. Lee urged him to stand firm and keep working at his Warwick River dams to produce "the happiest results," Magruder kept a careful watch upon the constant flow of men and matériel onto the peninsula before and after the *Monitor-Merrimac* showdown. "I presume that now Yorktown will be the object of attack by the *Monitor* and the fleet, and I am doing my best to provide against this new danger," he told Lee on March 16. Earlier, on March 6, he had informed Richmond of the arrival of troop transports off Newport News; he may not have realized the full scope of the federal reinforcements, but he was witnessing the first preparations for McClellan's advance on the Confederate capital. Undeterred by the awesome force amassing on his front, Magruder addressed his own troops with characteristic bombast:

Your country, invaded by an insolent foe, again demands your help. Your homes are violated, your fireside polluted by the presence of a mercenary enemy or silent in the desolation; many of our friends in captivity or in exile; our people slain, and the very altars of our religion desolated and profaned. The restless tyrants who have dared to invade us have vowed our conquest and destruction. It is for you to rise and avenge our slaughtered countrymen or nobly share their fate. Of what worth is life without liberty, peace at the expense of honor, the world without a home. . . .

Grand words, these—Bonaparte himself could not have done better while addressing his legionnaires.

As he went about his war preparations, Magruder relied increasingly on the bottle to steady his nerves, and the unconcealed drinking caused many of his own men to question his command abilities. Try as he might, Prince John could not escape his reputation as a drinker either in Virginia or afterward. "Does he leave the whiskey alone now?" one of his troopers at Yorktown, Private Charles W. Trueheart, wrote to his mother in February 1863, after Magruder had assumed his new duties in Texas. "That was a very serious failing with him on the Peninsula." Nor were Trueheart and his comrades overly impressed with Magruder's military prowess. "He is not one of our great generals. In these parts he is considered a second rate general; not comparable to Lee, Jackson, Bragg, and Longstreet."[2]

Yet Magruder could rise to the occasion when circumstance demanded. For some weeks prior to the March 9 fight between the *Monitor* and *Merrimac,* he had watched and indeed participated in the unfolding drama that led to history's first naval engagement involving ironclad ships. Virginia military forces had overtaken the great naval base at Norfolk on April 20–21, 1861, before the Old Dominion voted an Ordinance of Secession; the state had done the very same thing at the outbreak of the Revolution to prevent British use of the vital facility. In April 1861, as the followers of former governor Henry A. Wise seized the yard at the onset of the Civil War, Virginia and later the Confederacy found herself in possession of a United States screw steamer, the 170-foot *Merrimac.*

Shortly renamed the *Virginia,* although Magruder always called the ship by her original name, she was refurbished as the South's first ironclad. When finished, "her hull was cut down to the water line and 170-foot long superstructure with sides sloping at about 35 degrees from the vertical was built." Her twenty-two-inch-thick oak super-structure was covered with iron bars in a crisscross pattern. Then, continues one account, "forward and aft of this 'citadel' the decks were just awash when the 263-foot ship was in fighting trim, giving it the appearance of a floating barn roof." She was also fitted with "six 9-inch smoothbores [Dahlgrens] and four rifled guns of 6- and 7-inch bore."[3]

The *Merrimac* was not ready for action until early March 1862— nearly a year after capture of the once-sunken vessel—which prompted Magruder as commander on the peninsula to blast the "criminal tardiness." Secretary of the Navy Stephen R. Mallory at one point was obliged to prod Captain Smith Lee, naval superintendent at Norfolk and Robert E. Lee's older brother, to quicker action on the ship. "The crisis demands the extraordinary exertions of all loyal men, and if your subordinates fail from lack of zeal we must supply their places at once." Magruder initially thought the ship might sup-port his flanks on the York and James rivers, particularly the latter, but his enthusiasm waned as the project neared completion. "I am also satisfied that no one ship can produce such an impression upon the troops at Newport News as to cause them to evacuate the fort," he wrote to Adjutant General Cooper on February 26. "No important advantages can be obtained by the *Merrimac* further than to demon-strate her power, which, as she is liable to be injured by a chance shot at this critical time, had better be reserved to defeat the enemy's se-rious efforts against Norfolk and James River."[4]

Three hundred miles to the north, meanwhile, at the Brooklyn Navy Yard, federal workers worked at breakneck speed to ready a new ship popularly known as "Ericsson's Folly." The brainchild of naval engineer John Ericsson, the radically designed ironclad is known to history as the *Monitor*. Ericsson's ship was 172 feet in length by forty-one feet at the beam; moreover, her unique design made it nearly impossible to damage her two-sectioned hull by ramming. When completed, the *Monitor* sat low in the water, with her deck nearly awash; her most distinctive feature was a steam-driven turret conceived by the Swedish-born Ericsson. In his own words, the tur-ret "was simply a short cylinder resting on the deck, covered with a grated iron roof provided with sliding hatches. This cylinder is composed of eight thicknesses of wrought-iron plates, each one inch, firmly riveted together." The turret, which sat on a metal ring embedded in the deck, not only had its own engine for power, but also sported two eleven-inch smooth-bores to confront her enemies. A three-foot, ten-inch rectangular pilothouse also protruded above her nearly submerged deck. Powered by steam, the *Monitor* left her New York berth on the morning of March 6 and arrived off Newport News during the night of March 8–9.[5]

As Confederate naval officers anxiously awaited the federal ironclad's appearance on the Chesapeake, Magruder remained as skeptical as ever. On March 2 he told Richmond that he was unable to assist the *Virginia* and her captain, Franklin Buchanan, because poor roads prevented his moving artillery to the coast. And Magruder thought the vessel should be used as an adjunct to the Warwick line; "I have the honor to state for General Magruder, who is in the field . . . that he recommends that the *Merrimac* be stationed a little above Newport News, to prevent the gunboats coming up the swash channel leading into Warwick River and turning the right flank of his line of defense," his aide, Henry Bryan, telegraphed to General Cooper. Magruder wanted the ship as little more than a "floating battery" to reinforce his land positions. When Buchanan sent a formal appeal, he was just as rebellious: "It is too late to co-operate with my army in any manner below with the *Merrimac*, even if the roads will permit it, which they will not, for the enemy is very heavily reinforced both at Newport News and Fort Monroe with infantry and six batteries of light artillery," he told the beleaguered captain on March 3. "It would have been glorious if you could have run into these as they were being landed from a Baltimore boat and a commercial transport," he added with smug confidence.

The "fight of the ironclads" commenced at about 1:00 P.M., March 8, when the *Merrimac* steamed into Hampton Roads from her Norfolk berth and attacked the arc-positioned federal fleet in front of Fort Monroe and Newport News. The Confederate vessel, which was hampered because of Chesapeake water depths, managed nonetheless to ram and sink the thirty-gun *Cumberland*; force the *Congress* to surrender after a blistering fire; and cause three other ships to run aground. Buchanan withdrew to Norfolk at about 5:00 P.M., with every intention of renewing the fight on the morrow. Then, on March 9, with Magruder watching from the Virginia shore, Buchanan encountered his long-anticipated nemesis and the battle was on. The encounter itself was inconclusive, although a radical departure in naval warfare had opened, with the *Monitor* easily outmaneuvering her cumbersome opponent. "The Federal boat withdrew to resupply ammunition, and the engagement was renewed about 11:30," writes one authority. In the ensuing melee the *Merrimac* concentrated her guns on the *Monitor*'s exposed pilothouse. After a shot struck the sighthole, blinding her helmsman, the fight was broken off by the withdrawal of both vessels. Magruder filed his own assessment of the battle one day later: "Finding, as I anticipated that the naval attack produced no effect upon the fort except to increase its garrison, I contented myself with occupying the most advanced posts, Bethel and Young's Mill where the troops are now." Prince John was plainly not impressed with the military significance of "the glorious achievement of the Confederate states war-steamer Virginia" and what he termed "Ericsson's battery."[6]

Although the *Merrimac* remained in Hampton Roads as a deterrent to Yankee transports plying the lower Chesapeake, its fight with the *Monitor* proved a mere sideshow to the larger campaign, except that it forced McClellan to abandon any immediate notion of moving up the James River. As Magruder watched more and more federal troops stream onto the peninsula, before and after the *Monitor-Merrimac* tussle, events shaping the campaign shifted to Washington and Abraham Lincoln's impulse to end the war by marching on Richmond. Four months after the federal disaster at Manassas, Lincoln had placed McClellan in charge of the Army of the Potomac and inadvertently commenced his own wearing search for a suitable commander until the spring of 1864, when Ulysses S. Grant took charge. Nearly twenty years younger than Magruder, the two warriors had served together in Mexico; McClellan, known throughout the army as Little Mac, had attracted Lincoln's notice after a successful campaign in the mountains of western Virginia at the same time Magruder labored at his peninsular defenses.

The new Yankee commander became a controversial figure almost from the moment of his November 11 appointment. When he failed to act on Lincoln's wish to invade the Confederate capital by crushing Johnston's army clustered around Centreville, McClellan became the object of intense scrutiny by the Northern press and Republican politicos. To the exasperation of Lincoln, he took several weeks to develop a strategy for landing the federal army at Urbanna, on the Rappahannock River. Although he would not march on Richmond by that avenue, his continued dalliance prompted Lincoln's famous quip, "If McClellan is not going to use his army, I would like to borrow it from him." The headstrong and secretive McClellan, who once openly snubbed Lincoln by going to bed during a presidential visit to his home, finally developed a scheme for marching on Richmond by the "lower Chesapeake." He submitted the formal plan on February 3, and though Lincoln had serious reservations, he agreed with several stipulations, including the mandate that sufficient troops be left on the Potomac to safeguard Washington. McClellan was told to initiate his forward movement no later than March 18, and by March 17, one day short of the deadline, his transports were on their way south from their Potomac staging areas.[7]

"Little Mac" himself arrived at Fort Monroe on April 2 to lead his 100,000-man army toward Richmond, and John Bankhead Magruder, who had been warning his superiors for months about the impending peril, was the only Confederate in his path, with a mere 11,000 men. Actually, McClellan's ready force was somewhat smaller than the 100,000 men ascribed by many writers and historians, though it shortly exceeded that figure with reinforcements. "I had five divisions of infantry, Sykes's brigade of regulars, and a portion of the reserve artillery disembarked," he wrote after the war. "Another cavalry regiment and a part of the fourth had arrived but were still on shipboard; comparatively few wagons had come." McClellan, to his unbelievable disgust, learned on the day of his arrival that Lincoln had resolved to keep 37,000 troops under Irvin McDowell near the capital, and that he could not employ several thousand men under Wool stationed around Fort Monroe. The presidential mandate was prompted by Stonewall Jackson's March 23 entry into the lower Shenandoah, and though beaten at Kernstown, that intrepid warrior remained encamped within fifty miles of Washington. Flag Officer Louis M. Goldsborough, commanding the federal fleet, also greeted McClellan with news that he could expect no naval support for an offensive because of the *Merrimac*'s continued presence. The April 2 conference took place aboard Goldsborough's flagship, the *Minnesota*, which had been targeted for destruction by the *Merrimac* had the *Monitor*'s appearance not thwarted further action. "I thus found myself with 53,000 men in condition to move," McClellan continued, as he stared out at Magruder and the peninsula defenses.[8]

Intelligence reports of Magruder's preparations had played a role in the federal planning from the onset; "a rapid movement from Urbana [Urbanna] would probably cut off Magruder in the Peninsula, & enable us to occupy Richmond before it could be strongly reinforced," Lincoln had written in a February memorandum. And detective Allan Pinkerton fed McClellan's discomfort with a somewhat exaggerated report dated March 29, although his information derived from an October 1861 finding: "General Magruder (whose headquarters were at Yorktown) commanded all the forces on the Peninsula bounded by James and York Rivers, and also those on Gloucester Point, his command at that time including twenty-seven regiments of infantry, 1,200 cavalry, and four field batteries from four to six guns, iron and brass, rifled and smooth bore." McClellan himself put Magruder's total force at fifteen to twenty thousand when he reached Fort Monroe. Prince John's gun emplacements and redoubts—some dating from the Revolutionary War—caused the overly cautious commander to abandon his plans for a frontal assault. "By marching troops around groves of trees and shuttling cannon from place to place creating an impression of enormous strength," asserts one scholar, Magruder was able to dupe his opponent. And, notes Edward Porter Alexander, the Confederate artillerist and war chronicler, "Magruder, who was expecting reenforcements [*sic*], made the bravest possible display, exhibiting the same troops repeatedly at different points." Whether Magruder's bluff or overcaution by McClellan determined the outcome, the latter did not charge the Confederate entrenchments despite his great superiority in numbers.[9]

From April 4, when McClellan opened his assault, until Joe Johnston was placed in command, Magruder faced the whole fury alone; he had been on the peninsula for eleven months against Benjamin F. Butler, John E. Wool, and now McClellan. Before the decision to reinforce him by Davis and Lee, Magruder had known that the Yankee hordes at Fort Monroe would move in his direction. When Robert E. Lee returned to Richmond from his ill-fated campaign in western Virginia, Magruder wrote to congratulate his appointment as "Commander in Chief of Confederate forces"; although Lee was renamed military adviser to President Davis, Magruder relayed that he was happy to be under his command and would "execute your orders with alacrity and zeal." Yet all was not well. "Should the enemy advance I should be compelled to withdraw at once the few troops I have in front to my main line of defense behind Warwick River, the left resting on Yorktown and the right on Mulberry Island," reads a March 14 communiqué to Lee. "That line is too long for the few troops I have, being over 8 miles to the mouth of the Peninsula, known as Mulberry Island, and about 14 miles from Yorktown to Mulberry Point, which is the corresponding work on James River." Then, two days later, Magruder fired another ominous warning: "The enemy again drove in the pickets to-day on the Warwick road after exchanging fire. He appears to be operating with a considerable advance guard, supported by heavier bodies, between it and Newport News, so that it is difficult to cut off the advanced troops without entangling my handful of men with very superior forces lying in wait." And Magruder repeated his earlier alarm: "So, if the enemy persevere, I shall be compelled in a very short time to withdraw the regiments which are now in front of the second line, viz, from Yorktown to Mulberry Island."[10]

As the Confederate high command started a steady flow of troops mostly from northern Virginia toward the peninsula, Magruder did what he could in spite of an earlier directive from Secretary of War Judah P. Benjamin to send 5,000 of his men across the James to Suffolk. Throughout the period leading to McClellan's advance, Magruder was mightily concerned with his position at Lee's Mill, which sat astride a vital road crossing of the Warwick, a mile or so south of Yorktown; he placed Major J. Thompson Brown and his thinly spread artillery between Yorktown and the Mill. He also admonished Brown to make sure sufficient horses were available to move the guns at short notice. When D. H. Hill returned as part of James Longstreet's command during the Southern buildup, he became critical of Magruder's artillery. "Hill was distressed by the poor quality of the Confederate guns and ammunition," comments his biographer. "The guns were made of flimsy metal and sometimes burst when fired. Many shells either exploded at the cannon mouth or failed to explode at all." Upon receiving a brigadier's star after the Big Bethel melee, Hill had

been assigned to Johnston's army in northern Virginia, but soon returned to the peninsula; ever obstinate, Hill complained so boldly
about "foul play" in the ordnance department headed by Josiah Gor-
gas that Secretary of War George Randolph, who had replaced Benjamin, and had himself been an artillerist at Big Bethel, had to assure
him "that not treachery but a shortage of good metal" explained the
difficulty.[11]

Young's Mill was likewise critical to Magruder's strategy; he relied
upon Lafayette McLaws to hold that position about two miles beyond Warwick Court House where the road from Newport News
crossed Deep Creek. "I wish Young's Mill held to the last without
fighting for it," Magruder wrote to Colonel Alfred Cumming, who
held the place under McLaws's command. "I am maneuvering to give
the enemy the idea we are in great force." But following a misunderstanding over who was in charge, Magruder was obliged to tell
Cumming that he should defer to McLaws; and in a March 13 memorandum Magruder ordered him to stop "attaching his signature to future communications" from the post. Cumming thereupon acted
quickly to remove any notion that he was usurping McLaws. "The
momentary doubt under which I labor . . . was entirely dispelled by
the command from General McLaws received this morning," he
wrote the following day. "And neither before nor since that time have
I thought it necessary to demand a more explicit instruction from the
major general [Magruder]."[12]

Although Joseph E. Johnston did not appear at Magruder's headquarters until April 13, McClellan opened his offensive on April 4
when both armies clashed for the first time; sporadic contact continued, but Little Mac's thrust at Richmond degenerated into the siege
of Yorktown that lasted until May 3–4, when Johnston decided to
break off the stalemate without a fight. Magruder's theatrical marching and countermarching produced the desired effect upon the ever-
timid McClellan. He took one look at the Confederate fortifications,
and chastened by Lincoln's decision to withhold McDowell's command, the federal chieftain resolved upon a prolonged siege instead
of a headlong thrust. In other words, McClellan decided to do nothing of significance for the next month while his troops and former
slaves hauled his heavy guns into place. "In our front was an entrenched line apparently too strong for assault, and which I had . . .

no means of turning, either by land or water," McClellan wrote after the war.

> Whatever might have been said afterward, no one at that time—so far as my knowledge extended—thought an assault practicable without certain preliminary siege operations. At all events, my personal experience in this kind of work was greater than any officer under my command; and after personal reconnaissances more appropriate to a lieutenant of engineers than a commanding general, I could neither discover nor hear of any point where an assault promised any chance of success. We were obliged to resort to siege operations in order to silence the enemy's artillery fire, and open the way to an assault.

When he was at last ready to move, McClellan had upwards of a hundred heavy guns, mostly Parrotts, howitzers, and mortars, within firing range of Yorktown.[13]

While he entrenched, McClellan approved the use of Hiram Berdan's U.S. Sharpshooters to pummel Magruder's lines. The New York–born Berdan, a national rifle champion before the war, was described by one associate as "unscrupulous and totally unfit for command"; yet during much of the siege his handpicked shooters spared no one. Every time a Confederate trooper moved his head, they were ready with deadly aim. "Dragging their rifles beside them, the distinctive green-clad snipers stealthily took to tall treetops and secluded stone pits just a few hundred yards from the enemy," writes historian Charles Bryan. Using the cover of darkness, they typically awaited the coming dawn to open fire. "The astonished Rebels," Bryan continues, "scattered as Berdan's boys cut down on everyone in sight, including Southern slaves carrying ammunition to the front." Throughout McClellan's siege, Berdan personally surveilled Magruder's positions in search of the best opportunity. "I feel amply repaid," reads his official report, "for the danger I ran in reconnoitering the ground fire, posting the men, encouraging and directing them through the day, by the confident feeling that we must have killed and wounded several hundred rebels." Berdan was particularly proud of his work, he added, because "the rebels are trying to destroy our country."[14]

John Bell Hood likewise had a fearsome contingent of sharpshooters and snipers, who gave as good as they got during the siege. As the long-range artillery bursts and sharpshooting continued, participants on both sides attest to the difficult weather. McClellan says that the rain began a steady downpour at the beginning and that the resultant mud played havoc with his operations. "From April 4 to May 3 this army served almost without relief in the trenches," Magruder notes in his battle summary. "It rained almost incessantly; the trenches were filled with water. The weather was exceedingly cold; no fires could be allowed; the artillery and infantry of the enemy played upon our men almost continuously day and night; the army had neither coffee, sugar, nor hard bread, but subsisted on flour and salt meat, and that in reduced quantities, and yet no murmurs were heard." Magruder also confirmed that new troops began "to pour in," which relieved his anxiousness about McClellan's numbers. His total strength grew to about 33,000 during the Yorktown operations, according to Joe Johnston. While he continued to await the onslaught, it became obvious to Magruder and, indeed, to his superiors in Richmond, that any federal commander other than Little Mac would have advanced at once. "Every preparation was made in anticipation of another attack by the enemy; the men slept in the trenches, but to my utter surprise he permitted day after day to elapse without an assault," Magruder continues. "In a few days the object of his delay was apparent. In every direction; in front of our lines, through the intervening woods; and along the open fields, earthworks began to appear."[15]

Even though Magruder's bravado and carefully planned fortifications held Lincoln's war machine at bay, Jefferson Davis and Robert E. Lee acted to remove him from command. President Davis, like Abraham Lincoln, had more than a little difficulty during the early part of the war in deciding upon a suitable general; and once the men had been chosen, they could not be persuaded to act. In the first weeks of 1862 he finally settled upon Joseph Eggleston Johnston for command at the critical point; but Johnston was his own man, with an inflated notion of his military capabilities. Virginia-born in 1807, he had graduated thirteenth in the West Point class of 1829—one year behind Davis himself and one year before Magruder. Johnston had served in Mexico with Lee, Davis, and Magruder, and in the moribund service of the 1850s he had gained a brigadier's star as quartermaster general of the army shortly before the outbreak of the war; of all the officers who joined the Confederate standard, only Johnston had already attained general rank. He had passed Lee, who was still a brevet colonel, and, of course, Magruder, a mere captain/brevet lieutenant colonel of the Washington garrison.

In April 1861, before Virginia joined the new government, Johnston had bypassed the military forces of Virginia headed by Robert E. Lee and traveled to Montgomery, where he was commissioned directly into the Confederate army. But when the official rankings were posted, he was listed fourth behind Samuel Cooper, Lee, and Albert Sidney Johnston. Johnston not only fancied himself betrayed, but also developed a deep-rooted antipathy for Jefferson Davis that lasted straight through the war and, indeed, until the deaths of both men— Davis in 1889 and Johnston in 1891. It was an animosity that caused irreparable harm to the Confederate war effort. In 1861, however, Johnston was dispatched to Harpers Ferry, where he took the reins from Tom Jackson and where he achieved some success by keeping the aged General Robert Patterson from a linkup with Irvin McDowell on the eve of First Manassas. And when he marched over the Blue Ridge with Jackson and E. Kirby Smith to join the Confederates gathering in front of McDowell's advance into Virginia, although in nominal command, he deferred to the Louisiana Creole P. G. T. Beauregard to conduct the actual battle. Then, as Magruder struggled on the peninsula, Johnston took charge of the Southern forces clustered about Centreville to watch Virginia's northern frontier. But even here he had no stomach for a vigorous defense, and began falling back toward the Rappahannock without bothering to tell the president.[16]

The first contact between Magruder and McClellan occurred on April 4, and one week later Johnston was summoned to the Richmond office of Jefferson Davis; following the meeting, in which his Virginia command was expanded to encompass the forces of Magruder as well as those of Benjamin Huger at Norfolk, Johnston headed for the front. Before his leaving, however, Davis should have expected trouble when he asked that both Magruder and Huger receive orders to concentrate all of their troops behind the Warwick. At Yorktown, Johnston took one look at Magruder's defenses and decided they could never contain McClellan and his siege guns. After one day on the ramparts, he returned to Richmond convinced that a concentration of troops nearer the capital was the only military option. "I recollect being present at the discussion during the Spring of 1862, which you mention, and believe that you were fully sensible of all the difficulties of meeting Genl. McClellan's advance up the Peninsula, and you were not at the time favorably impressed with Magruder's line, but I do not recollect that you proposed a plan of operations instead," Lee told Johnston in 1867, two years after the war, and added a postscript about airing dirty linen in public: "I very much regret the revival of these questions now, as I do not think it will produce good." Although Lee did not think much of Johnston's arguments during April 1862, Johnston himself maintained that Magruder's "little works" were not only inadequate for defense, but that the ponds impounded by his dams also thwarted offensive operations.[17]

When Johnston returned to Richmond for the conference described in Lee's letter, he was again ushered into the presidential office for a renewed strategy session; also present were Lee, Secretary of War Randolph, Gustavus W. Smith, and James Longstreet. Magruder apparently did not follow his new boss to the meeting, but he was clearly a part of the protracted deliberations. "[M]y intention was to suggest that we leave Magruder to look after McClellan, and march, as proposed by Jackson a few days before, through the Valley of Virginia, cross the Potomac, threaten Washington, and call McClellan to his own capital," Longstreet notes in his postwar memoir. Although Longstreet confesses that the president only asked his views "through a polite recognition of my presence," Johnston dominated the proceedings with his unrelenting demand to abandon the peninsula in favor of a gathering of forces nearer Richmond.

Lee and Randolph, however, favored combat as far from the capital as possible, with Randolph stressing that a withdrawal from the lower peninsula would force the abandonment of Norfolk and its naval facility, thereby opening Richmond to attack from the James. They too, as well as Davis, had seen Magruder's lines on numerous occasions, and obviously had some respect for them; Lee, after all, had encouraged him to keep improving the Yorktown defenses. "In the end Davis made the decision. He turned down Johnston's plan and also refused to go ahead with another one submitted by Smith, a wholly impractical suggestion to barricade and defend Richmond with as few troops as possible while the bulk of the army invaded the north," writes a Davis biographer. "In this, one of the most important strategy conferences yet held by Davis, he listened fully to the views of all present and made up his own mind and stood with Lee and Randolph." There was only one problem: Joseph E. Johnston had no intention of carrying out the president's wishes.[18]

Magruder, meanwhile, kept up the pressure as the Richmond talks unfolded; he had anticipated difficulty by recalling his advance troops at Young's Mill to the Warwick and cutting orders for his surgeons to "make requisitions on the medical purveyor at Williamsburg for supplies of medicine." Magruder, who made his headquarters at Lee's Mill, or Dam No. 1, almost in the center of his defenses, not only moved Thompson Brown to the Warwick but also ordered Major Stephen D. Ramseur to march his artillery command to Yorktown in order to bolster D. H. Hill, who held the Confederate left. Then, on the dawn of April 16, McClellan unleashed an attack on Lee's Mill, which Magruder considered his weakest point.

The fight opened with six federal batteries and dozens of sharpshooters pouring a withering fire from across the river; during the early morning melee, the Confederates were able to train only one six-pounder from Cobb's Legion on the attackers. The piece, under the command of Lieutenant Pope, Magruder records, "was served with the greatest accuracy and effect and by the coolness and skill with which it was handled the greatest odds against us were almost completely counterbalanced." McClellan even tried to silence Pope's gun by sending a massed infantry charge against it; but Lafayette McLaws, alerted by the heavy musketry and artillery fire, rushed reinforcements into the fray and was able to blunt several additional infantry thrusts. The affray ended with the onset of darkness, after Magruder—who was present—ordered up more troops. As had been the case for some months, Prince John relied upon McLaws to do the heavy work. "The dispositions of General McLaws were skillfully made," he telegraphed headquarters. "His whole being and conduct is deserving of the highest commendation."[19]

The fight at Lee's Mill—also known as Burnt Chimneys—was Magruder's last as commander of the Army of the Peninsula. Johnston, newly arrived from Richmond, proceeded to reorganize the command two days afterward as the siege of Yorktown settled into a standoff and McClellan continued to bring up his heavy guns. Magruder was given "Command of the right of the positions commencing at Dam No. 1 & extending to the [James] River." The center was assigned to James Longstreet, while D. H. Hill had Johnston's left wing at Yorktown and the York River inlets; G. W. Smith, who shortly superseded Johnston for a brief time during the Battle of Seven Pines, was given command of the reserve. All four—Magruder, Longstreet, D. H. Hill, and Smith—were newly minted major generals in the Confederate army. But while the army fought incessant rains and held a few dress parades to relieve the tedium of siege warfare, Johnston became increasingly defeatist in outlook. "Gen. Johnston appreciated that we could not afford to become entangled in siege operations with McClellan before Yorktown, for the river flank was too weak," writes Edward Porter Alexander, who fought under Longstreet. "He was willing to be assaulted by the main force, but, as soon as it appeared that McC. would not venture that, he began to prepare to evacuate our lines and to retreat up the Peninsula."[20]

There can be no doubt that pressure was building on Johnston at the very moment McClellan was employing the hot-air balloons of Professor Thaddeus Lowe to observe his lines and then use the cover of night to float his guns up the rivers. Johnston, according to his own battle summary, had no thought of challenging McClellan's army: "Before taking command of the Peninsula I had the honor to tell the President my opinion of the defects of the position then occupied by our troops there." And he added an exercise in self-justification: "After taking command I reported that the opinion previously expressed was fully confirmed." Throughout those last weeks of April he chose to ignore Jefferson Davis as he sped forward his withdrawal scheme. "Johnson showed no interest in correlating the action on the other fronts—Norfolk, the Rappahannock, and the Valley—with his planned evacuation," writes a campaign historian. Lee was informed on the twenty-fourth that he might have to fall back; "on April 27 he went a little further, and two days later came right out with it: 'We must abandon the Peninsula soon. As two or three days, more or less, can signify little, I think it best, for the sake of the capital, to do it now.'" His mind fixed, and with McClellan ready to open a heavy bombardment of his lines, Johnston ordered "the troops to move toward Williamsburg on the night of [May] 3rd by the roads from Yorktown and Warwick Court-House." Three days earlier he had started wagons and ambulances carrying his sick and wounded toward Richmond.[21]

Magruder, meanwhile, had been largely ignored in the unfolding drama; and he was incapacitated during the last phases of the siege, probably from overwork, anxiety, and renewed drinking. After Johnston's reorganization of April 18, he appears to have taken little part in the army's day-to-day command decisions. "Magruder was commander of Johnston's right wing, responsible for 16,000 men—almost a third of the entire army." But he was clearly unhappy with the new scheme. "He feuded with the army's deputy commander Major General Gustavus Smith. He did not get along with Johnston, either," observes a recent biographer. Within days of Johnston's final order to retreat toward Richmond, Magruder had to be relieved of his command. Hugh Thomas Douglas, his engineering officer, has left a poignant memoir of Magruder's last hours behind the Warwick: "I shall never forget the morning that Gen. Magruder, lying on his sick bed worn out by the arduous duties of three weeks, a strain enough to have killed any ordinary man, summoned me to his room and directed me to prepare for the move," Douglas wrote fifty years later. "The tears coursed down the old man's cheeks and rising on one arm with dramatic effect, he pointed to his little army, and said 'Sic transit gloria, Peninsula.'" Still, Magruder marched with his troops from Dam No. 1 when the army moved during the early-morning hours of May 3.[22]

Johnston's withdrawal order came with the certain knowledge that the big federal guns were finally in place; one day before the evacuation decision, "McClellan ordered battery #1, composed of 200-pounder Parrotts to open fire on Yorktown and its docks. One Rebel recorded that when the huge shells came thundering in, it seemed as if the whole world was falling apart," notes a student of the siege. "Ironically, the shelling caused few casualties; one shot blew a sleeping soldier twelve feet in the air, but other than rudely interrupting his nap, it left him uninjured. The only deaths were a few of the hundreds of wild hogs that congregated in town during the winter." But Johnston had heard enough, and he left in such a rush that precious stores had to be discarded, including seventy-seven artillery pieces, although most of the guns were outdated naval ordnance taken at Norfolk the previous year. At a time when ordinary citizens were being implored to make sacrifices for the army, the quick retreat and abandonment of food, wagons, and supplies of every description added fire to the festering disagreements between Johnston and President Davis.[23]

Magruder's precise movements during the initial phases of the withdrawal are confused in the official dispatches. He was temporarily removed from command of Johnston's right wing and replaced by David Rumph Jones, a South Carolinian who had hauled down the Stars and Stripes during the surrender of Fort Sumter; the only question is when. Since Magruder is silent about the episode in his own writings, the biographer must rely upon his contemporaries; Longstreet says that when the army reached Williamsburg Magruder was told to "march at two A.M. on the 5th with D. R. Jones's and McLaws's divisions, to be followed by the divisions of G. W. Smith and D. H. Hill." Yet H. T. Douglas, who visited his sickroom and who readied his division for the evacuation, says flat out that Magruder was too ill to lead his men.[24]

Interestingly, none of his contemporaries, including Jefferson Davis, gives any hint about the nature of his complaint, nor do any of them suggest that the difficulty was rooted in his drinking. According to Joe Johnston, however, Magruder must have led his division out of its Warwick River entrenchments: "I directed the troops to move toward Williamsburg on the night of the 3rd," his official report reads. "They were assembled about Williamsburg by noon on the 4th, and were ordered to march by the road to Richmond, General Magruder leading." But he was unable to move at the appointed time, which likewise delayed G. W. Smith. When he finally marched out of Williamsburg, part of his men under McLaws turned to contest McClellan's lead columns at Fort Magruder, about half the distance to Yorktown. An ailing Prince John took no part in the mean fighting of May 4; in the battles that lasted through the fifth, speculates Colonel R. L. Maury, "the mistake, growing out of ignorance or carelessness, might have been avoided had General Magruder been assigned to defense of the rear on that day, for he and his troops were perfectly familiar with the whole country—they had been there all the previous autumn and winter and had themselves laid out and built those very fortifications." A meaningful role in the withdrawal, instead of being sent ahead of everyone else by Johnston, could well have aggravated Magruder's feelings of dejection and his continued drinking.

Colonel Maury says further that Magruder was "ordered not to halt at all and that the other divisions should take up their march [on the 5th] to the Chickahominy at early dawn—Longstreet being in the rear." Thus Maury and Longstreet agree that Magruder was still in the saddle when the troops left Williamsburg. But the march out of Yorktown must have been an ordeal for everyone. "The horrible roads are well remembered even now by all who passed them on that dark and rainy night," Colonel Maury wrote in 1880 about the pullout from Magruder's lines. "The mud and water were ankle and sometimes knee deep, and infantry were often called to help the weary horses drag wagons from holes and ruts in which the wheels had sunk to the very axles." It was a slow, thankless march, with hungry troopers often dropping by the roadway to catch a few moments' sleep before proceeding.[25]

Magruder was relieved sometime during the march from Williamsburg; Johnston, in his official report of the campaign, composed two weeks afterward, seems to suggest that Magruder was still in command when "his division moved at daybreak on the 5th in heavy rain and mud." But in his war memoirs, published in 1874—four years after Magruder's death—Johnston included a slightly altered version. "The four divisions were assembled at Williamsburg about noon of the 4th," he wrote. "Magruder's division temporarily commanded by Brigadier General D. R. Jones, was ordered to move on in the afternoon, by the 'New Kent Road,' and to turn off at the 'Burnt Ordinary,' toward the Diascund Bridge; to be followed by G. W. Smith's which was to keep the New Kent Road." Yet all agree that D. R. Jones was in charge of the division when the lead columns halted at Barhamsville, eighteen miles up the road toward Richmond. Johnston, however, was in slight error because Jones, who graduated in the West Point class of 1846 with Stonewall Jackson and George B. McClellan, like Magruder, was already a major general. Although he "successfully withdrew" Magruder's division from the peninsula and played a role in the Seven Days campaign, Jones suffered from a heart ailment that took his life in January 1863.[26]

"On the 9th of May," reads Longstreet's memoir, "the Confederate army halted; its right near the Long Bridge of the Chickahominy River; its left and cavalry extending toward the Pamunkey through New Kent Court-House." While Johnston's force waited and licked its wounds within sight of Richmond, Magruder's division, still under Jones, was put under the command of G. W. Smith on May 12; the army's proximity to the capital also permitted Jefferson Davis and Robert E. Lee to make frequent inspection of the sprawling encampments. Lee, remembering their cadet days at West Point, decided to visit his old comrade's sickroom. Thereupon, writes a Lee relative, "he found him cheerful and comfortable; at last John appealed to him to have a lot of monkeys removed from the room over head, whose playful noises disturbed his sleep." The "anaecdote [*sic*] Gen. Lee told of him," suggests that Magruder was suffering from delirium tremens and hallucinations associated with the uncontrolled use of alcohol. Others indicate that his nervousness and halting performance during the subsequent fighting from Seven Pines through Malvern Hill was abetted by a specially prepared medication containing morphine; the age-old remedy for drunken stupors accompanying prolonged drinking bouts almost certainly caused him to experience a painful if not debilitating reaction.[27]

As Magruder joined the retreating columns, Joe Johnston turned to fend off his pursuers on May 5 in the vicinity of Williamsburg. With the Confederates desperately urging their wagon trains along the muddy, nearly impassable roads, and McClellan attempting to halt their exodus by landing additional troops at White House on the York, Johnston decided to contest the retreat without Magruder's help. Although this forward disembarkation of troops could well have cut off the march to Richmond, it was not accomplished until May 7, following a battlefront visit by Abraham Lincoln and his secretary of war, Edwin Stanton; and by that time Johnston had made good his escape. Near Williamsburg, however, the armies clashed around Fort Magruder, where the Confederates blundered badly from failure to utilize several of Magruder's neighboring redoubts. Not only Colonel Maury, but Davis and Longstreet, wrote separately that lack of precise knowledge about the defensive positions hampered the battle. In the hard fighting of May 5, D. H. Hill and Longstreet bore the brunt of the federal onslaught; Jeb Stuart, the cavalryman par excellence, even sent "the Gallant" Pelham into the fray with his mobile batteries from the horse artillery. John Pelham, one of the war's truly romantic figures, killed at Kelly's Ford in March 1863, idol of countless Richmond belles, soon became the hero of Fredericksburg when he used his guns to bludgeon Ambrose Burnside's initial attack on Marye's Heights.

Longstreet sets the numbers "engaged as Confederates, 9,000; Union 12,000." Johnston had 1,500 aggregate casualties, to 2,300 for McClellan. The fighting around Fort Magruder continued until late evening when Longstreet gave the order to march for the Chickahominy. "We advanced along the edge of the wood to the left of Fort Magruder, and about 11 o'clock we saw emerging from the little ravine to the left of the fort a swarm of Confederates, who opened on us with a terrible and deadly fire," writes Private William Goss. "Then they charged us with their peculiar yell. . . . We were none of us too proud, not even those who had the dignity of shoulder-straps for support, to dodge behind a tree or a stump. I called to a comrade, 'Why don't you get behind a tree?' 'Confound it,' said he, 'there ain't enough for the officers.' "

While Goss observed that Union officers used their rank to visit the rear as the fight unfolded, it ended when Brigadier General Winfield Scott Hancock and 1,200 federals were able to hurl back a determined though futile charge by Jubal A. Early of D. H. Hill's command. "I cannot think of it, till this day, without horror," D. H. Hill wrote after the war. "The slaughter of the Fifth North Carolina Regiment was one of the most awful things I ever saw and it was caused by a blunder." The blunder resulted in part from an incomplete knowledge of the pits and redoubts surrounding Fort Magruder; and Magruder, the soldier who designed and maintained the whole Confederate defense system, was not there.[28]

Johnston's withdrawal from the peninsula also led to Benjamin Huger's pullout from Norfolk, as Secretary Randolph had foreseen. With the army gone, Flag Officer Josiah Tattnal, who had taken over from Buchanan, had no choice but to destroy the *Merrimac*, because her deep draft precluded moving up the James to safety, although attempts were made to lighten the vessel. "The ship was accordingly put ashore as near the mainland, in the vicinity of Craney Island, as soon as possible, and the crew landed," Tattnal told a board of inquiry. "She was then fired, and after burning fiercely fore and aft for upwards of an hour blew up a little before five on the morning of the 11th." With some of his units already ashore well up the York, McClellan moved quickly to take control of the James. A flotilla of five federal ships, including the *Monitor,* was sent up the river on May 14–15; at Drewry's Bluff, within six or seven miles of Richmond, the Confederates had barricaded the river and were able to turn back the gunboats following a four-hour engagement. Richmond could have been in real danger had McClellan's naval venture been properly supported by land troops, but a combination of heavy guns on the bluffs and sharpshooters along the shore was enough to save the capital.[29]

Within three days of the Drewry's Bluff episode, Magruder was back in command of his old division as the army lay encamped along the Chickahominy; and he threw himself back into the fray with renewed enthusiasm. In two firmly worded letters of May 18 and 21, he asked Randolph to appoint Captain Henry Bryan as his adjutant general and Lieutenant Colonel John B. Cary as inspector general; both, written in his own hand from Richmond's Fairfield Race Course, were signed "J. Bankhead Magruder, commanding, Right Wing." Bryan, tragically, had to be relieved after suffering two wounds in the Seven Days battles. And from "Mr. Belcher's House" at the race grounds, Magruder wrote to William Nelson Pendleton, his old roommate at West Point, on May 21, asking that he find a place for "Mr. Bernard Casler, a very estimable and accomplished gentleman," in his commissary department. Some days later—during the Battle of Seven Pines—he implored Pendleton, now chief of artillery for the army, to dispatch several experienced men for his own artillery force.[30]

Magruder had his division—still calling itself the right wing—concentrated around the New Bridge over the Chickahominy during the days leading to Seven Pines. When he asked to reposition his forces closer to Richmond, on an arc between Mechanicsville and the Meadow Bridge, he met with opposition from G. W. Smith. "It is now obvious as there is no enemy in Charles City County that the whole of the enemy's forces are marching upon the Rail Road and by a dash they could even get into our works to the left before we could, from our advanced positions," Magruder told his unappreciative superior. "Would not it be better to night [*sic*] to withdraw your division nearer to the town and extend it to the left & ought not the whole army to move to the left flank to arrest this new movement of the enemy?"

That Smith had little patience with Magruder's suggestions was related to his larger troubles with Davis and Lee. On May 23 Magruder had been summoned to Davis's office in Richmond for assignment on the Texas coast. The president, writes his most recent biographer, "regarded the Trans-Mississippi as something of a dumping ground, and in the summer of 1862 he began a war-long policy of sending discredited generals there to command or using it to shelve personal favorites who were too controversial to keep in the East." Davis was piqued at Magruder because of his drinking, but he was after all a Confederate major general with long military experience, and he offered him command of a western subdistrict composed of Texas, Arkansas, and Louisiana west of the Mississippi. Prince John was overjoyed with the job offer, but pleaded with Davis to let him stay in Virginia for McClellan's inevitable offensive. Although Davis temporarily withdrew the appointment when several generals and politicians offered strenuous objection, Lee sent a May 26 order to General Paul O. Hebert, commanding in Texas, informing the onetime Louisiana governor that Magruder would replace him "as soon as relieved from his present position."[31]

The war office must have been in virtual turmoil regarding Magruder throughout May 26; following Lee's communiqué to Hebert, Assistant Adjutant General A. P. Mason issued General Order 117: "Maj. Gen. Lafayette McLaws is assigned to the command of the troops heretofore commanded by Major General Magruder, the latter having been relieved." Joe Johnston, of all people, fired off a wire to Randolph objecting to Magruder's treatment by headquarters. "Your letter is calculated, I think, to give the impression that I have done Major-General Magruder injustice," he told the war secretary, also on the twenty-sixth. "Let me remind you that my order in question was given in obedience to yours assigning General Magruder to the command of a department, and directing him to report for instructions. . . . I had no option, but was bound to obey it. If injustice was done, it was not by me." Johnston said the affair placed him "in a false position in relation to Major General Magruder and the army." Then, still on May 26, a new order came down that said Magruder would not only stay with his command, but that he should report to Johnston for immediate posting.[32]

Two days later, Magruder conferred with Johnston as the army prepared for battle. He issued a few orders from his position north of the Chickahominy, including the movement of several units under D. R. Jones to other sectors of the field. Johnston remained anxious that Irvin McDowell was marching on Richmond from the north, which would have placed Magruder at the center of battle. But Johnston altered his battle plans after Jeb Stuart's cavalry patrols reported that McDowell had veered off toward Fredericksburg. When Erasmus Keyes was discovered isolated from McClellan's main force north of the Chickahominy, the decision was made to attack. As part of the reconcentration to meet the new objective, Magruder, along with A. P. Hill, was ordered to assume a position south and facing the river. At Longstreet's suggestion, G. W. Smith's "wing" was placed in reserve to guard the Confederate left, which extended into the capital itself. Magruder thus held the only reserve at the Battle of Seven Pines, and as the fight unfolded, he was removed from the center.[33]

Johnston attempted to maneuver several columns into a concentrated attack on Keyes, now reinforced by Samuel P. Heintzelman, near "a clump of trees" known locally as Seven Pines, where the Nine Mile and Williamsburg roads intersected. Longstreet with 14,000 men, D. H. Hill 9,500, and Huger 5,000 with W. H. C. Whiting in support of Longstreet, were instructed to converge on Keyes and the Union front south of the river. The irascible artillerist E. P. Alexander affirms that the plan was straightforward, but that botched orders and Longstreet's unwillingness to march as expected nearly spelled disaster. "The result was a poorly managed battle, in which the Confederates succeeded in driving Keyes' corps back a few miles, but utterly failed to inflict the kind of defeat that might have disrupted McClellan's advance," writes a Johnston biographer. "Johnston had 55,000 men at his disposal to deal with an isolated corps of 15,000 Federals, yet he never succeeded in getting more than 14,000 of his men into the battle."

Most of the fighting was done by D. H. Hill, who grew tired of waiting for Longstreet and opened the battle at around one-thirty in the afternoon. The aged Edwin Sumner, a soldier since 1819, managed to get one of his divisions across the Chickahominy in time to help blunt Hill's attack. As the fighting unfolded, first Robert E. Lee and then Jefferson Davis came on the field, but Johnston could see that his chance of destroying Keyes had evaporated, and chose to avoid the president by riding away on some pretended errand. In spite of a peculiar battlefield phenomenon that prevented Johnston from hearing the raging musketry along Hill's front, he personally rode into the battle with Whiting's command. No sooner had he left for the fray, reads Davis's account, than "General Johnston who had gone further to the right where the conflict was expected, and whither reenforcement from the left was marching, was brought back severely wounded, and, as soon as an ambulance could be obtained, was removed from the field." Twice wounded—the second time by an exploding artillery blast—Johnston "fell heavily from his horse" as stretcher bearers sloshed across muddy fields to take him to a place of safety. A Chickahominy swollen to overflowing by torrential rains had induced Johnston to attack in the first place.[34]

Although Gustavus Smith assumed immediate command until the following day, when he was replaced by Lee, accounts of Magruder's movements throughout May 31 are sketchy at best. Prince John himself submitted no written account, but Jefferson Davis records that he went looking for him after Johnston's misfortune. "After a personal reconnaissance . . . , I sent one, then another courier to General Magruder, directing him to send a force down by the wooded path, just under the bluff, to attack the enemy in flank and reverse," he notes. "Impatient of delay, I had started to see General Magruder, when I met the third courier, who said he had not found General Magruder, but had delivered the message to Brigadier-General [Richard] Griffith, who was moving by the path designated to make the attack." Smith, who took command when Johnston left the field, suggests in his carefully reasoned account that Johnston had sent for Magruder's reserve earlier: "Just before dark the only troops of Magruder's command that were within reach—when I transmitted General Johnston's order for them to be brought up—arrived on the field; but it was then too late to put them in action." But where was Magruder, who did not accompany his troops? He uncharacteristically left their employment to a subordinate officer, which suggests that he may have been yet incapacitated from anxiety and/or illness.[35]

Losses were severe on both sides at Seven Pines, totaling 6,100 for Johnston and 5,000 for McClellan. Largely because of Longstreet's bungling on the march, a sizable part of McClellan's army escaped destruction. Whether Magruder's prompt arrival on the field when ordered up by Davis and Smith would have altered events must remain a moot question as a new commander emerged to lead the Army of Northern Virginia; and Lee had already acted on Davis's instruction to send him to the faraway Gulf coast. The next morning, writes John Coxe, who fought with Hampton's Legion, "there was no fighting on our front . . . , though about 8 A.M., a lively fight began over on our right, but it died out completely by 10 A.M., on that first of June, 1862." Longstreet, the man designated to spearhead the abortive fight of June 1, and who was blamed for the failure to destroy Keyes, wrote after the war that Magruder had agreed with him that Johnston's plan to concentrate his disparate columns at Seven Pines had been unworkable from the beginning. It was the first major battle around Richmond, and Johnston entered the fray without issuing careful instructions for his commanders and without a clear knowledge of the terrain over which he asked them to fight. Magruder, although he was unaccountably absent from his command at the critical moment, like other officers, suffered from Johnston's poorly thought-out plans for battle. Since he has nothing to say about his own movements, it is easy to speculate that the drinking which plagued him during Johnston's retreat up the peninsula flared anew while his men sat out the battle.[36]

7

The Seven Days

ALTHOUGH MAGRUDER YEARNED to undertake his new duties in the West, he remained with the army in Virginia for the defense of Richmond; he fought through the Seven Days campaign, however, only to see his command broken up and assigned elsewhere, as Robert E. Lee took the army northward to draw McClellan's forces from the capital. Troubles with President Davis and Lee over his conduct in the subsequent battles very nearly destroyed his opportunity for command in the Trans-Mississippi. Yet Magruder again found himself in the forefront of the Virginia fighting despite a continuing public and official perception that his drinking and constant agitation hampered his performance on the battlefield. During the twenty-six-day interval between Seven Pines and Lee's opening battles to hurl Mc-Clellan from the peninsula, even a cursory examination of the printed record reveals that Prince John played an important, if somewhat secondary, role in the Confederate game plan. He initially maintained his headquarters at the racing grounds east of Richmond, but like his fellow commanders he was soon confronted with a near rebellion when Lee set his troopers to digging trenches and erecting earthworks before the growing federal army. The Mexican War had impressed upon Lee the necessity of defensive works in the face of superior numbers, and, writes one biographer, "the use of entrenchments for infantry was Lee's greatest contribution to military art." As McClellan, supplied by the Richmond & York River Railroad, methodically but hesitatingly brought up men and siege guns for a renewed assault, Lee, too, was preparing for his own attack. The unfolding drama through

163

June 1862 found Magruder in daily communication with not only Lee but also the Confederate war office.[1]

The clash of titans that culminated in the Seven Days campaign, lasting from June 25 through July 1, 1862, took place in a swampy region within sight of the capital, dominated by the Chickahominy and its chief tributary, White Oak Swamp Creek. The Chickahominy, which originates a few miles north of Richmond, follows a southeasterly meander until it strikes the James between Charles City and Williamsburg; its poorly defined banks in the low-lying tidewater form a nearly impenetrable barrier during periods of excessive rainfall. White Oak Swamp Creek, which meets the Chickahominy a few miles east of Richmond, is likewise a sluggish, marshy stream with heavy, tangled undergrowth that caused problems for both armies in 1862. From Magruder's headquarters, several bridges spanned the Chickahominy in the immediate vicinity of McClellan's advance: the New Bridge, Duane's Bridge, Grapevine Bridge, the Richmond & York River Railroad Bridge, and finally the easternmost Bottom's and Long Bridges. At least five thoroughfares transversed the region, including the Nine Mile Road from Richmond to Fair Oaks Station, a distance of nine miles from the Richmond city limits; the Williamsburg Pike, which crossed the Chickahominy by Bottom's Bridge, and the Charles City Road, which ran south of White Oak Swamp. Northernmost was the Mechanicsville Pike, which crossed the river east of Magruder's encampment. "I was in command of three Divisions," he wrote, "those of Maj. Genl. McLaws, Brig. Genl. D. R. Jones, and my own, each consisting of two Brigades, the numerical strength being about (13,000) thirteen thousand Men." As the crescendo approached, Magruder "slept near my troops," but he unfailingly signed his numerous dispatches to Lee and the war office, "Major General, Commanding Right Wing," a holdover from his command farther down the peninsula.[2]

When Lee took charge on June 1, Magruder and his fellow commanders were soon caught in a new wave of enthusiasm that swept the ranks. It was obvious from the beginning that Lee meant to fight; "commanders of divisions and brigades will take every precaution and use every means in their power to have their commands in readiness at all times for immediate action," read his Special Order No. 22, issued on June 1. "They will be careful to preserve their men as much

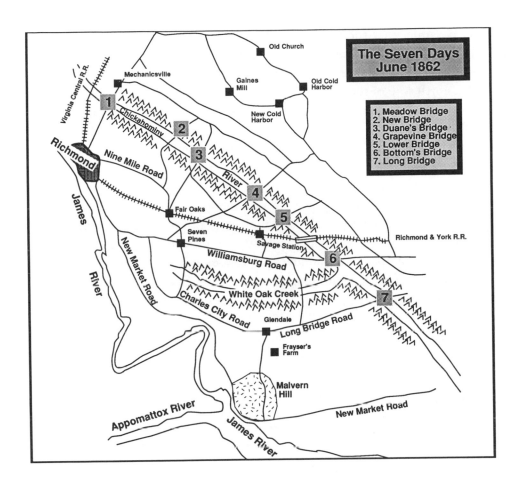

The Seven Days June 1862

1. Meadow Bridge
2. New Bridge
3. Duane's Bridge
4. Grapevine Bridge
5. Lower Bridge
6. Bottom's Bridge
7. Long Bridge

as possible, that they will be fresh when called upon for active service." Yet when he summoned his generals together at his new headquarters "in a modest house owned by the widow Dabb, set back on the north side of the Nine Mile Road about one and a half miles from the edge of Richmond," Lee found that pervasive gloom gripped the officer corps. Johnston's withdrawal up the peninsula before McClellan's advance had clearly taken its toll on fighting élan; and Longstreet says that Lee was bombarded by incessant carping from his brigadiers. W. H. C. Whiting, one of Magruder's comrades, even presented an elaborate map to demonstrate the futility of further resistance by constructing parallels. Still, Lee kept the troops digging; and when Jefferson Davis happened on the officers' meeting he, too, noted the rampant despondency. "I expressed in marked terms, my disappointment at hearing such views, and General Lee remarked that he had, before I came in, said very much the same thing," Davis wrote in his postwar memoir. "I then withdrew and rode to the front, where, after a short time, General Lee joined me, and entered into a conversation as to what, under the circumstances, I thought it most advisable to do."[3]

Lee and Davis unhesitatingly resolved to press the enemy with every resource at their disposal. The artilleryman E. P. Alexander was certain that Lee's positive spirit had shifted the advantage away from McClellan before the battles opened on June 26. Lee also began to send Magruder pointed notes urging him to stand firm; when his command failed to drive off several working parties from his front, Lee told him on June 5—three days after the big conference—that he was unwilling to issue specific orders for defense. But, he added, "the army would not recede from a position when only threatened," because "our artillery could as effectively damage the enemy as he could injure us." He told Magruder to resist any Yankee attempt to capture "Mr. James Garnett's place," near his forward positions south of the Chickahominy. The following day, June 6, Magruder strengthened his lines by directing Whiting and D. R. Jones to reposition their units to cover the ground between the river and the railroad. His aide-de-camp, Major Joseph L. Brent, confirms that Magruder was drawn into the new scheme: "Very soon and almost imperceptibly, the net work [sic] of the general organization was cast over the whole army, and we were bought into a far closer connection with headquarters."[4]

Lee's reorganization, writes his aide and early biographer General A. L. Long, soon contained a line that "extended from Chaffin's Bluff, on the James River, crossing the river road about four miles, and Darby Town, Charles City, Williamsburg, and Nine Mile Roads, about five miles from Richmond to a point on the Chickahominy a little above New Bridge, and then continued up that stream to Meadow Bridge." Lee, according to Magruder's old messmate from Fort Leavenworth, could draw upon six divisions: "Longstreet's division formed the right, while those of Huger, D. H. Hill, Magruder, Whiting, and A. P. Hill in the order named, extended to the left." With Magruder positioned about where he had been through the Seven Pines imbroglio, and A. P. Hill on the extreme left, Lee opened his campaign. And his thoughts soon turned to Thomas Jonathan Jackson, whose small force of "foot cavalry" had been savoring victory after victory with its lightning marches through the Shenandoah Valley. For some weeks—even before he assumed command of the Army of Northern Virginia—Lee had been collaborating with "Stonewall" to worry Lincoln into withholding men and supplies from McClellan's peninsula army. The nearness to Washington of Jackson's Shenandoah triumphs over James Shields, Nathaniel P. Banks, and John C. Frémont had nearly paralyzed Lincoln with fear.

Now, however, Jackson was needed in front of Richmond to reinforce Lee's army for the grand thrust. With considerable fanfare, troops were withdrawn from the Richmond defenses and dispatched to Jackson with the intent of deceiving the ever-cautious federal commander into thinking an assault from the north was in the offing. Although Magruder lost no men in the venture, he was obliged to reposition his command to fill the vacuum created by their withdrawal; "with regard to Gen. Whiting's division being in your control, the commanding general desires me to say that your command does not extend beyond those of McLaws' and Jones'," Lee's adjutant informed Magruder on June 10. "He thinks that by continuing the system of division commanders greater harmony may be preserved throughout the army, as all questions involving differences of opinion may be referred to a common superior and promptly resolved." A flap must have developed between Magruder and Whiting, himself a West Point man, class of 1845. "In any disposition that will be made I feel confident of my ability to co-operate with General Whiting," Magruder informed headquarters the same day, June 10, about the request to widen his command. "These differences are not accompanied by anything unpleasant between General Whiting and myself; but are such as will necessarily arise between two independent minds when neither commands, and produce inconvenience in little matters too unimportant to be referred to the commanding general." Another communiqué, the following morning—this one signed by Lee— reached Magruder: "Two brigades of General Smith's division, under General Whiting, have been selected to temporarily re-enforce General Jackson." Magruder was ordered to close the gap caused by their departure by making sure that his lines reached the railroad. Lee again admonished: "Make the movement quietly, if practicable, consulting the comfort of the troops as well as the good of the service, which I know your good government will insure." At this point Lee still had confidence in him as the army prepared for battle; but he also included his usual remarks that Prince John should remain attentive to his duties.[5]

Then, as Magruder worked with A. P. Hill to implement Lee's directives, Jeb Stuart was sent on his famous ride to pinpoint McClellan's exact positions. "You are desired to make a secret movement to the rear of the enemy now posted on the Chickahominy, with a view to gaining intelligence of his operations, communications, etc.," Lee instructed his twenty-nine-year-old cavalryman. "Another objective is to destroy his wagon trains, said to be daily passing from the Piping Tree Road to his camp on the Chickahominy."

With a hastily assembled force of 1,200 horsemen, Stuart started one of the war's memorable adventures on the morning of June 12. Four abreast, his men rode north from Richmond. Infantrymen said they, too, were headed for the Shenandoah, but their direction soon shifted to the east. Next it was through Hanover Court House and a two-day running battle with the federal cavalry under Stuart's own father-in-law, General Philip St. George Cooke, until they recrossed the Chickahominy behind McClellan. Although couriers were dispatched to Lee's headquarters with detailed findings, Stuart completed his encirclement of the Army of the Potomac by galloping up the New Market Road into the capital on the fifteenth. When he reached the governor's mansion, records Emory Thomas, Stuart said,

" 'he had been to the Chickahominy to visit some of his old friends of the United States Army, but they, 'very uncivilly turned their backs on him.' "[6]

Lee now knew that Yankee general Fitz-John Porter held McClellan's right flank north of the Chickahominy, and that here would be the focus of his attack. The federal chieftain, on the other hand, discounted Stuart's ride for public consumption, but the episode probably saved his command from annihilation. "The Confederates had made him painfully aware that his lifeline from White House Landing to the Chickahominy was vulnerable," continues historian Thomas. Although McClellan was slow to act, Lee's threatening preparations for battle forced him to abandon his York River depots and shift his base of operations to the protective guns of the federal navy at Harrison's Landing. And his quick move to the James set the groundwork for Lee's great diagonal thrust eastward across the peninsula from the Richmond entrenchments.[7]

Stuart's intelligence convinced Lee that Porter's separated right wing could be destroyed, and on June 16, one day after the cavalryman's return, he dispatched the famous summons for Jackson to leave the Shenandoah. Although Jackson with his foot cavalry did not reach Ashland on the railroad to Fredericksburg until the twenty-fifth, the *Official Records* indicate that Magruder was in near-constant communication with Lee about his own role in the unfolding drama. And while he waited for Jackson, Lee began to concentrate Longstreet and the two Hills near the Mechanicsville Bridge for a cross-Chickahominy assault on Porter, while Magruder and Huger were again posted to a holding action against McClellan's left wing under Franklin, Sumner, Heintzelman, and Keyes; during the buildup, Magruder continued to watch the front between the Chickahominy and the railroad to the York. "Under present disposition of troops, Maj. Gen. J. Longstreet is charged with the military movements and operations of his own and Maj. Gen. D. H. Hill's division," read Lee's order No. 71, dated June 22. "Maj. Gen. J. B. Magruder those of his division, to be composed of Cobb's and Griffith's brigades and the divisions commanded by Maj. Gen. McLaws and Brig. Gen. D. R. Jones— Semmes' and Kershaw's brigades constituting McLaws' division and Toombs' and Anderson's, Jones.' " Stonewall Jackson, meanwhile, arrived at Lee's Dabb House headquarters the next day following an exhausting ride ahead of his troops for the famed conference with Lee, D. H. Hill, Longstreet, and A. P. Hill. Although Magruder was close by, he was not invited to the strategy-making session; he remained on the sidelines, in a subordinated position, as Lee turned to other, steadier men for the hard fighting ahead.[8]

Magruder's copy of Lee's Order No. 75, issued June 24 and marked "Confidential," can still be examined in the Museum of the Confederacy archive in Richmond. Jackson was to close the vise on Porter by approaching the Union right wing from the north; everything depended upon Stonewall's timely appearance so that A. P. Hill could cross the Chickahominy by the Meadow Bridge upon hearing Jackson's opening gun. D. H. Hill and Longstreet were assigned to cross in support of Jackson and Powell Hill, respectively, once Mechanicsville and the Chickahominy crossings had been secured. While Lee's commanders were forcing Porter down the Chickahominy, "the divisions under Generals Huger and Magruder will hold their positions in front of the enemy against attack, and make such demonstrations Thursday [June 26] as to discover his operations." Lee also told Magruder, "Should opportunity present, the feint will be converted into a real attack, and should an abandonment of his entrenchments by the enemy be discovered, you will closely pursue." It was a complicated maneuver at best—one that necessitated tight cooperation by widely separated units.[9]

Although the scheme went wrong from the beginning, Lee managed to salvage a final triumph from the initial confusion. Stonewall Jackson, accustomed to quick marches along the well-manicured Valley Turnpike with the ever-present Blue Ridge for direction, became confused when he charged into the low country along the Chickahominy; he did not arrive on the field until the following day, despite efforts by soldiers native to the area to find the right byways for him. But McClellan had learned from a deserter about Jackson's approach, and, fearful lest the Valley Army tip the balance against his force of 100,000-plus, he opened the fight on June 25 instead of waiting for Lee to do so. In what became known as "the affair at Oak Grove" or King's School House, the Union commander moved his army south of the river—except for Porter's Fifth Corps—and began his assault on Richmond by attacking Magruder and Huger. Magruder's written reports—privately printed and official—make no mention of the engagement, because most of the fighting fell upon Huger, who held the keep south of the railroad. McClellan afterward wrote that "General Heinzelman was directed to drive the enemy's pickets from the woods in his front, in order to give us command of the cleared fields further in advance." In the mean scrap that followed, both Lee and McClellan were on the field before it ended with the onset of darkness. "The bill for advancing his picket line some 600 yards was costly however: 68 dead, 503 wounded, and 55 missing, a total 626," reads a recent account of the campaign. Confederate losses numbered about 440 casualties, mostly from Huger's command. "For a fight over advanced picket lines to generate more than a thousand casualties suggested just how intense any fighting between these two armies was likely to be."[10]

Costly though it was, McClellan, by his own confession, lost interest in the Oak Grove affray when intelligence reached him that Jackson was approaching from the north; when June 26 dawned over the peninsula, Stonewall and the foot cavalry were nowhere in sight, as Lee searched the horizon in vain for his opening announcement. Hours lapsed as McClellan conferred with Porter on how best to counter the threat, until A. P. Hill and the Confederate Light Division settled the dilemma for him. At 3:00 P.M., tired of waiting, an impatient Hill crossed the Meadow Bridge on his own initiative. As Lee watched through his field glasses from afar, Powell Hill, with Field, Pender, Anderson, Archer, and Gregg at his side, and four extra horses clevised to each gun, managed to drive the federals out of Mechanicsville.

A. P. Hill, who was reinforced by Longstreet and D. H. Hill, soon ran into difficulty when Fitz-John Porter withdrew his 30,000 bluecoats behind defensive works beyond Beaver Dam Creek. Actually, two nearly parallel streams—Beaver Dam and Powhite Creeks, each of which had a gristmill, Ellerson's and Gaines respectively—flowed into the Chickahominy from the north. Following brutal combat along Porter's right and center, "an attempt was made to turn our left lower down the creek, which failed disastrously," wrote the Yankee historian Alexander Webb. "Two regiments of Ripley's brigade, with Pender's brigade, endeavored to flank the position of [Ellerson's] mill, but being exposed to the magnificent Union artillery, were repulsed with heavy loss." Roswell Sabine Ripley, a South Carolinian who frequently argued with his superiors, had his command badly cut up; one Georgia unit lost 335 out of 514 men when they mistakenly charged directly into Porter's entrenched positions. Jackson's non-arrival left the Confederates without a clear-cut victory, and, worse, Fitz-John Porter remained at his guns, although word reached him during the night to fall back on Powhite Creek with the dawn.[11]

"Hold your trenches at the front of the bayonet to night [*sic*] if necessary," a handwritten note from Lee implored Magruder as the fight unfolded. "If we reach the New Bridge, I will let you know. Keep a watch for a signal at that place." Although Magruder remained at this post south of the river—between the Meadow and New Bridges—he grew increasingly anxious as the day wore on; during the early-morning hours his artilleryman, Stephen D. Lee, opened on the enemy with his guns, but the action was soon terminated when the superior firepower of Franklin and Sumner drove him back. As Magruder looked around and discovered that he was alone after D. H. Hill and Longstreet crossed the Meadow Bridge to join A. P. Hill, he dispatched his aide, Major Brent, to learn what was afoot. Brent, a peacetime lawyer who had sorted out Magruder's legal entanglements in California, rode eastward and across the Meadow Bridge, where he found Lee and his staff dejected by Jackson's continued absence. Lee told him to have Prince John keep the pressure on Heintzelman and Franklin, but Brent took one look and resolved to tell Magruder that A. P. Hill would never reach the New Bridge by nightfall. That Magruder could expect no succor from north of the Chickahominy as he faced the bulk of McClellan's invaders became obvious. Yet as evening approached he directed S. D. Lee to open once more upon his tormentors.[12]

Repeated assurances that Magruder's vigorous showmanship prevented a direct assault on Richmond from south of the river during the Mechanicsville engagement have been exaggerated over the years. Lee's report on Mechanicsville does not even mention Magruder, nor does that of McClellan. Lafayette McLaws, when he filed his report on July 20, says only that his command remained inactive throughout June 26. As the Yankee generals plotted their options in a late-night strategy session, Joseph Hooker and George Sykes wanted to attack Magruder on the morrow; although his position was vulnerable, McClellan said no. Jackson, he stated, was sure to join

Lee on the twenty-seventh, and the Union army would forget Magruder and reinforce Porter instead.[13]

During the Gaines Mill fight on June 27, however, it was a different tale; as the strengthened Yankees north of the Chickahominy fought a desperate battle to save Porter's extreme right from destruction, Magruder, ever the audacious showman, carried out Lee's command to harass McClellan's southernmost flank. Throughout the day, observes Jed Hotchkiss, "Magruder performed his part well in holding the Federal troops south of the Chickahominy, marching and countermarching his infantry in deceptive movements and keeping his artillery in constant action." After his inactivity on the twenty-sixth, Magruder recorded his own actions as the Gaines Mill struggle—Lee called it the Battle of the Chickahominy—raged within his line of sight north of the river: "In obedience to these instructions [from Lee]," he wrote, "I caused the pickets and skirmishers to observe the utmost vigilance, attacked the Enemy's pickets from time to time, and opened a frequent fire of Artillery on his works to Ensure a free knowledge of the position, Strength and Movements." Put another way, Magruder's 13,000-man troop held the combined corps of William B. Franklin and Edwin Voss Sumner, nearly 35,000 men, at bay throughout the twenty seventh.

While the fighting raged north of the river, McClellan sent an urgent request for both commanders to cross in support of the beleaguered Porter. But, Jed Hotchkiss continues, "Franklin replied that for him to send any troops was not 'prudent,' and Sumner, threatened by the brave Magruder, replied, 'hazardous.'" The brigades of William H. French and Thomas F. Meagher, a mere 5,000 men, finally crossed late in the evening. Porter had already been routed and was preparing for a general retreat toward the James before either man joined the federal rear. When Lee, who became increasingly disenchanted with Magruder, submitted his campaign report the following year, he uncharacteristically said nothing about Prince John's demonstrations. Yet, one might argue, Magruder's vigorous posturing had tipped the balance in Lee's favor.[14]

The extra troops were needed because the combined forces of Longstreet and the two Hills—bolstered by Jackson and the Valley Army—were pounding Porter unmercifully. Fitz-John Porter had reestablished his lines a few hundred yards beyond Powhite Creek, behind another swampy stream named Boatswain's Creek; and he did so upon McClellan's order, without Jackson ever firing the first cannon. Porter's units were centered around a bluff known locally as Turkey Hill, adjacent to Boatswain's, which flowed east and southward into the Chickahominy near a gristmill owned by Dr. Gaines. Throughout the twenty-seventh, while Magruder blasted away at Franklin and Sumner, Lee, who was personally on the field, sent his columns against the federal entrenchments. Jackson, after initial difficulty finding the battle front, ordered Whiting and his own Stonewall Brigade into the fray to nearly decimate Porter's right wing. Although McClellan's big siege guns from south of the Chickahominy tore at Longstreet and A. P. Hill, Lee's gray divisions not only held their ground but also pressed the advantage. But Magruder's artillery, directly across the river in Lee's line of sight, was powerless to halt the fierce cannonading. Finally, as darkness approached and the brigades of French and Meagher arrived to help a crumbling Porter, Lee called upon John Bell Hood and his Texans to charge straight into the Union center atop Turkey Hill.[15]

After a battlefield conference with Lee, Hood ordered his men across Boatswain's Creek and up the bluff; the hill which butted the swamp reached a staggering sixty feet above the surrounding countryside. "Moving down a precipitous ravine, leaping ditch and stream, clamoring up a difficult ascent, and exposed to an incessant and deadly fire, these brave and determined men pressed forward, driving the enemy from his well-selected and fortified position," none other than Stonewall Jackson wrote later about the advance of Hood and Colonel Evander M. Law. It was a glorious day for Southern manhood. Writes his recent biographer, "Hood heard a great shout from the top of Turkey Hill. Mounting he rode forward to find that the Fifth Texas had captured almost the entire New Jersey Regiment, that the Fourth Texas and the Eighteenth had overrun and captured the enemy artillery, and that a gallant charge by the Fifth United States Cavalry had been repulsed with a terrible slaughter among the horsemen." The onset of darkness, Jed Hotchkiss reasoned, saved Porter from total destruction, although Hood lost nearly 1,000 men in the encounter. Porter had no choice but to retreat south of the river, and he destroyed a number of bridges as he rushed to join McClellan's main force.[16]

Lee had won a great victory in spite of his 8,700 casualties to Mc-Clellan's 6,800. Yet the general commanding found himself in a precarious situation when Porter destroyed those Chickahominy River bridges. With Powell Hill, Longstreet, Jackson, and D. H. Hill north of the river without a convenient crossing point, Lee's main force was separated from Magruder and Huger, who suddenly found themselves confronted with the whole fury. Notwithstanding the arguments by Lee apologists that he had no fear that a timid McClellan would attack along the Richmond thoroughfares, Magruder moved quickly to remedy the impasse. "After the battle of Friday the 27th of June, on the opposite bank of the Chickahominy, it was ascertained that the Enemy had withdrawn his troops to the right bank and therefore the whole of his force were massed in front of our lines and that he had destroyed the bridge over the river, thereby separating our army and concentrating on his own," Magruder put in his handwritten report for August 12. "I immediately ordered without awaiting instructions the Bridge to be rebuilt which was done by the troops under Brig. Gen. Jones in order to establish at least one line of communication between the two portions of our army. This was completed on Saturday the 18th." Although Magruder had difficulty when Robert A. Toombs opened an unsuccessful attack without his authorization, his order to repair the New Bridge certainly abetted Lee's plans to pursue the federal army. "General Magruder is under a misapprehension as to the separation of the troops operating on the north side of the Chickahominy from these under himself and General Huger on the south side," Lee wrote six weeks later, to refute Prince John's assertions. "The bridge referred to and another about three-quarters of a mile above were ordered repaired before noon on Friday, and the New Bridge was sufficiently rebuilt to be passed by artillery on Friday night. . . . Besides this, all other bridges above New Bridge and all the fords above that point were open to us." Slowly but steadily, Lee continued to lose faith in Magruder's command potential during the Seven Days, even though more unpleasantness would arise between the two warriors.[17]

"From the time at which the enemy withdrew his forces to the south side of the Chickahominy and destroyed the bridges to the moment of his evacuation, that is from Friday [June 27] until Sunday Morning [June 29], I considered the situation of our army as

Extremely Critical and Perilous," reads Magruder's report. But Saturday, June 28, according to Major Brent, was "a wasted day," as McClellan and Porter raced toward the James via Grapevine and Lower Bridges and the protective cover of the federal navy. Magruder, like the rest of the army, had no idea where McClellan was heading for much of the day, although he hurried Brent on another early-morning jaunt to locate Lee for instructions. After crossing the New Bridge, "I found Genl. Lee upon an eminence, overlooking both the northern and southern sides of the river," Brent relates. "He formed one of a cluster of officers. He was a superb figure, calm and unruffled, as he was becoming a repository of great power. I felt the admiring influence of the success he had achieved, and regarded him with complete assurance that he was equal to any emergency." Though Brent could never transmit the commander's great composure to his own chief, James Longstreet, who joined the impromptu assembly, like Lee, grilled the major about Magruder's condition. After a few moments, Brent continues, "I then left, bearing a message to Genl. Magruder that he should be very cautious." Magruder himself related that "I received repeated instructions during Saturday night from Genl. Lee's Head Quarters, enjoining me upon my command the utmost vigilance, directing the men to sleep on their arms, and be prepared for what ever [*sic*] might occur."[18]

No further orders were received from Lee on the twenty-eighth, as both armies looked at each other across the Chickahominy; Brent insists that Magruder's front was inactive through the daylight hours. Perhaps a day of rest, or at least one without combat, was needed after the twenty-seventh, when he had "shifted his troops here and there and back and forth." There can be no doubt that his aggressiveness had contributed to McClellan's discontent. "One of his more imaginative ploys," continues a campaign chronicler, "was unmasked by Samuel K. Zook, the enterprising colonel of the 57th New York in Sumner's corps, who personally scouted far out in front and caught a glimpse behind the enemy lines." To his surprise, he discovered a contingent of blacks "parading, beating drums, and making a great noise" to distract the federals. June 28, however, was another day—one on which North and South buried their dead after the Gaines Mill bloodbath. Magruder's force remained bivouacked around Goulding's farm, below the Chickahominy, while the federal Goliath completed its Southern exodus not far from his lines. McClellan had temporarily given the slip not only to Magruder but also to Lee, as his engineers hurried to construct bridges across the nearly impassable White Oak Swamp during his headlong drive for the James.[19]

By the small hours of Sunday, June 29, both Magruder's pickets and Lee's staff officers knew that Heintzelman and Sumner had abandoned their trenches. "Col. Chilton who rode into my camp on Sunday morning hurried me off to see Genl. Lee on the Nine Mile Road, and I gave while riding with him, the necessary orders to put in motion my whole command which extended to a distance of some miles," Magruder wrote later. But Lee also revealed his plans to hit McClellan before he reached the White Oak morass: A. P. Hill and Longstreet would cross by the New Bridge and pass behind Magruder to intercept the retreat; Magruder was directed to attack eastward toward Savage Station, a depot on the Richmond & York River Railroad, to crush the federal right wing composed of Sumner and Franklin. That was after Stuart and the cavalry had been on another foray to pinpoint the enemy if possible, and Richard S. Ewell was ordered to Despatch Station, north of the Chickahominy, to see if McClellan might return to his old refuge at White House. As they talked, Lee plainly conveyed the notion that Jackson would reinforce Magruder's left flank as he advanced down the river. Even General Long, who was present, stresses that "Jackson was directed to cross the Chickahominy and relieve Magruder in the pursuit," but that Stonewall did not arrive until the next morning, thereby leaving him unsupported.[20]

When Magruder returned to his command and discovered that his old comrade from the Mexican War would not join the attack, he rushed Major Brent to seek additional troops from Lee. Although Brent's writing is never derogatory toward Magruder, he nonetheless leaves the impression that Marse Robert was less than pleased with the request and, indeed, with Prince John's general conduct:

> When I delivered my message, he seemed surprised and a little incredulous. He said his information was that the enemy was in rapid retreat, and he thought that his rear guard would scarcely deliver battle at the point indicated. And he said, "Major, have you yourself seen and formed an opinion upon the number of the enemy?"

> I replied that I had made no personal reconnaissance.
>
> "But what do you think? Is the enemy in large force?"
>
> I was surprised at the question, and after a moment's reflection, I replied, "Genl. Magruder has instructed me to say that he finds the enemy in strong force in his front."
>
> Genl. Lee looked at me with an amused expression, as if he appreciated the loyalty that declined to express an opinion contrary to the message I bore.

Unable to turn his back on a colleague, Lee relented long enough to order two of Huger's brigades for Magruder's use but only upon the stipulation that both be returned to their original duty if the enemy had not been engaged by 2:00 P.M.[21]

General Long sets the time for Magruder's "unsupported advance" at noon, while Brent says it came at two o'clock. After Huger sent a note recalling his brigades, and a message arrived from Jackson that he was not coming—that he was not only occupied with rebuilding the Grapevine Bridge, but also had other orders, Prince John issued the forward march.

> Thus, the forces which Genl. Lee had left to operate against the enemy being reduced from some Thirty five or Forty thousand to some Thirteen thousand men, I was compelled, to abandon the plan of capturing any large portion of the enemy's forces, and directed that Semmes' Brigade [McLaws's division] should be placed on the Williamsburg road and Cobb's on the left of the Rail Road, in line with Kershaw's—Jones's Division being on the Extreme left—& Barksdale's Brigade marching in reserve behind the centre.

So reads Magruder's formal report, which then continues, "I ordered the whole to move to the front, and each command to attack the enemy in whatever force or works he might be found." A huge gun mounted on a railroad car with suitable armor plate, "under the able command of Lt. Barry," also moved down the tracks with Magruder's 13,000 men. In the vicinity of Savage Station the federals turned to meet the onslaught. The Confederates, however, missed an opportunity to deliver McClellan a stinging blow when Magruder, who was "a bundle of nerves" throughout the day, did not press the contest.[22]

It commenced at around 4:30 P.M., when the brigade of Joseph B. Kershaw, a South Carolina lawyer-legislator as well as a veteran of the

Mexican War, made contact with the enemy. Magruder personally directed the action from a convenient railroad bridge until "darkness and a severe thunderstorm" halted the battle. Kershaw was repulsed south of the railroad in a counterattack by the Fifth Vermont, but, wrote Augustus Dickert, a member of his command, not before the "great siege gun" blasted holes in Sumner's ranks. Dickert, who received a nasty thigh wound, reports that Kershaw's ranks simply fell apart during the heated engagement, "nor was the railroad battery idle, for I could see the great black, grim monster puffing out heaps of gray smoke, then the red flash, then the report, sending the engine and car back along the track with a powerful recoil." Although their lines held in spite of the shelling, the federal decision to withdraw toward White Oak Swamp, rather than press the Savage Station fight, conceivably saved Lee from a major setback. When Prince John failed to press the advantage because of Jackson's absence, McClellan did not order up reinforcements from his considerable reserve.

Why Jackson lethargically spent June 29 rebuilding the Grapevine Bridge within sight of Magruder's struggle along the Chickahominy remains one of the war's mysteries, when that fighter was wont to seize every opportunity. "He probably knew that the river was fordable at that position but preferred to pass his men over dry shod," a charitable Longstreet included in his postwar memoir. Clearly, Jackson's reticence for whatever reason left Magruder in the lurch at Savage Station; "if Jackson had repaired the 'Grapevine Bridge' over the Chickahominy as early as Lee expected, and if he had crossed and joined forces with General Magruder, who was advancing down the Williamsburg Road, Sumner and Franklin would have been in difficulty," writes Kenneth P. Williams, a Northern historian. "But the danger passed, and during the night the Second and Sixth Corps crossed the swamp and destroyed the bridges."[23]

Although Lee remained uncritical of Jackson's lapses, he surely singled Magruder out: "General Magruder is under a misapprehension as to the withdrawal of any part of the force with which he was to operate." The misunderstanding arose, according to Lee, "as to the road by which General Huger was to march on Sunday, June 29, and from the erroneous report with regard to a change in General Jackson's movements." Lee found that Jackson had not been ordered to other duty, and he told President Davis that Magruder was immediately apprised of the mixup in communication; but the unalterable truth remains that Prince John fought without a single man from Stonewall's command. And, despite his hesitancy throughout the day, the Confederates suffered only 626 casualties in the Savage Station fight, to 1,590 for the enemy, who left behind a trove of supplies, including a fully equipped field hospital.[24]

The fierce struggles since Seven Pines continued to take their toll upon Magruder, who confessed to Major Brent that he was not only ill but also that narcotics were aggravating his condition. What he had witnessed, though, was enough to unnerve stronger, more relaxed soldiers. "In passing Savage Station there is a dead man sitting on a large box, his legs drawn up and leaning against another one. Some distance on there is a man sitting behind a large oak tree; his head is shot off," observed Corporal Orlando Hanks, Company K, First Texas Infantry, Hood's Brigade, as he marched to the front. Hanks and his fellow Texans were following in pursuit of McClellan's bluecoats, who retreated through White Oak Swamp during the night of July 29–30. After a late-evening conference among Magruder, Lee, and Jackson—the latter managed to cross long enough to parley—Lee fashioned a three-pronged attack for June 30. Jackson was instructed to cross the swamp and form the extreme Confederate right—but that warrior once again evaded the contest by marching to the edge and firing blindly into the ranks of W. F. Smith and Israel B. Richardson from the bank.

Since the enemy had drawn themselves into an inverted L, with Franklin and Sumner at right angles (and reaching southward) to Smith and Richardson, Longstreet and Powell Hill were told to ram McClellan's right by marching down the Long Bridge Road; Huger was to advance by the Charles Court House Pike in support of Longstreet. "Next morning early [Monday] I received orders from Genl. Lee in person to proceed with my command to the Darby Town road, and a guide was furnished by him to conduct me thither," Magruder says about his part in the advance. This path would have put him in the rear of A. P. Hill; Magruder marched promptly, as ordered, reaching "Timberlake's Store," about twelve miles distant, at around 2:00 P.M., and as his men took a brief bivouac, a bevy of conflicting orders commenced to bombard him. And, writes a campaign historian, "Lee expected to employ his divisions in one concerted effort to destroy the Union army, but such was not the case. Huger's timidity, Magruder's vacillation, and Jackson's lethargy—plus poor staff work and the difficulties of concentrating forces directly on the field of battle—combined to thwart his wishes."[25]

Once the new battle opened around the crossroads hamlet of Glendale—also near the chief plantation of the countryside, Frayser's Farm, where the federals became entangled because of congested roads—Magruder became hopelessly confused, not only from his own indecisiveness but also owing to muddled directives from Lee and his staff. Major Brent has left a sad portrait of his chief throughout June 30, when he failed to bring his forces to bear upon the enemy, although he managed to capture several hundred prisoners:

> Genl. Magruder was on horseback, galloping here and there with great rapidity. He seemed to me to be under a nervous excitement that strangely affected him. He frequently interposed in minor matters, reversing previous arrangements and delaying the movement he was so anxious to hasten.
>
> I looked on with great sadness at what seemed to me a loss of equilibrium in a man whom I knew to be earnest and indefatigable in the discharge of duty. This was soon a matter of conversation with the staff. Major Bryan and others referred to it in my presence, and at last Major Bryan said to me that I ought to speak to the General and endeavor to calm him. . . .
>
> I had felt a certain degree of mortification at the apparently nervous excitement of the General, and as I entertained a sincere esteem for him and a high appreciation of his military ability in certain directions, I gave heed to the suggestion of Major Bryan and determined that I would act upon it, although I felt a certain reluctance to undertake it.
>
> "General," I said, "I am sorry to see that you are not feeling well this morning."
>
> "Why do you think so?"
>
> "Because," I continued, "I have never seen you act as you have this morning."
>
> "What have you seen me do, different from my usual habit?"
>
> "Well, General, I hope you will pardon me, but I have never seen your usual calmness so much lost by an extreme irritability, sometimes exhibited without any apparent cause, and hence I inferred that you must be feeling badly."

"Well, Major, you are right. I am feeling horribly. For two days I have been disturbed about my digestion, and the doctor has been giving me medicine, and I fear has given me morphine in his mixture, and the smallest quantity of it acts upon me as an irritant. And beside that, I have lost so much sleep that it affects me strangely; but I fully appreciate your kindness in speaking to me, and I will endeavor to gain my self control."

Magruder, Brent confirms, showed no animosity following the tête-à-tête, but his behavior unquestionably reverberated through the army, reaching Lee, who was in personal contact with him during the day, and no doubt to President Davis himself.[26]

Magruder's difficulties commenced when he was directed to march cross-country to join Theophilus H. Holmes on the New Market or James River road; that order was interrupted by a summons from Longstreet to reinforce him after Holmes, who had just arrived from south of the James, got into trouble with McClellan's lead units. Longstreet wanted Magruder's 13,000 men because he feared that Holmes would be overwhelmed "by the fire of thirty field guns and the gunboat batteries," which might threaten the entire Confederate advance. Lee's adjutant, Colonel Robert H. Chilton, found Magruder on the Darbytown Road and ordered him back toward Holmes on the James and immediately adjacent to a small rise on the otherwise flat peninsula called Malvern Hill; then more conflicting commands arrived from Lee and Longstreet, with Magruder himself galloping through the dense underbrush to sort out Paul J. Semmes's brigade, which had lost its way trying to reach Holmes. After a personal encounter with Lee amid the mounting confusion, he was directed to reinforce Longstreet along the Confederate left. "After night fell Magruder was called to relieve the troops on the front of my line," Longstreet writes. "His march during the day was delayed by his mistaken guide." Longstreet's charitable assessment notwithstanding, Magruder was at the front, making troop dispositions, until 3:00 A.M. Monday, and Brent is positive that he had no food the entire day. If he was not under enough pressure, a part of his command became intertwined with that of Jackson approaching from the north, although luckily no shots were exchanged.[27]

Already excited, Magruder was under tremendous pressure during June 30, and the biographer of 130 years later can only speculate that his frantic wish to reach the front fed his anxieties; when Lee filed his official battle summary, he simply stated that "Magruder who reached the Darbytown road, was ordered to re-enforce Holmes, but being at a greater distance than had been supposed, he did not reach the position of the latter in time for an attack." But when Prince John found himself under official scrutiny after the campaign and sought to justify his behavior throughout the Seven Days, Lee was a bit more generous with his old companion-in-arms: "General Magruder was ordered to relieve the troops under General Longstreet Monday night, June 30, after the latter had been operating all day, had repulsed the enemy, and won the position contended for." Lee added that the front "was clear" through the night, but that Magruder had been called forward "to have fresh troops to discover the enemy." Although Lee put him forward as the battle drew to a close, Magruder's command had again avoided the fray at Frayser's Farm when Longstreet, supported by A. P. Hill, had borne the brunt. At three-thirty on Monday morning, July 1, Magruder writes, Jackson appeared in person at his command post along Longstreet's front and assured him that reinforcements were near at hand. "I then slept an hour—the first in forty eight," he put in his report.[28]

During the night, McClellan had withdrawn his last units through White Oak Swamp and arranged them along the crest of Malvern Hill. The gentle rise, about 150 feet above the surrounding plain, was amphitheatrical in shape and not only a natural platform for McClellan to defend against the pursuing Confederates, but also within easy reach of the heavy naval guns lurking in the James. Two precipitous ravines on the eastern and western flanks of Malvern Hill meant that Lee would have to attack up the northern slope. In quick order, McClellan's artillery chief, Colonel Henry J. Hunt, who had been schooled by Magruder at Fort Leavenworth, arranged several hundred guns in tiers to rake every conceivable approach. It was a formidable defensive position in any soldier's book, but Lee had driven "those people"—his name for the enemy—over six days running, and he meant to destroy them before his adversaries could reach the safety of the federal navy. Lee's brigades were obliged to attack across open fields into Hunt's murderous crossfire, although Longstreet had convinced him that the Confederate batteries could "soften up" the federal lines. With the breaking dawn, Lee resolved to command his legions forward, but "confusion in the delivery of these orders meant that the attack was disjointed, with brigades advancing individually rather than together," writes the historian James McPherson. "This enabled Union artillery to pulverize nearly every attacking unit, allowing only a few enemy regiments to get close enough for infantry to cut them down."[29]

Magruder, Brent relates, was up before daylight without breakfast, when Lee rode into his bivouac; joined shortly by Jackson, the three generals planned their strategy amid great cheering as Lee and Jackson rode through the massed Confederate ranks. After calm had been restored, Lee unfolded a worn, misdrawn map to explain his movements, and Magruder's misfortunes for the remainder of the day started with a misunderstanding of the document. Lee's left was assigned to Jackson, newly arrived from White Oak Swamp; D. H. Hill had the center, while Magruder was instructed to march by a locally known route called the Quaker Road to form the right flank. Longstreet and A. P. Hill were held in reserve after the heavy fighting of June 28–30; Huger was told to fall in behind Magruder. "In a little while, the generals halted, and then General Lee, touching his cap, rode away. I doubt whether it was 10 A.M. when Jackson and Magruder rode back to regain their commands and make dispositions for the determined battle, which Genl. Lee had ordered," Brent continues. "Genl. Magruder was an energetic man, never delaying in the forming or execution of his plan, and in a very little time his staff and his division commanders were employed in making ready for the march." Despite his troubles on the thirtieth, Prince John lost no time in carrying out Lee's wishes.[30]

Up at an early hour, Magruder faced another grueling day, marked by confused orders not only from Lee's staff but also from Longstreet, who soon joined the fray; although it was later determined that Lee's map showed the Long Bridge Road as the Quaker Road, Magruder relied upon local guides to lead him down the latter. Jed Hotchkiss, a man who knew about maps, wrote that "it so happens that there are two roads in the region having the same name; he had taken the wrong one and finding out his mistake had countermarched, but did not reach the field of battle until late in the day." Afterward, when Magruder sought to defend himself from charges that he had joined the assault on Malvern Hill later than Lee anticipated, he submitted sworn affidavits from three local guides that he had proceeded along the correct path. "I am an enlisted man, member of the Henrico Southern Guards, was a resident of Henrico County; I was detailed to report on the morning of July 1, 1862, as a guide to Major-General Magruder; did so report, and was with him on that morning," asserts Private L. T. Gatewood. When Magruder marched out with S. B. Sweeny, another Henrico County man, as guide, he consulted Gatewood about the local roads. "I told him that [Quaker Road] left the Long Bridge road to the right and just above Nathan Enroughty's gate and ran diagonally across to the Charles City road, and that I indicated to him the same road as that along which he was afterward conducted by S. B. Sweeny." As he tramped southward with Sweeny and another guide named Watkins, Magruder soon realized his error—that he was marching away from Lee's point of attack.

The whole affair, according to Brent, served to confuse and agitate Magruder, and he reports that Longstreet suddenly rode unattended into his line of march:

> Genl. Magruder immediately explained his trouble, saying that there was an error somewhere. Longstreet said he thought so also, and Magruder asked him if he would give him an order to move back, but Longstreet said he could not give the order, but that he would say that Genl. Magruder was not moving in accordance with Genl. Lee's intention, and he that had passed the position it was intended for him to occupy.

Finally, on his own initiative, Magruder ordered his troops to retrace their steps. After a lapse of "two or three hours" he reached "a wood" on the right flank of Malvern Hill and deployed for combat. "What Genl. Lee said, I now well remember was that Magruder should advance upon 'the Quaker Road' [and not the Old Quaker Road]," Brent wrote forty years later in response to a correspondent who wanted to know about the "dearth of maps" during the Malvern Hill episode.[31]

Magruder reached the mark sometime after 4:00 P.M. and, following what amounted to a confrontation with Huger, who flatly refused to support his advance, moved against the enemy, reinforced by William "Little Billy" Mahone; although a part of Huger's command, Mahone, an intrepid fighter to the end of the war and later a United

States senator from Virginia, decided to act on his own and accompany Magruder into battle. Robert H. Chilton, apparently also acting on his own, again issued conflicting orders—Brent labels him a "marplot"—calling on Huger to move toward Jackson. Augmented by Mahone and Lewis A. Armistead—who fell dead the next year at Gettysburg—Magruder joined in Lee's uncoordinated piecemeal assaults on Malvern Hill. Like other units, his troops suffered a bloody repulse in the face of Hunt's guns. Billy Mahone verifies that the slaughter was awesome: "The brigade carried into this battle 93 commissioned officers and 1,133 non-commissioned officers and privates, and lost in killed 4 officers and 35 men; wounded 13 officers and 151 men; missing, 120 men."

Magruder was constantly in the field from 5:00 until 8:30 P.M., when darkness halted the uneven contest. "Round shot and grape crashed through the woods, and shells of enormous size, which reached far beyond the headquarters of our gallant commander-in-chief, burst amid the artillery parked in the rear," he wrote in his official report. "Belgian missiles and minié balls lent their aid to this scene of surpassing grandeur and sublimity. Amid all, our gallant troops in front pressed on to victory, now cheered by the rapid fire of friends on their left, as they had been encouraged in their advance by the gallant brigades on the right, commanded by Generals [Ambrose R.] Wright and Mahone." Magruder had a passion for the word "gallant" while describing the actions of his subordinates, but he was forced to conclude, "The enemy, from his strong position and great numbers, resisted stoutly the onset of our heroic bands, and bringing into action his heavy reserves, some of our men were compelled to fall back."[32]

Reinforced by troops from A. P. Hill's command (Wright's Brigade), Magruder by his own measure "concluded to let the battle subside and to occupy the field, which was done to within 100 yards of the enemy." The next morning, Brent writes, Prince John had no fear that McClellan would renew the fight; but, his trusted aide continues, "he looked badly, and he told me that he had hardly slept. Some of the veins in his face seemed swollen, and were absolutely purple, and he evidently suffered from the chilly weather." And when Brent carried an inconsequential dispatch to headquarters that rainy morning of July 2, Lee told him that Magruder "must not be discouraged," because the enemy was in rapid retreat toward his gunboats on the James.

Malvern Hill had been a bloody affair, and though Magruder came on the field later than Lee would have liked, he played a significant part in the commander's drive to crush McClellan and the Army of the Potomac. Confederate losses reached a staggering 5,300 men, while federal casualties totaled about 3,200. It was the concluding fight in the Seven Days campaign, and though Lee saved the capital and, indeed, was hailed as a hero by its inhabitants, he had not destroyed the Northern engine threatening the Southland. But when he saw that his adversaries no longer posed a threat, he not only began a general withdrawal from the peninsula, but also commenced preparations to move northward. And it was apparent from the start, as Stonewall Jackson, followed by Longstreet, took the van toward Cedar Mountain, the Second Manassas, and Antietam, that Magruder would have no place in the new fighting scheme. "I have determined to retain for the present in their present positions the commands of Magruder, Huger, D. H. Hill, and Ransom," Lee informed the president on July 3.[33]

Although charges amounting to cowardice and incompetency were soon hurled at him, Magruder had his new command in the West on his mind. On July 2, one day after Malvern Hill, he wrote to Secretary of War Randolph that he was ready to proceed, and it is apparent that extensive conversations with Davis took place about the assignment before his departure. The Trans-Mississippi had been and would remain a source of frustration for the Confederate president; this fact came to the fore during a heated exchange between Davis and General Sterling Price. A former Missouri lawyer/congressman as well as a popular soldier in the West, Price had traveled to Richmond during mid-June for a session with Davis in which he sought high command beyond the Mississippi. Upset that some of his Missouri troops had been summoned across the river for the Shiloh campaign, he nearly exploded when Davis retorted that "Price and his men for the time being must remain on the east side of the river for that is where they were most needed." Then, continues his biographer, "as for the Trans-Mississippi command, that had been assigned to Major General John Bankhead Magruder."

When Price stormed out of the presidential office, banging a table with his fist, Davis told a subordinate that the headstrong Missourian was "the vainest man he had ever met." Yet Davis had second thoughts about the influential Price, and recalled him within days for another interview. During that interval, Davis and/or Randolph must have conferred with Magruder, who was then preoccupied with McClellan's advance on Richmond. Not only was Price's resignation from the army rejected, but he was also told that General Braxton Bragg would return his Missouri troops at the earliest practical time. "In addition, Randolph informed him that he would be appointed second in command to Magruder in the Trans-Mississippi, and Magruder in turn promised to make an immediate and all-out effort to liberate Missouri." Thus Magruder, unaware that renewed difficulties in the peninsula fighting and continued intrigue about the Trans-Mississippi would cause him trouble, readily agreed to the presidential concessions for Price. Command of the vast Trans-Mississippi, a region stretching from the great river to the reaches of Texas, New Mexico, and Arizona, was a signal honor, and Prince John did not hesitate to seize the prize.[34]

A persistent and more serious problem, however, was Magruder's drinking. Major Brent was not the only person to notice the "purplish, swollen veins" in his face during the Malvern Hill combat. Lingering charges of alcoholism would not go away, and Magruder sought out a medical officer in one of the Georgia regiments when he was obliged to defend himself. "Concerning his condition in reference to intoxication, I can say most positively that if he was under the influence of liquor I failed entirely to see it, and from my knowledge of his usual appearance and manner . . . , had he been laboring under such influence I must have noticed it," testified Dr. E. J. Eldridge, who had been under Magruder's command for eight months. "I saw him again in the vicinity of the battlefield after the engagement was over . . . and assisted him in deciphering a badly-written order by candlelight, and noticed his calm deportment then, and am positive, as far as my judgment goes, that he had not even taken a drink—most certainly was not the least excited from any cause." When he reached Raleigh, North Carolina, on his journey to the West, a fragmented letter in the Duke University archive, dated July 17, notes his appearance two weeks later: "Strange as it may seem he did not have any fine trappings about him, no fine uniforms," writes an unidentified correspondent who speculates that he had been recalled to Richmond because of drunkenness. "He is noted for the amount of gold lace he can put on his uniforms. He looked gloomy, reserved and dignified."

While the Tarheel correspondent says nothing about strong drink at the time, Robert E. Lee's daughter-in-law verifies the prevalent notion about his departure for the Trans-Mississippi. "What do you think of Huger's being laid on the shelf? & poor McGruder? the [illegible] people say he is to be ct. marshalled for being drunk, at the time he ordered the charge in which Capt. Akinson [sic] was killed," Charlotte Wickham Lee, the wife of Rooney Lee, wrote on July 19. Although Lee had a particular fondness for Rooney's wife, mother of his first grandchild, she does not mention a conversation with her father-in-law following the battles before Richmond when he called on the family. The popular perception of Magruder aside, his journey to the Gulf Coast was halted abruptly when Davis telegraphed Brigadier General S. B. French, commanding at Wilmington, North Carolina, that Prince John should return immediately to confer with the president.[35]

Young Magruder. (1913 Year-Book of the American Clan Gregor Society; courtesy of the Mitchie Co., Charlottesville, Va.)

T. J. (Stonewall) Jackson during the Mexican War, when Magruder introduced him to the light artillery. (Courtesy of Massachusetts Commandry Military Order of the Loyal Legion and the U.S. Army Military History Institute)

Robert E. Lee, shortly after the Mexican War. (Courtesy of West Virginia State Archives)

Stonewall Jackson, 1862, around the time when he failed to assist Magruder during the Seven Days. (Courtesy of National Archives)

Popular wartime lithograph of Robert E. Lee. (Courtesy of Massachusetts Commandry Military Order of the Loyal Legion and the U.S. Army Military History Institute)

John Bankhead Magruder in civilian clothes. (Courtesy of
Massachusetts Commandry Military Order of the Loyal Legion
and the U.S. Army Military History Institute)

Joseph E. Johnston, Magruder's replacement on the lower peninsula. (Courtesy of Massachusetts Commandry Military Order of the Loyal Legion and the U.S. Army Military History Institute)

James Longstreet, who said Magruder had done the right thing on the peninsula. (Courtesy of Massachusetts Commandry Military Order of the Loyal Legion and the U.S. Army Military History Institute)

Sterling Price of Missouri, Jefferson Davis's reject for Magruder's command in the Trans-Mississippi. (Courtesy of the U.S. Army Military History Institute)

Jefferson Davis, President of the Confederacy, 1861–1865. (Courtesy of
Massachusetts Commandry Military Order of the Loyal Legion and the
U.S. Army Military History Institute)

E. Kirby Smith, Magruder's superior in the Trans-Mississippi.
(Courtesy of Massachusetts Commandry Military Order of the
Loyal Legion and the U.S. Army Military History Institute)

Francis R. Lubbock, Texas governor and warm supporter of Magruder.
(Courtesy of Archives Division, Texas State Library)

Hamilton P. Bee, Magruder's faithful subordinate throughout the Texas fighting. (Courtesy of Archives Division, Texas State Library)

John S. "Rip" Ford, an old Indian fighter who captured the Rio Grande Valley for Magruder. (Courtesy of Archives Division, Texas State Library)

John A. Wharton, shot dead in Magruder's Houston headquarters. (Courtesy of Massachusetts Commandry Military Order of the Loyal Legion and the U.S. Army Military History Institute)

Simon Bolivar Buckner, Magruder's fellow commander in Louisiana and his friend after the war. (Courtesy of Massachusetts Commandry Military Order of the Loyal Legion and the U.S. Army Military Order of the Loyal Legion and the U.S. Army Military History Institute)

Governor Pendleton Murrah, who withheld his Texas troops from Magruder, but accompanied him to Mexico following the surrender. (Courtesy of Archives Division, Texas State Library)

Confederate generals in Maximilian's Mexico. Standing: Magruder and
William R. Hardeman. Seated: left to right, Cadmus Wilcox, Sterling
Price, Thomas C. Hindman. (Courtesy of U.S. Army Military Institute)

White Sulphur Springs, West Virginia, 1869. Seated, left to right: Blacque Bey, Turkish minister to Washington; Robert E. Lee; millionaire George Peabody; banker W. W. Corcoran; Judge James Lyons of Virginia. Standing, left to right: Generals James Conner of South Carolina; Martin W. Gary of South Carolina; Magruder; Robert D. Lilley of Virginia; P. G. T. Beauregard of Louisiana; Alexander R. Lawton of Georgia; Henry A. Wise of Virginia; Joseph L. Brent of Louisiana. (Courtesy of Greenbrier Collection)

John Bankhead Magruder after the war. (Courtesy of Confederate Memorial Hall, New Orleans, Louisiana)

8

Galveston

UPON HIS RECALL TO RICHMOND in the last weeks of July, Magruder went into conference with Davis to learn that "a junior officer" had leveled charges of misconduct against him. Over the next weeks he constructed an elaborate defense for his actions during the Seven Days, complete with several pages of notarized testimonials from other campaign participants. The exercise was designed to demonstrate that he had not been under the influence of liquor and that his command decisions had been in compliance with higher authority. Although his report (August 13) and a follow-up (September 5) contain detailed accounts of his troop maneuvering, Magruder, as always, is most complimentary toward the officers and men under him. One can easily see why his staff and subordinates stayed so intensely loyal, even though his fellow commanders and superiors had differing views of his abilities. When Lee read the first document, he added a terse comment before forwarding the reports to the president: "He had many difficulties to contend with, I know. I regretted at the time and still regret that they should not have been more readily overcome." The popular notion that Magruder left Virginia because Lee wanted to be rid of him does not tell the whole story; he had been handed command of the Trans-Mississippi well before the Seven Days, and though he asked Lee to keep him for the campaign to save Richmond, he had started for the West before the accusations began to fly. And the fact remains that Jefferson Davis, a man who kept a close eye on the Confederate war machine, allowed him to proceed within days of Savage Station and Malvern Hill.[1]

Still, Magruder was obliged to linger in Richmond while Lee and the Army of Northern Virginia fought the titanic struggles at Second Manassas and Antietam without him. After the recall from the Trans-Mississippi, Magruder took no further part in the Virginia campaigns. By October 10, when orders were cut for him to take charge in Texas, Davis and the Confederate high command had obviously regained confidence in his talents; and he had other admirers who wanted his services. Governor Francis W. Pickens wanted him to command at Charleston, South Carolina, when John C. Pemberton was transferred to the West—a decision one scholar labels as the worst one that Jefferson Davis made during the war. Adjutant General Samuel Cooper, who visited South Carolina, recommended Magruder for the post, but Lee told the president that "Huger was the best man for the job." It is unclear whether Lee thought him unsuitable for the assignment, or whether he wanted him in Texas, far removed from the Army of Northern Virginia.[2]

The South Carolina prospect faded when Magruder did not press the issue, but awaited his fate in the capital; it is also apparent that Davis had second thoughts about placing him over the entire Western theater. When Earl Van Dorn, Davis's first commander in the West and a nephew of Andrew Jackson, heard about the appointment, he informed Richmond on July 9 that "I learned a day or two since that General Magruder has been ordered to command the Trans-Mississippi District, and immediately telegraphed to you not to send any one at present." Van Dorn, shot dead by an irate husband some months later, thought Sterling Price was a better prospect for the post because "the love of the people of Missouri is so strong for [him], and his prestige as a commander there so great, that wisdom would seem to dictate that he be put at the head of affairs in the west." Davis, unwilling to accept Van Dorn's recommendation, had already tapped Prince John, with Price as his second-in-command. That followed Van Dorn's transfer east of the river, and the appointment of General Thomas C. Hindman to command the department, but the Arkansan was not a West Point man—which, coupled with his questionable tactics, led to his replacement by Magruder. The outcry against Hindman prompted Van Dorn to warn against any appointment, while Magruder's troubles during the Seven Days led Davis to name his old friend and West Point classmate Theophilus Hunter Holmes to take over the entire Trans-Mississippi. The July 16 order, which directed Holmes to make his headquarters at Little Rock, was issued at the same time Magruder made his way back to Richmond.[3]

Three months after Holmes—who did not want the job—took charge, Magruder was named to command in Texas, replacing Brigadier General Paul Octave Hebert; his October 10 appointment, signed by Secretary of War Randolph, ordered him to establish a headquarters in San Antonio, ending his long wait at Richmond. Although Magruder decided to command from Houston, he found himself embroiled from the beginning in a difficult situation created in part by the unpopular Hebert, who had been forced to guard the state's 600-mile coastline with inadequate manpower and supplies; and he had been forced to make some hard choices while dealing with a near rebellion fomented by a large Unionist population as well as a sizable German contingent that did not share the Confederate vision of a slaveholding South. Hebert was a West Point man, class of 1840, but his command and administrative tactics proved anathema to the proud, individualistic Texans. Just twenty-five years earlier, Anglo stalwarts had defeated the Mexican armies of Santa Anna, and now many of those very men were confronted with a disagreeable leader of French ancestry. "What they found most repulsive about him was the fact that he was 'a man of no military force or practical genius' who 'preferred red-top boots, and a greased rat-tail moustache, with a fine equipage, and a fine suit of waiters, to the use of good, practical common sense,' " finds historian Stephen Oates. "Because they abhorred his European red-tapism and because they suspected him of cowardice, they became tired and disgusted with him and began to complain." Governor Francis R. Lubbock, who later went to Richmond as an adviser to President Davis, was moved to write: "In response to the general desire for a change in military commanders, The Confederate States government finally sent us Gen. J. Bankhead Magruder, of Virginia."[4]

For all of his faults in Texan eyes, Hebert sought to cope with hostile segments in the state by a proclamation of martial law—but in doing so he managed to alienate loyal Confederates as well. "Every white male person above the age of sixteen years, being temporarily or otherwise, within the aforesaid limits [of Texas], shall upon a summons issued by the provost marshal, promptly present himself . . . to have his name, residence, and occupation registered, and furnish such information, as may be required of him," reads Hebert's document of May 30, 1862, issued nine months after he assumed command. Any effort to circumvent Confederate authority, he continued, would be "dealt with summarily." Otherwise, "non-interference with the rights of loyal citizens, or with the usual routine of business, or with the usual administration of the law will be permitted except when necessary to enforce the provisions of this Proclamation." While thousands of Texans enthusiastically embraced the Stars and Bars, serving with valor under John Bell Hood, Benjamin Franklin Terry, Henry E. McCulloch, and other Southern leaders, thousands more either joined the Union army or flaunted Confederate authority. It was the latter recalcitrants and shirkers that Hebert sought to contain, and Magruder himself was afterwards forced to grapple with open hostility and insurrection by reimposing martial law in several German counties around LaGrange, Texas, to stop rampant evasion of Confederate conscription laws.[5]

In November 1860, when the pro-slavery presidential candidate, John C. Breckinridge of Kentucky, carried the state by 47,000 votes, against 15,400 for John Bell, the Constitutional Union standard bearer, Governor Sam Houston, ever the quintessential Texan but stout Union man, had been hounded into summoning the legislature dominated by Confederates, which in turn authorized a secession convention. Although Houston attempted to circumvent the extremists by stalling as long as he could, because he knew that otherwise he "would be asking for hot-headed action and certain secession," the convention assembled on January 28. By a lopsided vote, the secessionist-dominated gathering overrode a small, determined minority that fought to keep Texas in the Union and rammed through an Ordinance of Secession two days later. Then, in rapid succession, a popular referendum confirmed the convention's mandate and by March 5, 1861, Texas had been formally admitted to the infant Confederate States of America. No matter that nearly 15,000 Texans had voted to remain under the old flag. But when the secession convention adopted a resolution that all state officeholders take an oath in support of the new scheme, Sam Houston balked.[6]

On that fateful day, March 5, Houston retired to the executive mansion in Austin and went to his bedroom on the "upper floor, removed his coat and vest and remained alone throughout the night during which he did not sleep," records his daughter. "Instead he walked the floor of his bedroom and upper hall in his sock feet, wrestling with his spirit as Jacob wrestled the angel until the purple dawn shone over the eastern hills." The next morning Houston told his wife that he "would never do it," and resigned in favor of Lieutenant Governor Edward Clark, who took over the reins of government. While the rapidly aging Houston, who later warmed to Magruder's handling of Confederate Texas, withdrew quietly to his home in Huntsville, plenty of Union sympathizers and others challenged the new regime from the outset.

Prominent Unionists like E. J. Davis and A. J. "Jack" Hamilton left the state, as others commenced what amounted to civil disobedience. "As the war progressed, the fringe of the frontier became the gathering place of a furtive, migratory population of Unionists, pacifists, and of deserters, intermixed with the ever-present scattering of renegades," notes one scholar. "They congregated across Red River in Indian Territory, in the back country of Denton and Wise counties 'where Union sentiment was strong,' farther west along the Wichita Rivers, and to the south on the headwaters of the Concho. From these stations, they were able to commit scattered depredations, and more serious, to keep outlying communities in constant fear of their disastrous raids." Unlike older, more settled parts of the Confederacy, the vast, sparsely peopled portions of Texas afforded hundreds of hiding places for those opposed to the Stars and Bars. First Van Dorn and Hebert, followed by Magruder during his tenure in Texas, found it necessary to contain the dissidents. And more than a few blacks suspected of aiding the Unionists were brutally executed or lynched by frightened Confederates, including one poor fellow accused of attempting "to poison 'war widows' whose husbands were in the service." Opposition to Confederate rule became so widespread that General Ben McCulloch posted a notice throughout his subdistrict in North Texas during July 1862 that read, "All disloyal persons and persons whose expressions, conduct, or presence is regarded as injurious to the interests of the Government of the Confederate States, will be arrested."[7]

According to federal pension records, "an estimated 2,132 whites and 47 Negroes from Texas sought and found service in the Union armies." Mostly they fled the state during the war to serve in a cavalry unit raised primarily in New Orleans by Edmund Jackson Davis, a man Magruder would get to know well following his arrival on the Gulf Coast. A native of St. Augustine, Florida, he was described as "a tall, slender, graceful sort of man, six feet two and a half inches, of fair complexion and possessing a rather fine face and delicate blue eyes suggesting a generous character." Once settled in the Lone Star, Davis became a practicing attorney, and in 1861, when Texas left the Union, he was serving as district judge at Brownsville, in the lower Rio Grande Valley. Identifying himself with the Unionist cause from the beginning, Davis traveled to New Orleans by way of Mexico, where he formed the First Texas Cavalry, composed, said the Confederates, of "refugees and renegades." Later, after Magruder emerged victorious in the Battle of Galveston, he learned to his disgust that Davis and the First Texas had been aboard the USS *Cambria*, which narrowly escaped capture off the Galveston bar. "The vessel, which contained E. J. Davis and many other apostate Texans, besides several hundred troops and 2,500 saddles for use of the negative sympathizers, succeeded in making her escape," Magruder informed Richmond after the incident. Although Davis remained the most prominent Texan in the federal army, reaching general rank, other units were commanded by John L. Haynes, who, like Davis, became a leader in Reconstruction Texas. In a strange twist, when the "apostate Texans" became political leaders after the war, Davis was serving as governor and chief of the state's infant Republican party at the same time Magruder spent his last, sad days in a Houston hotel.[8]

Another source of trouble for the Texas secessionists was the state's numerous German population. German settlers—primarily from the Rhineland—began filtering into the state during Mexican rule, and encouraged by Sam Houston, the flow continued under the Texas Republic, 1836–1845; with the backing of immigration societies or unions, the migration continued until the eve of secession; indeed, additional Germans entered the state throughout the nineteenth century. By the outbreak of the Civil War, several thousand Germans had settled in the hill country west of a line extending through San Antonio, Seguin, and Austin; and numbers more were situated farther east in the San Bernard, Colorado, Lavaca, and Guadalupe watersheds. Several counties with significant German populations reached almost to Magruder's Houston headquarters. By and large, the Germans had not been assimilated into the dominate Southern culture with the outbreak of hostilities, so that they opposed slavery and secession almost to the man. Those who streamed into the region after the abortive revolutions of 1848 to establish a liberal constitution in the German states were especially strident in their opposition to the Confederacy and its conscription laws. Hundreds left the state to form the backbone of Davis's First Cavalry, while many others joined the resistance at home.

As Magruder awaited his fate in Richmond, German antipathy to Confederate Texas reached a climax in something called the Battle of the Nueces, on August 10, 1862. On that occasion a company of sixty-five Unionists from the German communities around Fredericksburg and Comfort, commanded by Fritz Tegener, were headed for Mexico when they were run down by "ninety-four mounted Confederates." The ensuing melee soon turned into outright slaughter. "One survivor said that after the first Confederate charge had been repelled, only six effective Germans were left to meet subsequent onslaughts," reports a battle chronicler. "Major Tegener was wounded early in the battle but escaped capture. At the conclusion of the encounter the number of German dead was approximately thirty with twenty wounded." Although Lieutenant C. D. McRae, in charge of the Confederate troopers, sent to Fort Clark, a few miles northward, where Magruder had commanded eight years earlier, for medical help, "the Germans were left unburied, 'prey to the buzzards and coyotes.'" Not content with the massacre, in which several Confederates were also killed, Confederate soldiers executed a number of the wounded Germans on the spot.

Already enraged with the secessionists—one leader had branded them "a bunch of damned abolitionists"—the German resistance hardened its stance as word of the massacre spread across the Lone Star. Besides the troubles around Fayette County and LaGrange, its county seat, that confronted Magruder during January 1863, the upheaval among the German counties remained widespread. "Eyewitnesses described a meeting of more than five hundred at Roeder's Mill (Austin County) at about the same time," records Claude Elliot. "The Germans are concentrating at Frelsburg (Colorado County) with the avowed purpose of resisting conscription," said another account. Similar incidents bombarded Magruder from the moment he relieved Hebert, creating an insolvable dilemma. Confederate authorities could do little more than declare martial law and hope for the best, although the Germans at large never embraced the Confederacy.[9]

Surely the most notorious backlash against the Texas Unionists took place in a vigilante atmosphere during October 1862, as Magruder made his way west. "The Great Hanging at Gainesville," the county seat of Cooke County on the northern border with the Indian Territory, grew out of something called "the Peace Party Conspiracy." After the state legislature created several districts in late 1861 to police internal security, Brigadier General William Hudson became suspicious of pro-Union activity in his command, which covered eighteen north Texas counties, most of them having cast an antisecession vote. A mole was sent to infiltrate a clandestine group that had its own secret handshake and passwords. Acting on information fed to them, Confederate military units rounded up "sixty to seventy men throughout the district and jailed them at Gainesville, but six or seven miles south of Red River." A hastily summoned jury of twelve townsmen, writes historian Sam Acheson, "tried and found guilty thirty-nine of those charged with conspiracy and insurrection, disloyalty and treason, or a combination of such charges." Thomas Barrett, one of the jurors forced to flee the county because of hatreds originating out of the affair, tells what happened next:

> The time for the hanging arrived, and I left the prison. I took my seat at the northeast corner of the square, for I knew that the men would be hauled in a wagon down California Street to that old historic tree, which is now dead (1885) and lies still where it has been hauled as the bodies of the men who were hung on its long limbs lie in the grave.
>
> I had not been there long, till I saw the death wagon coming with two of the prisoners. I saw men with guns on each side of the wagon guarding, to prevent escape, and see that the hanging was done, and this continued until late in the evening before the last one was hung. . . .

Barrett had no stomach for the actual executions, and he says he did not watch the gruesome business; he considered any attempt to save the accused as "hopeless," demonstrating anew that Confederate Texas was not only a divided place but also one that meant to crush opposition to the Southern war effort.[10]

Meanwhile, Major General John Bankhead Magruder wound up his affairs in Richmond by saying farewell to members of his old staff who had not been assigned to the fighting in northern Virginia. One week after his October 10 appointment, Prince John received a note of appreciation from Major William Norris, a longtime member of his official family. "A congress knife" accompanied the letter as a going-away present from his peninsula associates. "I know I could not speak with a distinct voice my grateful acknowledgments for the unvarying kindness and appreciation, which, during the past year, I have received at your hands," wrote his former signal officer. Although several staff members joined him in Texas, others did not. Major Brent moved to a post in Louisiana, while Norris remained at the war office in Richmond as chief of the Signal Bureau.[11]

Magruder had reached Mobile, Alabama, by October 30, where he wrote to his kinsman, Major Smith P. Bankhead, about a command in Texas. Bankhead, who subsequently took over one of his Texas subdistricts on the western frontier, with his headquarters at San Antonio, was admonished to contact General Leonidas K. Polk, under whom he was serving at Jackson, Mississippi. Get Polk's recommendation, Magruder added, and "go with it to Richmond & urge your claims & say to Mr. Randolph that I want you with me—I will write to him today." The ploy must have worked, because Bankhead was in charge at San Antonio by April 1863. Since Magruder told Bankhead to write him at Vicksburg, he reached Texas by way of Arkansas and the Indian Territory. With New Orleans under the control of his old adversary Benjamin F. Butler, it was not feasible to reach the state by the normal sea routes to Galveston and Indianola. Magruder entered the state by the old Central National Road, established fifteen years earlier to connect the infant Republic of Texas with St. Louis. Whether he conferred with Theophilus H. Holmes is not clear, but within months he would dispatch some of his Texas units over the same route to bolster John C. Pemberton's defense of Vicksburg. When he did reach the Lone Star, Magruder chose to ignore his Richmond instructions and established his headquarters at Houston— probably with Holmes's approval, "until further notice."[12]

While Confederate newspapers across the state, as well as most politicians, greeted his coming with enthusiasm, his old nemesis had followed him westward. "Some persons are fearful that Gen. Magruder . . . is incapacitated for energetic attention to business by reason of drunkenness," editorialized the *Dallas Herald* on November 29. The piece—reproduced from the *Houston Telegraph*—relates that a group of Virginia parents had petitioned President Davis to remove him from command at Big Bethel, lest their sons be corrupted by his imbibing. When Davis forwarded the remonstrance to him, the story goes on, Magruder "from that day to this has not drank an intoxicating draught." If true, the *Herald* continued, "it speaks volumes for his head and heart." The pro-Confederate organ was likewise confident that Magruder had with him stands of small arms and several artillery batteries to strengthen the state's defenses.[13]

The Dallas paper may have been a bit optimistic, because Thomas North, a traveler through Texas who visited Houston during this period, labeled him as "the gay, dashing, festive, Magruder"; other indications abound that Prince John enjoyed the high life in both Texas and Arkansas before the Confederate collapse of 1865. North, however, is emphatic that his demeanor "suited Texas," and John Salmon "Rip" Ford, the old Indian fighter who served Magruder on the Rio Grande, reports that when word spread across the state that he was coming, it was worth an additional 50,000 men. "Professor Frenzel," in a patriotic outburst, even composed a new march to commemorate his arrival; and Magruder unquestionably exhibited a positive, go-get-'em attitude from the beginning. When a group of "wealthy Texas planters" presented him with "a noble charger," Magruder not only thanked them in a public letter, but also said what the state wanted to hear: "Sustained by the confidence of Texas, I do not doubt the repulse of the enemy from every portion of her soil. . . . This holy influence—the inspiration of mothers, wives, and daughters—has given our cause an irresistible strength," he touted after less than a week in Houston. And he would fight to safeguard their homes. "With you and with them is my whole heart—the honor of our country and the public safety my only thought, and such abilities as I possess will be devoted to their preservation, with unwearied energy and entire confidence of success."[14]

After finding that he "belonged partly to that class of men whose genius, being unshackled, was capable of achieving the most brilliant result; but when overshadowed by authority became paralyzed," A. L. Long confesses that Magruder's zeal won him "the confidence and affection of the Texans." And though Prince John remained outwardly exuberant in his public utterances and gathered some initial successes, he soon encountered the hard realities of holding Texas for the new nation. By year's end he called for what amounted to a scorched-earth policy when he issued "a proclamation to the citizens of Texas calling upon those living on the coast to remove at once all of their property of every description that can be moved." Then, one week after his capture of Galveston on New Year's Day, 1863, he informed Richmond, "There are about 12,000 men organized in this state, about 6,000 armed, and these indifferently." He found that the sheer size of the place made it impossible to administer, much less defend, with the troops at hand. Magruder, like Confederate commanders elsewhere, began demanding additional men and supplies as well as "competent officers" to oversee the reinforcements. And to his dismay, he learned that "disaffection in this country was greater than had been related to me."

A veritable checklist of difficulties confronted him from the start, and more than grand rhetoric would be required to hold the enemy at bay. In addition to the deteriorated military situation with the federals at Galveston and threatening other coastal locations, widespread opposition to the Confederate draft required his immediate attention. The pervasive lack of manpower rendered him nearly helpless to combat Yankee forays into the state, and Governor Lubbock as well as other Texas politicos resisted efforts to transfer state troops to other parts of the Confederacy. The Rio Grande border was virtually denuded of men with chaotic caciques threatening from across the river in northern Mexico, as well as the French occupation further south. On the far frontier, Indians were a constant menace, compounded by an ongoing debate between Richmond and Austin about how to handle the problem. An equal dilemma for Confederate Texas was the necessity of keeping the cotton trade flowing into Mexico from the state, and indeed from Arkansas and Louisiana as well, to ensure the receipt of vital war supplies from abroad, coming back across the

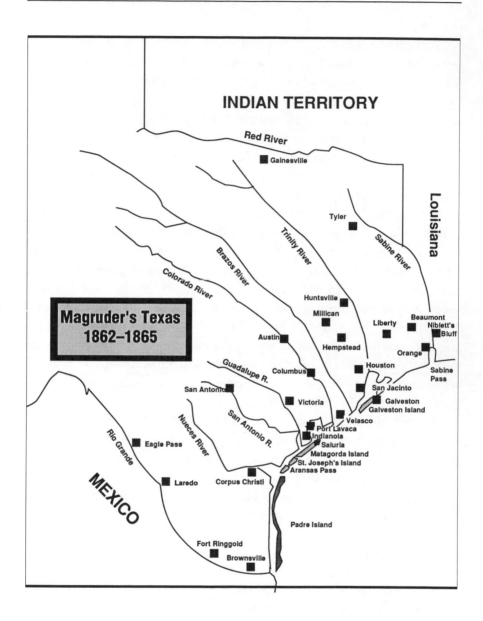

INDIAN TERRITORY

Red River

■ Gainesville

Louisiana

Tyler ■

Trinity River

Sabine River

Brazos River

Colorado River

Huntsville ■

Millican ■

Liberty ■

Beaumont ■

Niblett's Bluff ■

Magruder's Texas 1862–1865

Austin ■

Hempstead ■

Orange ■

Guadalupe R.

Columbus ■

Houston ■

Sabine Pass

San Antonio ■

Victoria ■

San Jacinto ■

Galveston ■

Galveston Island

San Antonio R.

Velasco ■

Port Lavaca ■

Nueces River

Indianola ■

Eagle Pass ■

Saluria

Rio Grande

Matagorda Island

St. Joseph's Island

Aransas Pass

Laredo ■

Corpus Christi ■

MEXICO

Padre Island

Fort Ringgold ■

Brownsville ■

border. In the months ahead, Magruder would be called upon to deal with these and other threats, including relations with worrisome foreign consuls at Galveston and Brownsville.[15]

Magruder quickly set about the task of organizing his command to meet a renewed thrust at the Texas coast by Nathaniel P. Banks, who had replaced Butler at New Orleans. Prince John's Order No. 1, issued November 29, 1862, directed every subordinate officer to send an accurate accounting of his troops, including Sibley's Brigade, despite its disastrous attempt to plant the Confederate banner in New Mexico and Arizona; Colonel Henry Hopkins Sibley, West Point class of 1838, a Louisiana native and inventor of the famed Sibley tent, led an abortive expedition into the Santa Fe country during 1861 and early 1862. Although he routed the federals under his brother-in-law, E. R. S. Canby, in the so-called Battle of Valverde, and was successful in reaching both Albuquerque and Santa Fe, he was unable to hold his gains. After "a slow and painful retreat" back into Texas, Sibley and his men were not only removed from Magruder's command, but also ordered to Louisiana. Fortunately, part of his brigade had not marched for its new posting, and was able to assist in the pending defense of Galveston. Magruder's initial order also named his headquarters staff, which included Captain Edward P. Turner, who remained by his side to the very end, as adjutant, along with Major A. G. Dickinson. His nephew, George junior, who followed him from Virginia, served as aide-de-camp.[16]

Magruder had been in Houston less than a week when he informed Adjutant General Cooper that "an expedition has sailed from New York for Texas," and that additional men and artillery were necessary to repel the invaders. At the urging of Abraham Lincoln, the federals had indeed been aiming at the Texas coast for several months. Not only Lincoln but also Secretary of War Edwin Stanton had urged a new force into the Gulf under the command of Nathaniel P. Banks, Massachusetts politico and onetime speaker of the House of Representatives, with the dual purpose of threatening the French in Mexico and establishing a foothold in Texas as a means to encourage its Unionist population. Accompanying this mass of men and ships was Andrew Jackson "Jack" Hamilton, a confidant of Lincoln, recently named military governor of Texas. Hamilton, an Alabama native, had been a lawyer/politician in Texas for fifteen years at the outbreak of the Civil War; moreover, he held a seat in the Thirty-fifth Congress that he refused to give up when the state withdrew from the Union in February 1861. As a staunch Union man, he gained the president's attention as early as March, and he even embarked on a speaking tour across upstate New York in support of Lincoln's war policies. Although Banks was reluctant to move so hastily, it was largely through Hamilton's badgering that he ordered the Galveston expedition of late December 1862.[17]

Shortly after Lincoln's proclamation of April 18, 1861, creating a naval blockade of Southern ports, authorities at Galveston began erecting breastworks and drilling the local militia. Federal blockaders appeared at random intervals through early 1861, and on August 3 the island was shelled by Yankee warships. An effective blockade continued until May 15, 1862, when Captain Henry Eagle, commanding the federal force off the city, demanded its surrender. Although Hebert advised Colonel J. J. Cook, the local commander, to surrender and evacuate the place, the Confederates held their ground until the invasion threat passed. Hebert thereupon imposed martial law, requiring all males between the ages of eighteen and fifty-five to register for military service. The sweeping edict came in the wake of a mass exodus to the mainland by frightened civilians; expecting an artillery duel to erupt between Cook's defenders and Eagle's flotilla, hundreds had fled in the aftermath. "This expectation was strengthened by an order for all non-combatants to leave the island in a given time," observes Thomas North. "The next few days witnessed a general stampede of people and valuables up country, the writer and his family with the multitude, to save them from the dangers of flying shot and shell. Every available vehicle was brought into requisition to convey people and goods from the city. Anything that could freight a thousand pounds or more, could easily command five dollars a load, four miles to the bridge where the cars stopped."[18]

The naval quarantine continued, in spite of an occasional blockade runner, until October 4, 1862, when the federals moved to end the stalemate. A new Union commander, William H. Renshaw, reinforced by additional vessels, sent the steamer *Harriet Lane* into the harbor under a white flag, demanding the surrender of Cook and his garrison. Although Hebert, who had been ordered to transfer the bulk of his command to Arkansas, still counseled withdrawal from the island, a four-day truce was arranged, under which, according to Joel Hoovestol, "all who wanted to go were now removed from Galveston and virtually all machinery of any value was taken away."

But the Confederates never totally abandoned the city; "communication with the Island was maintained by planking over the railroad bridge and protecting it on the island side were a redoubt and rifle-pits, occupied by a detachment of infantry and artillery," writes Xavier Blanchard DeBray, commanding officer of the 26th Texas. His command, "ordered to Virginia Point, by frequent patrols, day and night, satisfied the Federals that we still claimed the city and prevented them from visiting it." Federal reinforcements were landed, DeBray continues, "on one of the wharves and took quarters in its warehouses, strongly barricading themselves, but they never ventured into the city." By December 29, Colonel Isaac Burrell was forced to admit that he controlled the place only in daytime; at night, he told his superiors in New Orleans, "owing to our small force (as the balance of my regiment has not yet arrived), I am obliged to draw in the pickets to the wharf on which we are quartered." Contrary to the estimates of Thomas North, Burrell reported 3,000 Galvestonians still on the island after Cook's evacuation.[19]

Meanwhile, North continues, Magruder "saw that Texas expected him to retrieve the disgraceful loss of Galveston, Metropolis of the state." Forgetting about pressing civil and administrative matters, Prince John, eager to regain his tarnished image from the peninsula, traveled to Virginia Point, opposite the island, within two days of his arrival, for a personal inspection of Galveston and its occupiers. Following a visit to his Houston headquarters by Governor Lubbock, who urged action, Magruder bent his energies to recapturing the island city. In rapid order, slaves were removed from the coast; fearful lest Confederate cotton fall into enemy hands, it too was shipped inland. Besides summoning every available trooper, Magruder had lighthouses destroyed at Pass Cavallo, Padre Island, and Saluria on Matagorda Island, as a hindrance to an anticipated naval incursion. At Port Lavaca, which had been shelled by federal ships in November, extra precautions were taken, including demolition of the railroad to Victoria about thirty miles to the west. Magruder also informed Theophilus Holmes at Little Rock on December 15 that he had acted to ensure a steady flow of cotton into Mexico, that he would impress

wagons to freight government cotton, and as a means of thwarting unscrupulous buyers and traders, he had ordered every bale stopped at
the Rio Grande that did not have General Hamilton P. Bee's stamp of
approval.[20]

Magruder was a busy man through the last days of December as
he prepared to act; on the twentieth of the month he issued a popular appeal, in which, in the words of Lubbock, he exhorted the state
"to fight to the last extremity, and showing, by a review of [Benjamin
F.] Butler's rule in Louisiana, that no submission, however abject,
would save them from insult and spoliation of property, if the enemy
were permitted to once gain control of the State. 'The line of the
seaboard, from Sabine to the Colorado,' said he, 'must be held at all
hazards.' " Mostly he concentrated on military preparations for a combined land-sea strike at the federals in Galveston. "A few miles below the city of Houston, on Buffalo Bayou, at a point of narrows,
where the huge forest trees on either bank locked arms across the
waters, and the ever creeping old ivy, might have been seen three or
four old steamer hulks being transformed into rams and gun-boats,
whose sides were barricaded with compressed cotton bales," North
relates poetically. When completed, Magruder's fleet was composed
of two refurbished vessels: the *Bayou City*, which boasted a thirty-two-
pound rifled gun; and the smaller *Neptune*, fitted out with two twenty-
four-pounders. After a month of feverish, often secret preparations,
Magruder was ready to strike on the night of December 31. Good
Confederates said he gave Texas a New Year's present.[21]

Magruder had a rough idea of the pending battle because he had
already been in the city; when he visited Virginia Point during the
first week in December, he had taken a squad of eighty troopers into
Galveston proper, under cover of darkness, for a thorough inspection
of the enemy's defenses. The Confederates knew what they were up
against on that New Year's Eve, and, wrote Colonel DeBray, "all dispositions having been perfected on land and water, on the 31st of December, by nightfall, the column was set in motion to Galveston, over
the railroad bridge, on a six-mile silent march by a dim moonlight."
Magruder himself was surprised that Burrell had left the two-mile-
long railroad span intact, although the federals probably did not have
the manpower to destroy it. Major Leon Smith, commanding the
naval expedition, had been instructed by telegraph to commence his

thirty-mile voyage down Buffalo Bayou and across Galveston Bay, while Magruder personally led the land assault.

The attacking force of nearly 4,000 men, composed of units under J. J. Cook, William R. Scurry, and H. H. Sibley, was under the overall command of General Tom Green. A railroad flatcar had been fitted out with an eight-inch Dahlgren and moved "to a point within a few hundred yards of the *Harriet Lane*" and the federal gunboats in the harbor; because Burrell had barricaded his men into "Kuhn's Wharf at the end of Eighteenth Street" and destroyed the passageway leading to it, Magruder had fifty specially constructed scaling ladders to help his troops reach the enemy. Besides "entrenching tools" to build breastworks opposite the harbor as protection against the northern fleet, "a large quantity of cotton bales" accompanied the attackers. "In addition I had fourteen fieldpieces, some of them rifled and some of them smooth-bore," Magruder wrote later, to augment his six large guns, the largest of which weighed 5,400 pounds. "Three of the heaviest of the siege guns had to be transported 9 miles, the others 7 miles, between sunset and 12 o'clock, under cover of darkness over very difficult roads." When all was ready, Prince John's guns and men extended about two and a half miles from Fort Point, at the northernmost tip of the island, to the western limit of the city, along the railroad from the mainland.[22]

On Magruder's extreme right—opposite Fort Point, about two miles away, was Captain Sidney T. Fontaine, supported by several "dismounted dragoons" from Lawrence T. Pyron's command; in the city proper he placed the railroad ram, also on his right, "at the upper wharf." George R. Wilson's battery of six fieldpieces was in front of the "center wharf," while J. J. Cook, with 500 men, was placed opposite Kuhn's Wharf, where Burrell was ensconced in an abandoned warehouse with 264 men and officers of the 42nd Massachusetts Infantry. Cook was supported by William H. Griffin's battery and several dozen sharpshooters. Lieutenant Colonel J. H. Manly held the far left, guarding the bridge to Virginia Point. Spread out across the city was a reserve force under General W. R. Scurry, who had marched with Sibley on the ill-fated expedition into New Mexico. At the attack, Magruder's force pointed toward the mainland and the enemy fleet in Galveston Harbor. Facing him at nearly point-blank range beyond the wharves was Renshaw's fleet of six federal gunboats: "the

Westfield, flagship with six guns, another converted ferry boat, the *Clifton*, with eight heavy cannon, an altered merchant ship, *Sachem*, mounting five guns, the *Owasco*, only regular warship of the fleet, armed with four cannon, a small schooner with one gun, the *Corypheus*," in addition to the *Harriet Lane*, mounting five heavy guns.[23]

With the approach of battle, according to Lieutenant L. J. Storey, Magruder must have been once more in an agitated state; as Storey, who later served as lieutenant governor of Texas, urged his own unit into position, he was overtaken by Prince John and Colonel DeBray, accompanied by several staff officers.

> When General Magruder in a most abrupt and commanding voice spoke to me as no southern gentleman would have spoken to his negro [*sic*] and as I had never been spoken to in my life before, and asked, "Who are you, sir, and what are you doing here?" I replied in the same tone of voice: "I am Lieutenant Storey, sir, in command of this advanced guard, placed here by order of General Magruder, delivered to me by Col. DeBray, sir." He replied in a very pleasant voice: "All right, lieutenant, proceed cautiously" and rode away.

In the predawn hours, Magruder personally torched the center gun as a signal for the general assault; four years after the war, he told his adversary, Burrell, now a general, that "it was a 6 or 12 lb ball, which passed through the house where your men usually slept." No matter that Burrell had moved his force to safer quarters, the formidable firepower of Renshaw's fleet was aroused by that opening shot.[24]

Burrell's sentries had already detected what appeared to be Confederate troop movements, and the Massachusetts infantrymen on Kuhn's Wharf plainly heard puffing locomotives as men and supplies rolled into position. While moonlight silhouetted both armies, Magruder says it had disappeared before he fired the first shot, although "the still light of the stars enabled us to see the Federal ships." Subsequent scholarship indicates the moon went down that first day of January 1863 shortly after 2:00 A.M., and that the battle commenced afterward, probably at around four o'clock. Whatever the precise moment, Magruder himself tells what happened next: "The enemy did not hesitate long in replying to our attack. He soon opened from his fleet with a tremendous discharge of shell, which was followed by grape and canister. Our men, however, worked steadily at their guns under cover of darkness." Meanwhile, Cook's command plunged into the federals on the wharf, only to discover that their scaling ladders were too short for the job. Following a stubborn contest in which Confederate sharpshooters had been posted on both flanks to distract Burrell's men, the attackers were forced to withdraw.

Although Magruder's motley contingent kept banging away at the bluecoats, a concentrated fire from the superior naval guns caused his gunners and infantrymen to seek cover. "As daylight, which was now approaching, would expose these men still more to the enemy's fire, and as our gunboats had not yet made their appearance, I ordered the artillery to be withdrawn to positions which afforded more protection, but from which the fire could be continued on the adversary with greater advantage to us," the euphoric commander put in his official report. General Scurry took over the artillery pullback, as Magruder commenced preparations "for the immediate fortification and occupation of the city." No matter that his hastily assembled force—he even had adventure-seeking civilian volunteers joining the attack—was being pounded by the federal ships, Magruder had come to stay, and stay he would; one of his gentleman volunteers was John R. Baylor, the governor of Confederate Arizona, who served at one of the fieldpieces. At the critical moment, however, "Magruder's navy" steamed across the bay and changed the course of battle.[25]

When Leon Smith appeared with the Confederate ships, the *Bayou City*, with her "cotton armor" and hundred-man force, was commanded by Captain Henry Lubbock, brother of Texas governor Francis R. Lubbock; a company of sharpshooters armed with shotguns and assorted rifles—some of then brought from Virginia by Magruder—was also on board. The *Neptune*, also cotton-clad, carried 150 men, sharpshooters from Sibley's command, "all of the brigade having stepped forward as volunteers anxious to take part in the affair." Two other ships, "the *Lady Gwinn* and the *John F. Carr*, accompanied the expedition as tenders. On the *Carr* were a number of troops and volunteers; and on the *Gwinn* a number of spectators who were prepared to take part if necessary," writes a naval historian. "The cutter *Dodge* and the *Royal Yacht* were present but did not take part in the fight." Smith did not waver for a moment, but sent the *Bayou City* straight at the *Harriet Lane*, which, along with the *Owasco*, had sent the "hail of iron" into Galveston that had caused Magruder's land force to give ground. With every sharpshooter emptying his piece, the *Bayou City* commenced firing at the *Lane* with her thirty-two-pounder, which knocked a hole in the vessel's side; but the rifled gun soon exploded, killing Captain A. R. Weir and several others standing nearby. The ship's pilot thereupon decided to use her as a ram, although a "strong ebb-tide" caused him to miss the *Lane*, nearly dead in the water for lack of steam.[26]

The *Harriet Lane*, centerpiece of the Yankee task force, was next rammed by the *Neptune*, although the Confederate ship was also damaged by the impact and by the *Lane*'s guns. The ill-fated cotton-clad was soon scuttled near the harbor, where she went down in eight feet of water without serious loss of life. Before she sank, however, the *Neptune* joined in a final thrust at the *Lane* when the *Bayou City* made a second attack, ramming the sidewheeler with a force that locked the two vessels together. Riflemen on board both Confederate vessels— protected by their cotton barriers—poured such a fire into the *Lane* that surrender was immediate. Among the dead were the commander, J. M. Wainwright, and Lieutenant Edward Lea, son of Major A. M. Lea, Magruder's old friend from West Point; young Lea had remained in the federal navy at the outbreak of war. The body was removed to Magruder's headquarters in Galveston before burial in the Episcopal Cemetery, where Magruder himself would be laid to rest eight years later. Wainright and Lea were buried together "with appropriate honors, in the presence of many officers of both armies and many citizens, all of whom expressed their deep sympathy with the bereaved father, who said the solemn service of the Episcopal Church for the burial of the dead."[27]

Meanwhile, as the Confederates worked to haul the *Harriet Lane* to shore in order that the dead and wounded might be removed, a three-hour truce was called after Magruder's emissaries to Commodore Renshaw demanded a surrender of the remaining enemy ships. But Renshaw had been killed when his flagship, the *Westfield*, ran ashore near Bolivar Peninsula, across the bay from Galveston. An attempt to destroy the vessel by dousing the decks with turpentine resulted in a premature explosion that not only killed the fleet commander, but also destroyed his ship. "There was a plunging noise in the water, such as occasioned by the falling of a heavy body, and then

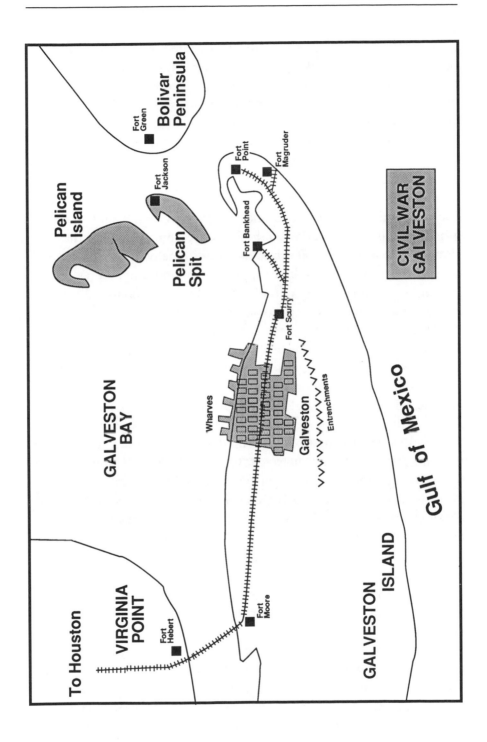

To Houston

VIRGINIA POINT

Fort Hebert

Fort Moore

GALVESTON BAY

Pelican Island

Pelican Spit

Fort Jackson

Fort Green

Bolivar Peninsula

Fort Point

Fort Magruder

Fort Bankhead

Fort Scurry

Wharves

Galveston

Entrenchments

GALVESTON ISLAND

Gulf of Mexico

CIVIL WAR GALVESTON

for a radius of four or five hundred feet there was a shower of frag-
ments which sounded like falling rain," writes Thomas Scharf. "The
Westfield was seen to part or burst forward, like a chestnut burr, and
when the smoke cleared away there was no sign of life about her."
Magruder came down to the waterfront personally to accept surrender of the remaining federal ships, only to see three of them, *Clifton,*
Owasco, and *Sachem,* disregard his capitulation ultimatum and steam
out to sea. Although Magruder was powerless to check the Yankees,
he was able to write in his official battle summary, "We captured one
fine steamship, two barks and one schooner. We ran ashore the flagship of the commodore, drove off two war steamers . . . all of the U.S.
Navy, and took 300 or 400 prisoners." Additionally, his men captured
fifteen naval guns as well as a supply of coal and other stores left on
Pelican Spit, a small island in the harbor. Magruder reported his losses
in the naval action at twenty-six killed and 117 wounded.[28]

Once the federal ships had been destroyed, captured, or driven
from the scene, Burrell and his troops had no choice but surrender.
Magruder, always the gracious commander, designated General
Scurry to receive the formal capitulation. Afterwards, Burrell said that
he surrendered immediately after the *Harriet Lane* raised the white
flag, and that only one trooper had been wounded and none killed in
the aftermath. Although some Confederates continued to fire after
the white flag had been hoisted, Burrell believed the shooting was
done without the knowledge of Scurry and Magruder: "This statement is made in justice to General Scurry, who by his gentlemanly
conduct and uniform kindness to officers and privates is entitled to
the grateful remembrance of the whole command."

But Magruder and his men could afford to be magnanimous in
victory; "perhaps no battle of the war was followed by a fuller abne-
gation of all unkindness between the opposing elements, nor more
sympathy manifested at the interment of fallen foes," commented the
Dallas Herald.

Prince John Magruder was clearly not a man to carry grudges. "No
military man of whatever rank or experience could have made better
arrangements, and displayed more ability than you and your troops
did in the most trying and embarrassing situation that I have ever
seen officers and men placed in," he told Burrell in his 1869 letter,
following the Confederate collapse. Magruder had won a much-
needed triumph, which, ironically, would be his last, but others in the

North did not share Burrell's generosity. Admiral David G. Farragut branded the Galveston episode a disaster that "did more injury to the Navy than all the events of the war"; and Augustus Fox, Lincoln's assistant secretary of the navy, called Magruder's victory and the loss of Galveston "too cowardly to place on paper." Mostly, the federal setback goaded Lincoln to establish another beachhead on the Texas coast, although several months would elapse before the next invasion attempt.[29]

As Magruder was inspecting repairs on the *Harriet Lane*, a picturesque figure known as Nicaragua Smith suddenly appeared alongside; the onetime adventurer with William Walker's failed filibuster into Central America during 1856, Smith—really Thomas Smith—accompanied a federal task force transporting E. J. Davis and the First Texas Cavalry as reinforcements to Burrell's small force. He had been sent from the USS *Cambria* in search of a pilot to bring the fleet into Galveston. Unaware that Magruder had retaken the city, Smith was instantly recognized as a deserter from a Confederate unit and placed under arrest; he had likewise been accused of setting several fires about Galveston before going over to the federals. Not only Smith's arrival, but also that of the "apostate Texans" wearing Northern uniforms, raised a sensation among the defenders. Although Magruder's official report says the hapless fellow had come to escape the federal provost marshal, he ordered him shot for desertion. "When standing in front of twelve messengers of death, the lieutenant in charge of the execution of the death sentence, advanced to him, and asked if he had any last word or message," recounts the traveler Thomas North. "He said, 'Yes,' and gave it, but the character of it forbids its mention here. He died as he lived, with unmentionable wickedness on his lips—a sad spectacle of depravity, unwept and unregretted by all."[30]

Magruder announced triumphantly that the federal blockade was lifted on January 5:

> Whereas the undersigned has succeeded in capturing and destroying a portion of the enemy's fleet and in driving the remainder out of Galveston Harbor and beyond the neighboring waters and thus raising the blockade virtually, he therefore proclaims to all concerned that the harbor of Galveston is open for trade to all friendly nations, and their merchants are invited to resume their usual intercourse with this port.

Commodore H. H. Bell, however, issued his own warning two weeks later "to all concerned" that a federal quarantine still existed at Galveston, Sabine Pass, and indeed along the entire Texas coast: "Any merchant vessel appearing off the aforesaid ports or attempting to pass out from the said ports under any pretext whatever will be captured." The northern blockade was never lifted entirely, although the timely appearance of Raphael Semmes and the Confederate raider *Alabama* in the Gulf following the Battle of Galveston frightened Yankee seamen enough to call a temporary halt to federal incursions along the coast; and blockade running into Galveston and Sabine Pass continued sporadically after Magruder's victories. Semmes had word that a federal fleet was approaching the Texas coast, and came to ply his craft; after sinking the USS *Hatteras* in plain sight of Galveston, and unaware of the city's recapture, he withdrew quickly to avoid the remainder of Bell's ships.[31]

Magruder, undeterred by the continuing blockade, put his energies to rebuilding the Galveston defenses before his departure for Houston on February 13. In spite of occasional shots thrown into the city by Bell's squadron, Prince John again became the master of deception. On the peninsula, Magruder had duped the federals by marching his troops to create the illusion of great numbers, and now he placed "Quaker guns," or painted logs, at conspicuous locations around the waterfront and "blocked the harbor's entrance with piles, torpedoes, and other obstacles." Colonel Arthur Fremantle, a British officer who visited Galveston during the construction activity, reports that 150 whites and 600 slaves from surrounding plantations worked at the fortifications under Magruder's direction. When a random shell burst over the city, "all of the negroes [*sic*] ran, showing every sign of great dismay, and two of them in their terror, ran into the sea, and were unfortunately drowned." Following vociferous complaints from foreign consuls, Bell finally ceased his shelling activities; Galveston, thanks to Magruder's aggressive posturing with the limited resources at hand, for the moment was secure for the Confederacy.[32]

"From Albert Bail's store, on the Strand, to Hindley's building (the latter included), we understand that not twenty panes of glass remain," reported a Galveston newspaper. "The jarring of our guns and the explosion of shells broke the glass windows by the thousands. When the firing first began some of our men thought the houses were falling, so startling was the rattling of broken glass." While shattered windows appeared to be the only substantial damage, Magruder and his compatriots launched into a frenzied extravaganza following Burrell's surrender. "The Grand Seignior" led the joyous Confederates through the glass-strewn streets with abandon. "Magruder with blood upon his garments, a bullet wound upon his body and victory upon his standards danced until there was daylight in the sky," says his chronicler Mark Grimsby. The war-weary Texans, unaccustomed to victories of any kind, were willing to forgive Prince John's exuberance. He had accomplished what previous lackluster commanders had not—he had beaten the enemy. It was a "signal defeat," declares O. M. Roberts, an ardent secessionist who presided over the convention that took Texas out of the Union, and later became governor. Another of his officers, X. B. DeBray, a Frenchman who had graduated from the French military academy, argues that Magruder's triumph "raised popular enthusiasm to the highest pitch."[33]

His work done at Galveston, Magruder returned to his Houston headquarters on February 23; when he departed to look after his fiefdom in Texas, New Mexico, and Arizona, DeBray was left in charge. Magruder was at the height of his glory in the afterglow of Galveston, "a fine soldierlike man of about fifty-five, with broad shoulders, a florid complexion, and bright eyes," notes Fremantle, who met him a few weeks afterward. "He wears his whiskers and mustaches in the English fashion, and he was dressed in a Confederate uniform." Prince John had sent "an electric shock" through the state when it was most needed. In response to his first dispatch after the battle, Jefferson Davis had fired back the obligatory congratulations: "Your success has been a heavy blow to the enemy's hopes, and I trust will be vigorously and effectively followed up." Other laudatory words followed as the president implored him to allay "domestic discontent" across the state. Although he harbored reservations about Confederate efforts to hold not only the Texas coast but the eastern Gulf as well, Davis writes in his 1881 memoir that Magruder's victory won the South's "grateful admiration."[34]

Among the accolades streaming into Magruder's office was a true appreciation from Sam Houston; that old warrior had renounced the Confederacy, but had not lost his zeal for the Texas he loved. "You, sir, have introduced a new era in Texas by driving from our soil, a ruthless enemy. You deserve, not only my thanks, but that of every Texan," wrote the hero of San Jacinto. "We hope that Texas, with so gallant a leader as you are, General, will yet show to the world that she is capable of defending her own soil, notwithstanding that she has been drained of her resources, which have been transferred to other battlefields." Houston, amid his congratulations, had found a raw nerve—too many men were going elsewhere to fight, and it was a dilemma that plagued Magruder throughout his stay on the Gulf Coast.

Early 1863, however, was a time for platitudes, and the Texas legislature sent its own glowing tribute on March 30: "The thanks of the legislature are hereby extended to General J. B. Magruder and the officers and men under his command for the brilliant victory." Literally thousands of messages rolled into his headquarters from Texans of every stripe. "The whole people of Texas," wrote S. Lee from Cuero, De Witt County, "desire to express gratitude and admiration to you, under God, for the beneficence and energy of your administration in their affairs, but in especial for the redemption and disenthralment of their principal harbor from the hands of the enemy." Lee even included an elaborately drawn shield to commemorate the battle that can still be seen in the University of Texas archive. It features an alligator symbolizing "secrecy, wisdom, and courage," fighting with a horse, denoting "strength, speed, and chivalrous honor." Lee placed a smoking warship in the background and emblazoned the whole with the motto of the Confederacy: *"Pro Aris et Focis."* Showman and fighter that he was, Magruder relished the adulation.[35]

9

"The People of Texas Have Made a Demi-god of Him"

MAGRUDER HAD NO SOONER driven the Yankees from Galveston than he faced another crisis at Sabine Pass, located on the Texas-Louisiana border; since the Union navy also kept a blockading squadron at Sabine as well as Galveston, he acted to drive them out shortly after establishing his headquarters as part of his plan to regain the Texas coast and Rio Grande Valley. "In December, 1862, Captain [Charles] Fowler was instructed by Gen. Magruder . . . to proceed to the Sabine River and there make selection of two or three steamboats, for the purpose of attacking the Federal gunboats that were in possession of Sabine Pass," wrote Mrs. M. Looscan, whose husband took part in the subsequent battle. "Having been vested with full power of impressment of such materials as might be necessary for carrying out the proposed plans in the shortest possible space of time, Captain Fowler selected the steamboats *Josiah H. Bell* and *Uncle Ben*, the former about 180 feet long and the latter probably 135 feet, both about ten years old." Since the overhaul work was completed at Orange, Magruder dispatched additional troops and war supplies from Houston, including "an eight-inch rifled Columbiad" for service with the cotton-clad armada. The supplies were sent to nearby Beaumont via the Texas & New Orleans Railroad.

Once the boats were refitted with fourteen-by-fourteen timbers extending into the hulls, "Magruder's navy" set sail under the overall command of Major Oscar M. Watkins; also aboard were sharpshooters from A. W. Spaight's command. But the federals, suspecting trouble, had withdrawn seaward, and, writes Alwyn Barr, "outside the pass lay two Federal blockaders, a sloop, *Morning Light*, armed with nine heavy guns, [and] the schooner *Velocity*, mounting two light how-itzers." The chase commenced at daylight on January 21, with the federals running for the open sea, although both were sailing vessels easily overtaken by the steam-driven Confederate craft. "Two gun-boats which I fitted up on the Sabine, have captured the enemy's blockading squadron, consisting of a 12-gun ship of war and a schooner of two guns, commanded by officers of the U.S. Navy," Ma-gruder said in effusive praise of his men three days later. "Our boats pursued the enemy 30 miles at sea, during which time a running fight was kept up. Finally, getting them under fire of our Enfield rifle, they surrendered." Both Yankee ships were returned to Sabine Pass, al-though the *Morning Light* was later burned when she could not be towed across the bar. Watkins, who did not lose a single man, took 129 prisoners—some of them wounded—as well as thirteen heavy guns, and enemy stores valued at $100,000.[1]

First Galveston, then Sabine Pass had been wrested from the enemy with little effort, and a euphoric Magruder became the toast of Texas after his disappointments in Virginia. In spite of the recent glories, however, Galveston remained his chief concern as his engi-neering officers Valery Sulakowski and John Kellersberg worked day and night to improve the city's defenses throughout January. Union fleet activity subsided briefly in the aftermath of the *Alabama-Hatteras* imbroglio—Magruder even included a note in his report to Richmond that workmen had retrieved wreckage from the Yankee warship on nearby beaches while working at their Quaker guns and other fortifications. And a certain civility was maintained between the Confederates and Galveston's blockaders during the respite from actual combat. "Colonel [J. J.] Cook, of the Galveston garrison went to the Federal fleet on January 24, 1863, to take letters so that they could be forwarded to the northern states," finds one scholar. As a graduate of the United States Naval Academy, Cook found a warm reception aboard the enemy flagship "and met many of his old ac-quaintances," who assured him that an earlier bombardment had re-sulted from an unintentional mixup. Upon his return, Cook "reported that all of the Federal officers had told him that they were tired of the war." But Magruder's struggle was far from over when he left the Gulf Coast during the first weeks of February for his Houston headquarters, which he had scarcely occupied since his arrival in November.[2]

During Magruder's first weeks in Texas, General Holmes, still in charge of the Trans-Mississippi, had granted him a virtually free hand to drive the enemy from the coast. "Consider [yourself] invested with all the authority I can confer, and use it for the defense of Texas," he told Magruder upon his arrival in the Lone Star. Yet Holmes warned him to avoid any entanglements in civil affairs without the approval of Governor Francis R. Lubbock. The commanding general was not only partially deaf, but also getting on in years. He had been born in 1804, so that he communicated with Magruder and Richard Taylor in Louisiana "infrequently and usually on routine matters, leaving military operations in their districts almost entirely to their discretions," finds a Holmes scholar. When Holmes was removed on January 14, and sent to command the North Carolina reserves, he was replaced by Lieutenant General E. Kirby Smith. For the next two years, until the last days of Confederate Texas, Smith and Prince John developed at least a working relationship that enabled Magruder to fend off any serious Yankee incursions into the state until the spring of 1865.[3]

Pressing civil and military matters notwithstanding, Magruder decided to enjoy his new-found acclaim by embarking upon a tour that took him to Austin, San Antonio, and the Rio Grande Valley; he had not been in the interior of Texas since his stint at Fort Clark during 1856. Although the *Houston News* called him "a man of strictly abstemious habits" in an effort to offset the reputation for high living that plagued him, Magruder unquestionably savored the trip. "We have had a very gay time lately," a correspondent of Mrs. Edward C. Wharton observed from Austin. "The visit of Gen. Magruder made quite an excitement. Of course there were Parties, Tableaux, Concerts, and a musical entertainment given at the Governor's." Governor Francis R. Lubbock, unlike his successor Pendleton Murrah, maintained a high opinion of Magruder that lasted until he left office to become a personal adviser to Jefferson Davis in Richmond. "A firm and skillful hand was at the helm of military affairs in Texas, and the hopes and expectations of the people rose accordingly," Lubbock noted in his massive autobiography.[4]

Magruder was welcomed to the capital city by Alexander W. Terrell, who reintroduced him to Dr. Josephus M. Steiner, a prominent

Austin physician. Terrell, an Austin lawyer and judge, afterwards served under Prince John as lieutenant colonel and colonel of a cavalry regiment. During the drive into Mexico City sixteen years before, when young Preston Johnstone had both legs torn off by a cannon shot, it was Steiner who worked in vain to save his life as Magruder and the future Stonewall Jackson looked on. As the battle raged around them, Magruder determined that the Mexicans "were firing copper balls." Steiner was busily ligating Johnstone's arteries when Magruder, according to Terrell's memoir, looked at several dead and disabled horses and called out, " 'Doctor, come quick and cut a ball out of this dead horse—I believe they are firing copper balls.' Steiner with his long red knife handle in his hand turned quickly to his commander, and said, 'Damn you, I am not a horse doctor; don't you see that I am trying to save Johnstone's life?' " Although bad blood had persisted between the two since the incident, they met, Terrell proclaims, "with the consent of both parties."[5]

When Magruder arrived in San Antonio with his entourage, the partying flared anew. "San Antonio has just had a visit from the commanding Gen. Magruder. He and his Staff, attachés, *amateurs*, body guard, a long train of ambulances, baggage wagons, etc., reached here about a week ago on a military tour of inspection en route for Brownsville on the Rio Grande," wrote Mrs. Ada Bankhead, wife of his kinsman in command at the Alamo City. "This trip is so mixed up with amusement and pleasure that it can scarcely be called one of military necessity or duty." She continued, somewhat skeptically, "He was received here in the most gratifying manner. The people of Texas have made a demi-god of him and fairly worship him." Colonel Bankhead met the party with an honor guard outside the city and escorted Magruder into San Antonio, where he was welcomed by the mayor on "the balcony of the Menger House." "He responded in a most happy and acceptable manner, upon which 8 guns from the Battery were fired on the plaza in his honor. This reception was followed by a most magnificent supper." The deprivations of war aside, social life under the Confederacy flourished in San Antonio with a steady round of balls and parties.

Magruder, who had only one lady in his company, the wife of an aide, surely enjoyed "the exaggerated form of the hoop skirt" that dominated the city's wartime fashions. A popular San Antonio ditty of the day proclaimed:

> Now crinoline is all the rage with ladies of whatever age
> A petticoat made like a cage—Oh, what a ridiculous fashion
> 'Tis formed of hoops and bars of steel or tubes of air which lighter feel.
> And worn by girls to be genteel, or if they've figures to conceal.
> It makes the dress stretch, stretch far out, a dozen yards or so about
> And pleases both the thin and the stout—Oh, what a ridiculous fashion.

His partying done, Magruder "went on his way" after attempting to cajole Bankhead and his wife into joining his company. "I can but rejoice that we have escaped the pleasure and pain" of the trip, Mrs. Bankhead said. She had no desire to leave the comforts of San Antonio for the 180-mile jaunt across south Texas to the Rio Grande.[6]

During his tour of the interior, Magruder was confronted with the realities of civil administration; partying in the aftermath of his military triumph on the coast was soon overshadowed by the frustration of having to cope with another kind of command decision. While he was in San Antonio, at least two problems demanded his attention: Indian raiding along the frontier, and cotton trading across the Rio Grande. Governor John R. Baylor had alerted him to Indian troubles as early as December, while he was preparing for the recapture of Galveston. "Arizona has been kept in poverty by Indian depredations. Not a cow, sheep or horse can be raised there now except by being herded day and night," Baylor wrote. "It is equally notorious that on numerous occasions the women of our State have been taken prisoners, and, after being subjected to every outrage that the brutal passions of the savage could prompt, they were murdered in cold blood, and their scalps used to ornament the shield of the Indian warriors. As one of the hundreds of sad proofs of such scenes of horror I myself have seen an Indian shield on which were the scalps of twenty-two different unfortunate women."

Baylor said further that, having spent his life from boyhood on the frontier, he was convinced that it would be "cheaper (were it possible) to board the savages in first-class hotels" than to continue the reservation system. Abolitionists in Kansas, he proffered, were agitating several tribes—including "Cherokees, Creeks, Seminoles, and other smaller ones in addition to the Northern Comanches, and Kiowas." Although a Confederate presence in Arizona and New Mexico had been lacking since Sibley's withdrawal the previous summer, both territories were, after all, in Magruder's jurisdiction, and he was not long in organizing a campaign to relieve their suffering. On April 15, however, E. Kirby Smith, upon hearing "a rumor" that an expedition was under consideration, sent a pointed command: "If a movement into Arizona should have been contemplated you will promptly check it, as it cannot under existing circumstances be authorized."[7]

Although Smith refused to help Arizona and New Mexico because of manpower shortages, conditions were just as traumatic on the Texas frontier. "Ever since 1856, hostile Indian war parties had been harassing homesteads along the fringe of Texas settlements," writes a biographer of Smith. "Most of the raiders were Comanches, but several bands of Apaches, Kiowas, Lipans, and Kickapoos shared in the harvest of scalps. By 1858, fifty ranches in Webb County were abandoned, and there was only one white family left in Montague County." The federal army that included Robert E. Lee and Magruder himself contained the marauders after a fashion before the war. With secession and the exodus of able-bodied men to join the Confederate cause on other fronts, the troubles started anew. The state legislature had responded by creating something called the Frontier Regiment to replace the older Texas Mounted Rifles commanded by Ben McCulloch, an old Indian campaigner who had led his troopers to other theaters. From the beginning of the Confederacy, a heated debate had developed between Austin and Richmond over responsibility for calming the 600-mile frontier extending from the Red River and Indian Territory to the Rio Grande.[8]

By the time Magruder reached Texas in November 1862, Colonel James N. Norris—appointed by Lubbock—had been in charge of the Frontier Regiment for several months. Norris, wrote a regiment chronicler, was a poor commander who did not have the respect of his men, although he maintained a vigorous patrol system through the spring of 1862 that managed to kill twenty-one hostile Indians and capture 200 horses. Texas had intended from the start that the Confederate government should assume responsibility not only for Indian defense but also for the frontier units. Finally, on March 11, 1863, Lubbock, acting on instructions from his legislature, formally tendered the regiment to Magruder, who jumped at the chance to have additional troops under his charge and accepted the offer without consulting E. Kirby Smith or Richmond. Lubbock made the transfer with the explicit codicil that the troops remain on the frontier and not leave Texas.

"With little regard for conditions on the frontier, [Magruder] ordered Brig. Gen. Hamilton Prioleau Bee, commanding the Submilitary District of the Rio Grande, to prepare to take charge of five companies of the Frontier Regiment, and to post them at Ringgold Barracks, on the Rio Grande, in anticipation of a supposed federal invasion of the lower Texas Coast." Magruder told his subordinate, W. R. Scurry, who was Bee's superior, to assume control of the entire regiment; what ensued demonstrated the continuing dilemma in balancing pressing military needs with the aspirations of Texas civil authorities and his Confederate superiors. "As the plans progressed for Confederate military authorities to assume responsibility for the frontier, word arrived in Austin from President Davis," writes historian David Smith. "He still refused to accept the Frontier Regiment if bound by the condition that it remain under the direction of Texas rather than the Confederacy. Once Davis had spoken, Magruder had no choice but to withdraw from the controversy. But the reluctance of Davis and Lubbock to reach a mutual accommodation meant that the frontier—for the moment—would remain an obligation of state authorities." Lubbock's immediate successor, Pendleton Murrah, eventually worked out an understanding the following year, when the Frontier Regiment became the 46th Texas Cavalry, attached to Colonel Smith P. Bankhead's command.[9]

If corralling warlike Indians was a headache for Magruder, the dilemma of buying cotton within the state, transporting it to the Rio Grande, and selling or exchanging it for guns and food to supply his troops became a nightmare. From the moment he set foot in Texas, he was confronted with three conflicting interests vying for the state's cotton supply: agents of the Texas Military Board, created in 1861 to provision the state's civilian and military needs; Confederate treasury and army agents trying to buy and resell enough cotton to supply

Magruder's command; and private speculators bent on turning a buck by outbidding state and Confederate operatives. "His principal reason for visiting Brownsville was to settle rivalries about the cotton trade," commented Colonel Fremantle, who met Magruder on the roadway between San Antonio and the Rio Grande. A British officer traveling through Texas, Fremantle encountered Prince John's company a few miles north of Brownsville and was invited to return with him.

"We sang numerous songs," Fremantle wrote, referring to a gala fête at which he was given the seat of honor next to Magruder. "Both the General and his nephew sang, and his entire staff live with their chief on an extremely agreeable footing and form a very pleasant society." Major George A. Magruder remained with his uncle in Texas and Arkansas until the war ended in 1865. Amid the gaiety, Prince John revealed something of his propensity for the spirited life: "I had a long and agreeable conversation with the General, who spoke of the Puritans with intense disgust, and for the first importation of them as '*that pestiferous crew of the Mayflower.*' " The anything-but-puritanical Magruder also relished the ruses he had used against his old adversary McClellan during the peninsula campaign. Fremantle added that Magruder not only presided over the festivities with aplomb, but "wore a red woolen cap for the occasion."[10]

Cotton, however, dominated his travels to the southernmost corner of the Confederacy, because it was here that the precious commodity was sold for cash or traded for war matériel. Both Paul O. Hebert and Theophilus H. Holmes had attempted to regulate its flow across the border, and Paul N. Luckett, commanding on the lower Rio Grande, imposed a five-dollar-per-bale tax during June 1862. The levy was designed to pay for maintaining Confederate garrisons at Fort Brown and other locations along the border. Although Holmes had issued an October 1862 mandate that no cotton could be sold across the border except by Confederate agents, Magruder arranged a December conference in Houston with Governor Lubbock, General Bee, Major Simeon Hart (representing the Confederate war department), and Luckett, at which it was agreed that all transshipped cotton require Bee's stamp of approval. Magruder issued a later order reaffirming the strictures imposed by Holmes and implemented by Bee and Luckett.

On March 31, before he left San Antonio, he fired off a communiqué to Adjutant General Cooper in Richmond, proclaiming that he "had not meddled in these matters except under orders from my superiors." But his position was undercut when Secretary of War James A. Seddon issued an edict countermanding the earlier restrictions on transborder cotton sales by Holmes and Bee that had been endorsed by Magruder himself. There was nothing in Confederate law, Seddon said, to prohibit the buying and selling of cotton by any citizen of the new government. Seddon's order, which resulted in a free flow of cotton into Mexico, Magruder added, "may make it necessary for me to fall back from the Rio Grande and give up that frontier to the enemy from the difficulty of supplying the troops there except through the means of cotton." By the time he reached Brownsville, however, Magruder had learned what others already knew—that conferences and military edicts were meaningless. "The competition among Confederate agents, Texas agents, and private contractors of every stripe drove the price of cotton always higher," writes historian Fredericka Meiners. "Even with the exorbitant transportation fees, speculators could pay up to twenty-five cents per pound in the interior because they had the cash." All government agents were powerless to meet the going price, which in some instances reached astronomical levels at the border. What was worse for Magruder and his own cotton procurers, Mexican traders and foreign ship captains were reticent to accept Confederate or Texas script.[11]

As Magruder worked to solve the dilemma, the Confederate congress alleviated some of the problem with the Impressment Bill of March 26, 1863; actually, Confederate authorities had been impressing all manner of items since 1861 under the guise of military necessity, with no legal underpinning, and in so doing had incurred the wrath of civilians and politicians alike. "So indefensible did this practice appear to even the most loyal Confederates," writes E. Merton Coulter, that "congress passed a highly complicated and involved law regulating in great detail the method of impressing supplies and fixing prices in several states." Magruder was clearly ambivalent from the beginning about what would be the best procedure. On May 7 in Brownsville he issued General Order No. 65, which permitted the continued purchase of cotton by Confederate agents; but six weeks later—after his return to Houston, he was obliged to inform

Hamilton P. Bee that "doubts having risen as to the legality of impressing cotton under the 'Impressment Bill' [I have] referred the matter to Lieut. Gen. Kirby Smith for a decision—the authority given you, therefore, in [my] letter of May 21, 1863, from Corpus Christi . . . to impress Cotton, is for the present revoked, and you will cause all cotton that may have been impressed under authority from these headquarters to be returned to the owners."[12]

Matters came to a head in early June when the *Sea Queen*, a British ship carrying a cargo of Enfield rifles, arrived off the Rio Grande; following an exchange of communiqués with E. Kirby Smith, Magruder was told to proceed with impressment of 14,000 bales of cotton not only to pay for the guns but also for other items aboard the vessel. Smith went further on June 27—one week after Magruder's directive to Bee—and scored him for failure to proceed with impressment of the *Sea Queen* cotton because "of the odium that must attach itself to such a measure." The anticipated loss of Vicksburg as Grant tightened the noose around its defenders, Smith added, made the move more necessary than ever to finance operations in the Trans-Mississippi; but Magruder, who did not want to offend state officials, was reluctant to act. "Lest it should be otherwise, feeling as I do, with the peculiar temperament of the Texas people, the importance of maintaining your popularity, I am perfectly willing that the odium of the measure, if any, should fall upon myself, and that your usefulness in the district should remain unimpaired. You can, therefore, or through General Bee, make all the above impressments in my name and under my orders." The carte-blanche instruction to impress brought a quick response from Guy M. Bryan, representing the Texas Cotton Bureau, who secured an order from Smith instructing Magruder to exempt cotton owned by the state.[13]

Magruder continued to rely upon Bee to carry out the nuts and bolts of impressment, but he was never totally committed to the policy because it alienated the state's farmers and politicians; yet cotton was needed to supply his men, although he viewed traders and middlemen as his chief obstacles. In short, he was forced to brush aside civilian outcries in the name of military necessity. "Magruder intended to impress temporarily every bale in sight, even state cotton . . . until the merchants agreed to advance the cotton to the army." And, continues historian Meiners, "on the border . . . Bee resorted to his own tactics to obtain the cotton. Magruder's ideas, arriving several days to two weeks after he wrote them, simply did not apply to the situation." The whole tangle became moot during the first week of November, when Banks sent a landing force to occupy Brownsville and the lower Rio Grande, although some attempt was made to transport cotton through Eagle Pass and Laredo, farther upriver. By the time Confederate control was reestablished in the region, Magruder had been reassigned to command in Arkansas; following the return to his old post in March 1865, the war was drawing to a conclusion, which rendered continued concern over impressment useless.[14]

While Magruder struggled with cotton on the Rio Grande, an urgent summons arrived from E. Kirby Smith to march his army toward Louisiana; the appeal came in response to Banks's renewed effort to implement his dual mission in the Gulf: to establish a federal presence in Texas, and to help clear the Mississippi River of Confederate control. Although Texas Unionists persistently urged a thrust into the state, Banks shifted his attention to the capture of Port Hudson, a few miles north of Baton Rouge, which dominated the lower Mississippi. And he would not march until the west bank of the river was cleared of Confederate forces. When General William B. Franklin, who had commanded one of Ambrose Burnside's Grand Divisions at Fredericksburg, was sent up the Atchafalaya and Bayou Teche with an expeditionary force to capture Opelousas and Alexandria, Confederate general Richard Taylor was able to hold him in check at the battles of Irish Bend and Fort Bisland during April 12–14. Taylor soon withdrew into Opelousas as the first Red River campaign fizzled, but an alarmed Kirby Smith was taking no chances on a further penetration into Louisiana. "Some 15,000 of the enemy are now about the Teche," reads his April 16, 1863, missive from Alexandria to Magruder. "You will immediately move all your disposal force toward Opelousas," and to placate his Texas commander, Smith added, "These troops will not be removed from West Louisiana, and will be returned to your district as soon as the necessity for their presence here ceases to exist."[15]

Magruder unhesitatingly complied with Smith's directive as he cut orders for Bee and Scurry to hurry their commands eastward. And he informed headquarters on May 7 that 5,000 troops were on their way to the Sabine. But here he balked. Although it would become acute under Lubbock's successor, Magruder accurately perceived that many, if not most, of the Texans were reticent to fight elsewhere. Anxious to preserve his standing among them, he did not wish to press the issue. A letter from Elijah S. C. Robertson, the son of an early Texas impresario and himself a state soldier/politician, indicated that he was ready to serve his country but did not wish to follow his old chief, Ben McCulloch, across the Sabine. Governor Lubbock, who was normally supportive, wrote to Magruder in July asking that he not force the question of troop transfers. "I am here in a great degree disliked," he said as he reminded "the Major General Commanding": "Should the barrier of the Mississippi River fall into the enemy's hands, we will surely make every sacrifice to destroy him on our own soil; and in anticipation of that work, prepare our facilities to accomplish great things." As the Texans concentrated around their Niblett's Bluff rendezvous, Magruder used every ploy short of insubordination to keep his troops at home, thereby provoking a feud with Richard Taylor, commanding in Louisiana, who faced the threat imposed by Banks and the federals. "Magruder's stubborn reluctance to dispatch his Confederate and Texas regiments to Taylor's relief only worsened relations between the two district commanders," writes a Smith biographer. Later in the year, when Banks did move in force against Texas, Magruder blamed the fall of Brownsville on E. Kirby Smith's concentration of his troops in east Texas.[16]

Magruder had a valid argument in seeking to retain his men at home when Banks launched two thrusts against the Texas coast, while at the same time his troops were ordered to reinforce Taylor. Although both raids were admittedly nothing more than pinpricks, they demonstrated anew the extreme vulnerability of Texas to such incursions by U.S. naval forces despite the elaborate fortifications at Galveston as well as at several points between Matagorda Bay and Corpus Christi. The first occurred on April 18—just two days after Kirby Smith's order for Magruder's forces to march for Louisiana—when "13 men in two small boats landed at about 600 yards from the [Sabine Pass] light-house." Then, continued Colonel William H. Griffin, the commanding officer assigned by Magruder, "Three of the men approached very cautiously to within a few yards of the lighthouse, when, upon a demand they surrendered; the other men having 400 yards advantage of my men started at the double quick step for their boats." Griffin's garrison ran down the intruding Yankees, capturing or killing all but three, who managed to escape. The probe by the Union navy at the Sabine was an attempt to gather detailed reconnaissance for a later full-scale operation.[17]

Two weeks later, on May 3, the federals attempted a landing on St. Joseph's Island, where Magruder had first set foot in Texas during the Mexican War. Captain Edwin E. Hobby, whose son, W. P. Hobby, became a twentieth-century governor of the state, had a company of twenty-eight men—members of his brother Alfred Marmaduke Hobby's Eighth Texas Infantry, on the island during the assault. When approximately forty of the enemy approached in "three launches," Hobby reported the capture of two landing craft, although "the bark opened fire on us." The attackers lost, according to Confederate estimates, twenty men killed, wounded, or captured. As two of the Union boats heaved from the island, Hobby's troopers saw "at least two men fall overboard" when they fired at the retreating enemy. A jubilant Magruder quickly telegraphed his congratulations to the "heroic gallantry" of his troops in a proclamation issued from Corpus Christi two days after the set-to: "Major-General Magruder feels sure that those of the troops who have been ordered to Louisiana bore with them willing hearts and strong arms . . . and begs to assure those who remain that he feels confident that Texas will be nobly defended while her sons stand between the enemy and their loved homes."[18]

Upon his return to Houston, Magruder was joined by Lubbock for a tour of the Galveston defenses, which continued to be his highest priority; the two even visited the old battleground at San Jacinto, where Sam Houston had defeated Santa Anna twenty-seven years earlier to establish Texan independence. Lubbock, obviously pleased with fortifications on the coast, was moved to comment in his memoirs: "Magruder had a little bluster in his composition, which at times served a good turn in scaring the enemy." Although most of his troops had departed or were on their way to the Sabine, Magruder held "a grand ball in Cobb's schoolhouse," Lubbock continues, "with a good share of the representative belles of Houston and Galveston being present." Not even the press of war could dissuade his unquenchable humor, and in those last weeks before the state's isolation, imposed by the fall of Port Hudson and Vicksburg, Magruder issued one of his broadsides: "When I arrived in Texas, about the last of November,

1862, I found her Islands and a portion of her coasts in the possession of the enemy, and her territory threatened on all sides," he informed Lubbock in a public declaration. "The divine Ruler has vouchsafed success to our efforts to drive the foe from our soil, and at this moment every Island, and all the passes on the coast are in our possession." Yet he harbored no illusions about the perils ahead:

> Late events in a neighboring state, demonstrate plainly the objects of the enemy, which are to open the navigation of the Mississippi, and to push their light draught gunboats into every navigable bay and bayou of Louisiana and Texas, to liberate the negroes [sic], to lay waste the country, destroying not only crops, but farming implements, to slay or impress the men and to subject our women to every species of insult and brutality.[19]

The fall of Vicksburg, on July 4, 1863, induced Magruder to ask for an additional 10,000 state militia, which Lubbock did his best to supply. The scarcity of manpower and the difficulty of provisioning those already in the field led to some uneasy moments on August 13–14, when units of the Galveston garrison rose in revolt. "The only issue now given consists of beef, molasses, and corn-meal," Colonel E. F. Gray, commanding the Third Texas Infantry, reported on August 4. "The latter, even when good, is exceedingly heating in its effects on the blood, and when, added to this, it is sour, dirty, weevil-eaten, and filled with ants and worms, and not bolted (and the troops without means of sifting it themselves), it becomes wholly superfluous to add that it is exceedingly unwholesome." Three days earlier, X. B. DeBray had warned Magruder that many troops at the garrison were in poor health because of their rations, and that Colonel Sulakowski estimated an additional 1,200 men were needed to man the Galveston defenses properly. Although a more serious defiance occurred a year later, the outbreak of August 1863 was over rations when Gray's men refused muster or to work on the fortifications for a couple of days. "The commanding General received with feelings of deep mortification the intelligence of the mutinous and insubordinate conduct of a portion of the troops guarding the city and island of Galveston," Magruder announced on the twenty-fourth; and he let it be known that no further refusals to obey orders would be tolerated— that he would "never yield to force even that which his sense of justice and propriety would have dictated." While a true mutiny had not taken place, General P. N. Luckett, who had been dispatched by Magruder to investigate the incident, reported everything "perfectly quiet" on August 16.[20]

The already dismal manpower situation in Texas, and indeed throughout the Trans-Mississippi, was exacerbated when E. Kirby Smith ordered Magruder to transfer all available troops to Arkansas in anticipation of another federal move toward that state as well as into east Texas from Louisiana. Magruder once more complied under protest during the continuing threat to the coast; and he was in east Texas supervising his men when word arrived that another powerful force had assaulted Sabine Pass in the first weeks of September. The necessity for more men prompted Magruder to flirt with an idea advanced by Colonel Valery Sulakowski, his chief engineer at Galveston. A native of Poland, Sulakowski got up a scheme to recruit a 5,000-man army among Polish exiles living in Germany, France, and England following an abortive revolt against Russian domination of their homeland. But when he asked that Texas grant each recruit 200 acres of land after the war, Governor Lubbock "allowed the proposal to become buried in his files." Nor was Magruder able to count on the state's slave population as a source of additional soldiers; although General Patrick Cleburn, serving in the Army of Tennessee, spearheaded a drive to enlist blacks into the Confederate service during January 1864, and President Davis later embraced the idea, the Texans remained adamantly opposed. The governors of Virginia and Louisiana sided with Davis, but Lubbock informed Magruder during the summer of 1863 that under no circumstances would Texas be a party to slaves serving under state or Confederate banners. Magruder did, however, issue several orders summoning Texas plantation owners to supply bondsmen for service as teamsters in the cotton trade and to work on coastal defenses.[21]

Intelligence reports and rumors bombarded Magruder that Banks had assembled a massive force at New Orleans. These convinced him that the Yankee fury was about to strike once more along the Texas coast. Although Banks wanted to move eastward toward the Mississippi and Alabama coasts, Abraham Lincoln told him he must direct his legions at Texas, as Magruder had anticipated. "Recent events in Mexico," the president told his commander on August 5, "render early action in Texas more important than ever." Lincoln wanted

Union forces on the Gulf Coast for reasons other than military up-manship. "Specifically, Banks's presence there would discourage the ambitious Emperor of the French, Louis-Napoleon or Napoleon III, whose troops were already taking Mexico and might soon point to-ward the Lone Star State," writes a Banks biographer. The Confed-erates, too, had been weary of the intruders below the Rio Grande, although Magruder sought their help in driving the federals away from Brownsville and the lower Texas coast. E. Kirby Smith granted permission on August 30 for him to deal with the French in order to increase supplies not only for Confederate units in the state but else-where as well. In the unfolding drama, however, Prince John had lit-tle time to chase after assistance from Maximilian, but delegated that task to Hamilton P. Bee. "As regards our foreign relations," he told his captain on the Rio Grande, "General Smith leaves the course to be pursued by you in your intercourse with the French entirely to your discretion and wisdom which have heretofore characterized your con-duct toward that nation and the Mexicans."[22]

Throughout the first days of September, Magruder made his headquarters at Millican and several other spots in east Texas, but his mind was never far from Banks and his army at New Orleans. "In re-gard to your letters relative to the contemplated invasion of Texas, I [must] inform you that Niblett's Bluff, Orange, Beaumont, Liberty, Houston, and Columbus have already been made depots of supplies; some of them are already fortified and being fortified," he told Bee on September 1. Although he had given his kinsman Smith P. Bank-head command of troops headed for Arkansas, he was busy with his own plans to save Texas from the invaders. Magruder found himself in the anguished position of having to determine what to defend with his limited manpower. He clearly did not have the resources to secure the entire coastline, and two or three days before his missive to Gen-eral Bee, Peter W. Gray, the Confederate treasury agent for Texas, warned that Prince John "could hardly have more than 5,000 effec-tives at his disposal—many of them militia—and but poorly armed."[23]

"The 5,000 troops sent to Louisiana left me about 11,000 men, exclusive of State Troops, the latter not available under present or-ders," he reported to Kirby Smith on September 4. "This is the force with which I have to defend a coast of about 400 miles, besides the Louisiana frontier." Although he put his troop numbers higher than the public perception, Magruder had already resolved to give up the coast from Aransas and Corpus Christi to the border, and if necessary even to abandon Brownsville and the Rio Grande, even though he thought Bee had sufficient numbers to defend himself. But he also told Bee that Saluria had to be maintained at all costs, "otherwise Galveston will be turned and the troops caught." Situated on the "northeastern bulge of Matagorda Island," Saluria had been a Texas settlement since 1845. It contained Fort Esperanza, which guarded the entrance into Matagorda Bay, Port Lavaca, and Indianola with their port facilities and road connections to San Antonio and the interior. "If I cannot sustain myself at Saluria," Magruder told Kirby Smith, "I intend to concentrate still further by taking the line of the Brazos [holding its mouth] on the west and the Sabine on the east, defending the Brazos country and the Caney, if possible, and removing everything from San Antonio, should that place be likely to fall into the hands of the enemy." Caney Creek, an old bed of the Colorado River, emptied into the Gulf of Mexico a few miles up the coast from the Brazos. By falling back to Saluria, Magruder reasoned, he would reduce the defended coast to about 150 miles.[24]

As Magruder made his war preparations by sending troops to the vital points, Yankee general William B. Franklin set sail from New Orleans on September 5 with 1,500 troops aboard several transports for another try at Sabine Pass. Although supplies and reinforcements had been sent to Orange and Beaumont, the garrison at Fort Griffin on the Sabine numbered fewer than forty-five men when the federal armada reached the river. Griffin, shortly dubbed Fort Dowling, was positioned about 3,000 yards from the Gulf on the Texas shore; opposite the installation was a low-lying oyster reef that divided the Sabine into two channels. Mudflats lined both sides of the river below the fort to the open sea. Fort Griffin "was an unfinished work on the Texas side of the pass, destitute of any outer defenses, presenting three bastioned sides on the east, south, and west, with the north and rear enclosed by a redoubt about four feet above the level," reads a contemporary account. "The work occupied the high ground and commanded both the Texas and Louisiana channels. The former about 300 yards; the latter at a distance of three-fourths of a mile."

Upon Franklin's arrival, Lieutenant Richard Dowling, a twenty-four-year-old native of County Galway in Ireland, was in command,

and he was about to become a genuine Texas hero. Dowling had been a participant in the recapture of Galveston as well as in several other coastal operations; after the war he maintained, with his brother, a Houston drinking establishment known as "The Bank." In September 1863, however, he was in charge of the Davis Guards, finds Frank X. Tolbert, composed of "forty-one Irishmen (plus two 'outsiders,' a cavalry surgeon and a young engineering officer)." Although Magruder had ordered the garrison to spike the fort's six guns—"two 32-pounder smooth bores, two 24-pounder smooth bores, and two 32-pound howitzers," and to fall back on Beaumont, where it was thought the enemy could be easily defeated, Dowling eagerly disregarded his instructions. Not only that, but his Davis Guards used rails from a nearby railroad to strengthen their gun emplacements, and they drove wooden stakes across the shallow Sabine to sight their pieces with what proved to be uncanny accuracy. Dowling and his Irish compeers thus laid the groundwork, comments the prestigious *Handbook of Texas*, "for the most spectacular military engagement in Texas during the Civil War."[25]

The federals had apparently profited little from their earlier sortie into the Sabine because Franklin sent two of his four gunboats forward to find a suitable landing site for the transports. Of the four warships—*Arizona, Granite City, Sachem*, and *Clifton*—the last two had taken part in the Battle of Galveston. In the absence of Captain Frederick H. Odlum, the post commander, Dick Dowling, held his fire until the federals steamed within 1,200 yards of the fort, then opened on the *Clifton* as it sailed up the Texas channel, forcing it to raise the white flag within minutes; the *Sachem* then capitulated in the Louisiana passage when the vessel encountered a fierce pounding from "a powder-blackened" Dowling and his gunners; and Commodore Leon Smith, aboard the Confederate "cottonclad" *Uncle Ben*, joined the fray by steaming down the Sabine. It was over in forty-five minutes from the opening shots, as the *Granite City* and *Arizona* turned back to the Gulf, accompanied by the troop-laden transports *Suffolk* (Franklin's flagship), *St. Charles, Landis, Exact, Laurel Hill, Thomas*, and *General Banks*. Five of the seven troopships had actually crossed the bar, but did not come within range of Dowling's guns. Without the loss of a single trooper, Dowling had not only averted Franklin's attempt to gain a foothold on the coast, but had also blocked a serious threat to much of east Texas. The small company of Irishmen had thrown back 1,500 federals and captured two enemy gunboats—neither of which was severely damaged—and 300 prisoners. They also took thirteen guns from the *Sachem* and *Clifton*—guns that Magruder used afterwards to strengthen his fortifications up and down the coast. Governor Lubbock likened the Davis Guards to the defenders of the Alamo during the Texas Revolution, and news of the victory on the heels of Port Hudson, Vicksburg, and Gettysburg raced across the disheartened South like an electric stimulus.[26]

Magruder could scarcely contain himself when word of Dowling's triumph reached him in east Texas, and he lost no time in reaching Fort Griffin. At least five or six of his dispatches to various Confederate leaders can be found in the *Official Records*, and all of them characteristically praise Dowling and his men. "Almighty God in his divine mercy has given us another signal victory over our enemies," reads his September 10 proclamation to "The Men of Texas." And, two days later, writes historian Tolbert, "Magruder indulged in his love of theatricals." In an open-air ceremony at Fort Griffin, he presented sabers to Dowling and his fellow officers, proclaiming that "each member of the garrison was to wear 'Sabine' embroidered in a wreath design on his hat or cap."

While Magruder made his temporary headquarters aboard the "C.S. Steamer Clifton, Late of the U.S. Navy," he was clearly anxious that more federals were on their way to the Sabine; documents had been uncovered on the *Clifton* and *Sachem* suggesting that 15,000 troops had been allocated for the occupation of Texas. "I expect their return soon with ironclads, and hope to be prepared to meet them successfully," reads his September 26 report to Richmond. "The prisoners all stated that they were bound for Houston, and will yet get there. I trust, however, my dispositions of all the available forces under my command will thwart them, although very small in number." But, once beaten at "the Mud Fort on the Sabine," Banks and Franklin showed no inclination to renew the campaign. After lingering a few days off the bar, the federals withdrew to New Orleans for a regrouping. Unbeknownst to Magruder, who pleaded with Kirby Smith and Richard Taylor for troops to fend off a renewed assault, Banks had resolved to descend upon the Rio Grande Valley. And, significantly, when Congress voted a resolution of thanks "to Captain

Odlum, Lieutenant Dowling, and the men under his command, "no mention was made of Prince John, even though "this defense . . . preventing the invasion of Texas, constitutes, in the opinion of Congress, one of the most brilliant and heroic achievements of this war."[27]

Three hundred federals had been captured aboard the *Sachem* and *Clifton*, and this presented Magruder with a problem of housing his prisoners of war. In early October, Governor Lubbock asked that he send "one or more companies" to protect the state penitentiary at Huntsville from enemy raiders; "an attempt against the Institution would be made by cavalry," he argued, because "its destruction would entail incalculable evil." But Magruder's follow-up suggestion that the stockade, established in 1847, be used to contain Union prisoners brought a firm rebuff from Lubbock that it would surely invite its obliteration: "Were the penitentiary not a Manufacturing facility (the sole one for clothing, too, in the Trans-Miss. Dept.) as well as a place of confinement for prisoners, I could entertain no objection to your proposition," Lubbock told him on October 14. "As it is I cannot incur the risk."[28]

Although the creation of Camp Ford at Tyler, Texas, in late 1863, eased the prisoner dilemma for Magruder, he soon found himself in a controversy with Banks over the treatment of Confederates taken by Union forces. Some POWs had been interned at a makeshift camp near Millican—at the northern terminus of the railroad from Houston until a yellow fever epidemic forced their dispersal into smaller groupings. After the fall of Brownsville in early November and Banks's subsequent foray up the Texas coast, several civilians had been retained by the enemy and a number of Confederate officers held at Saluria after they approached the Union lines under a flag of truce to ascertain the status of several men taken in the fighting around Aransas Pass. Magruder's wrath knew no bounds when he addressed a December 10 letter to Banks about the incident. "No prisoner of war has ever received even a momentary insult, and all have been cared for as well as the circumstances of the country would permit. It is my desire to do this in the future, and I am determined that the civilized world shall know that the black flag and its horrors cannot with truth be attributed to me." And he continued: "I have the honor to remind you that I have several hundred prisoners of war on my hands, including officers of the rank of colonel in the army and lieutenant commander in the navy of the United States, and that my treatment of these prisoners will be rigorously and mercilessly regulated by your adherence to or departure from the known laws of civilized warfare." When Banks delegated Major General C. C. Washburn (who became governor of Wisconsin after the war) to respond, Magruder was informed that the two private citizens had been returned to their homes. "Your threat of 'merciless retaliation,' and the disclosure of your intention to raise the black flag, I do not deem it important to advert to, neither to the general tone and temper of your dispatch," Washburn said. "The desperate fortunes of a bad cause induce me to pardon much, which, under other circumstances would not be lightly passed over."[29]

The continued total separation of Texas and the Trans-Mississippi from Richmond emboldened Unionist and German elements to resist Confederate authority and to work for a federal takeover. A general deterioration of the state's social fabric and the need to protect his home front caused Magruder to take strong action during the fall of 1863 as he awaited the enemy's next military thrusts. "I have discovered a well-laid and I fear widespread conspiracy, with an understanding with the Federal army, through the federal prisoners at Hempstead, by which our cause is greatly endangered on this side of the Mississippi," he informed Kirby Smith on October 11. Five men—"Dr. Richard Peebles of Hempstead, D. J. Baldwin and A. F. Zinke (a German printer), Reinhardt Hilderbrand of Fayette County, and E. Seeliger of Austin County"—were arrested on Magruder's order and incarcerated in one of his military stockades. Prince John thereupon sent the five to San Antonio as a means of avoiding a writ of habeas corpus, and pleaded with Kirby Smith to declare martial law. When Smith refused, Magruder said he would do it on his own in Texas, and that he had already suspended habeas corpus. "Boldness and promptness are absolutely necessary. As you are really the Government on this side of the River, cut off as we are from the President, I think you would be perfectly right to exercise the power conferred upon him by the Congress," he implored Shreveport. "I agree with you that we should be more particular, in our isolation in exercising any authority not possessed by us, unless absolutely necessary; but I think the President would fully justify it if the public safety were clearly in jeopardy by a combination of traitors."

When Peebles obtained a writ of habeas corpus from a local magistrate, the Texas civil courts demanded his release and that of his cohorts. But their freedom was short-lived, as Major J. H. Sparks, on Magruder's authority, promptly took them into custody under the guise of military necessity. Following an unbelievably complicated appeals process, the matter worked its way to the Texas supreme court, which returned a verdict against Magruder. "The situation of the country . . . forbids our attempting to punish him by imprisonment. We feel that it would illy comport with the dignity of the court to visit its penalties upon the subordinate offender [Sparks] while the principal is enabled to go unwhipped of justice," the justices ruled from Tyler, where the court sat on circuit. "We shall therefore, discharge the rule in this case, with judgment against the defendants merely for costs." Guilty though he was, Magruder escaped a serious confrontation with the Texas courts. After the release of Peebles and the others from Confederate jurisdiction, the high court "looked the other way," as Sparks again took the Unionists into custody. "On July 20 [1864], Magruder with no legal authority and without any attempt to stage even a drumhead court-martial, ordered the prisoners exiled forever from the territory of the Confederate States," comments historian Robert L. Kerby. "Escorted by a troop of cavalry they were conducted to Eagle Pass, and on August 14 driven across the Rio Grande into Mexico."[30]

A more serious threat to Confederate Texas occurred in November 1863, when Banks made a landing in force—this time on the Rio Grande. Although Magruder confessed to E. Kirby Smith that he had "7,000 men without any arms, and one half of the rest badly armed," and commenced preparations to contain the mischief with state troops, it was also apparent that the assault caught him off guard. A November 2 message from Shreveport hinted of a federal move up the Red River Valley, and implored him to cooperate with Richard Taylor in Louisiana; but, Smith added, "if Texas should prove the object of the enemy's movement, General Taylor is prepared to assist you."

Magruder himself addressed a letter on the same day to governor-elect Pendleton Murrah, who did not replace Lubbock until November 5, in which he made no mention of the Rio Grande expedition. Instead he reiterated Smith's contention that an enemy excursion from Louisiana via Niblett's Bluff was entirely possible, although some Confederate troops remained at the Sabine crossings. "The Red River Valley once in the enemy's possession, a movement upon the wealthy and productive portion of Eastern Texas above the line of the San Antonio road, becomes practicable." And, ironically, while making a plea for militia to bolster his meager command, he sought to reassure the new governor that a shipment of 5,400 Enfield rifles was on its way north from the Rio Grande. As Magruder sat in his Houston headquarters, it was soon obvious that a strategic mistake had been made by transfer of the Valley garrison to east Texas as a counter to the federal threat from Louisiana. General Hamilton P. Bee dispatched another missive, dated November 2, to Magruder: "I was advised by express from the mouth of the river this morning, at 3:30 A.M., that the enemy had made their appearance in seven steamers off the mouth of the Rio Grande at 7 P.M. yesterday."[31]

Banks, who accompanied the armada in person, arrived with such force that Bee had no choice but flight; Magruder wanted him to withdraw toward Roma—about half the distance to Laredo—but he abandoned that idea on November 5 because "I cannot go up the river with so small a force, as the whole country will be against me." Bee had only nineteen men at Fort Brown after the bulk of his command had been summoned to east Texas, although the arrival of James Duff's cavalry raised his total to about 100 men as he headed north toward the ranch of Richard King and safety. Sickness and anxiety gripped Bee from the moment of Banks's appearance, and his "pent up nervous tension caused him to panic," writes a chronicler of the operation. "He dumped his siege guns into the river and started a supply wagon train hurrying north while he put the torch to Fort Brown and its cotton." Chaos and wild abandon overtook Brownsville as the Confederates pulled out. "Behind him, the fires of Brownsville got out of hand. Hysterical mobs choked the single road to Matamoros and the ferry where men pulled guns to force passage for women and children," continues James Irby. A tremendous explosion of stored gunpowder wreaked more destruction on the town. Banks arrived the next day, November 2, to find Fort Brown not only consumed by fire but also ravaged by "looters and plunderers."[32]

Although Abraham Lincoln told Banks to stay out of Mexico for fear of precipitating an incident, his newly appointed governor, A. J.

Hamilton, opened channels with followers of Benito Juarez, who were locked in a death struggle with the Emperor Maximilian, whom Magruder and the Confederates had been courting. Hamilton had not accompanied the invasion force, but came later to establish Union civil authority in Texas, which proved to be short-lived; he was forced out when Magruder dispatched John S. "Rip" Ford a few months later to regain the Rio Grande. When Mrs. A. J. Hamilton and her children, who remained on the family homestead outside Austin during much of the war, petitioned to join her husband behind federal lines, Governor Lubbock informed Magruder on October 22 that he knew of no charges against her and thought she should be allowed to go. But, he added, the matter was one of Confederate jurisdiction and that Prince John would have to determine her fate. Some months earlier, however, when Mrs. Hamilton had first initiated her appeal, the governor had taken a different tack with Magruder: "Circumstances might arise should the contemplated invasion of our state take place, headed or aided by Hamilton, that his family could be held as hostages . . . the military should control and determine the necessary action." The affair dragged on until May 1864, when Magruder, always the chivalrous gentleman, gave his permission for her departure. Yet Mrs. Hamilton was not allowed to join her husband until December 1864, and only then with the intervention of Governor Santiago Vidaurri of Nuevo León.[33]

As future governor Edmund J. Davis and Colonel John L. Haynes, the latter another "apostate" Unionist destined for a political career in Reconstruction Texas, used the Second Texas Cavalry, with its large contingent of Mexican-Americans, to establish rapid control over the lower Rio Grande, Banks decided to send his troops northward along the coast. Unlike his effusive outpourings over Dick Dowling's exploits, Magruder's dispatches to Richmond and Shreveport are strikingly silent—almost nonexistent in the *Official Records*—about the Brownsville episode. Despite his feelings of near helplessness, because there were no more victories after Sabine Pass, federal troops landed on Mustang Island during the night of November 16, only two weeks after their arrival on the Rio Grande. Their destination was Port Aransas, situated at the northern extremity of Mustang Island, which lay off the coast between Padre and St. Joseph's islands. Banks had leapfrogged past A. M. Hobby's garrison at Corpus Christi to attack Aransas, which guarded the inlet into Corpus Christi and Copano bays.[34]

Hamilton P. Bee, who received the news at a temporary bivouac on San Fernando Creek, in present-day Nueces County, as he made his way north from Brownsville, wrote to Magruder on November 17: "They [the enemy] arrived in a fleet of nine vessels, six steamers and three sail, from the direction of Brazos Santiago, and before dark that evening, over 500 had landed." Although Bee reported a total available force of "355 men—five companies of the thirty-third Cavalry, one company Eighth Infantry, and one company cadets," Banks soon had more than 1,500 troops on Mustang Island; following a twenty-mile trek up the island from the landing site, they captured Port Aransas on November 17. When the word reached Magruder, he commenced an immediate plan to reinforce the coast "in time to save Saluria and Velasco, two most important points." A federal withdrawal from New Iberia, Louisiana, at around the same time, convinced him that more Yankees were on their way to Texas—that Brownsville and Aransas were the opening wedge in a grand invasion scheme. An obviously perplexed Prince John dashed off a November 21 missive to Richard Taylor in Louisiana: "I must have re-enforcements. By rapid marches to Niblett's Bluff, your forces may reach Texas in time, and I urgently desire that you will advance with the utmost rapidity to my relief." Taylor, however, did not respond.[35]

Magruder was alone and, for all practical purposes, cut off from E. Kirby Smith and reinforcements, when additional federals landed thirteen days later at Saluria on Matagorda Island, about sixty miles north of Port Aransas. For all the talk about holding Fort Esperanza at Pass Cavallo as a means of protecting Port Lavaca and Indianola, the post garrison—the Eighth Texas Infantry commanded by John M. Ireland, a future governor of Texas, withdrew to the mainland upon the enemy's approach. Although Colonel W. R. Bradfute, commanding on the coast, escaped from Corpus Christi aboard the steamer *Cora* when Port Aransas fell, and made his way to Saluria before the Yankees, he had no intention of offering battle with Ireland's hopelessly outnumbered ranks. Bradfute, however, did spike the fort's guns before the withdrawal. "No fight occurred before the evacuation, with the exception of a few shots from the enemy from some batteries planted on the land below the fort at a distance of 1½ miles," reported George P. Finlay, an assistant inspector general at the place. "Left the fort yesterday [November 29] at 10 o'clock. Everything was quiet then, though early in the morning the enemy had thrown about a dozen shells from a rifled 6-pounder, most of which passed harmlessly over the fort, only two striking it." With the capture of Fort Esperanza, Banks had firm control of the Texas coast southward to the Mexican border.[36]

Magruder quickly placed Colonel Smith P. Bankhead in charge at Houston, and made his way to Indianola—on the mainland opposite Saluria—where he established a temporary headquarters. The federal advance produced some uneasy moments not only in Texas but in Shreveport as well, although E. Kirby Smith informed Magruder on December 15 that "General Banks, in person, had returned to New Orleans." As a sop to his pleas for help, Tom Green's contingent was ordered back to Texas, Smith added, to help turn the tide. "After conferring with Taylor, Kirby Smith concluded that the situation in Texas was not so desperate as pictured by Magruder, especially since there was no reliable information that more than 6,000 troops had left Louisiana for the coast of Texas," writes a Smith biographer. "No further re-enforcements [*sic*] would be sent to Magruder at that time, and the Texas commander was instructed to make no change in the organization of Green's cavalry division, as it might be necessary to recall it from Texas on short notice." His alarmist cries for additional men aside, Magruder moved his headquarters to the plantation home of John C. McNeel in Brazoria County. Here, a few miles from Velasco, where the first Anglo-Texans had established themselves as members of Stephen A. Austin's colony, Magruder began to concentrate his forces for a defense of Houston and what he considered the state's breadbasket. But he vastly overstated Union strength when he apprised Governor Murrah on December 19 that "the enemy's force on the coast is from 15,000 to 20,000 men, of which about 15,000 are already stationed at Decrow's Point [Matagorda County] and Saluria." And, he added, "Immediately upon the evacuation of Saluria, I ordered the commanding officer to destroy the wharves at Lavaca and Indianola as might be of service to the enemy, and also to destroy the railroad to Victoria." At Christmas time while he remained at the McNeel homestead he told Kirby Smith, "No matter what might happen" that he would support his decisions.[37]

Magruder remained popular with secessionist Texas in the afterglow of Galveston and Sabine Pass, but widespread disenchantment with the war by Unionists, Germans, and the non-slaveholding classes had grown to alarming levels by year's end; William Pitt Barringer, who remained his loyal supporter, confided that he feared "a reaction against the Revolution and the slaveholders." Although the partying and headquarters frivolities would return soon enough, Magruder's preoccupation with Banks left little time for lighthearted amusements. Increased dissensions and failures on the Rio Grande and along the coast, however, did not detract from Magruder's standing among the Texans. Throughout his stay, Prince John was able to capitalize on his connections with several prominent families in addition to his military associations from the Mexican War and service in the old army. He was a kinsman of Mrs. Thomas Affleck, whose husband was a widely known writer on agricultural policy in Texas and the South. And through the Afflecks he enjoyed an association with "the Mother of Texas," Mrs. Jane Herbert Wilkinson Long, so called "because she was the first known woman of English descent to enter Texas and bore the first known child of such parentage in the State." Magruder was likewise linked to Jared Groce, one of Stephen F. Austin's original settlers as well as the owner of a vast plantation above Houston.[38]

When he filed his end-of-year report, Magruder assessed his total numbers at 9,700 Confederate and state troops. Although Banks held most of the Southern coast, the federals soon departed for other theaters; the famed Red River campaign of 1864 not only siphoned enemy forces from Texas but the bulk of Magruder's command as well, when he was summoned to assist Kirby Smith and Richard Taylor in Louisiana. The Union failure to invade east Texas through the Red River Valley was followed by Abraham Lincoln's decision in March 1864 to place Ulysses S. Grant in charge of all Northern armies, which inadvertently relieved Magruder from having to defend the Lone Star State, because Grant at once branded federal pinpricks along the Gulf Coast as useless, and ordered Banks to direct his efforts elsewhere.[39]

10

"You May Fully Depend on Me"

ALTHOUGH EVENTS IN WASHINGTON AND LOUISIANA relieved the pressure on Texas, Magruder remained fearful not only about a renewed invasion, but also for the state's internal security. The continued isolation of Texas and the Trans-Mississippi following Confederate failures at Port Hudson and Vicksburg, with federal steamers plying the Mississippi from New Orleans to St. Louis, caused many to abandon the fight; a general malaise gripped much of the army as common soldiers by the hundreds deserted the ranks for home and family. In January 1864, Magruder told Governor Pendleton Murrah that "day after day numerous requests" were pouring into his headquarters from enlisted men and their families seeking assignment to the Texas state guard for service nearer their home communities. With reports reaching Houston that Banks was amassing a 40,000-man force around New Orleans, he was obliged to reject all such requests, which only encouraged more desertions. Murrah, apparently for political considerations, implored him to grant some transfers as distraught family members bombarded the gubernatorial office with calls for relief. Magruder sent General Tom Green into "Polk, Angelina, and adjacent cos.," where an entire regiment had "deserted almost in a body" during the last weeks of January. Later, as Texas troops were ordered across the Louisiana border to help check the federal drive toward Shreveport, he informed E. Kirby Smith on March 8 that "a very dangerous feeling had engulfed portions of the army"; by that time, Magruder told his superior, "two veteran regiments of cavalry" were needed to carry out his orders.[1]

Magruder's running battle with Governor Francis R. Lubbock and, after November 1863, with his successor Murrah, over use of state troops, intensified through the first months of 1864. Murrah, a South Carolina lawyer who had been in Texas since the 1840s, was a "strong state rights man" who refused to cooperate with Magruder and Smith on implementing conscription laws enacted by the Confederate congress. The tug-of-war was closely associated with the confiscation of cotton by Confederate authority, and literally dozens of letters concerning both issues—letters now preserved in the Texas state archives—passed between Murrah and Magruder from the former's inauguration until Prince John's departure for Arkansas in August. As always, Magruder's letters are excited and repetitious; both before and after a February conference with Murrah and Smith that proved fruitless, he continually warned of dire consequences if additional help from Texas officialdom was not forthcoming. "It is my plain duty to inform your Excellency that without the aid of the State Troops now in the field, I have but little hope of my ability to defend any large portion of Texas against the foe," he told the new governor on November 2. "If after the months of ardious [*sic*] toil spent in organizing these Troops they are to be disbanded just as the campaign opens, the country need not expect to be spared the scenes of desolation which are presented in Missouri, Arkansas, and parts of Louisiana."[2]

The grand rhetoric aside, Murrah in effect ignored Magruder's appeals for additional men. "How do you propose to turn over the State Troops to the Confederate authorities," Magruder asked in a February 8 letter. And he pointed out that Confederate law required each new company to have "at least sixty-four men and battalions not less than five companies and Regiments not less than ten." Although he was trying to check Murrah's piecemeal transfers of men, matters became increasingly difficult two weeks later when the Confederate congress enacted a revised conscription statute demanding induction of all able-bodied men between the ages of seventeen and fifty. A recalcitrant Murrah told Magruder during mid-March than he would employ his own "judgment and discretion to some extent in complying with your request in sending to the field all the state troops to the age of fifty years." Murrah even used the old canard that transferring Texas units to Magruder's command would leave the state "defenseless on the frontier." The worsening military situation following the Red River campaign caused Murrah to relent somewhat as Magruder prepared to leave the state for Arkansas. His change of heart, which resulted from a personal meeting with E. Kirby Smith in the east Texas town of Hempstead during late July, was short-lived; while he told a Houston newspaper that Smith and the Trans-Mississippi had his "full and unreserved support," he continued to ignore the new conscription law. "Murrah's refusal to cooperate with Magruder made the act a dead letter in Texas," wrote former governor Lubbock. "General E. Kirby Smith sustained Magruder and remonstrated with the Governor, but in vain."[3]

The Trans-Mississippi commander was required to walk a tight-rope in his role as mediator between his commanders and not only Murrah but other civilian authorities as well. But Smith developed reservations about Prince John at the same moment the latter was locked in his confrontation with Murrah. "Magruder has ability and great energy; he acts by impulse, commits follies, and has an utter disregard for law; he has no facility for drawing around him good men, and his selection of agents is almost always unfortunate; he has no administrative abilities, though he is active and can do a large amount of work," Murrah told Arkansas senator Robert W. Johnson in a confidential letter on January 15. "He would be a better commander of a corps, but no reliance could be placed upon his obedience to orders unless it chimed in with his own plans and fancies." Whimsical or not, Magruder did make concessions in his firm policy of never releasing Confederate troops for other undertakings. He consistently spurned requests for men to work at agricultural pursuits, despite desperate pleading from relatives and neighbors, but other troops were dispatched to work in a private pistol factory. That operation, located at present-day West Columbia, Texas, sold its sidearms to the government for $100 each, which caused an outcry from several citizens who wanted their menfolk furloughed to work on family farms. And, at Magruder's order, men from Hamilton P. Bee's command were hurried to oversee work on the public highways and "to impress nigroe [sic] wagons for the purpose." Although these activities were military-related, Murrah and others, aware of his frolicsome nature, were often inclined to reject Magruder's nearly constant appeals for additional levees upon scarce manpower.[4]

General William R. Boggs, Smith's chief of staff, thought his boss "made a great mistake" by keeping Prince John in command, because of his questionable antics. Several of Magruder's own troops joined in the laxity surrounding his regime in Texas. An abortive mutiny took place at Galveston during March 1864 to protest "the banquets and soirées given by the ladies of Galveston for General Magruder and his staff." An outbreak among the Galveston encampment the previous summer had forced him to reestablish order through the use of strong measures, despite pleas from the ranks for regular paychecks and better food. Although his general orders of March 24 said nothing about his own partying while his men made do with short rations, Magruder moved quickly to punish the mutineers as the Red River campaign raced to a climax. After learning that "gross offenses against the rights and property of several citizens, male and female," had been committed, he ordered three or four officers and a sergeant broken in rank as well as a stern warning read to the entire company: "The major general commanding [Magruder had a fondness for that term] announces to the army that he will not hesitate to dismount any corps that disgraces itself by plundering and damaging the property of any citizen and that he will remove the colonels, majors, and captains, if necessary, of those regiments, battalions, and companies which commit such crimes, holding always the officers highest in rank responsible for the conduct of their inferior officers and men."[5]

Not only in Texas but also across the South throughout 1864–1865, a paradox began to unfold before Magruder and his fellow commanders. Every available man was needed to combat the encroaching Yankees, yet war-weary Confederate soldiers were either deserting the ranks or becoming increasingly unruly. In extreme north Texas, "devils" reported to be deserters from Quantrill's Missouri irregulars raised so much havoc that Magruder summoned Henry E. McCulloch to chase down the marauders. And it was not only deserters that caused manpower shortages throughout the spring. Troops from A. W. Spaight's Battalion had to be used for bridge repairs in several counties, and slaves were impressed in six or seven counties along the Red River for roadwork, even though most slaveholders in the region found ingenious ways to withhold their laborers. While Magruder wrestled with domestic issues, Murrah on April 5 again refused to release state troops under his control. E. Kirby Smith may have questioned his performances in Texas and Arkansas during the Confederate breakdown, but former governor Lubbock, who joined his staff as lieutenant colonel upon leaving office, thought otherwise: Magruder was in the saddle every day during the spring, surrounded "by a bright, active corps of young officers," he comments. "I found him a considerate, as well as active, energetic commander."[6]

As Magruder was escorting the ladies, ordering what was left of his Texas troops, arguing with Murrah, attempting to check Confederate desertions and increasing Unionist activity, as well as worrying about Indian depredations along the frontier, plans for the momentous Red River campaign began to unfold in Washington and the Southwest. While Abraham Lincoln and his war cabinet still labored to create loyal state governments in Texas, Louisiana, and Arkansas, and to confiscate huge cotton stockpiles in east Texas, a military thrust through the Red River Valley began to foment in the presidential mind; a federal presence in east Texas, so the reasoning went, would also threaten the French in Mexico and secondarily lead to the capture of a large Confederate prison camp at Tyler, Texas. In early January 1864, Lincoln's general-in-chief, Henry W. Halleck, began issuing orders for a four-column attack under Nathaniel P. Banks—the same general who had spearheaded the earlier invasion of the lower Rio Grande. Although Banks himself thought the capture of Mobile would produce greater results, like all military men he was required to obey orders. Halleck and the generals who surrounded him directed Banks to secure "military possession of Shreveport, secession capital of Louisiana and headquarters of the Trans-Mississippi Department of the Confederacy," notes a Banks biographer. "Shreveport carried with it control of the Red River, the shortest and best line of defense for Louisiana and Arkansas, and . . . a base of operations against Texas." Murrah, meanwhile, remained unmoved by Confederate appeals for additional Texas troops as Banks fell short of his goal, but the federal invaders did manage to get within twenty miles of the Louisiana-Texas border.[7]

Halleck's master plan called for Banks to move northward by Bayou Teche to Shreveport, while Frederick Steele led a 15,000-man force from Arkansas toward the prize. William Tecumseh Sherman was instructed to detach another 10,000 troops under General A. J. Smith from the Army of the Tennessee to accompany the gunboats of Commodore D. D. Porter from Natchez and thence up the Red River. Halleck realized from the inception that capture of Shreveport depended upon the caprices of the river, and therefore he delayed the start of the campaign until "there was sufficient water in the Atchafalya and Red Rivers." While the scheme looked good in the abstract, it had serious flaws. Sherman would only permit Smith to be across the Mississippi for one month before his return; and Steele reduced the Arkansas contingent by 3,000 men on his own initiative because of Halleck's poorly-drafted instructions. Besides the uncertainties of the river itself, an unrealistic schedule for this difficult concentration of forces had been conceived, which complicated matters for Banks.[8]

The two-and-a-half-month interval between the formation of Halleck's plan and the start of the campaign afforded E. Kirby Smith and his generals sufficient time to concentrate their own forces before the Yankee onslaught. Increased military maneuvering by the bluecoats led to considerable speculation among the Confederate high command, although Smith and Richard Taylor, the son of Zachary Taylor and still Smith's commander in Louisiana, soon deduced Banks's destination. Magruder, however, remained convinced that the federal buildup around New Orleans, and indeed along the Eastern Seaboard, was preparation for another thrust at the Texas coast. "The enemy, between 30,000 and 40,000 strong, is advancing from his present base of operations at Berwick Bay in the direction of Opelousas. Should he fail to diverge for a moment upon Texas, by way of Niblett's Bluff, his whole force will be thrown upon Genl. Taylor's army in his front, and thence up the Red River Valley to Shreveport," he told Murrah on November 22 before Halleck had issued his marching orders. Although he was attempting to secure the release of state troops, Magruder warned, "The Red River Valley once in his [Banks's] possession, and a movement upon the wealthy and productive portions of Eastern Texas becomes practicable." Two months later he advised his district commander, Hamilton P. Bee, that the Yankees had 20,000 men "at the mouth of the Mississippi," and that they were headed for Galveston. Bee, brother of Barnard Bee, slain at First Manassas and the officer who reportedly tagged Thomas Jackson with the immortal sobriquet "Stonewall," was told to hold his command in readiness for a movement toward the "vital Point."[9]

In a lengthy letter to W. R. Boggs on January 22, Magruder repeated his assertion that Banks was preparing to descend on the Texas coast with "20,000 additional troops at the mouth of the Mississippi. The lieutenant general being thoroughly acquainted with my views for the defense of Texas," he continued, "I do not think it proper to present them again." Only 9,000 men, including 3,000 state troops, were available, Magruder went on, for the defense of Texas in the inevitable invasion. Unimpressed with Magruder's arguments, Smith ordered him to concentrate his available forces in east Texas for a quick march to Niblett's Bluff—situated on the Sabine River boundary with Louisiana, when it became clear that Banks's object was Shreveport and the Red River Valley. And though he had no choice but to obey superior commands, Magruder made his own preparations along the coast with the resources available to him. He ordered a small troop concentration at East Bernard, on the lower Colorado not far from the coast, to meet any attack. The troopers were admonished to "work with a will upon the defenses so necessary for their protection" because, he added, it was more than probable that an enemy thrust at Galveston would be launched within the month.[10]

The main show, however, was east of the Sabine, and Magruder was told to hurry General Tom Green toward Alexandria on March 5, a full five days before A. J. Smith left Vicksburg aboard Porter's flotilla. Magruder's Special Order No. 66, issued the following day, set Green's division in motion on March 7; the Texans were instructed to march from Hempstead "via Montgomery, Woodville, Burkeville, Huddleston, and Hurston, La. to Alexandria La." Supplies of corn and subsistence, Magruder added, were available along the way; Green's marching orders forbade all furloughs and leaves of absence.

Boggs, acting on Smith's behalf, sent daily communiqués imploring Magruder, who remained in Houston, to speed the movement of men and supplies. Smith, anxious to meet the enemy, called for all available small arms in Texas, as well as horses to assist his ill-equipped troopers. Although Green was able to sustain his men, the sad state of Texas and the Trans-Mississippi, which led to increased desertions and a general feeling of desperation, confronted his command on the eastward trek. "The distance to be traversed in reaching headquarters in Louisiana exceeded 300 miles. Heavy rains had fallen, the muddy roads were cut all the way by the passage of wagon trains, and part of the region I had to pass through was stripped of food and forage by the march and countermarch of armies," wrote Governor Lubbock, who left Magruder's headquarters on March 10 to join his fellow Texans. "The country along the roads wore an air of desolation. Old men, boys, women, children, and a few cripples were occasionally met with, but no able-bodied men."[11]

Green did not join Richard Taylor at Mansfield, Louisiana, until April 5, although A. J. Smith and Commodore Porter had arrived on the lower Red River by March 14 to open the campaign. And Magruder dispatched additional Texas units as E. Kirby Smith positioned his meager force to meet the onslaught. "Heavy columns of the enemy are marching from Little Rock, the Mississippi River, and Brashear City [present-day Morgan City]," Boggs had telegraphed on March 12, after the order to send Green forward. Magruder, who was given "the option" of accompanying his troops or remaining in Houston, was directed to send "all the force at your command in the Eastern Sub-District of Texas to Louisiana, reducing the garrisons to a minimum." Kirby Smith urged him to approach Murrah anew for a release of state troops, and to keep a communication with his Shreveport headquarters by courier and telegraph. "These orders," Boggs added, "must be carried out without delay." Within two days Magruder informed Smith that all available troops would be "hurried forward as soon as possible."[12]

When Tom Green, a graduate of the University of Tennessee and Princeton, who had practiced law in Texas for several years before the war, reached Taylor, his contingent bolstered the Confederate force to a total of 16,000; the well-known Green, who had manned one of the famed cannon called the "twin sisters" at the Battle of San Jacinto, was killed a few days later at Blair's Landing on the Red River. Other Texas outfits, under Camille Armand Polignac, a French-born officer who had served in the Crimea, and Hamilton Bee, soon arrived to reinforce Smith's force. Polignac, who commanded a cavalry unit known popularly as Polignac's Brigade, reached Taylor during the retreat toward Shreveport on April 1, seven days before the decisive battle at Sabine Crossroads, three miles southeast of Mansfield; the federal rout was partly the result of newly arrived units from Magruder. The Texans, including the division of John G. Walker, fought again the following day, April 9, at Pleasant Hill when Taylor renewed his attack on the federals struggling to find their way south. Here, seventy miles south of Shreveport, another hard-fought engagement ended in stalemate. "As darkness rapidly enshrouded the scene, both armies lost the will to continue the killing," writes Richard Taylor's biographer. E. Kirby Smith, who came on the battlefield to encounter a dispirited Taylor, ordered a Confederate retreat northward at the same time Nathaniel P. Banks started his columns back down the Red River.[13]

As the armies of Taylor and Banks jockeyed for position, Magruder told an unidentified correspondent that he waited with "impatience"—that he could not then (March 11) leave his Houston headquarters. On March 31 he again appealed to Murrah for additional troops: "I beseech your Excellency to throw aside any other considerations." The same missive carried a warning that E. Kirby Smith feared a raid by federal cavalry—5,000 strong "upon Marshall, and the destruction of our Manufacturers and Supplies there, as well as the devastation of that region of the country." A vigorous Magruder-Murrah correspondence continued throughout the Red River fighting: Smith (Boggs) would telegraph Prince John for more troops and supplies, and Magruder would thereupon petition the governor for state levies; Murrah, who either ignored Magruder or found a means to evade the requests, remained adamant. "Relying upon the patriotism and spirit of concession which you have met me on several occasions, my hopes [remain] of an ability to meet the enemy successfully, should he invade Texas," Magruder appealed on April 4. Finally, on the seventh, Murrah relented: "As you have declined receiving State troops as State Troops, I shall be forced in view of the dangers surrounding the State and Country, to co-operate with you in organizing them under the recent law of Congress." That came two days after Murrah told Magruder that the troops had already been organized into marching units for the front.

His intentions aside, the Texas governor, facing renewed Indian threats along the frontier as well as a general uneasiness throughout the state, continued to withhold support when reports of the federal withdrawal from the campaign reached Austin. On April 28, two weeks after Pleasant Hill, Magruder informed Murrah that E. Kirby Smith had ordered him to command in Arkansas; although he had surely despaired of getting additional men from Texas, Magruder

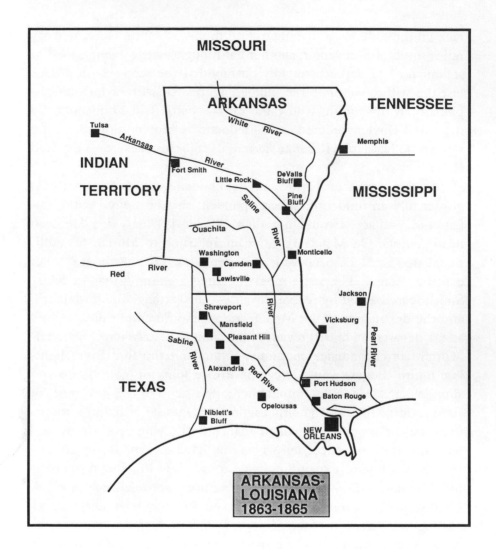

MISSOURI

ARKANSAS   TENNESSEE

White   River

Tulsa

Arkansas

Memphis

INDIAN   River

Fort Smith

Little Rock   DeValls
Bluff

TERRITORY   Pine
Bluff   MISSISSIPPI

Saline

Ouachita   River

Washington   Monticello

Camden

Red   River   Lewisville

River

Jackson

Shreveport

Vicksburg

Mansfield

Pleasant Hill   Pearl River

Sabine

River   Alexandria   Red River

TEXAS   Port Hudson

Opelousas   Baton Rouge

Niblett's
Bluff

NEW
ORLEANS

**ARKANSAS-
LOUISIANA
1863-1865**

took the occasion to stroke his adversary in the hopes of better relations: "I cannot leave this Desk . . . without expressing to you my high appreciation of your patriotism and ability." Magruder's departure from Texas, however, was delayed by a May 2 telegram from Smith telling him to stay put for the present. Smith, who was in Arkansas himself, directing an attack on Frederick Steele's federal army after its withdrawal from the Red River fighting, apparently had second thoughts about the transfer.[14]

Following Pleasant Hill, which was fought within twenty-five miles of the Texas border, the Trans-Mississippi commander faced a dilemma: Should he attack the fleeing columns of Banks and Porter, or should he drive into Arkansas and destroy Steele? Although Taylor wanted to pursue Banks down the river, Smith, after more than a little soul-searching, resolved to attack northward, where Steele had not advanced beyond Camden. Here, a good 110 miles northeast of Shreveport, the Union commander had remained in place upon learning about the fight at Pleasant Hill. To the eternal disgust of Taylor, Smith started his lead units into Arkansas on April 14, and two days later he took the road northward himself. Constantly harassed by Price's cavalry and dangerously low on supplies and forage, Steele abandoned the Camden defenses on April 27 and started his wagon trains toward the safety of Little Rock. Although Magruder would soon make his Arkansas headquarters in the Ouachita River town, Smith pressed through the place after the retreating Steele.

At Jenkins Ferry three days later, Smith overtook his prey in the muddy bottoms along the Saline River; Steele managed to extricate himself after a nasty little fight in which Walker's Texas division alone lost seventy-four killed, 266 wounded, and one missing. "The Battle of Jenkins Ferry," writes a state historian, "for all practical purposes ended the military campaigning in Arkansas." The Texas troops sent from Magruder's Houston headquarters had once more tipped the scales, as they had done along the Red River; yet Smith told Prince John to remain at his old station until Confederate operations had been sorted out in the aftermath of Lincoln's attempt to invade northwestern Louisiana and east Texas.[15]

Meanwhile, Richard Taylor started his chase after Banks and Porter with what forces he could muster, including the Texas commands of Bee and Tom Green; but Taylor had a cancer eating at his soul because of Smith's decision to attack into Arkansas with part of the army. "My plans for following and driving the enemy were to a great extent based upon the assurances that Walker's division would be at my disposal," he told Smith afterwards. As Smith headed into Arkansas himself, he appointed Taylor lieutenant general, subject to the approval of Jefferson Davis. "Of the three district commanders, Major Generals Magruder, Price, and Taylor, the latter is the junior, and the one of the three I consider suitable to take charge of affairs in the department," he told the president on April 16. "Should the contingency arise to which I have referred the good of the country and the cause demand that he should succeed to command." Although Smith clearly preferred Taylor, Magruder wrote a hearty word of congratulation to his fellow commander following "Your glorious success in the brilliant affair of the 8th and 9th inst., and in several subsequent engagements." Magruder's April 16 note to Taylor also carried word that his differences with Murrah had been patched over and that "2,000 or 3,000" additional troops would soon find their way to Louisiana—troops that never arrived. All was apparently forgiven between the two on a personal level, despite earlier feuding over precious manpower.[16]

Although Magruder took no personal hand in the Red River operation, on April 12 disaster struck at Blair's Landing, where Taylor had ordered Tom Green forward with his cavalry to block Porter's gunboats: "With loud yells the Texans jumped into their saddles and followed their brave commander, rushing to within twenty feet of one gunboat, but a fierce shelling forced them to withdraw some distance," notes Green's biographer. Other vessels soon appeared on the river as Green renewed the attack. "Suddenly fate caught up with the Texas commander. As he stood beside his horse some forty feet from the *Osage*, a cannon shell struck him in the forehead tearing away the upper portion of his skull and killing him instantly." More jousting and fighting with the enemy by Taylor's men continued as Banks sped toward safety. Although Porter had boasted that his "gunboats could go 'wherever the sand was damp,'" low water above the Alexandria rapids produced some tense moments as federal engineers strove night and day with their famous sluice dams to raise the water level; and more dams were needed at points on the lower river.

Constant skirmishing took place until the final action at Yellow Bayou on May 18 near the mouth of the Atchafalaya River, and by May 26 Banks had reached Donaldsonville on the Mississippi south of Baton Rouge. Besides the sorrowful loss of Tom Green, William R. Scurry, who had fought at Magruder's side during the recapture of Galveston, also fell in the Louisiana fighting. Hamilton P. Bee, another of his faithful lieutenants from the moment of his arrival in Houston, ran into difficulty when Taylor charged him with incompetence while skirmishing along the Cane River, and removed him from command; although Bee "remained under a cloud" for the remainder of the war, he was later posted to a subordinate command on the Texas frontier. As the Red River fighting drew to a close, it was clear that the Texas units played a major role in the defeat of Banks as well as Smith's successful foray into southern Arkansas. Magruder had taken a marginal role in both actions, but, concludes Texas historian Alwyn Barr, an estimated 3,000 of his men were lost in the effort.[17]

While the Red River campaign was under way and, indeed, until his departure for Arkansas in mid-August, Magruder had good reason to worry about a renewed federal thrust at the Texas coast; Banks had a formidable army at his disposal as well as a naval armada to ferry him into the western Gulf. "The commanding general announces to his troops that the enemy having failed in his attack upon Mobile renders it more than probable that he may make one on Galveston in the next month," he proclaimed on April 19. "And the necessity for agricultural purposes of most of the negroes [sic] being kept upon the plantations has induced him to call upon his troops to work with a will upon the defenses so necessary for their own protection, as well as that of the country." The next day he told Boggs that he had not accompanied his men to Louisiana because "I could not abandon my district at the moment when my presence was most necessary." By his own reckoning, the enemy had 5,000 troops on the shores of Matagorda Bay and another 4,000 on the lower Rio Grande. Fearful that enemy troops along the coast would march on Houston, Magruder put his remaining 4,000 or so men to preparing defensive barriers.

While he fretted and prepared for the onslaught that never arrived, however, an appreciated missive arrived from General Howell Cobb, one of his comrades from the Virginia fighting. "I have witnessed your successful career in Texas," Cobb told him, although he wrote to commend John A. Wharton, recently transferred to the Trans-Mississippi from the East. "I assure you dear General your friends and officers who served under you in the Peninsula can never cease to regard with interest their esteemed commander," the one-time Georgia governor added. If Magruder had his detractors on both sides of the Mississippi, he also had a reservoir of support; just as E. Kirby Smith would soon rely upon him to tidy up what remained of Confederate Arkansas, few men who served under him could forget his barracks-room bonhomie. Alexander C. Jones, another associate from the East, joined Magruder's staff in early 1864 as inspector general. While he traveled to Galveston and through other parts of Texas during the summer, Magruder came to rely upon Jones to maintain his Houston headquarters.[18]

When Kirby Smith journeyed to Hempstead in east Texas some weeks after the close of his Arkansas venture to once again confer with Governor Murrah, Jones tended to much of the preliminary planning. The June meeting dealt with the distribution of cotton proceeds between Texas and the Trans-Mississippi commands, whereas the earlier confab at Houston between Smith, Murrah, and Magruder had concerned the use of Texas state troops; under an agreement they worked out, the State Cotton Bureau would retain one half of all Texas cotton, while the remaining half would be exempted. Nor would Smith and Magruder interfere with the transportation of cotton to the Rio Grande for transshipment abroad. Proceeds from cotton sales were still the chief means to equip and supply Confederate forces in the Trans-Mississippi, and not only under Magruder's command. Murrah left the meeting determined to cooperate in the division of monies garnered from the sale of impressed cotton. The importance of this revenue source was more than obvious when Magruder told Smith and Boggs on June 6 that he required 200 bales to outfit a new regiment under Sherod Hunter for service on the frontier; their sale, Magruder reasoned, would yield $10,000 in specie. The Confederate congress, however, resolved the persistent dilemma for both soldiers a few weeks later, when all cotton-related matters were handed over to civilian treasury officials.[19]

Smith gave his blessing for Magruder to concentrate his forces for the defense of Sabine Pass, Galveston, and Velasco, although Union forces occupied a good portion of the lower Rio Grande when the Hempstead conference took place. Constant probing by the Union navy during May, June, and July fed his anxieties about another Yankee incursion. As early as May 20—in the last days of the Red River campaign—Magruder had warned Shreveport "that the troops left in the State of Texas are totally inadequate to its defense in case General Banks should move upon our coast as I believe he will do." Texas units in Louisiana, Magruder said, would require more than a month to return, and he pointed out that barely 200 men were posted between Matagorda Bay and San Antonio. Even before operations on the Red River, he had watched a naval bombardment of Indianola during late February; and the federal navy ventured into Matagorda Bay, creating havoc and consternation for the meager defenders left at Saluria. On April 20 Magruder was able to tell Smith that the Yankee flotilla had been driven off "after a fight of one and a half hours."[20]

The federals had also shelled Velasco, at the mouth of the Brazos, on March 21, but like other thrusts at the coast, the raid had not been followed by an invasion force. The enemy, however, kept nearly constant pressure on Galveston with an intense blockade throughout 1864; it remained the chief port of entry for Texas and a place close to Magruder's heart after its recapture the year before. And by mid-June the blockading squadron was comprised of twelve warships of varying drafts. Yet Confederate vessels—often flying the flags of other nations, including the Swiss Republic—were able to elude the blockaders with some regularity. One small ship, reported the Galveston newspapers in early June, "took French Leave of the Yankee fleet outside on Saturday night last. She slipped out as she came in, just as easy as falling off a log." Although the "little blockade runner" was bound for Havana with 300 bales of cotton, other ships, like the *Isabel*, which made "upwards of twenty successful trips between Mobile and Galveston," were not as fortunate. The *Isabel*, run down and captured by the USS *Admiral* on May 28, was found to be carrying a cargo of powder, arms, percussion caps, hardware, and medicine."

Daring federal commanders occasionally chased the runners into Galveston harbor, including "a large schooner from Havana [which] ran the blockade this morning about 3 o'clock," reported the *Galveston Tri-Weekly News* on June 6. Her pursuers fired nine shots before she found safety at the dockside. If maintaining a flow of ships and war supplies into Galveston and, indeed, the rest of Texas remained a dilemma for Magruder, he had a solution for keeping the blockaders at bay. "Go on with the new works and open upon the ships as soon as the guns are planted, if the enemy comes within range," he ordered General James M. Hawes, commanding at Galveston, on July 6. Although Magruder ordered several siege guns transported to Houston in August 1864, Hawes, who reported that he had 3,600 effectives on July 31, retained command until Magruder departed for Arkansas. And Prince John had other means of coastal defense: "Oddly enough for a Confederate general, Kirby Smith possessed a naval department, or at least a 'Marine Bureau,' under the immediate command of his subordinate Magruder," writes a careful student of the Trans-Mississippi. His bureau had been established shortly after the Battle of Galveston under the direction of Leon Smith, whom Magruder always called "Commodore Smith." By early 1864, William R. Geise continues, Smith had "thirty-five vessels, twelve of them armed steamers, two armed schooners, and the rest transports, dispatch boats and police boats, all located on the bays and bayous of the coast of Texas." But Magruder's armada with its high number of ships that were hardly seaworthy, manned by disgruntled soldiers doubling as sailors, was simply no match for the federal blockaders.[21]

His efforts to retake the lower Rio Grande Valley were much more successful during the summer. A residue of Banks's army under Francis J. Herron remained ensconced around Brownsville when Magruder summoned John Salmon "Rip" Ford, his chief conscription officer at Austin, to lead an expedition toward the Mexican border. The popular Ford, who held no Confederate commission, assembled several hundred men in San Antonio, and by March 17 he was ready to advance. By April 17 he had reached Laredo, on the Rio Grande, some 170 miles upriver from Brownsville. Ford immediately found himself embroiled in the complicated tug-of-war between the French and their Mexican allies on the one hand, and the patriot Benito Juarez and his supporters on the other. Upon reaching the valley, Ford sent word to Magruder in Houston that he would avoid crossing into Mexican territory because "it would be tantamount to a declaration of war by the Juarez government against the Confederate States." At the end of May, however, Ford was able to purchase guns and other supplies from beyond the Rio Grande through his superb diplomatic overtures with both warring factions.

With a force numbering about 1,500 men, including troops from Confederate Arizona, he moved down the river to Ringgold Barracks at present-day Rio Grande City; Ford also engaged in a heated disagreement with the local agent for the Texas Cotton Bureau, who refused to release funds for the expedition as Magruder had instructed him to do. After he eventually secured the funds through drafts, Ford reached Hidalgo on June 21; at the ranch of Las Rucias, "twenty-four miles up river from Brownsville," the Yankees turned to contest the Confederate columns. "Federals were at Las Rucias awaiting an attack from Hidalgo," writes a scholar of the border clashes. "So sure were they Ford would strike from up river, they had taken no precautions to cover the Brownsville road to their rear. So the Confederates were able to work their way by means of an obscure trail toward the Union rear. . . . The brief but fierce battle which followed ended with the routing of the Federals, who escaped to the Mexican side."

Following the Las Rucias fight, which included federal troops from the command of Edmund J. Davis, Ford had an unobstructed path into the prize at Brownsville. "Your course and efforts meets [*sic*] with . . . most perfect satisfaction . . . none could have conducted the operations with greater success," an ecstatic Magruder wrote on July 12. "We soon learned that the Federals had fixed an ambuscade on the Brownsville Road for our special entertainment. There were cannon, infantry, and cavalry prepared in fine style to kill us off. We did not go where they expected us," Ford writes in his 1897 memoir. "On July 29 the Unionists evacuated Brownsville and Fort Brown and moved down river to Brazos Island to embark for other points." And, Ford adds, "the Yankee line of retreat was marked by the articles of clothing that had been cast off." Fearful that Ford would overwhelm him, Herron had withdrawn his army to the low-lying islands at the mouth of the Rio Grande, rather than risk an all-out fight. With the extraordinary diplomatic and military exploits of his trusted subordinate, Magruder was able to inform Shreveport that the Rio Grande was free of enemy forces when the Confederates barreled into Fort Brown on July 30—that Ford's mission had been accomplished with surprisingly few men. Although Boggs had rushed troops from Louisiana to help in the fight, Colonel Henry M. Day, commanding the 91st

Illinois Infantry at Brazos Santiago, told his superiors on August 15, "The entire force of the enemy, consisting of about 900 cavalry, have left Brownsville, with the exception of about 80 men who are guarding the place."[22]

On August 4, less than a week after Ford's triumph, Magruder's fate took a dramatic turn when E. Kirby Smith held "a grand pow-wow" with Sterling Price and Missouri governor Thomas C. Reynolds at his Shreveport headquarters. At that meeting it was determined to launch Price upon an expedition to reestablish Confederate authority in Missouri, which created a power vacuum because a major general senior to Price was needed to command the considerable body of Confederate troops in southern Arkansas. Since Magruder was the only officer qualified in the district, and since Smith was gratified by his performance along the Mexican border, he was posted to Arkansas the same day. John Walker was tapped to replace him at Houston, and Simon Bolivar Buckner was ordered to Louisiana following Richard Taylor's departure to join the Army of Tennessee. Magruder, however, was unable to leave until August 17, when he turned over temporary command of Texas, New Mexico, and Arizona to Paul O. Hebert, the man he had replaced twenty-two months earlier. Although the Red River campaign had delayed his leaving Texas for several weeks, Prince John had done good service for the Confederacy along the Gulf Coast and the Rio Grande. "All I ask is that you will give the same cordial support to my successor which you have afforded me, and that you will not relax in your efforts to preserve that which you have so nobly won," Magruder said with characteristic panache as he told his Texans farewell. "I found your State in danger, I leave it in security. I found the people in despondency, I leave them in hope. I found traitors exultant; I leave patriots triumphant. . . ."[23]

Magruder may have left the Lone Star full of optimism, but Governor Murrah remained unmoved. "I agree as to the importance of maintaining a state force, which may be thwarted, judgeing [sic] from the movements of Maj. Genl. Magruder," he informed Guy M. Bryan, now adjutant on E. Kirby Smith's staff; his confidential memo, however, trusted that Smith would be more favorably disposed toward Texas. Although Magruder traveled to his new headquarters by way of Shreveport for a tête-à-tête with Smith, who apparently retained confidence in him, Major F. R. Earle, commanding the 34th Arkansas

Infantry under Thomas J. Churchill, greeted the transfer with guarded enthusiasm: "Genl. Magruder has command of us here. As far as we have seen he has been well received," Earle told his wife from Camden. "I hope his career may be glorious, not particularly for his sake, but for the sake of all the people." Camden and much of Arkansas where the Confederate impulse was strongest had suffered mightily under Steele's occupation. One resident said the federal departure for Little Rock a few weeks before Magruder got there "left many without any livestock or any means to support themselves." Magruder's coming, with his well-known buoyancy, was received with hope.[24]

During his layover in Shreveport, Magruder applied himself to the duties ahead. Unfortunately, Smith was still locked in his tiff with Richard Taylor throughout his stay; at one point the Trans-Mississippi commander warned Jefferson Davis that either he or Taylor had to go—that both men could not remain west of the river. After John A. Wharton proclaimed that federal gunboats were so thick that a bird could not fly undetected across the Mississippi, Smith informed his nemesis on August 22 that he could take no troops with him when he reported east of the river—he would have to proceed on his own. Smith's preoccupation with affairs of greater moment left Magruder to his own devices. "Since my arrival here I have endeavored to obtain from the best sources all possible information relating to the positions and strength of the enemy's forces in Arkansas, and to the means which are expected to be placed at my disposal for operations against them," he wrote to Boggs on August 30. He estimated enemy troops in Arkansas at 16,000; with federals positioned between De Valls Bluff and Pine Bluff, Magruder was convinced that he should attack Steele's communications and supply lines because insufficient Confederate troops existed for a direct assault on Little Rock. To accomplish his purpose, he told Boggs, "it is necessary that our army should cross the Arkansas River in such force as to make it as certain as a pitched battle can ever be that we should be able to fight the enemy with success, for the country between the Arkansas and White Rivers becomes, it is said, utterly impracticable after a rain, and the Arkansas River will be between it and [our] base of Camden."[25]

Although Magruder did not reach Camden until the second week in September, Sterling Price, who had been in charge since the

Confederate recapture of the place, left for his Missouri raid on August 30; one day earlier Price had issued a proclamation that Prince John was about to take over: "The major-general commanding congratulates the people and the army of the district on the assignment of this distinguished officer to its command," he told the Arkansans. "The troops he is about to control have won unfading laurels on many well-fought fields. Under this able, gallant, and active leader they will garner still more." While he tarried in Shreveport, Magruder not only wished to confer with Price personally, but also promised Kirby Smith that he would cooperate with the Missouri venture in any way necessary to insure success. But Price marched before a one-on-one understanding between the two soldiers could be established, and that fact alone may have contributed to Price's failure.[26]

Magruder was in Camden by September 9, more than a week after Price had gone northward, and he would make the town his headquarters until December 1, when he relocated in the Hempstead County hamlet of Washington. Following the retreat of Steele's force at Jenkins Ferry—a few miles north of Camden—the heavily entrenched town had been securely in Confederate hands. Although the surrounding countryside had been stripped clean of forage and sustenance for any army, the Ouachita River town dominated the region south of the Arkansas River because of its excellent communications with Louisiana and the lower Mississippi. Situated on the Ouachita fifty miles northwest of its juncture with the Saline and forty miles north of the Louisiana border, "the town upon a high bank on the left side of the river had been fortified by the Confederates, completely as against any force except a gunboat fleet, to which it would have offered a tempting goal." Then, continues John M. Harrell, "the Ouachita River from Camden down is like an estuary from the sea." Steamboats regularly called from New Orleans and Banks would surely have taken the place, had the Red River campaign not fizzled. Magruder had been correct in his earlier assessment from Shreveport that southeastern Arkansas, with the Ouachita, Saline, Arkansas, and White rivers flowing parallel to each other in a southeasterly direction, would make difficult campaigning for either army. While Price was on the prowl in Missouri, everyone but Magruder himself realized that he was perfectly safe from the enemy. Frederick Steele was content to remain behind the Little Rock defenses, eighty-five miles away, while the Missouri drama played out.[27]

Magruder had no sooner arrived in Camden than he became Prince John once more. Just as the ladies of Galveston "saw fit to give Gen. McGruder and other high officers of the army a supper and a ball, or party," wrote Private H. C. Medford, one of his Texas troopers, Magruder appeared to ignore the deprivations of his enlisted men as the Confederate war effort commenced to falter. And, Medford continues, "the soldiers told [him] that it was no time for feasting, fiddling, and dancing." Six months after the "Galveston mutiny," which had required "one regiment and a battalion" to squelch, the overwhelming scarcity of provisions—in a state more ravaged than Texas had ever been—must have caused his Arkansas command to look askance upon his renewed partying. At Camden, but also at Washington, which became the state capital after Governor Harris Flanagan's retreat from Little Rock, and was Magruder's later headquarters, the good times rolled. "The pretty girls of that refined and hospitable community had the presence of officers once more. . . . His nephew and aide-de-camp was as great a beau as his uncle in former days—and would be now. He [Magruder] wore a Confederate uniform, made and finished in regulation style in Paris," noted Colonel Harrell. "The parlors of these two chivalrous representatives of the old south were the scene of many costly and elegant festivities during the winter of 1864–65." General Boggs, ever critical of Magruder, says that Prince John's departure for Texas before the war's end was related to the partying or lack thereof: "The style of living in Arkansas was not in accord with Magruder's taste and in a very short time he was at department headquarters and closeted with General Smith." While Boggs is adamant about his return to Texas the following March, others realistically point out that the war was over in Arkansas and that he returned to Houston as a replacement for John Walker, who had become unpopular with the Texans.[28]

Amid the "elegant festivities" that started immediately after he reached Arkansas, Magruder was the worried and worrisome commander; imaginary disaster threatened him at every turn, and in a replay of his incessant communiqués about an invasion of the Texas coast, he opened a bombarding correspondence with Smith and

Boggs regarding enemy intentions from the moment he reached his new assignment. Nor could he be accused of being a grudging subordinate. He reported almost daily troop movements, accompanied by his own assessment of their meaning. "Seven thousand men are reported to have landed on the island at the mouth of White River, where the enemy I am informed, have a depot," he told Boggs on September 10. "I estimate those who went up the river on eleven transports at 6,000, call the former 5,000, the latter 4,000, and Steele will have 9,000 reinforcements." Magruder put Steele's total force at 12,000, excluding those at Fort Smith, and he not only asked for additional troops, but also reminded Shreveport, "When Price left there were but 3,000 men (armed) in Arkansas; stretched from Washington to Monticello, and of these only about 250 cavalry." The September 10 appeal closed with an evaluation of his situation in Camden and southern Arkansas: "The very great object is to beat the enemy at any sacrifice, and unless we hold the Arkansas Valley we cannot subsist an army except joining Red River, without immense means of transportation."[29]

Arkansas was in such poor shape that few if any offensive maneuvers could be mounted by the Confederates. Even Magruder was forced to admit that "the country between the Ouachita and the Arkansas is almost a desert, without corn, or grass or man or beast." The nearly total lack of corn for horses prompted the removal of several cavalry units to Texas before the end of the year. Thousands of state residents left for Texas after abandoning their farmsteads and their slaves, many of whom were left to their own devices to reach areas held by the federal army. The resultant breakdown in law and order caused great patches of the state to be abandoned as the lawlessness and general scarcity of food spread north and south.

"Much of the theft and murder that took place ultimately had no military or political motive behind it," writes an Arkansas historian. "In one such raid a band of armed men entered the home of John and Ellen Buchanan of Washington County searching for gold. When the Buchanans refused to tell where their property was hidden, the raiders burned the feet of the mother and father and then hanged one of their sons from a nearby tree." Although the remainder of the family escaped with their lives, Magruder was powerless to check the spreading mayhem and suffering; yet E. Kirby Smith hoped that he could mount an assault upon Frederick Steele's encampment at Little Rock. But, he added in a September 22 note, "You cannot expect further accession to your force."[30]

Magruder was concerned that Benjamin H. Grierson would move his cavalry from Memphis for an attack upon his garrison clustered around Camden; even so, Kirby Smith remained convinced that "the reinforcements reported to have joined Steele, will find occupation in Missouri, and should leave you strong enough for offensive operations." While he pondered his next moves, Magruder opened communications with Governor Flanagan on September 11, only two or three days after his arrival at Camden. He was too involved with an anticipated enemy thrust "from Pine Bluff toward Monticello," he said, for a personal visit. Magruder also asked Flanagan if he would concentrate "five companies of State troops at Arkadelphia" to "push their reconnaissance toward Little Rock as far as possible, pick up stragglers, deserters, and persons liable to conscription." Throughout the war, Flanagan cooperated with Confederate authorities, although he was inclined to pardon Arkansas militiamen who broke ranks or deserted as the conflict wound down. Unlike Murrah, who was always worried about Indian atrocities on the frontier and along the Rio Grande, the Arkansas governor willingly placed his state troopers at Magruder's disposal.

Upon the initial federal occupation of Little Rock, Flanagan had moved his seat of government to Washington, "along with his assistants and the archives." The New Jersey–born governor, who had been in Arkansas since 1836, kept his capital there until 1865, and from there he issued repeated calls for militia companies to resist the federals: "I ask the people of Southwest Arkansas to make an effort to save their homes from destruction. [You] are a proud and daring people," he proclaimed in 1863. For all of his good intentions, Flanagan had difficulty maintaining his government. With most of the state under Union control after mid-1863, "only 8 of the 25 senators and 31 of 75 representatives" reached the new capital for an opening session of the legislature. But the state supreme court "declared an emergency quorum present, so that the legislative business could proceed." As Flanagan struggled to sustain a semblance of state government, Magruder switched his headquarters to Washington in early December 1864. After leaving Camden on November 21, he was alternately at Lewisville and Spring Hill before becoming firmly established at Flanagan's side.[31]

Before Magruder's move from Camden, Kirby Smith met him for a strategy session at Lewisville on November 3; Smith implored him to march on Little Rock as a means of relieving the pressure on Price. If that proved "impracticable," he was told to attack Fort Smith. General Samuel Bell Maxey, commanding in the Indian Territory and a U.S. senator from Texas after the war, was ordered to assist with both operations. Little Rock and Fort Smith were firmly in Union hands, rendering a meaningful assault next to impossible. At year's end Magruder reported his total strength at 12,700 effectives under five subordinate commanders: Thomas J. Churchill, Mosby M. Parsons, John A. Wharton, John S. Marmaduke, and James A. Fagan. He did manage to launch several raids, including a January 1865 assault upon an enemy position at Dardanelle, situated on the Arkansas River roughly midway between Little Rock and Fort Smith. The expedition not only overwhelmed and destroyed a steamer, the *New Chippewa*, but also captured "1 officer and 29 men of the Fiftieth Indiana, 40 negroes [*sic*], [as well as] the captain, crew, and a large number of refugee families from Fort Smith." Magruder reported Confederate losses as one killed and fifteen wounded; he set federal casualties at twenty-seven killed and wounded "besides those who drowned" while attempting to flee aboard two additional steamers. More than 100 Yankees were taken prisoner. Another incursion by Parsons's command destroyed a mill at Pine Bluff, "capturing one company, thirty-seven strong, [along with] a number of horses, arms, etc."[32]

Magruder's isolated thrusts were nothing more than pinpricks in the sides of the Union occupiers; and as he ordered the destruction of Confederate cotton to keep it out of enemy hands and sent his cavalry into northwestern Arkansas to bring out Southern loyalists, he kept a close eye on the East, where the war was winding down. With Robert E. Lee stalled behind his defensive works in front of Petersburg, and William Tecumseh Sherman wreaking havoc in the Carolinas, both Jefferson Davis and Abraham Lincoln reluctantly consented to the famed Hampton Roads conference on February 3. The meeting, aboard the steamer *River Queen*, between Lincoln himself and three Confederate leaders—Vice President Alexander H. Stephens, R. M. T. Hunter, a prominent Virginia secessionist, and Assistant Secretary of War John A. Campbell—resulted in Lincoln's firm declaration that nothing short of complete surrender would end the war. Although an honorable termination of the conflict appealed to many Confederate politicos, and talk of capitulation raced through the Southland, Davis could not accept Lincoln's ultimatum, and Magruder pledged his support in a February 12 letter:

> In this crisis in our affairs, when Editors of news papers [*sic*] and men of mere expedients are levelling their attacks against your Excellency, I think it proper that those generals who agree with your Excellency in the opinions which you have Expressed as to peace negotiations, and in your general policy should assure your Excellency of their cordial support. I am one of those; and I beg leave to say, that you may fully depend on me. . . .

Magruder promised to use his "influence" in support of Davis and the Confederate cause. With the Civil War racing to a climax, Magruder's fellow cadet at West Point from almost forty years before found no time to answer his commander in Arkansas.[33]

In the midst of rampant desertions throughout the Trans-Mississippi, E. Kirby Smith reported only 36,000 effectives under his command by early March; that, coupled with fears that E. R. S. Canby, who had replaced Banks as federal commander in Louisiana, might hurl his considerable force toward Galveston and the Texas coast prompted Smith to speed troops toward the region, including the command of John H. Forney. Simon Bolivar Buckner, later governor of Kentucky, had been appointed lieutenant general, which left Magruder as senior major general in the West and also an officer upon whom Smith and Davis could rely; invasion alarms by this time were strong enough that he was hurried back to Texas as a replacement for Walker, and instructed to erect works for the defense of Houston. As early as March 8, Magruder was ordered to relinquish his command in Arkansas to James F. Fagan and "come here [Shreveport] on your way to Texas." Before his formal proclamation of March 31 placing him back in charge of Texas, New Mexico, and Arizona, Smith told Magruder to cooperate with H. T. Douglas, now chief engineer for the Trans-Mississippi, on "construction of an interior line of fortifications, extending from the Brazos to the Trinity." Magruder, whose last weeks in Arkansas were taken up with preparations for a court of

inquiry to censure Sterling Price's conduct in Missouri, and with minor troop dispositions to counter probes by Steele's cavalry units, was
back in Houston by April 4. Although alarmist when he first arrived
in Arkansas, he had settled down to what was essentially garrison duty
for the next six months. While he had been unable to drive the federals from Little Rock, Fort Smith, and the Arkansas River Valley, his
generalship thwarted any serious effort by the enemy to invade southern parts of the state.[34]

11

Last Things

WHEN MAGRUDER ISSUED an April 4 order reestablishing his headquarters in Houston and naming a staff that included Captain Edward P. Turner as well as his nephew George, the Confederate war effort was clearly spent; at the end of February 1865, Robert E. Lee had only four out of ten major generals at his side to man the Petersburg defenses outside Richmond. With Sherman closing on the Army of Northern Virginia from the south, Lee attempted a March 25 sortie against Grant's encircling columns by ordering John Brown Gordon to assault a Union strong point called Fort Stedman in a last try to break the siege. Gordon was hurled back after a brief success, and seven days later, at Five Forks on April 1, Lee and Grant fought the last battle of importance. Completely overpowered by the enemy's superior numbers and firepower, Lee started his westward flight along the Appomattox River toward Joseph E. Johnston's remaining army in the Carolinas. News of Lee's surrender on April 9 swept across Magruder's domain like a death knell, prompting an accelerated desertion by officers and common soldiers alike. "There were no lonely chimneys standing in Texas amidst the ashes of houses burned in the vandal-like marches of the enemy as they had seen in Louisiana. There were no farms, homes and towns made desolate by the ravages of cruel warfare," wrote Oran M. Roberts, soldier and future governor. "It was easy even for soldiers of the line to understand that if Grant should thrust his armed hosts upon Texas, its broad domain would be laid in ruins, and they would be powerless to prevent it even by the sacrifice of their lives in defense of their homes and country."[1]

As Magruder faced incessant disillusionment mixed with periods of boundless optimism until the final surrender of June 2, tragedy struck his official family within days of his return to Houston. A violent argument erupted between Generals John A. Wharton and George W. Baylor in an upstairs room of the Fannin Hotel, where Magruder maintained his headquarters. Trouble between the two had started in Arkansas following the Red River campaigning, when E. Kirby Smith had pursued Frederick Steele northward. "I sent his sadale [*sic*] bags with a change of clothing but forgot to send the Pistol which I have bitterly regretted since, it would at least have given him a chance for his life," Wharton's wife told William Pitt Barringer, after her husband left their Hempstead, Texas, home on his way to join Magruder. Although Magruder had gone upstairs in a vain attempt to quiet the pair, Baylor shot and killed Wharton on April 6 when Prince John returned to his downstairs office. A Tennessee native, Wharton married a daughter of South Carolina governor David A. Johnson, although he had lived in Texas from childhood; a strong secessionist, he had been a Democratic presidential elector in 1860 as well as a member of the Texas secession convention. Baylor was likewise an early advocate of the Southern cause, who reportedly hoisted the first Confederate flag in the capital city of Austin. Despite Mrs. Wharton's attempts to brand him "a murderer," Baylor managed to overcome the unfortunate incident by becoming a Texas Ranger as well as a state legislator before his death in 1916. In April 1865, however, Magruder ordered a military funeral with full honors for his fallen comrade, and personally conducted the procession down Houston's Main Street to the depot, where the remains were dispatched to his wife.[2]

One week later Magruder, obliged to confront the realities of war, issued an address "to the patriotic citizens of Texas." The proclamation, signed by his adjutant, Turner, was an attempt to rally sagging spirits, and it was Prince John at his flamboyant best. "The enemy threatens our coast and will bring his great undivided resources for a successful invasion of the State. Let him be met with unanimity and Spartan courage, and he will be unsuccessful. . . . Let him be met at the water's edge, and let him pay dearly for every inch of territory he may acquire." After saying that forty-two Irishmen had hurled back 15,000 federals at Sabine Pass, Magruder continued, "There is no reason for despondency, and if the people of Texas will it, they can successfully defend their territory for an indefinite period." Yet he presented a different picture in an April letter to E. Kirby Smith. Although Magruder pledged his "cordial support" to carry out Smith's commands, he was plainly worried. "The soldiers are excited against certain classes of citizens, and nothing but military power, vigorously wielded, can save us from deserters, far more to be dreaded than the worst the enemy can inflict upon us." Texans around Houston, he thought, could be relied upon to check the military breakdown and to stand firm for the Confederacy.[3]

Magruder pleaded with Smith to keep Brownsville open for foreign trade by dispatching an expeditionary force to the lower Rio Grande; the Trans-Mississippi, he speculated, offered a firm base to continue the war after Jefferson Davis arrived to establish a reorganized government, but an avenue to the larger world was plainly needed. Yet Magruder told Shreveport that he did not know the president's whereabouts as Davis, accompanied by Secretary of State Judah Benjamin, Postmaster General John H. Reagan, and a stash of Confederate gold, made his way southward from Richmond. Davis was on the run through Salisbury and Charlotte, North Carolina, during late April and early May until his capture on May 10 at Irwinville, Georgia, forty miles north of the Florida border. The notion that Davis might somehow create a Confederate redoubt, under the aegis of E. Kirby Smith and Magruder, was nothing more than a pipe dream. Prince John may have proffered the hope of Texas resistance on April 28, but the following day he told Smith that his troops were "deserting by the tens and twenties a night."[4]

Before Kirby Smith's coming to Houston, Magruder became embroiled once more with Governor Murrah—this time over Confederate specie. "I have never given any order to Col. Jones, or anyone else to interfere in any manner with the public monies at San Antonio, or else where [*sic*]," he told Murrah on May 26. The governor had gotten word that Colonel A. C. Jones, now in command at San Antonio, had been distributing Confederate gold to his troopers. And, Magruder added, "these monies I have never had control over in any way; they being exclusively under the orders of the Treasury agent Judge

[P. W.] Gray, and the Commanding General of the Dept., Genl. Smith." The day before, he had informed Murrah that he was obliged to surrender several steamers—ostensibly owned by Texas as part of Magruder's marine bureau—if the terms of capitulation granted Simon B. Buckner in Louisiana were applied to Texas. Although Kirby Smith did parcel out $1,700 "to Generals Magruder, Forney, Walker, Hawes, and Drayton" when the war ended, the question of Confederate resources in the West continued to haunt the reputations of Smith and Magruder for years.[5]

A festering dilemma over the secessionist treasury plagued leaders in the East as well. As late as 1882, John H. Reagan, then a Texas congressman, scolded Joseph E. Johnston for declaring that Jefferson Davis had absconded with "$2,500,000 in Confederate coin." Reagan declared that Davis had approximately $860,000 in coin and bullion when he left Richmond. "About $100,000 or more of the coin was paid out to soldiers before [Davis] reached Washington, Georgia." Although Reagan ordered between $600,000 and $700,000 to be burned, "the most of the balance was turned over to two naval officers with directions to secrete it until matters were quieted and then to get it out at some port and take it to Bermuda, Nassau, or Liverpool to some of our depositories to be held for use of the Confederacy." But that money never found its way to the remote shores of Texas; presumably Magruder's share of the $1,700—about $350 of Secret Service gold under Kirby Smith's control—was paid in lieu of back pay and constituted his total funds upon the final collapse. Charles R. Benton, who was present at the June 2 surrender in Galveston harbor, avows that Magruder left Houston for Mexico with "about $200, barely enough to carry him to the frontier."[6]

Meanwhile, when word reached the Trans-Mississippi that Johnston had capitulated to Sherman on April 18 at Durham, North Carolina, followed by Richard Taylor's surrender to E. R. S. Canby in Alabama on May 4, Magruder and Smith took differing tacks. Prince John said he thought news from the East was "untrue" as he issued another address "To the People and Army of Texas" on May 4, the very day of Taylor's submission. It was classic Magruder who implored his district to "stand by your venerated and illustrious President in his misfortunes, and above all present to your foe a united, firm, and defiant front, and to the world the spectacle of an army of citizen soldiers determined under any circumstances to be true to their duty, to be faithful to their beloved Confederacy, and ready at any moment to put down depredators of their innocent fellow citizens and traitors to their country who seek by every means to undermine your fidelity." E. Kirby Smith was a bit more realistic when he summoned Governors Henry W. Allen of Louisiana, Murrah of Texas, Harris Flanagan of Arkansas, and Thomas C. Reynolds of Missouri into conference at Marshall, Texas, to assess the deteriorating military situation. "Since the evacuation of Richmond, the seat of government of the Confederate States has not been fixed, and it may be transferred to the western side of the Mississippi," proclaimed Smith's call to the governors. It was impossible to confer with President Davis, Smith continued, and though he had a formidable army yet under arms, he had no wish to usurp civil authority; "without proferring any suggestions," Smith asked the assemblage "to indicate such policy as you may deem necessary to maintain with honor and success the sacred cause in which we are engaged."

Magruder did not make the 200-mile journey to Marshall, but remained at his Houston headquarters with Murrah; because of illness, Murrah, too, did not attend the conclave, but sent Guy M. Bryan in his place. With Smith in attendance to "furnish any information in my power which might be useful in your deliberations," Allen, Flanagan, and Reynolds issued a separately drafted appeal for action. Bryan signed the joint memorandum by Flanagan and Reynolds that called upon Smith to consult U.S. authorities "with a view to making a complete pacification of the Trans-Mississippi Department." While the governors expressed "complete confidence" in Smith's judgment, he did not return to his headquarters in Shreveport, but headed south to join Magruder. Smith made his way via Hempstead, where his wife had given birth to an infant daughter, as Magruder not only tilted with Murrah but also watched the continued evaporation of his army.[7]

Three days after the Flanagan-Reynolds-Bryan appeal, Magruder telegraphed his own call to Smith. "For god's sake <u>act</u>, or let me <u>act</u>! [Underlining in Magruder's hand.] I have excited myself more than I ever did to instil [*sic*] a spirit of resistance into the men but in vain," he told his chief on May 16. "I but make myself antagonistic to the army and an object of their displeasure. Nothing more can be done except to satisfy the soldiers to induce them to preserve the organization and to send them in Regiments to their homes, with as little damage to the community as possible." He also confided that on the night of May 14, 400 troops had left en masse from the garrison at Galveston. Matters indeed worsened! As units came apart, wrote A. W. Sparks, who became a straggler himself, or a soldier without a command:

> I want to say that all of the military starch is knocked out of a soldier when he straggles. Yes! and a straggler looks bad and feels worse. No citizen can realize how bad a straggler feels but in order to convey to you some idea of how he feels you may take him as he looks and multiply that by about 400 and you will then have a slight conception of an army straggler. Low down, cowardly, mean, shirk, not worthy of the name of a man, much less a soldier. That was the kind of crowd I felt to be in, so I just quit.

Little wonder that Magruder himself began to entertain notions of quitting.[8]

Unbelievably distressing news bombarded Houston in the days that followed. James S. Slaughter, Magruder's commander at Brownsville, sent word that his troops were leaving in droves. "They say," Slaughter reported, "we are whipped. It is useless for the Trans-Mississippi Department to accomplish what the Cis-Mississippi has failed to do." On May 22 and again on the twenty-fourth, Magruder dispatched telegrams to Smith, who was making his way through east Texas. Magruder told him to hurry, as he was needed in Houston. Kirby Smith reached headquarters on May 27 and immediately sent a pathetic telegram to Buckner in Louisiana: "Just arrived. Texas troops all disbanded. Public property all seized. Galveston will probably be occupied by the enemy this morn. No supplies for maintaining the troops. Discharge them and send them to their homes. When shall I expect you[?] Will any troops accompany you[?]"[9]

Smith's presence in Texas, where he reestablished headquarters for the Trans-Mississippi, unquestionably contributed to the dismal atmosphere pervading the region. Although diehard officers, including Sterling Price, Jo Shelby, and William Preston, a member of Magruder's command, plotted to arrest Smith and take control themselves rather than surrender, E. Kirby Smith's designated representatives met with E. R. S. Canby, who had hurried to New Orleans from the Alabama capitulation of Richard Taylor. "On the morning of May

25, Canby, Steele, and Major General F. J. Herron met Generals
Simon Bolivar Buckner, Sterling Price, and J. L. Brent [Magruder's
aide during the peninsula fighting] at the St. Charles Hotel," writes
Canby's biographer. "At a late hour in the evening, the conference
ended in the surrender of the last Confederate forces in the field."
They included, at least in theory, troops in Texas, even though Smith
and Magruder formally surrendered that part of the Trans-Mississippi
a few days later.

One day earlier, on May 24, Magruder, apparently on his own initiative, had appointed Colonel Ashbel Smith, his commander at
Galveston, and William Pitt Barringer as an embassy to Canby: "You
are hereby appointed to proceed to New Orleans or such other place
as may be necessary to negotiate with the Genl. commanding the
Federal Troops at or near that place, or with the proper authorities of
the United States and the District of Texas & on the terms confided
to you." Ashbel Smith, Yale-educated, had been secretary of state for
the Republic of Texas, and possessed vast experience in diplomatic
dealings with Mexico and various European nations; he was particularly fitted to represent not only Magruder but also Texas. Magruder
likewise made arrangements with the federal fleet commander at
Galveston for their safe passage. E. Kirby Smith's coming on May 27,
and news of the Canby-Buckner agreement, precluded their departure for the Crescent City.[10]

"I found on my arrival here that the Troops of this District had
disbanded and were making their way home," Smith wrote to Governor Murrah on May 30. "That they had possessed themselves of the
public property; that much of this had been scattered here, and there
over the State; and that some of it in the shape of ordnance stores, artillery, etc., remains unmolested." And he asked Murrah to use Texas
state troops yet under his command to protect what Confederate
property he could. Smith dispatched an equally poignant note to
General John W. Sprague, commanding federal forces along the Red
River in North Texas: "When I gave you, at Shreveport, a memorandum which I hoped might be the basis of negotiations with the
United States Government, I commanded an army of over 50,000 and
a department rich in resources. I am now without either." With nothing left to command, Smith added, "The department is now open to
occupation by your Government. . . . I plan to go abroad until future

policy of the United States Government toward the South is announced." Unquestionably, Smith and Magruder had discussed their move to join Maximilian south of the Rio Grande before Smith instructed his lieutenant to appoint commissioners to treat with federal authorities for the surrender of Confederate Texas.[11]

The fateful session took place aboard the USS *Fort Jackson* on June 2. Edmund J. Davis, future Reconstruction governor of Texas, received the surrender in Galveston harbor after Smith and Magruder arrived by special train from Houston. "They went out to the fleet & stayed all day and late into the night—perhaps they spent one night aboard—I don't exactly remember," Magruder's ordnance officer, Charles R. Benton, wrote sixteen years later. Benton, who was present along with Captain Turner, says that he made three copies of the surrender document at his Galveston office and then met with Magruder late in the evening. "He asked me for the last time if I would go with him to Mexico, saying he would make me a full Colonel of arty [i.e., artillery] in charge of the arty and ordnance on his staff under Maximilian." Although this suggests that Magruder had already been in contact with the Emperor's representatives, Benton also wrote of the late-night meeting: "Our Genl. Magruder was very sorrowful—stern & thoughtful—But very quiet—saying little or nothing while Kirby Smith was walking up and down the office of the Washington Hotel very rapidly & in an excited manner." Two days after the surrender, Magruder told Smith that E. J. Davis had offered him "transportation to New Orleans which he declined since he had duties to perform in carrying out the convention," and he expressed a desire to return to his family, whom he had not seen since the journey to Europe in 1860–1861. An 1867 article in *The New York Times* hints that his wife and children were in New Orleans, awaiting his arrival.[12]

Within a day or two, however, he set out for Mexico in the company of several officers, although he asked Davis to transport his personal baggage to New Orleans aboard the U.S. fleet. Confederate senator Williamson S. Oldham wrote that "five men dressed in Confederate uniforms" were encountered searching for Magruder among his Houston lodgings after the surrender; Oldham, at least, was convinced the intruders were Yankees in disguise, with a warrant for Magruder's arrest. When they passed through Colorado County on July 10, Magruder and his staff were heavily armed. With not only disgruntled Unionists but also brigands roaming the countryside, he carried "four six shooters and a rifle" as he headed for the Rio Grande. Magruder confirms that he intended to cross at Matamoros, but highwaymen forced him farther upriver. Prior to leaving Houston, however, he later told a *New York Times* correspondent, he had issued an order, "probably the last of the war," which condemned "in the strongest terms the formation of guerrilla parties, and urging all to support the laws and obey the orders of the United States authorities with an honest, zealous and loyal spirit."[13]

Magruder was not the only Confederate to make the trek south of the border in those chaotic weeks following the surrender; Jefferson Davis, after all, had been arrested, and many officers as well as civilian authorities were in a state of confusion. Although Confederate military men were not molested or detained by the victors, many of them, Prince John included, had little or no money to find a new life in Reconstruction America. The prospect of employment and new careers under a foreign banner had unquestioned appeal. Yet most rebel officers, with their educations at West Point and the University of Virginia—products of the plantation South with its aristocratic lifestyle—were sorely disappointed with their new surroundings. The shakiness of Maximilian's French-sponsored regime, coupled with Mexico's pervasive Roman Catholicism and the squalid conditions of the peasantry, offended the North American temperament. Very few ex-Confederates who sped across the Rio Grande found a permanent home, but returned to the United States at the first opportunity.

Magruder remained in Mexico for seventeen months, from July 1865 until November 1866, although he did not serve in Maximilian's military forces, but directed one of the emperor's governmental bureaus instead. And the modern reader can get a good grasp of his activities from a variety of sources. When he returned home without funds of any kind, Magruder embarked upon a lecture tour as a means of raising living expenses and also to sing the praises of Maximilian and his ill-fated wife, the Belgian princess Charlotte or Carlota. A transcript of his speeches appeared in *The New York Times* during April 1916 and also in the *1916 Yearbook* of the American Clan Gregor Society; while the documents are glowing accounts of the emperor and his impact upon Mexico, they also present a vivid, firsthand account of his days as a government official south of the Rio Grande. Likewise, several Confederate expatriates, including Alexander W. Terrell and Alfred Mordecia, have left glimpses of Magruder's Mexican sojourn in their own writings.[14]

After making his way to the Menger Hotel in San Antonio, he encountered a troop of 1,000 or so Confederates who marched with General Jo Shelby from Missouri; Shelby, an unredeemed rebel who proclaimed that he "entered the Confederacy with clean hands and would leave it the same way," used his cavalrymen to save several hundred thousand dollars during a famous shootout with bushwhackers in the subtreasury at Austin, and made his way into Mexico at Eagle Pass. According to Shelby's biographer, Magruder traveled with the entourage and no doubt took part in the famous ceremony in which a stone-laden Confederate flag was lowered into the Rio Grande; the Kentucky-born Shelby had sported a distinctive black plume on his hat throughout the Missouri fighting, which he laid inside the sunken banner as the "silent band" looked on. Rough travel lay ahead as Magruder and his companions made their way to Monterrey, 200 miles south of Eagle Pass. "The western portion of Texas and the northeastern frontier of Mexico were swarming with robbers and murderers," Prince John wrote afterwards. "I passed with safety, however, through Texas, though several highway robberies, attended with murder, were committed." Although "Mexican Liberals" under Benito Juarez "relieved us of part of our arms," he reached Monterrey on June 29, where he encountered the French garrison commanded by Jean Nigros (Jenningros).

His host immediately treated him to a lavish fête. In Magruder's own words: "Battalions of inviting French dishes, regiments of bottles of the most exquisite French wines, and barricades of boxes of the most fragrant Havanas were placed as it were, in battle array before us, but at the word melted away before the prowess of the wandering warriors of the Lost Cause like skirmish lines under the fire of serried infantry." Terrell says that Magruder reached Monterrey in an ambulance provided by Colonel George Giddings, a Texas admirer. A Texas lawyer who attained general rank as commander of the 34th Texas Cavalry, Terrell also noted that "no razor had touched the general's face for ten days, and his snow white beard looked strange on a face until then cleanly shaven, except for the moustache and side whiskers which were blackened." Magruder, already suffering from the heart condition that would take his life six years later, traveled with a personal band that included his nephew George junior, his aides Edward P. Turner and Alexander C. Jones, and Commodore Leon Smith and Major Oscar Watkins. "Two fine saddle horses that had borne him at Bethel and in the bloody fight at Gaines Mill" also accompanied him.[15]

Within days of his arrival, Magruder divided what money he had among members of his staff, each man receiving about $300; continued loyalty induced them to insist that Magruder keep the funds for himself, which he steadfastly refused to do. The lingering suspicion that Magruder and E. Kirby Smith—also in Mexico—had absconded with large piles of Confederate gold continued to spread through the country. Terrell, who observed Magruder closely during their stay in Mexico, says he was penniless upon crossing the Rio Grande; and Governor Henry W. Allen of Louisiana, editor of the *Mexican Times*, held that Prince John "was indebted to the generosity of friends for the scant means by which he was able to escape persecution." Yet Magruder found sufficient funds to host a July 4 banquet in Monterrey to celebrate "the Lost Cause" by drinking toasts to Robert E. Lee and Stonewall Jackson. Allen, who established the English-language newspaper in September 1865, totally discounted the notion that Magruder or Smith had profited from the "Mexican cotton trade." When Allen passed away in the spring of 1866, and others assumed publication of the *Times*, Magruder handled not only funeral arrangements but also transfer of the "sacred remains to New Orleans." But that lay in the future as Magruder prepared to leave Monterrey via San Luis Potosí for the capital during the last part of July. In fact he was one of the first Confederates from Texas and the Southwest to establish contact with the emperor.[16]

On August 5 Magruder reached Mexico City, where, according to Terrell, he immediately sought out Major Loysel, head of the French military cabinet, to arrange an interview with Maximilian; before leaving Monterrey, the assembled Confederates vowed to avoid service in the Mexican army. "At my suggestion," Magruder noted, "we adopted a resolution that under no circumstances would we accept service with either of the contending parties in Mexico, and that unlike other refugees we should abstain from plotting against our own country in any foreign country where we might find asylum." Although Maximilian had been in power roughly one year before Prince John's arrival, the Austrian-born monarch—younger brother of Emperor Franz Joseph—and his government were in trouble with the liberal-minded followers of Juarez at home as well as with the Lincoln administration north of the Rio Grande. Even before Napoleon III bowed to pressure from Washington and pulled his protective arm from him, Maximilian knew that his domestic policies found no favor among the disparate groups vying for power in Mexico, and that he must do nothing to alienate the Americans. "I have arrived at the conclusion, from which I will never vary, that no Government, of whatsoever form can exist permanently in Mexico which fails to win the good-will of the Government and people of the United States," the Emperor informed Magruder at their first meeting. "Under present circumstances your appointment to military positions in this country will give just cause of offense to your Government and people and therefore you must not expect it."[17]

Although the thirty-three-year-old Austrian and his wife commenced their ill-fated adventure in Mexico with noble intentions, Maximilian and his followers were creatures of the French from the onset. Roman Catholic Hapsburg nobility and French dreams of empire merged at a time when a war-torn United States was in no position to invoke the Monroe Doctrine; Maximilian, a grand admiral in the Austrian navy, who was forced to renounce any claim upon the imperial throne, had been approached by Mexican conservatives as early as 1859 about accepting the crown. In Mexico, a long saga of governmental instability that had persisted since the country gained its independence from Spain came to a head during 1859–1861, when the liberals under Juarez had taken the reins of power by not only seizing church lands but also by suppressing the religious orders. And the conservatives, who fled to Europe seeking the protection of Napoleon III and the Pope, exploded when parliament suspended interest payments on the nation's sizable debt for two years—a debt owed primarily to European banking houses.

A convention three months later between Great Britain, Spain, and France authorized armed intervention, and by December 1861, contingents of allied troops from all three countries began landing at Veracruz. British and Spanish forces were soon withdrawn from the venture, but the French—heavily reinforced by additional troops—commenced a torturous inland march. At Puebla on May 5—Cinco de Mayo—the Republic of Mexico "found its version of the Fourth of July" when General Ignacio Zarogoza temporarily stymied the French attempt to occupy Mexico City. Following a delay of several months and the coming of new commanders including François Bazaine, the French entered the capital on June 7, 1863. Although Mexico became a bottomless pit for the troops under Bazaine, a hastily summoned convention dominated by conservatives and their clerical allies set out to undo the work of Juarez and his followers; when a royalist government was established, Louis Napoleon lost no time in handing the imperial crown to Maximilian. Then, as the Union army drove Robert E. Lee southward toward Richmond and Magruder struggled to hold the Texas coast, Maximilian and his devoted but unstable wife of seven years took up the Mexican throne on July 17, 1864.[18]

An observation by Terrell that he had not seen one beggar in the South during the Civil War, yet that begging was rampant at every crossroads when the former Confederates arrived in Mexico, offers a powerful insight into the problems confronting not only the new regime but also Magruder and his companions. Even though Prince John is silent about his feelings toward Mexico, other than his life-long praise of Maximilian and Carlota, more than a few rebels who made their way southward in 1865 were perplexed by their new homeland. While other southerners suffered what modern writers label "culture shock," Magruder set out to build a new life for himself. Within days he had sold his ambulance to a Mexican cotton buyer, and secured funds from the British minister—a relative by marriage of his niece Helen Magruder (daughter of his brother George) to Lord Abinger of the English peerage. And he was shortly decked out in a wardrobe befitting a Confederate major general: "a suit of salt and pepper color, with a tall dove-colored hat, and patent leather boots." Terrell adds that Maximilian himself was observed shortly wearing the same outfit on the streets of Mexico City. From his rooms "on the first floor of the Iturbide Hotel," Prince John Magruder visited the great castle at Chapultepec, where the emperor and empress made their residence, and attended almost nightly productions at the National Theater.[19]

When he called at Chapultepec for the formal interview with Maximilian and his wife, according to his own account, both monarchs grilled him closely about United States policy toward Mexico; although he was reticent to discuss international affairs with "a lady," Magruder records that he told the Empress flat out the Monroe Doctrine precluded any relationship between their government and Washington: "She comprehended at once, the pale face broke into smiles, showing her dazzling teeth and eloquent dimples, the light of genius beamed from her expressive eyes, and her whole face seemed luminous with intelligence." Carlota, Magruder thought, "was at that moment incomparably beautiful." And he was equally taken with her husband: "Though tall and commanding in stature, his person was a model of manly beauty, and his face denoted greater strength than I expected from the photographs I had seen of him."

An important ingredient of Maximilian's domestic plans was the encouragement of immigration, particularly from the United States. "A few days after the interview" he organized a Bureau of Immigration and Surveys and placed it under the control of Carlotta, Magruder comments. "Captain [Matthew F.] Maury, the distinguished author of wind and current charts, formerly of the United States Navy, was appointed Commissioner of Immigration, and I became chief of the Land Office and Superintendent of Surveys." Maury, well known for his writings, later told his wife that he had recommended Magruder for the job at a salary of $3,000 per year, and that Carlota had readily accepted his suggestion. The September 1865 appointment was also influenced by Marshal Bazaine, who had encountered Prince John in the Crimea and had liked him. For the time being, Magruder's position ensured a regular income, but it also proved to be one of short duration. Before the post was abolished, however, hundreds of surveyors had been employed under his direction in the difficult task of clarifying titles for lands confiscated from the Church as Maximilian steadfastly refused to reverse the earlier policies of Juarez and the liberals.[20]

The *Mexican Times* labeled Magruder's appointment an enthusiastic success along with that of Maury. "The public lands will be surveyed, sectionized, and offered for sale according to the plan of the United States Land Office," the paper continued. "All the lands of the Government that have been acquired by purchase, forfeiture, confiscation or otherwise will be immediately brought on the market at very reduced prices, payable in a series of years—thus putting in the power of everyone to procure a home from 160 to 610 acres of land according to the size of his family." Although immigrants were encouraged to bring servants and their former slaves, slavery was forbidden throughout Maximilian's empire. Besides his annual salary, Magruder was granted a subsidy to carry out his mission: "$150 for office furniture, $1,200 a year for office rent, $500 for general expenses, and $300 for a special messenger." Since, as Maury noted, no survey of Mexican lands had ever been done, Magruder obviously faced a difficult job, although Carlota gave him a free hand to ascertain the number of engineers and surveyors needed. Still, he quickly became a great favorite among the ex-Confederates and Frenchmen gathering around the new government. "A boy of Sixty-four [actually he was fifty-eight], penniless, with a family in Europe, bereft of an avocation, he had grown gray in following; having no country and no calling, he, too, had come to choose his bivouac and receive [Maximilian's] protection," wrote John N. Edwards, one of Sterling Price's confidants. "The ranks opened for this wonderful recruit, who carried in his head so many memories of the land toward which all were journeying."[21]

While Magruder conducted frequent tours around the sites made famous during the American occupation of 1846–1847, Edwards reports that his lisp further ingratiated him "in as much as it lingered over his puns and caressed his rhetoric." Amid the partying, theatergoing, and bonhomie, his wife and younger children joined him in Mexico City. Mrs. Magruder was accompanied by Kate, aged thirty-one, and twenty-eight-year-old Henry, who once served in the Italian army during the family's residence in Florence and Rome. He met his family in Veracruz during March 1866, and accompanied them to the capital. "They had an uncomfortable and tedious journey up, and Mrs. M. has not been well since her arrival: I have consequently only seen the daughter and son who make a favorable impression, especially the daughter, quiet & lady like tho [sic] not at all handsome," commented Alfred Mordecia, a careful observer of the expatriate community. "They have a roomy & comfortable house, just near our office; but I imagine they are not the sort of people to enjoy the novelties of Mexico much." He thought they would return to Europe shortly.

Mrs. Magruder, Mordecia elaborated, regretted coming to Mexico. A month later he said the family was leaving for Italy and that he had no idea what Prince John would do, although they had thrown several "grand balls" in their home. Magruder, who had spent money he did not have to furnish a house, also learned during April 1866, along with Maury, that his office had been discontinued by the emperor. "This is a distressing thing to them, with nay means of support," Mordecia told his wife. The loss of income and position may well have influenced Mrs. Magruder's decision to depart. Upon her leaving, Magruder did not see his wife and younger children again before his own death, although he visited Isabell and Dr. Bucklin in their Baltimore home after his return to the United States.[22]

As Magruder went about his duties in the land office, which Mordecia felt Maximilian and Carlota failed to appreciate, several colonies of former Confederates sprang up around the country. The most ambitious of these, established by Sterling Price near Córdoba, had been, according to Edwards, secured through Prince John's influence. And when he called at the colony during his journey to meet his wife and children in Veracruz, Magruder returned to the capital with glowing praise for his onetime rival for command in the Trans-Mississippi. It was located about seventy miles from the Gulf of Mexico and nine miles southeast of Córdoba in a beautiful, verdant valley; Price had named the place Carlota in honor of the empress. A visiting *New York Times* reporter found "but three houses or rather bamboo huts," with five or six more under construction, when he visited Price in April 1866. A disastrous raid by a band of Juaristas, who branded all of the Confederates as enemies, nearly wrecked the enterprise, although the colony, with Magruder's blessing, struggled on until the last days of Maximilian's rule. Carlota only survived under the protection of a French regiment, and similar colonies under other impresarios found themselves in difficulty during late 1866 as the liberals spread their influence over much of Mexico.[23]

The world that Magruder and his fellow Confederates hoped to create for themselves came crashing down when Napoleon III bowed to influences at home and abroad to remove his troops from the country. Although Washington had never been comfortable with the

French presence beyond the Rio Grande, Abraham Lincoln had not pressed the issue because he viewed Maximilian's regime as a possible haven for disgruntled rebels as the war wound down. The Yankee president, who was never as vindictive as some members of his own party toward the South and her leaders, told a cabinet meeting on the very last day of his life, April 14, 1865:

> I hope there will be no persecution, no bloody work after the war is over. No one need expect me to take any part in hanging or killing those men, even the worst of them.
>
> Frighten them out of the country, open the gates, let down the bars, scare them off.

Whether Lincoln meant for them to migrate to Mexico is open to question, but in his December 1864 message to Congress he did not condemn Maximilian or the French occupation. "Mexico continues to be a theatre of civil war," he said. "While our relations with that country have undergone no change, we have, at the same time, strictly maintained neutrality between the belligerents." Although Ulysses S. Grant had been an invited guest at the April cabinet session, he did not share the president's view, nor did his cohort in arms, William Tecumseh Sherman. Both soldiers remembered that Confederate forces, particularly in Texas and the Southwest, had been supplied with foreign matériel through first Mexican and later French connivance. And a onetime "virtual understanding" between Magruder and Santiago Vidaurri, "once Juarist governor of Coahuila and Nuevo León," had permitted a rush of overseas goods into Texas during the war.[24]

Upon Lincoln's untimely death, however, new leaders emerged and, under the direction of William H. Seward, who remained as secretary of state under President Andrew Johnson, a diplomatic initiative was implemented to drive Maximilian from his throne; Sherman and Lewis D. Campbell, Johnson's minister to Mexico, were even dispatched on a mission to establish contact with Juarez, a move that had Grant's blessing. Although Sherman returned to the United States disgusted with the internecine nature of Mexican politics, orders were cut in January 1866 to halt all Confederates attempting to reach Mexico from New Orleans and Mobile; federal troops stationed along the Rio Grande kept a wary eye on those attempting to cross from Texas. Seward also bombarded Napoleon III with communiqués demanding the removal of French troops; Maximilian began to totter when Marshal Bazaine complained to Paris about the emperor squandering or at least mishandling monies sent from France. In response to these and other assaults, Maximilian had been forced to reduce his outlays during 1866 that led directly to elimination of Magruder's position at the land office. It was an economy measure dictated by a sweeping retrenchment to save what he could of the empire.[25]

Slowly the French ruler not only bowed to Seward's ultimatum but also to the realization that Bismarck and an energized Prussia were threatening his own throne within Europe. In the early months of 1866 he directed a withdrawal of French troops as he telegraphed Bazaine "not to force Maximilian to abdicate but on no account to delay embarkation as the ships [have] already left." Even a hurried trip to Paris by Carlota, who made a nuisance of herself with her paranoid appeals, failed to dissuade the sick and besieged Emperor of the French. In August 1866 Napoleon laid it on the line for his Mexican puppet: "It is necessary for your Majesty to come to a heroic resolution. It is henceforth impossible for me to give another *ecu* or another soldier." And, writes Napoleon's biographer, "he advised Maximilian to abdicate and sail for Europe with the French Army."[26]

Magruder probably spoke for most Confederates in Mexico when he wrote that "Napoleon affixed a stain upon the honor of France which will remain there for all time." The *Mexican Times* followed the lead of most southerners in the country with an editorial in May speculating that the French would not leave; if they did go, the blame was placed squarely on the emperor: "Napoleon the Third is a far-seeing and sagacious sovereign, but the mistake of his reign was not in fighting the battles of Mexico in Virginia, and guarding the line of the Rio Grande by holding the fords of the Potomac." Although the last French soldier did not leave until March 1867, the *Times* reported on November 19 that twenty transports were on their way to Veracruz to carry out the expeditionary force under Bazaine. When Maximilian decided to remain and face the Juaristas alone, he moved to Orizaba—about fifty miles from the coast—where Magruder called for a brief visit as he made his way out of the country. Here, surrounded by his Austrian troops, Magruder found him "without a Cabinet and with no one to consult, except his private chaplain, Father Fischer, a Roman Catholic priest, a devoted friend, an honest man."[27]

After making repeated appeals for him to leave, Magruder says that Maximilian consented to his issuing a statement that the Mexican venture had failed because of Napoleon—that he alone was responsible for the fiasco. And he implored Maximilian to take the railroad into Veracruz, where an Austrian steamer lay at anchor. In Magruder's own words:

> General, I will take your advice, but I wish you to be guided by my directions. Captain Graves, the Second Captain of the Austrian frigate, is here now. He will act under your orders at Vera Cruz. Leave here to-morrow morning at 4 o'clock and have cars ready for myself and escort the next day. Thus I will be on board by the day after to-morrow. In the meantime proceed by the French mail steamer to Havana and await my arrival there. I shall be with you in ten days.

In the days that followed, a Juarista raiding party destroyed a key railroad bridge, and during the unforeseen delay Maximilian resolved not to abandon his followers. Although Magruder had hoped to abet his escape, Maximilian marched from Orizaba with his pitifully small band of loyalists to become besieged at Querétaro, north of Mexico City. Appeals for mercy from throughout the civilized world after his capture, including that of Secretary Seward, failed to sway Juarez's sense of justice. Following "a show trial," Emperor Ferdinand Maximilian was executed by firing squad on June 19, 1867. By that time Magruder had made his way to the United States.[28]

Although he did not reach New York until January 1867, Magruder had an additional role to play in the saga of Maximilian and Carlota besides his well-known lecture tour during 1870. Two or three days after his November 17 landing in Havana "aboard a French Steamer," he met with Lewis D. Campbell, who was in the city awaiting the arrival of General Sherman before undertaking the mission to Juarez. In a long letter dated November 22, Campbell informed Seward about the encounter. "The day of my arrival in this port, I was informed by Mr. Miner, our consul general here, that an interview with me was desired by General Magruder, late of the so called confederate army who had arrived . . . from the city of Mexico and Vera Cruz." In a fit of pride, Campbell refused at first to see him, but when the two met "casually" in Miner's office, a prolonged exchange ensued. Magruder, who left Maximilian's capital on November 1, relayed his experiences with the emperor at Orizaba as well as the sad state of Mexican affairs. Primarily, however, he told Campbell about a conversation with Marshal Bazaine, who was preoccupied with the French pullout.

Campbell put in his report to Washington: "General Magruder further told me that at the close of his interview with Marshal Bazaine, when he was about to bid him adieu, the marshal said to him, 'You are about to visit the United States, general?' Reply: 'Yes.' 'You will see the President?' Reply: 'I probably shall.' 'If you do,' said Marshal Bazaine, 'deliver him this verbal message from me.' " Horribly upset over the havoc and chaos that he thought would result from the French abandonment of Mexico, Bazaine thought the United States should help to stabilize the country, since its "moral influence" had contributed to Maximilian's collapse. He proposed that President Johnson station "ten or fifteen thousand United States troops" in the northern part of the country, while a French presence was maintained in the south until a new government could take over. Bazaine's scheme was spurned by both governments, although Campbell felt it advisable to hurry Magruder's words to the president. Campbell must have been impressed by Magruder's performance; in concluding the report he wrote: "From his manner, and general tenor of his conversation, the impression was left in my mind that he was sincere, and that he desired in good faith to serve the interests of the government in communicating what he did."[29]

Magruder obviously had other, more personal matters on his mind than the fate of Mexico. On the very day of his arrival in Havana, he penned a letter to Maryland senator Reverdy Johnson seeking his help in securing an amnesty. Two months earlier Magruder had sent a formal application for pardon to John Van Buren, his attorney, but upon learning of Van Buren's death, he wanted Johnson to secure the documents from Van Buren's estate and present them to the president; and he again wanted it known that his position in Maximilian's government was not associated in any fashion with its domestic or foreign policies. His work in the land office, he emphasized, was nothing more than an administrative position.[30]

No less a Confederate than Robert E. Lee sought out Reverdy Johnson some months afterward to get his own reasons for joining the Southern breakaway before the public; the Maryland senator was a friend of the South and one of the few politicians from the region with an entrée to the new president, who subsequently appointed him ambassador to Great Britain as a replacement for Charles Francis Adams. When Magruder's boss, E. Kirby Smith, appealed to Ulysses S. Grant during 1865 for help in getting a pardon, he was told to come home and take the oath of allegiance like other Southern soldiers seeking a return to civilian life, and Prince John was obliged to take the same path, although, according to a correspondent for the *New York Herald*, he "remained some weeks in the country, having been invited to many plantations by friends to whom he had extended hospitalities formerly." The Cuban stopover, he declared, had "no connection to politics or business," his session with Campbell notwithstanding; Magruder likewise nixed the popular notion that he had intended to travel to England when he left the island. Instead he sailed directly for the United States, where he swore his allegiance to the government.[31]

While he remained in Havana, Magruder was vaguely involved with the disposition of the *Harriet Lane* and the *Pelican*, ships that had been confiscated by the Confederacy during the Texas fighting; but, commented the *Herald*, "ex-General Magruder having no interest in either of these vessels has himself no claims to establish." Although forces under his command had captured both ships three years earlier, he took the public stance "that whatever belonged to the United States at the time of the surrender of the Trans-Mississippi department, should be given at once to the [federal] government." The *Harriet Lane*, the more famous of the two, had been refitted as a Confederate blockade runner following her capture during the Battle of Galveston; but her recapture by the federal navy at Havana in 1864 had resulted in her condemnation and sale to private owners. The old ship—the pride of Magruder's navy in former days, plied the Atlantic coastal trade until 1881, when she was abandoned at sea following a disastrous fire.[32]

Magruder returned to the United States alone, without his family, with little or no money, and with no prospects for employment; after taking the prescribed oaths, he located in New York, yet he was almost constantly on the move over the next several months. Prior to his residence in Louisiana after 1869, he not only sought to open a law office, but also maintained a sporadic association with several

Confederate acquaintances. An April 1867 letter to Buckner in New Orleans indicates that he had been in St. Louis, but had been recalled to Baltimore on business and probably his daughter's increasingly poor health. When the press carried notice that he had accompanied General P. G. T. Beauregard on a tour of the New York Stock Exchange, Magruder dashed off "a card" to the *Times* complaining that he had been "misrepresentated"; not only did he deny any liaison with Beauregard, but he also insisted that he did not even know where the Stock Exchange was located. After a brief recapitulation of his role in the final Confederate surrender as well as his stay in Mexico, Magruder assured the paper that he had come home under terms granted by E. R. S. Canby allowing "commissioned officers of the Trans-Mississippi to select their residences within or without the limits of the United States." Once more he felt obliged to reiterate that his work with Maximilian was "a purely civil appointment." And, he added, "I returned to this country to work like a man for my personal independence, which I am now doing, without seeking or avoiding my former friends."[33]

Without revealing the nature of his work in New York, Magruder made his way to a conclave of Southern notables during August–September 1868 at White Sulphur Springs in West Virginia. It was the same fashionable watering place for the Southern moneyed class that he had visited with his young bride during 1833; with room rates at four dollars per day throughout the postwar period, he must have acquired some means following his return from Mexico. Although he did not sign a public manifesto issued by the gathering, and earned no mention about his attendance, a photograph of the participants has Magruder standing at Robert E. Lee's elbow. His close proximity to the Southern chieftains surely indicates his continued acceptance by the Confederate elite.

Union general William S. Rosecrans—then serving as ambassador to Mexico—had addressed an August 26, 1868, letter to Lee in which he asked how "good government" might be speedily reestablished in the Southern states; Rosecrans was seeking ammunition for the Democrats against Grant and the GOP in the upcoming presidential canvass. Lee's reply, signed by thirty-two Southern statesmen, included several with whom Magruder had been associated during 1861–1865: Beauregard, Charles M. Conrad, Virginia governor John Letcher, John

R. Baldwin, and James Lyons. Amid the turmoil of Reconstruction, Lee and his cosigners proclaimed that the South wanted peace and a return to secure democratic communities within the federal framework; southerners living in several unreconstructed states, Lee said, desired a restoration of orderly government. He conceded that " 'African slavery' and 'the right of a state to secede' were casualties of the late war,' " finds a Lee biographer. Moreover, Lee avowed that political power should not be placed in the hands of freedmen for "obvious reasons," which included the notion: "At present, the negroes [*sic*] have neither the intelligence nor the other qualifications which are necessary to make them depositories of political power."[34]

Magruder's onetime aide on the peninsula, Joseph L. Brent, was also a member of the White Sulphur Springs gathering; and it may well have been a renewed contact with the Louisianian that facilitated his move to New Orleans. Although Magruder had hobnobbed with a veritable galaxy of Confederate leaders in the West Virginia hills, he was Prince John once more upon returning to New York; after joining up with General Edward Higgins, another associate from the war, a frolic in a Broadway emporium nearly landed him in jail. Higgins, a Louisiana officer who had sailed ocean steamers in the 1850s, and later superintended John Pemberton's artillery at Vicksburg, finished the war as Confederate commandant at Mobile—a place Magruder knew well before and after 1865. The two had entered the store in a playful mood, where, said the manager, they "conducted themselves in a manner decidedly ungentlemanly, insulting the lady attendants and preventing by disparaging remarks the sale of goods on exhibition." When the storekeeper objected to the "ruffianly" outbursts, Higgins "raised his cane" while Magruder offered him moral support. Arrested and hauled into police court, the *Herald* reported, "General Magruder stoutly denied the allegations, assuring the Court that in visiting the establishment referred to they were on business, and that, although he did address the ladies present in relation to certain articles of a Bohemian ware there for sale, nothing was said that could offend the most refined and fastidious lady alive." The affair ended when Magruder and Higgins were ordered to post a $300 bond and "to keep the peace for six months."[35]

Unconcerned about his parole, Magruder made his way to New Orleans, where he not only continued his lectures on Maximilian and

Carlota but also established an office at the corner of Camp and Xavier Streets. And a July 10, 1869, letter to an admirer in the city leaves a hint that his health may have been in decline. "I have the Rheumatism and gout, yet my head is clear and my spirits good." Shortly afterwards he was back in Baltimore because of his daughter Isabell's death on July 20; although a local paper insisted that he had relocated there, he continued roving about the country until his own death, eighteen months later. He traveled to White Sulphur Springs in early August to join Generals S. B. Buckner and Alexander R. Lawton of Georgia for an outing; although he may not have attained position and financial stability himself, Magruder was able to visit and even party with men of standing: Buckner, for instance, had moved from New Orleans to become editor of the influential *Louisville Courier,* while Lawton was about to become president of the American Bar Association and after that ambassador to Austria. If he returned to Baltimore after the White Sulphur Springs interlude, it was for a brief stopover, because he had journeyed to Boston by early October and once more demonstrated his inherent generosity. While he stayed at the stylish Parker House, he reassured General Isaac S. Burrell who, as a colonel, had been his opponent in the Battle of Galveston, that his troops had performed in heroic fashion. Galveston had been Magruder's finest hour during the war, and he proudly proclaimed that he had torched the first cannon to open the fight.[36]

After a group of wealthy Texans offered to provide him with a plantation of his own, Magruder next visited Alabama and Louisiana on his way to Galveston. With the strong encouragement of Edward C. Wharton, he renewed his lectures during a brief layover in Mobile that attracted considerable notice. His February 29 presentation, which was repeated at least once, was given in the Odd Fellows Hall before "a very enthusiastic audience." A long account in a Mobile paper was reprinted in an altered version during 1916 by *The New York Times*; John A. Winston, a two-term antebellum governor as well as colonel of the Eighth Alabama Infantry under Magruder's command during the peninsula campaign, introduced him to the assemblage. Magruder opened with "a well turned compliment to the beauty of the daughters, and the spirit of the sons of the South," and then launched into a discussion of Mexican politics before the arrival of Maximilian. "The most interesting part of the lecture [was] General

Magruder's personal connection with the train of events which terminated so disastrously." When he added a discussion about the Mexican War exploits of Lee, Beauregard, Johnston, Stonewall Jackson, and even George B. McClellan, the crowd roared its approval. "Had the modesty which all brave men possess, not prevented it, the lecturer might have given equally interesting details of his own prowess," the *Mobile Register* added.[37]

Magruder must have been pleased with himself, because he rushed 500 stamped tickets to Wharton in New Orleans with instructions to engage the Hall of Science for additional lectures, and he asked him to employ someone to handle ticket sales. After a speech on March 2, when he was introduced by Wharton, Magruder used the Odd Fellows Hall for his subsequent appearances. Tickets for the events, which were "for sale at Hotels, Book and Music Stores, and at the door," cost one dollar. A paid advertisement in the *New Orleans Picayune* for March 10 gave the title as "Mexico, Maximilian and Carlotta," And the paper commented in a news clip, "The General, it will be remembered, delivers his lectures at the special solicitation of a number of his friends, and we may therefore expect a full house on the occasion." Because Magruder's presentations were "numerously attended," his several letters to Wharton suggest that he was also turning a dollar with his continued praise of the fallen Mexican leaders.[38]

Magruder traveled to Galveston throughout April–May 1870, and learned to his "sad disappointment" that the plantation or farm promised by his Texas admirers would not materialize. During the first week of May he heard about the attack that had been made upon him on the floor of the U.S. Senate. The attacker was Pennsylvania senator Simon Cameron, who, during a heated debate, had critcized his conduct as Abraham Lincoln's protector during the first days of Southern secession. Although Magruder addressed a letter to the *Philadelphia Evening Telegraph* retracing his movements during the upheavals of secession and his journey to Richmond, when *The New York Times* reprinted the piece, it got his name wrong: "Ex-rebel General James B. Magruder," it said, had written the letter to refute the statements of Simon, who had been Lincoln's secretary of war. Perhaps the misidentification was a harbinger of the sad events that followed. Sick and out of funds, Magruder moved into a Houston hotel with the support of his former aide Edward P. Turner, then a practicing attorney in the city. The five-story Hutchins House, considered one of the best hotels in the state, at the corner of Franklin and Travis streets, remained a Texas landmark until it was destroyed by fire in 1901. It was also Magruder's last home.[39]

"Another of the distinguished Confederate Generals has gone to his long home, there to form one of a bright circle, composed of Lee, Jackson, Johnston, Stuart, Hill, Cleburn, and other heroes," reported the *Galveston News* upon his death, on February 19, 1871. "Gen. J. Bankhead Magruder, having been unwell for several days, suffering from disease of the heart, breathed his last about 3 o'clock Saturday morning at the Hutchins House." Other papers reported that he had died alone, with only a servant boy as his sickroom attendant. Magruder's health had not been considered precarious until February 17, although he spoke briefly with a hotel employee on the eighteenth. When another guest heard heavy breathing and gasping, the manager summoned a physician, who arrived after his death. Following the rites of his church by "the Rev. Mr. Trader," he was buried in Houston's Episcopal cemetery.[40]

John Bankhead Magruder wavered during the Seven Days, but he had emboldened the Texans to great exertions after his recapture of Galveston. His fondness for strong drink caused some to view him as a rogue, yet he was Prince John to the last. Soldier that he was, with an undiminished devotion to the Confederacy, his life may have been summarized best by John F. Lee, kinsman of Robert E. Lee, who wrote in his 1871 account: "No mortal . . . was ever more unwilling to part with life, than poor John Magruder; though he did not make the right use of it—right use of hardly one hour of his Sixty years." Lee, a St. Louis lawyer, deplored Magruder's solitary death with a further observation: "Without prudence, and good conduct, & self denial which prefers the future good to the present gratification, there is small chance of happiness." He had made a shambles of his personal life, but he had been a dutiful military man for nearly forty years in the Union and Confederate armies, a legacy that deserves respect. Galvestonians, in particular, remembered his cool deliverance of their homes on that New Year's Eve eight years earlier; he was their hero, and as a final tribute to his bulldog determination, the body was reinterred in that city's Episcopal cemetery, where it now rests under a monument erected by the United Confederate Veterans.[41]

Notes

— 1. Youth —

1. C. R. Benton to E. C. Wharton, 29 March 1886, Edward C. Wharton and Family Papers, Louisiana and Lower Mississippi Valley Collections, Louisiana State University Libraries, Baton Rouge.

2. Jon L. Wakelyn, *Biographical Dictionary of the Confederacy* (Westport, Conn.: Greenwood Press, 1977), 305–306. William C. Davis, *Jefferson Davis: The Man and His Hour* (reprint, New York: HarperCollins Publishers, 1991), 413–414 (*New York Herald*, 20 February 1871).

3. "John Bankhead Magruder" Vertical File, Center for the Study of American History, University of Texas, Austin, unsigned newspaper clipping. David G. McComb, *Houston: A History* (Austin: University of Texas Press, 1981), 53. Mark Grimsley, "Inside a Beleaguered City: A Commander and Actor, Prince John Magruder," *Civil War Times Illustrated 21* (September 1982), 16.

4. John L. White, "Founder of Fort Yuma: Excerpts from the Diary of Major Samuel Heintzelman, U.S.A., 1849–1852" (M.A. thesis, University of San Diego, 1975), 152. A Regular, "The Soldiers' Temperance Movement," *Army and Navy Journal* 21 (20 October 1883), 243. Thomas M. Settles, "John Bankhead Magruder" in W. C. Nunn, ed., *Ten Texans in Gray* (Hillsboro, Texas: Hill County Junior College Press, 1968), 104. Timothy D. Spell, "John Bankhead Magruder: Defender of the Texas Coast, 1863" (M.A. thesis, Lamar University, 1981), 8–10.

5. Gary W. Gallagher, ed., *Fighting for the Confederacy: The Personal Recollections of General Edward Porter Alexander* (Chapel Hill: University of North Carolina Press, 1989), 74. Richard Taylor, *Deconstruction and Reconstruction: Personal Experiences of the Late War* (New York: D. Appleton and Company, 1879), 93. Stephen B. Oates, ed., *Rip Ford's Texas* (Austin: University of Texas Press, 1963), 343. Alexander Watkins Terrell, *From Texas to Mexico and the Court of Maximilian* (reprint, Dallas: The Book Club of Texas, 1933), 10–11.

6. Dumas Malone, ed., *The Dictionary of American Biography,* vol. 8 (New York: Charles Scribner's Sons, 1928), 204–205. William Croft Dickinson, *Scotland: From the Earliest Times to 1603* (London: Thomas Nelson and Sons, 1961), 376–377. Rosalind Mitchison, *A History of Scotland* (London: Methuen and Company, 1970), 171.

7. John Buchan, *Oliver Cromwell* (London: The Reprint Society, 1941), 320–341. Christopher Falkus, *The Life and Times of Charles II* (Garden City, N.Y.: Doubleday, 1972), 48. Ronald Hutton, *Charles the Second, King of England, Scotland and Ireland* (Oxford: Clarendon Press, 1989), 66–67.

8. Egbert Watson Magruder, ed., *Yearbook of the American Clan Gregor Society, 1913* (Richmond: Ware and Duke Printers, 1914), 39. Benjamin S. Ewell, "To Magruder-Ewell Camp," typescript, n.d., Richard Stoddert Ewell Papers (Washington, D.C.: Library of Congress), 1.

9. Magruder, ed., *Yearbook . . . 1913*, 39. Eber Worthington Cave, *Official Report of the Battles of Galveston and Sabine . . . With Sketch of the Life and Public Services of Maj. Gen. J. Bankhead Magruder* (Houston: Texas Printing Company, 1863), 18. William Broaddus Cridlin, "Caroline County Marriage Records," *Virginia Magazine of History and Biography* 38 (October 1929); ibid., 39 (January 1931), 39 (April 1931).

10. Cave, *Battles of Galveston and Sabine*, 18. Robert S. Garnett to Secretary of War, 4 February 1821, John Bankhead Magruder File, U.S. Military Academy, West Point, New York. Sarah P. Lee, ed., *Memoirs of William Nelson Pendleton, D.D.* (Philadelphia: J. B. Lippincott, 1893), 22.

11. John H. Gwathmey, *Twelve Virginia Counties: Where the Western Migration Began* (Richmond: Dietz Press, 1937), 342. Thomas M. Settles, "The Military Career of John Bankhead Magruder" (Ph.D. diss., Texas Christian University, 1972), 1. Henry Powell, *List of Officers of the United States Army from 1799 to 1900* (New York: L. R. Hamersly and Co., 1900), 177. James Bankhead to "Dear Sir," 5 February 1821, Virginia Miscellaneous Letters, Alderman Library, University of Virginia, Charlottesville. James Bankhead to James Breckenridge, 23 February 1815, James Breckenridge Papers, Alderman Library, University of Virginia.

12. Gwathmey, *Twelve Virginia Counties*, 179–191. Marshall Wingfield, *A History of Caroline County, Virginia: From Its Formation in 1727 to 1924* (Richmond: Trevvet Christian Company, 1924), 33, 59, 119.

13. Malone, ed., *Dictionary of American Biography*, vol. 8, 204. "A Short History of General J. B. Magruder," packed in Duke's Cigarettes (New York: Knapp and Co., 1888), copy in Alderman Library, University of Virginia. Mae Samuella Magruder Wynne, "General John Bankhead Magruder," *Yearbook of the American Clan Gregor Society, 1913* (Richmond: Ware and Duke Printers, 1914), 34. Douglas Southall Freeman, *Lee's Lieutenants: A Study in Command*, vol. 1 (New York: Charles Scribner's Sons, 1942), 15. Wakelyn, *Dictionary of the Confederacy*, 305. Grimsley, "Inside A Beleaguered City," 15. Settles, "Military Career of Magruder," 6.

14. Cave, *Battles of Galveston and Sabine*, 16. Paul Brandon Barringer, *The University of Virginia*, vol. 1 (New York: Lewis Publishing Company, 1904), 366. *New York Herald*, 20 February 1871. R. S. Garnett to Secretary of War, 4 February 1821, John Bankhead Magruder File, U.S. Military Academy Archives, West Point, New York.

15. Garnett to Secretary of War, February 4, 1821. Mary Rawlings, ed., *Early Charlottesville: Recollections of James Alexander, 1828–1874* (Charlottesville, Va.: Mitchie Co., 1942), 7. George Washington Lewis, Address Delivered Before the Literary Society and Students of the Rappahannock Academy and Military Institute, 30 July

1851 (Washington, D.C.: Gideon and Company, 1852), passim. Wingfield, *Caroline County*, 58–59. "John Bankhead Magruder," Vertical File, University of Texas, Austin.

16. Philip Alexander Bruce, *History of the University of Virginia, 1819–1919*, vol. 1 (New York: Macmillan, 1921), 52, 262. John Bankhead Magruder, Matriculation Card, University of Virginia Archives, Alderman Library, University of Virginia, Charlottesville. University of Virginia, Catalogue of Students, 1825 (Charlottesville: University of Virginia, 1825), 6.

17. Bruce, *History of the University of Virginia*, vol. 2, 33–35, 295. Barringer, *University of Virginia*, 290. Burwell Stark, "Reminiscences," *The Alumni Bulletin of the University of Virginia*, vol. 1 (Charlottesville: University of Virginia, 1894), 2.

18. Bruce, *History of the University of Virginia*, vol. 2, 321. Stark, "Reminiscences," 2.

19. Settles, "Military Career of Magruder," 3–6. J. B. Magruder, Matriculation Card, University of Virginia. Bruce, *History of the University of Virginia*, vol. 2, 144–147, 299.

20. University of Virginia, Catalogue of Students, 1826 (Charlottesville: University of Virginia, 1826), 2–4. Paul D. Casdorph, *Lee and Jackson: Confederate Chieftains* (New York: Paragon House, 1992), 169. Stark, "Reminiscences," 1–2. Malone, ed., *Dictionary of American Biography*, vol. 8, 206. See also Maximilian Schele de Vere, *Students of the University of Virginia* (Charlottesville: University of Virginia, 1878), unpaged; and Una Pope-Hennessy, *Edgar Allan Poe: A Critical Biography* (New York: Haskell House, 1971), 37–40.

21. University of Virginia, Catalogue of Students, 1826, 2–4. Stark, "Reminiscences," 2–3. Bruce, *History of the University of Virginia*, vol. 2, 32, 82. Magruder, Matriculation Card, University of Virginia.

22. J. B. Magruder to Secretary of War, 11 March 1825, Admission Records, United States Military Academy, West Point, New York. Joseph B. James, "West Point One Hundred Years Ago," *Mississippi Valley Historical Review* 31 (December 1944), 22–23.

23. Lee, ed., *Memoirs of . . . Pendleton*, 26. James I. Robertson, *General A. P. Hill: The Story of a Confederate Warrior* (New York: Random House, 1987), 11.

24. Lee, ed., *Memoirs of . . . Pendleton*, passim. J. B. Magruder to W. N. Pendleton, 21, 29 May 1862, William Nelson Pendleton Papers, Southern Historical Collection, University of North Carolina, Chapel Hill. Francis B. Heitman, *Historical Register and Directory of the United States Army, 1789–1903*, vol. 1 (Washington: U.S. Government Printing Office, 1903), 527, 988.

25. James, "West Point One Hundred Years Ago," 21–23. Ellsworth Eliot, *West Point in the Confederacy* (New York: G. A. Baker and Company, 1941), 2–3. Charles Dudley Rhodes, *Robert E. Lee: West Pointer* (Richmond, Garrett and Massie, 1932), 14–15.

26. Thomas J. Fleming, *West Point: The Men and Times of the United States Military Academy* (New York: William Morrow, 1969), 47–48. Stephen E. Ambrose, *Duty, Honor, Country: A History of West Point* (Baltimore: Johns Hopkins University Press, 1962), 69–74. *Register of the Officers and Cadets of the U.S. Military Academy*, June 1827 (West Point, U.S. Military Academy, 1884), 21–22.

27. Douglas Southall Freeman, *Robert E. Lee: A Biography,* vol. 1 (New York: Charles Scribner's Sons, 1934), 48 ff. Gilbert E. Govan and James W. Livingood, *A Different Valor: The Story of Joseph E. Johnston, C.S.A.* (Indianapolis: Bobbs-Merrill, 1956), 18–21. Clement Eaton, *Jefferson Davis* (New York: Free Press, 1977), 13–15.

28. T. H. Holmes to J. B. Magruder, 28 November 1862, Correspondence of General T. H. Holmes, vol. 358, Record Group 109, National Archives, Washington, D.C. Mark M. Boatner, *The Civil War Dictionary* (New York: David M. McKay, 1959), 406. Bruce, *History of the University of Virginia,* vol. 2, 78. Heitman, *Historical Register of the Army,* vol. 1, 527. Malone, ed., *Dictionary of American Biography,* vol. 2, 346–347.

29. Boatner, *Civil War Dictionary,* 156. Heitman, *Historical Register of the Army,* vol. 1, 571. Settles, "Military Career of Magruder," 17–19. See also Jerold N. Moore, *Confederate Commissary General: Lucius Bellinger Northrop* (Shippensburg, Pa.: White Mane Publishing Company, 1995).

30. Ambrose, *Duty, Honor, Country,* 187. Freeman, *Lee: A Biography,* vol. 1, 79–82. Rhodes, *Lee: West Pointer,* 20–21. Unidentified, "Recollections of Cadet Life," *Army and Navy Journal* 4 (3 August 1867), 794.

31. W. A. Croffut, ed., *Fifty Years in Camp and Field: Diary of Major General Ethan Allen Hitchcock, USA* (New York: G. P. Putnam's Sons, 1901), 37. Davis, *Jefferson Davis,* 36.

32. Davis, *Jefferson Davis,* 36. Haskell M. Monroe and James T. McIntosh, eds., *The Papers of Jefferson Davis,* vol. 1 (Baton Rouge: Louisiana State University Press, 1965), 73–75. Percy L. Rainwater, ed., "The Autobiography of Benjamin Grubb Humphreys, August 26, 1808–December 20, 1882," *Mississippi Valley Historical Review* 21 (June 1934), 238.

33. Ambrose, *Duty, Honor, Country,* 92–93. Rhodes, *Lee: West Pointer,* 19. Fourth Class Rolls, June 1827, vol. 1, 1817–1835 (Register of Merit), U.S. Military Academy Archives, West Point, New York. Ibid. Third Class Rolls, June 1828.

34. Delinquency Record of J. B. Magruder, Record of Delinquencies, 1822–1828, 544, U.S. Military Academy Archives, West Point, New York. *Register of Officers and Cadets of the U.S. Military Academy,* June 1829 (West Point, N.Y.: U.S. Military Academy, 1884), 21. Ibid., June 1830, 19. Lee, ed., *Memoirs of William Nelson Pendleton,* 27. William M. Polk, *Leonidas Polk: Bishop and General,* vol. 1 (New York: Longmans, Green and Company, 1915), 88.

35. Third Class Rolls, June 1828, vol. 1, 1817–1835 (Register of Merit). Muster Roll for 1828, Muster Rolls, Corps of Cadets, vol. 3, 1825–1830, U.S. Military Academy Archives, West Point, New York. Monroe and McIntosh, eds., *Papers of Jefferson Davis,* vol. 1, 93–94. William Marvel, *Andersonville: The Last Depot* (Chapel Hill and London: University of North Carolina Press, 1994), 12–19. Unidentified, "Recollections of Cadet Life," 794.

36. Ambrose, *Duty, Honor, Country,* 95. *Official Register of Officers and Cadets,* June 1829, 21. Muster Roll for 1829, vol. 3, 1825–1830.

37. Muster Roll for 1830, vol. 3, 1825–1830. Lee, ed., *Memoirs of William Nelson Pendleton,* 29. Julian Symons, *The Tell-Tale Heart: The Life and Works of Edgar Allan Poe* (New York: Harper & Row, 1978), 39–41.

38. First Class Rolls, June 1830, vol. 1, 1817–1835 (Register of Merit). Eben Swift, "The Military Education of Robert E. Lee," *Virginia Magazine of History and*

Biography 35 (April 1927), 104–105. James W. Pohl, "The Influence of Henri de Jomini on Winfield Scott's Campaign in the Mexican War," *Southwestern Historical Quarterly* 77 (July 1973), 86–88.

39. *Official Register of the Officers and Cadets of the U.S. Military Academy*, June 1830 (West Point: U.S. Military Academy, 1887), 19 (titles of the printed Register vary slightly from year to year). First Class Rolls, June 1830, vol. 1, 1817–1835 (Register of Merit). Ewell, "To Magruder-Ewell Camp," 2–3.

40. Rhodes, *Lee: West Pointer*, 23. Gerard A. Patterson, *Rebels from West Point* (New York: Doubleday, 1987), x, 159–160; James L. Morrison, *The Best School in the World: West Point, the Pre–Civil War Years, 1833–1866* (Kent, Ohio: Kent State University Press, 1986), 14–19.

—— 2. Lieutenant Magruder ——

1. J. B. Magruder to R. B. Taney, July 2, 1831, "Letters Received by the Office of the Secretary of War," National Archives M-221, reel 111. Canton Company of Baltimore, *Canton Days: The First Hundred Years or So* (Baltimore: Canton Company, 1928). Francis Fry Wayland, *Andrew Stevenson: Democrat and Diplomat, 1785–1857* (Philadelphia: University of Pennsylvania Press, 1949), 74–102, 169. *Baltimore Sun*, 10 December 1950.

2. Magruder to Taney, "Letters Received, by the Office of the Secretary of War," reel 111. Timothy Jacobs, *The History of the Baltimore and Ohio: America's First Railroad* (New York: Crescent Books, 1989), 14. James D. Dilts, *The Great Road: The Building of the Baltimore & Ohio: The Nation's First Railroad, 1828–1853* (Stanford, Calif., Stanford University Press, 1993), passim.

3. Secretary of the Society for the History of the Germans in Maryland, Sixth Annual Report (Baltimore: n.p., n.d.), 91. J. Thomas Scharf, *The Chronicles of Baltimore: Being a Complete History of "Baltimore Town" and Baltimore City* (reprint, Port Washington, New York: Kennikat Press, 1972), 285–286. Chapman Printing Company, *Genealogy and Biography of Leading Families of the City of Baltimore County, Maryland* (Chicago and New York: Chapman Printing Company, 1897), 159–160. *Baltimore American and Commerical Advertiser*, 19 May 1831.

4. "Ebbett," "John Magruder," *Army and Navy Journal*, 25 September 1880, 148. J. F. Lee to Unknown (1871?), Lee Family Papers, Virginia Historical Society Library, Richmond. T. R. Hay to W. M. E. Rachal, 23 July 1961, William Mumford Ellis Rachal Papers, Virginia Historical Society Library, Richmond. Edmund Jennings Lee, *Lee of Virginia, 1642–1892* (Philadelphia: Franklin Publishing Company, 1895), 402–405.

5. Association of the Graduates of the United States Military Academy, Annual Reunion, June 17, 1871 (West Point, N.Y.: U.S. Military Academy, 1871), 26. Walter P. Webb, ed., *The Handbook of Texas*, vol. 2 (Austin: Texas State Historical Association, 1952), 30–40. The Casemate Museum of Fort Monroe to the author, personal correspondence, 29 January 1993. Fitzhugh Lee, *General Lee* (New York: D. Appleton and Co., 1894), 27–28. Herbert Aptheker, *Nat Turner's Slave Rebellion* (New York: Humanities Press, 1966), 55, 152.

6. Alan D. Watson, *A History of New Bern and Craven County* (New Bern, N.C.: Tryon Palace Commission, 1987), 312. Adjutant General to J. B. Magruder, 26 September 1832, "Letters Sent by the Office of the Adjutant General, 1800–1890," National Archives Publication M-565, reel 8. Post Returns, New Bern and Beaufort, North Carolina, "Returns from U.S. Military Posts, 1800–1916," National Archives Publication M-617, Reel 828.

7. Norman G. Rukert, *Fort McHenry: Home of the Brave* (Baltimore, Bodine and Associates, 1983), 1, 52. Elizabeth Cometti and Festus P. Summers, *The Thirty-Fifth State: A Documentary History of West Virginia* (Morgantown, W.V.: University Library, 1966), 231. Adjutant General to J. B. Magruder, 19 August 1833, "Letters Sent by the Office of the Adjutant General," reel 8.

8. Jerome F. Morris, *The Brief Belligerence of Fort Macon* (Raleigh, N.C.: North Carolina Confederate Centennial Commission, n.d.), 1–5. Richard S. Barry, "Fort Macon: Its History," *North Carolina Historical Review* 27 (April 1950), 164–167. Richard S. Barry, "The History of Fort Macon" (M.A. thesis, Duke University, 1950), 101–103. Post Returns, Fort Macon, North Carolina, "Returns from U.S. Military Posts," reel 718.

9. Lawrence Lee, *The History of Brunswick County, North Carolina* (n.p., 1978), 94–98. S. G. DeR. Hamilton, "The Site of Fort Johnston" (copy of 1911 address in North Carolina State Library, Raleigh), 81–91. Post Returns, Fort Johnston, North Carolina, "Returns from U.S. Military Posts," reel 558.

10. *Raleigh Weekly Register and North Carolina Gazette*, 4 August 1835. *The Revised Statues of the State of North Carolina Passed by the General Assembly at the Session of 1836–7 . . .* (Raleigh: Turner and Hughes, 1837), 11. William E. Smythe, *History of San Diego* (San Diego: The History Company, 1907), 582–583.

11. Adjutant General to J. B. Magruder, September 28, 1835, 9 May 1836, 6 July 1836, "Letters Sent by the Office of the Adjutant General," reels 8 and 9. Amy Cheney Clinton, "Historic Fort Washington," *Maryland Historical Magazine* 32 (September 1937): 245–246. Morris L. Radoff, *The Old Line State: A History of Maryland* (Annapolis: Hall of Records Commission, 1971), 147. Post Returns, Fort Washington, Maryland, "Returns from U.S. Military Posts," reel 1382.

12. Marquis James, *Andrew Jackson: Portrait of a President* (reprint, New York: Grosset and Dunlap, n.d.), 245. Edward Pessen, *Jacksonian America: Society, Personality, and Politics* (reprint, Homewood, Ill.: Dorsey Press, 1969), 320–322. John K. Mahon, *History of the Second Seminole War, 1835–1845* (Gainesville: University of Florida Press, 1967), 75–76.

13. Mahon, *Second Seminole War*, 109–112. Holman Hamilton, *Zachary Taylor: Soldier of the Republic* (reprint, Hamden, Conn.: Archon Books, 1966), 120–124.

14. Post Returns, Fort Johnston, North Carolina, "Returns from U.S. Military Posts," reel 558. William L. Haskin, *The History of the First Regiment of Artillery from Its Organization in 1821, to January 1st 1876* (Portland, Maine: B. Thurston and Co., 1879), 52–55.

15. Haskin, *History of the First Artillery*, 59. J. B. Magruder to Adjutant General, 18 October 1836, "Letters Received by the Office of the Adjutant General, 1822–1860," National Archives Publication M-567, reel 128. Adjutant General to J. B. Magruder, "Letters Sent by the Office of the Adjutant General," reel 10.

16. Adjutant General to J. B. Magruder, 9 November 1836, "Letters Sent by the Office of the Adjutant General," reel 9. Thomas M. Settles, "The Military Career of John Bankhead Magruder" (Ph.D. diss., Texas Christian University, Fort Worth 1972), 30–31. G. E. E. Linquist, *The Red Man in the United States* (reprint, Clifton, N.J.: Augustus M. Kelley Publishers, 1973), 109. Jon M. White, *Everyday Life of the North American Indians* (New York: Dorset Press, 1979), 223.

17. Hamilton, *Zachary Taylor: Soldier of the Republic*, 121. Charlton Tebeau, *A History of Florida* (Coral Gables: University of Miami Press, 1971), 164–165; Mahon, *Second Seminole War*, 225.

18. Motte uses the spellings *Magruder* and *McGruder* interchangeably.

19. James F. Sunderman, ed., *Journey into the Wilderness: An Army Surgeon's Account of Life in Camp and Field During the Creek and Seminole Wars, 1836–1838 by Jacob Rhett Motte* (Gainesville: University of Florida Press, 1953), 155–178.

20. Mark Derr, *Some Kind of Paradise: A Chronicle of Man and the Land in Florida* (New York: William Morrow and Co., 1989), 289. Hamilton, *Zachary Taylor: Soldier of the Republic*, 129–133. Mahon, *Second Seminole War*, 232. Sunderman, ed., *Journey into the Wilderness*, 186.

21. Derr, *Some Kind of Paradise*, 289. Settles, "Military Career of Magruder," 33.

22. Derr, *Some Kind of Paradise*, 292. Haskin, *History of the First Artillery*, 667. Adjutant General to J. B. Magruder, 29 May 1844, "Letters Sent by the Office of the Adjutant General," reel 13.

23. J. B. Magruder to N. Callan, 27 March 1840, John Bankhead Magruder Papers, Perkins Library, Duke University, Durham, N.C. Adjutant General to J. B. Magruder, 10 December 1838, "Letters Sent by the Office of the Adjutant General," reel 11, 4 February 1846, 16 March 1846, reel 14.

24. Glyndon Van Deusen, *The Jacksonian Era, 1828–1848* (reprint, New York: Harper & Row, 1963), 135–139. Robert V. Remini, *Henry Clay: Stateman for the Union* (New York: W. W. Norton and Co., 1991), 522–523. Frederick Jackson Turner, *The United States, 1830–1850: The Nation and Its Sections* (New York: Henry Holt and Co., 1935), 471–473.

25. Major L. Wilson, *The Presidency of Martin Van Buren* (Lawrence: University Press of Kansas, 1984), 159–160. Thomas Jackson Arnold, *Early Life and Letters of General Jackson* (New York: Fleming H. Revell Company, 1916), 93. Frank E. Vandiver, *Mighty Stonewall* (New York: McGraw-Hill, 1957), 20. Post Returns, Plattsburg, New York, "Returns from U.S. Military Posts," reel 935.

26. Wilson, *Presidency of Van Buren*, 160–161. Adjutant General to J. B. Magruder, 10 December 1838, 25 February 1839, "Letters Sent by the Office of the Adjutant General," reel 11. William Chapman White, *Adirondack Country* (New York: Alfred A. Knopf, 1968), 81.

27. Haskin, *History of the First Artillery*, 285–287.

28. Wilson, *Presidency of Van Buren*, 165–166. Van Deusen, *Jacksonian Era*, 140–141. Haskin, *History of the First Artillery*, 72–73. Henry S. Burrage, *Maine and the Northeastern Boundary Controversy* (Portland: Marks Printing House, 1919), 328–342, and elsewhere.

29. Geraldine Tidd Scott, "Fortifications on Maine's Boundary, 1828–1845," *Maine Historical Quarterly* 29 (Winter/Spring 1990): 121–122. Cora Putnam, *The Story*

of Houlton (Portland: House of Falmouth, 1958), 60–62. Post Returns, Hancock Barracks, Maine, "Returns from U.S. Military Posts," reel 448.

30. Adjutant General to J. B. Magruder, 23 January 1843, "Letters Sent by the Office of the Adjutant General," reel 13. Robert L. Dabney, *Life and Campaigns of Lieut.-Gen. Thomas J. Jackson* (New York: Blelock and Company, 1866), 44. Haskin, *History of the First Artillery*, 74.

31. J. B. Magruder to Adjutant General, 3 January 1843, "Letters Received by the Office of the Adjutant General," reel 274. Adjutant General to J. B. Magruder, 23 January 1843, 10 May 1845, "Letters Sent by the Office of the Adjutant General," reel 14. Ebbett, "John Magruder," *Army and Navy Journal*, 25 September 1880, 148.

32. Francis B. Heitman, *Historical Register and Directory of the United States Army,* vol. 1 (Washington, D.C.: Government Printing Office, 1903), 1061. Thomas H. S. Hamersly, *Complete Army and Navy Register of the United States from 1776 to 1887* (New York: T. H. S. Hamersly Publisher, 1888), 879. Dumas Malone, ed., *The Dictionary of American Biography*, vol. 20 (New York: Charles Scribner's Sons, 1928), 536–537. W. J. Worth to W. L. Marcy, 29 January 1846, "Letters Received by the Office of the Adjutant General," reel 321. J. B. Magruder to Adjutant General, April 23, 1846, ibid.

33. Adjutant General to J. B. Magruder, 14 August 1845, "Letters Sent by the Office of the Adjutant General," reel 14. J. B. Magruder to J. Hooker, 14 July 1844, "Letters Received by the Office of the Adjutant General," reel 288. James A. Padgett, "Life of Alfred Mordecia in Mexico, 1865–1866, as Told in His Letters to His Family," *North Carolina Historical Review* 23 (January 1946), 85.

34. M. R. Stewart, M.D., to J. B. Magruder, 23 August 1844, "Letters Received by the Office of the Adjutant General," reel 289. William Power, M.D., to J. B. Magruder, 11 September 1844, ibid. H. S. Stinnecke, Surgeon, U.S.A., to Adjutant General, 12 September 1844, ibid. J. B. Magruder to Adjutant General, 12 September 1844, ibid.

35. Winfield Scott, memo, 17 September 1844, "Letters Received by the Office of the Adjutant General," reel 289. J. B. Magruder to Adjutant General, 12 October 1844, 7 December 1844, ibid.

36. Adjutant General to J. B. Magruder, 14 August 1844, "Letters Sent by the Office of the Adjutant General," reel 14.

____ 3. A Box in the National Theater ____

1. Seymour V. Connor and Odie B. Faulk, *North America Divided: The Mexican War, 1846–1848* (New York: Oxford University Press, 1971), 28–30. John M. Nance, *After San Jacinto: The Texas-Mexican Frontier, 1836–1841* (Austin: University of Texas Press, 1963), 227–230. John S. D. Eisenhower, *So Far from God: The U.S. War with Mexico, 1846–1848* (New York: Random House, 1989), xix.

2. Oliver P. Chitwood, *John Tyler: Champion of the Old South* (reprint, New York: Russell and Russell, 1964), 363. Thomas Bangs Thorpe, *Our Army on the Rio Grande* (Philadelphia: Cary and Hart, 1848), 38–41. Holman Hamilton, *Zachary Taylor: Soldier of the Republic* (reprint, Hamden, Conn.: Archon Books, 1966), 159.

3. William L. Haskin, *The History of the First Regiment of Artillery from its Organization in 1821, to January 1st 1876* (Portland, Maine: B. Thurston and Company,

1879), 78. Walter P. Webb, ed., *The Handbook of Texas,* vol. 2 (Austin: Texas State Historical Association, 1952), II, 529. George Meade, *The Life and Letters of George Gordon Meade* (New York: Charles Scribner's Sons, 1913), 27. W. A. Croffut, ed., *Fifty Years in Camp and Field: Diary of Major General Ethan Allen Hitchcock, USA* (New York: G. P. Putnam's Sons, 1901), 194.

4. J. B. Magruder to James Duncan, undated, James Duncan Papers, United States Military Academy Archives, West Point, New York. G. T. Mason to C. J. Couts, 27 October 1845, Cave Johnson Couts Papers, The Huntington Library, San Marino, California. Croffut, ed., *Fifty Years in Camp and Field,* 194, 203.

5. Adjutant General to J. B. Magruder, 23 January, 10 May 1845, "Letters Sent by the Office of the Adjutant General," National Archives Publication M-565, reel 14. Mark M. Boatner, *The Civil War Dictionary* (New York: David M. McKay Company, 1959), 47. William F. Barry, untitled piece, *Army and Navy Journal* 2 (August 1879), 11.

6. Lloyd Lewis, *Captain Sam Grant* (reprint, Boston: Little, Brown, 1991), 129; G. T. Mason to C. J. Couts, 24 December 1845, Couts Papers.

7. James Longstreet, *From Manassas to Appomattox: Memoirs of the Civil War in America* (Philadelphia: J. P. Lippincott, 1903), 20. U. S. Grant, *Personal Memoirs of U. S. Grant* (reprint, New York: Da Capo Press, 1982), 26–38. Meade, *Life and Letters,* 43–44.

8. Hamilton, *Taylor: Soldier of the Republic,* 173ff. Haskin, *History of the First Artillery,* 78–79. Meade, *Life and Letters,* 56.

9. Emma Jerome Blackwood, ed., *To Mexico with Scott: Letters of E. Kirby Smith to His Wife* (Cambridge: Harvard University Press, 1917), 34. J. B. Magruder to Adjutant General April 21, 1845, "Letters Received by the Office of the Adjutant General," National Archives Publication M-567, reel 321. Rhoda van Bibber Doubleday, ed., *Journals of the late Brevet Major Philip Norbourne Barbour, Captain in the 3rd Regiment, United States Infantry* (New York: G. P. Putnam's Sons, 1936), 24–25.

10. Jack Bauer, *Zachary Taylor: Soldier, Planter, Statesman of the Old South* (Baton Rouge: Louisiana State University Press, 1985), 166–180. Charles A. McCoy, *Polk and the Presidency* (Austin: University of Texas Press, 1960), 94. Robert S. Henry, *The Story of the Mexican War* (New York: Bobbs-Merrill, 1950), 400. War Proclamation, 13 May 1846, copy in "Letters Received by the Adjutant General," reel 321.

11. Hamilton, *Taylor: Soldier of the Republic,* 179–183. U.S. Congress, House Executive Document 60, 1st Session, 30th Congress, vol. 7 (Washington, D.C.: Government Printing Office, 1848), 3–6 (Taylor's Orders). Haskin, *History of the First Artillery,* 82. Zachary Taylor, *Letters of Zachary Taylor from the Battle-Fields of Mexico* (reprint, New York: Kraus Reprints, 1970), 1–4.

12. J. B. Magruder to Adjutant General, 31 August 1846 (reel 310), 15 September 1846 (reel 322), "Letters Received by the Office of the Adjutant General." Zachary Taylor's Orders No. 83, 7 July 1846, "Orders of General Zachary Taylor to the Army of Occupation in the Mexican War, 1845–1847," National Archives Publication M-29, reel 1. Adjutant General to James Bankhead, 17, 23 September 1846, "Letters Sent by the Office of the Adjutant General," reel 15. Doubleday, ed., *Journals of Philip Barbour,* 80.

13. Adjutant General to J. B. Magruder, 20 November 1846, "Letters Sent by the Office of the Adjutant General," reel 15. Robert W. Johannsen, *To the Halls of*

Montezuma: The Mexican War in the American Imagination (New York: Oxford University Press, 1985), 91. Eisenhower, *So Far from God*, 162–164.

14. J. B. Magruder to Adjutant General, 13 September 1846 (reel 322), 16 November 1846 (reel 323); Winfield Scott to Adjutant General, 28 November 1846, "Letters Received by the Office of the Adjutant General," reel 323. Adjutant General to James Bankhead, 29 November 1846, "Letters Sent by the Office of the Adjutant General," reel 15. Connor and Faulk, *North America Divided*, 106–110.

15. Adjutant General to J. B. Magruder, 30 August 1846, "Letters Sent by the Office of the Adjutant General," reel 14. George W. Cullum, *Biographical Register of the Officers and Graduates of the U.S. Military Academy . . . 1802 to 1890* (Boston and New York: Houghton, Mifflin and Co., 1891), 456. Haskin, *History of the First Artillery*, 608. Eba Anderson Lawton, ed., *An Artillery Officer in the Mexican War, 1846–7: Letters of Robert Anderson* (New York: G. P. Putnam's Sons, 1911), 43.

16. Meade, *Life and Letters*, 175, 185. Haskin, *History of the First Artillery*, p. 92. Lawton, ed., *Artillery Officer in Mexico*, 34. William Starr Myres, ed., *The Mexican War Diary of George B. McClellan* (Princeton: Princeton University Press, 1917), 50.

17. Haskin, *History of the First Artillery*, 92. Alfred Hoyt Bill, *Rehearsal for Conflict: The War with Mexico, 1846–1848* (New York: Alfred A. Knopf, 1947), 211–212.

18. Vincent J. Esposito, *West Point Atlas of American Wars, 1689–1900*, vol. 1 (New York: Frederick A. Praeger, 1960), 15. Henry, *Story of the Mexican War*, 267–269. Thomas Jackson Arnold, *Early Life and Letters of General Jackson* (New York: Fleming H. Revell Company, 1916), 84–85. Fitzhugh Lee, *General Lee* (New York: D. Appleton and Co., 1894), 35–37.

19. Bill, *Rehearsal for Conflict*, 211. Haskin, *History of the First Artillery*, 93–94. U.S. Congress, Senate Executive Document 1, 30th Congress, First Session (Washington, D.C.: Wendell and Van Benthuysen, 1848 [hereafter cited as Senate 1 (1848)]. J. B. Magruder to Adjutant General, January 12, February 25, 1847, "Letters Received by the Office of the Adjutant General," reel 368.

20. Connor and Faulk, *North America Divided*, 111. Henry, *Story of the Mexican War*, 283. Eisenhower, *So Far from God*, 272–283.

21. A. L. Long, *Memoirs of Robert E. Lee: His Military and Personal History* (reprint, Secaucus, N.J.: Blue and Grey Press, 1983), 52. U. S. Grant, *Personal Memoirs*, 63. Henry, *Story of the Mexican War*, 285–286. U.S. Congress, Senate 1 (1848), 263, 276, 282, 284.

22. [George Ballentine] *Autobiography of an English Soldier in the United States Army Comprising Observations and Adventures in the United States and Mexico* (New York: Stringer and Townsend, 1853), 215. John Esten Cooke, *Stonewall Jackson: A Military Biography* (New York: D. Appleton and Co., 1866), 14–15. Paul D. Casdorph, *Lee and Jackson: Confederate Chieftains* (New York: Paragon House, 1992), 79–82.

23. Bill, *Rehearsal for Conflict*, 257–259. Haskin, *History of the First Artillery*, 99. U.S. Congress, Senate 1 (1848), Appendix, 21. [Ballentine], *Autobiography of an English Soldier*, 221.

24. U.S. Congress, Senate 1 (1848), Appendix, 21. J. William Jones, *Life and Letters of Robert Edward Lee: Soldier and Man* (New York: Neale Publishing Co., 1906), 52. John Edward Weems, *To Conquer a Peace: The War Between the United States and*

Mexico (Garden City, N.Y.: Doubleday, 1947), 369–371. Arthur D. H. Smith, *Old Fuss and Feathers: The Life and Exploits of Lt. General Winfield Scott* (New York: Greystone Press, 1937), 286.

25. Bill, *Rehearsal for Conflict*, 258. Roy Bird Cook, *The Family and Early Life of Stonewall Jackson* (reprint, Charleston, W.V.: Education Foundation, 1967), 101–103. Smith, *Old Fuss and Feathers*, 298. Haskin, *History of the First Artillery*, p. 100–101.

26. Esposito, *West Point Atlas of American Wars*, vol. 1, 15–16. Cadmus Wilcox, *History of the Mexican War* (Washington, D.C.: Church News Publishing Company, 1892), 349–354. Winfield Scott, *Memoirs: By Himself*, vol. 2 (New York: Sheldon and Company, 1867), 460–463.

27. Justin H. Smith, *The War with Mexico*, vol. 2 (New York: Macmillan, 1919), 102–104. Long, *Memoirs of Lee*, 58–59. [Ballentine], *Autobiography of An English Soldier*, 249. U.S. Congress, Senate 1 (1848), Appendix, 101.

28. Henry, *Story of the Mexican War*, 332–336. U.S. Congress, Senate 1 (1848), Appendix, 101–102.

29. Smith, *The War with Mexico*, vol. 2, 105ff. Henry, *Story of the Mexican War*, 333. Eisenhower, *So Far from God*, 316–327. U.S. Congress, Senate 1 (1848), Appendix, 103–105.

30. Henry, *Story of the Mexican War*, 351–355. Blackwood, ed., *To Mexico with Scott*, 217. U.S. Congress, Senate 1 (1848), Appendix, 192. William Garrett Piston, *Lee's Tarnished Lieutenant: James Longstreeet and His Place in Southern History* (Athens: University of Georgia Press, 1987), 7.

31. U.S. Congress, Senate 1 (1848), Appendix, 133–134.

32. Henry Alexander White, *Robert E. Lee and the Southern Confederacy* (New York: G. P. Putnam's Sons, 1910), 43. Edward D. Mansfield, *The Mexican War: A History of Its Origin* (New York: A. S. Barnes and Company, 1849), 273. George W. Smith and Charles Judah, *Chronicles of the Gringoes: The U.S. Army in Mexico, 1846–1848* (Albuquerque: University of New Mexico Press, 1968), 257.

33. An Ex-Cadet [James Dabney McCabe], *The Life of Thomas J. Jackson* (Richmond: James E. Goode, 1864), 15–18. Casdorph, *Lee and Jackson*, 94–96. U.S. Congress, Senate 1 (1848), Appendix, 194–196. Robert L. Dabney, *Life and Campaigns of Lieut.-Gen. Thomas J. Jackson* (New York: Blelock and Co., 1866), 47–49. Cullum, *Officers and Graduates of the U.S. Military Academy*, 456.

34. Unidentified newspaper clipping, John Bankhead Magruder Vertical File, Center for the Study of American History, University of Texas, Austin.

35. *The Constitution of the Aztec Club of 1847 and the List of Members, 1893* (reprint, Louisville, Ky.: Lost Cause Press, 1980), 1–3. Alexander W. Terrell, *From Texas to Mexico and the Court of Maximilian* (reprint, Dallas: The Book Club of Texas, 1933), 58. Cooke, *Stonewall Jackson*, 14–16. Roy F. Nichols, *Franklin Pierce: Young Hickory of the Granite Hills* (Philadelphia: University of Pennsylvania Press, 1931), 213.

36. Haskin, *History of the First Artillery*, 116–117, 610. J. B. Magruder to Adjutant General, 26 November 1847 (reel 353), 17, 18 January 1848 (reel 382), George A. Magruder to Adjutant General, 23 January 1848 (reel 382), "Letters Received by the Office of the Adjutant General." Adjutant General to J. B. Magruder, 21 February 1848, "Letters Sent by the Office of the Adjutant General," reel 15.

— 4. "John Was Always Magnificent" —

1. George R. Stewart, *John Phoenix, Esq., the Veritable Squibob: A Life of Captain George H. Derby, U.S.A.* (reprint, New York: Da Capo Press, reprint, 1969), 53. Francis B. Heitman, *Historical Register and Directory of the United States Army, 1789–1903* (Washington, D.C.: Government Printing Office, 1903), 263. William L. Haskin, *The History of the First Regiment of Artillery from Its Organization in 1821, to January 1st 1876* (Portland, Maine: B. Thurston and Co., 1879), 321 (Boynton quote).

2. J. B. Magruder to Adjutant General, 1 August 1848, J. B. Magruder to I. B. Crane, 7 August 1848, J. B. Magruder, requisition, 16 September 1848, "Letters Received by the Office of the Adjutant General, 1822–1860," National Archives Publication M-567, reel 385. Heitman, *Historical Register of the Army*, 335.

3. J. B. Magruder to Adjutant General, 17 January 1848, "Letters Received by the Office of the Adjutant General," reel 382. Haskin, *History of the First Artillery*, 121.

4. J. B. Magruder to Adjutant General, 3 October 1848, "Letters Received by the Office of the Adjutant General," reel 385.

5. Adjutant General to J. B. Magruder, 5, 26 October, 30 December 1848, "Letters Sent by the Office of the Adjutant General, 1800–1890," National Archives Publication M-565, reel 16. J. B. Magruder to Adjutant General, 3 December 1848, "Letters Received by the Office of the Adjutant General," reel 386. Haskin, *History of the First Artillery*, 122. *Niles National Register*, 9 May 1849, vol. 75 (Philadelphia), 1.

6. Adjutant General to J. B. Magruder, 13 November, 7 December 1849, 7, 17 January 1850, "Letters Sent by the Office of the Adjutant General," reels 16, 17.

7. J. B. Magruder to Jefferson Davis, 13 December 1853, "Letters Received by the Office of the Adjutant General," reel 486. Benjamin S. Ewell, "To Magruder-Ewell Camp," typescript, n.d., Richard Stoddert Ewell Papers, Library of Congress, Washington, 2–3. Adjutant General to Allan B. Magruder, 3 May 1851, "Letters Sent by the Office of the Adjutant General," reel 17. See also A. B. Magruder to C. M. Conrad, 29 April 1851, ibid.

8. Haskin, *History of the First Artillery*, 122–123. Robert Stephen Milota, "John Bankhead Magruder: The California Years" (M.A. thesis, University of San Diego, 1990), 8–9.

9. Robert B. Roberts, *Encyclopedia of Historic Forts: The Military, Pioneer, and Trading Posts of the United States* (New York: Macmillan, 1988), 87–88. Fr. Zephyrin Englehardt, *San Diego Mission* (San Francisco: James Barry Co., 1920), 255–258. John Russell Bartlett, *Personal Narrative of Explorations and Incidents in Texas, New Mexico, California, Sonora, and Chihuahua*, vol. 2 (New York: D. Appleton and Co., 1854), 101–105.

10. Ed Scott, *San Diego County Soldiers-Pioneers, 1846–1866* (National City, Calif.: Crest Printing Co., 1976), 34, 39. Mark M. Boatner, *The Civil War Dictionary* (New York: David M. McKay, 1959), 623, 764, 801. Milota, "Magruder: The California Years," 74–79; both Milota and Thomas M. Settles, "The Military Career of John Bankhead Magruder" (Ph.D. diss., Texas Christian University, 1972), have searched deeply into California deed books and other records to present a detailed account of Magruder's land holdings.

11. Joseph L. Brent, *Memoirs of the War Between the States* (New Orleans: Fontana Printing Company, 1940), 5–8. Remi Nadeau, *Los Angeles: From Mission to Modern City* (New York: Longmans, Green and Co., 1960), 43. Milota, "Magruder: The California Years," 31–38, 74–76.

12. Adjutant General to E. A. Hitchcock, 9 July 1851, 1 December 1852, Adjutant General to J. B. Magruder, 30 November 1852, "Letters Sent by the Office of the Adjutant General," reel 17. McCall's report cited from Milota, "Magruder: The California Years," 66.

13. George H. Phillips, *Chiefs and Challengers: Indian Resistance and Cooperation in Southern California* (Berkeley: University of California Press, 1975), 91–94. Arthur Woodward, *Feud on the Colorado* (Los Angeles: Westernlore Press, 1955), 43. John L. White, "Founder of Fort Yuma: Excerpts from the Diary of Major Samuel Heintzelman, U.S.A., 1849–1852" (M.A. thesis, University of San Diego, 1975), 136–143.

14. White, "Founder of Fort Yuma," 168. Robert M. Utley, *Frontiersmen in Blue: The United States Army and the Indian, 1848–1865* (New York: Macmillan, 1967), 164. Woodward, *Feud on the Colorado*, 50.

15. Milota, "Magruder: The California Years," 57. Hamilton Cochran, *Noted American Duels and Hostile Encounters* (Philadelphia and New York: Chilton Books, 1963), 274–275. Stewart, *John Phoenix*, 121. Horace Bell, *Reminiscences of a Ranger: Or Early Times in Southern California* (Los Angeles: Yandell, Caystile and Mathes Printers, 1881), 74–78.

16. "Roll of Attorneys," handwritten ledger, California State Archives, Sacramento. Scott, *San Diego Soldiers-Pioneers*, 72, 86. Daniel H. Hill, "The Real Stonewall Jackson," *Century Magazine* 25 (February 1894), 624–625. Frank E. Vandiver, *Mighty Stonewall* (New York: McGraw-Hill, 1957), 43. Roy F. Nichols, *Franklin Pierce: Young Hickory of the Granite Hills* (Philadelphia: University of Pennsylvania Press, 1931), 213.

17. A. B. Magruder to C. M. Conrad, 7 August 1852, National Archives Record Group 94, file M-263, Records of the Adjutant General's Office, Washington, D.C. John W. Thomason, *JEB Stuart* (reprint, New York: Charles Scribner's Sons, 1958), 16–17. U.S. Congress, *Biographical Directory of the American Congress, 1774–1961* (Washington, D.C.: Government Printing Office, 1961), 1671.

18. Adjutant General to J. B. Magruder, 9, 21 June 1853, "Letters Sent by the Office of the Adjutant General," reel 17. C. M. Conrad to A. B. Magruder, 11 September 1852, Record Group 94, file M-264. Milota, "Magruder: The California Years," 77 (Sweeny citation). J. B. Magruder to Jefferson Davis, 13 December 1853, "Letters Received by the Office of the Adjutant General," reel 486.

19. *New York Times*, 12 July 1853. *San Diego Herald*, 8 October 1853, cited from Milota, "Magruder: The California Years," 77. *New York Herald*, 30 July, 29 September 1853.

20. Lynda Laswell Crist, ed., *The Papers of Jefferson Davis, 1853–1855*, vol. 5 (Baton Rouge: Louisiana State University Press, 1985), vol. 5, 38–43.

21. Ibid. *Richmond Enquirer*, October 8, 1853.

22. J. B. Magruder to Jefferson Davis, 13 December 1853 (two letters), "Letters Received by the Office of the Adjutant General," reel 486.

23. H. K. Craig to Jefferson Davis, 20 December 1853, "Letters Received by the Office of the Adjutant General," reel 486. Boatner, *Civil War Dictionary*, 206.

Jefferson Davis to J. B. Magruder, 22 December 1853, "Letters Received by the Office of the Adjutant General," reel 563.

24. E. L. Howe to Jefferson Davis, 22 December 1853, "Letters Received by the Office of the Adjutant General," reel 501. Jefferson Davis Memo, 23 December 1853, 21 April 1854, National Archives Publication M-444, "Orders and Endorsements Sent by the Secretary of War, 1846–1870," reel 002. Crist, ed., *Jefferson Davis Papers*, vol. 5, 209.

25. Unsigned newspaper clipping, John Bankhead Magruder, Vertical File, Center for the Study of American History, University of Texas, Austin. R. L. V. French Blake, *The Crimean War* (reprint, Hamden, Conn.: Archon Books, 1972), 147–148. Edward Hamley, *The War in the Crimea* (reprint, Westport, Conn.: Greenwood Press, 1971), 129. A. J. Barker, *The War Against Russia* (New York: Holt, Rinehart and Winston, 1970), 269. Richard Delafield, *Report . . . on the Art of War in Europe, 1854, 1855, and 1856*, Senate Executive Document, 36th Congress, First Session (Washington, D.C.: Government Printing Office, 1857), xiii.

26. Proceedings of the Special Meeting of the Medical and Chirurgical Faculty of Maryland in Relation to the Death of Dr. Riggin Buckler Held September 5, 1884 (Baltimore: Journal Publishing Co. 1884), 3. T. R. Hay to W. M. E. Rachal, 23 July 1961, William Mumford Ellis Rachal Papers, Virginia Historical Society Library, Richmond. *Baltimore American and Commerical Advertiser*, 23 July 1869 (Isabell Buckler obituary), *Baltimore Evening Sun*, 28 April 1955 (Riggin Buckler II obituary).

27. Adjutant General to J. B. Magruder, 18, 24 August 1854, "Letters Sent by the Office of the Adjutant General," reel 18. J. B. Magruder to Adjutant General, 2 April 1855, "Letters Received by the Office of the Adjutant General," reel 521. Jefferson Davis to Adjutant General, 6, 30 March 1855, "Orders and Endorsements of the Secretary of War," reel 003.

28. J. B. Magruder to Adjutant General, 2 April 1855, reel 521, 8 December 1855, reel 522, "Letters Received by the Office of the Adjutant General". J. B. Magruder, *Presidential Contest of 1856 in Three Letters* (San Antonio: Book and Job Office of the *San Antonio Texan*, 1856), 3. Roberts, *Encyclopedia of Historic Forts*, 155; Haskin, *History of the First Artillery*, 585.

29. Walter P. Webb, ed., *The Handbook of Texas*, vol. 1 (Austin: Texas State Historical Association, 1952), 622, vol. 2, 24. Roberts, *Encyclopedia of Historic Forts*, 768. J. B. Magruder Invoices, Fort Clark Records, Center for the Study of American History, University of Texas, Austin. Haskin, *History of the First Artillery*, 128.

30. Adjutant General to J. B. Magruder, 27 February 1856, "Letters Sent by the Office of the Adjutant General," reel 18. Lydia Spencer Lane, *I Married a Soldier: Or Old Days in the Old Army* (Philadelphia: J. B. Lippincott and Co., 1893), 85.

31. Magruder, *Presidential Contest of 1856*, 4. Jon L. Wakelyn, *Biographical Directory of the Confederacy* (Westport, Conn.: Greenwood Press, 1977), 292. Webb, ed., *Handbook of Texas*, vol. 2, 160, 340.

32. Magruder, *Presidential Contest of 1856*, 4–12.

33. Ibid., Philip S. Klein, *President James Buchanan: A Biography* (University Park, Pa.: Pennsylvania State University Press, 1962), 260. Eugene H. Roseboom, *A History of Presidential Elections* (New York: Macmillan, 1959), 166–167.

34. A. B. Magruder to Jefferson Davis, 29 December 1856, "Letters Received by the Office of the Adjutant General," reel 543. Roberts, *Encyclopedia of Historic Forts*, 328. Haskin, *History of the First Artillery*, 583.

35. Haskin, *History of the First Artillery*, 583–584. Richard O'Conner, *The Golden Summers: An Antic History of Newport* (New York: G. P. Putnam's Sons, 1974), 17–18.

36. Douglas Southall Freeman, *Lee's Lieutenants: A Study in Command*, vol. 1 (New York: Charles Scribner's Sons, 1942), 15. A. L. Long, "Memoir of General John Bankhead Magruder," *Southern Historical Society Papers* 12 (1884), 105–106. Adjutant General to J. B. Magruder, 29 December 1857, 24 April 1858, 29 April 1858, "Letters Sent by the Office of the Adjutant General," reel 19. *Newport Mercury*, 10 July 1858.

37. Tom Kneitel, *Directory of U.S. Army Forts, Camps, and Airfields, 1789–1945* (Commack, N.Y.: CRB Research Books, 1947), 22. *A Brief History of Fort Adams, Newport, R.I.* (n.p., n.d., copy in U.S. Naval War College Library, Newport, R.I.), 1–7. Adjutant General to J. B. Magruder, 24 May 1859, "Letters Sent by the Office of the Adjutant General," reel 19. *Newport Mercury*, 9 July 1859.

38. Adjutant General to J. B. Magruder, 31 October, 5 November 1859, 16 April 1860, "Letters Sent by the Office of the Adjutant General," reel 19. W. A. Swanberg, *First Blood: The Story of Fort Sumter* (New York: Charles Scribner's Sons, 1957), 36–38.

39. *History of the State of Kansas* (Chicago: A. T. Andreas, 1883), 418. Roberts, *Encyclopedia of Historic Forts*, 296–297. See also George Walton, *Sentinel of the Plains: Fort Leavenworth* (Englewood Cliffs, N.J.: Prentice Hall, 1973).

40. Post Returns, Fort Leavenworth, "Returns From U.S. Military Posts, 1800–1916," reel 611. Capsulized biographies of Elzey, Long, Taliaferro, and Hunt can be found in Boatner, *Civil War Dictionary*.

41. E. V. Sumner to Adjutant General, 24 January 1860, "Letters Received by the Office of the Adjutant General," reel 632. Adjutant General to E. V. Sumner, 10 March 1860, "Letters Sent by the Office of the Adjutant General," reel 19.

42. *History of the State of Kansas*, 419 (Callahan quote). A. L. Long, "Memoir of General John Bankhead Magruder," 106–107.

43. Adjutant General to J. B. Magruder, 27 January, 3, 18 February, 19 June 1860, "Letters Sent by the Office of the Adjutant General," reel 20. John Pegram to J. B. Magruder, 19 July 1860, Smith-Kirby-Webster-Black-Danner Papers, U.S. Army Military History Institute, Carlisle Barracks, Pennsylvania.

44. Adjutant General to J. B. Magruder, 11 October 1860, "Letters Sent by the Office of the Adjutant General," reel 20. J. B. Magruder to Adjutant General, 10 October 1860, National Archives, Record Group 97, Letters Received, M-385, 1860, Washington, D.C.

45. J. B. Floyd to J. B. Magruder, 11 October 1860, M-385, enclosure, National Archives, Record Group 97. Post Returns, Fort Leavenworth, "Returns of United States Military Posts, 1800–1916," reel 611.

46. J. B. Magruder to Adjutant General, 1 December 1860, National Archives, Record Group 97, M-463, 1860; 1 January 1861, M-221, 1861, ibid. (The latter is written on letterhead of the United States Legation in Paris.) Boatner, *Civil War Dictionary*, 26.

47. Haskin, *History of the First Artillery*, 587. Margaret Leech, *Reveille in Washington, 1860–1865* (reprint, New York: Time Incorporated, 1962), 59. David M. Potter, *The Impending Crisis, 1848–1861* (New York: Harper & Row, 1976), 485–513. E. Merton

Coulter, *The Confederate States of America, 1861–1865* (Baton Rouge: Louisiana State University Press, 1950), 1–33. William C. Davis, *"A Government of Their Own": The Making of the Confederacy* (New York: Free Press, 1994).

48. Ewell, "To Magruder-Ewell Camp," 4, R. S. Ewell Papers.

49. *New York Times*, 23 May 1870; Allan B. Magruder, "A Piece of Secret History: President Lincoln and the Virginia Convention of 1861," *Atlantic Monthly* 35 (April 1870), 438–440. Robert L. Dabney, "Memoir of a Narrative Received from Colonel John B. Baldwin of Staunton Touching on the Origin of the War," *Southern Historical Society Papers* 1 (January–June 1876), 445. J. B. Magruder to Colonel Lorenzo Thomas, 21 April 1861, National Archives, Record Group 97, M-82, 1861.

___ 5.   Big Bethel ___

1. *New York Times*, 23 May 1870. Charles H. Ambler and Festus P. Summers, *West Virginia: The Mountain State* (Englewood Cliffs, N.J.: Prentice Hall, 1957), 194. James C. McGregor, *The Disruption of Virginia* (New York: Macmillan, 1922), 176–177. George W. Cullum, *Biographical Register of the Officers and Graduates of the U.S. Military Academy at West Point, From Its Establishment, March 16, 1802, to the Army Reorganization of 1867,* vol. 2 (New York: D. Van Nostrand, 1868), 456.

2. *New York Times*, 23 May 1870. Philip St. George Cocke to John Letcher, 22 April 1861, miscellaneous correspondence, Virginia Historical Society Library, Richmond. Clifford Dowdey, *Lee* (Boston: Little, Brown, 1965), 145. Paul D. Casdorph, *Lee and Jackson: Confederate Chieftains* (New York: Paragon House, 1992), 169.

3. H. T. Douglas to S. T. C. Bryan, February 25, 1909, St. George T. C. Bryan Papers, Brockenbrough Library, Museum of the Confederacy, Richmond. Edward W. Callahan, ed., *List of Officers of the Navy of the United States and of the Marine Corps, from 1775 to 1900* (reprint, New York: Haskell House Publishers, 1969), 347. "George A. Magruder," typescript, Department of the Navy Library, Washington Navy Yard, Washington, D.C., Gideon Welles to G. A. Magruder, 23 April, 13 May 1861, "Resignations and Dismissals of Officers from the United States Navy, 1861," typescript (unbound on the shelf), Orders and Resignations, No. 31, Bureau of Ships, Department of the Navy Library, Washington Navy Yard, Washington, D.C.

4. Robert E. Lee, Jr., *Recollections and Letters of General Robert E. Lee* (Garden City, N.Y.: Garden City Publishing Company, 1903. Ambler and Summers, *West Virginia: The Mountain State*, 190. Secretary of War, *The War of the Rebellion: A Compilation of the Official Records of the Union and Confederate Armies*, series 1, vol. 2 (Washington, D.C.: Government Printing Office, 1880 ff.), hereafter cited as *O. R.* Jon L. Wakelyn, *Biographical Directory of the Confederacy* (Westport, Conn.: Greenwood Press, 1977), 305–306.

5. Lynda Laswell Crist and Mary Seaton Dix, eds., *The Papers of Jefferson Davis: 1861,* vol. 7 (Baton Rouge: Louisiana State University Press, 1992), 130–132. Clement Eaton, *Jefferson Davis* (New York: Free Press, 1977), 125–126. Mary Anna Jackson, *Memoirs of Stonewall Jackson by His Widow* (Louisville, Ky.: Prentice Press, 1895), 150. Craig L. Symonds, *Joseph E. Johnston: A Civil War Biography* (New York: W. W. Norton, 1992), 96–98.

6. *O.R.*, series 1, vol. 2, 709. Jennings C. Wise, *The Military History of the Virginia Military Institute, 1831–1865* (Lynchburg, Va.: J. P. Bell Company, 1915), 121, 146. Frank E. Vandiver, *Mighty Stonewall* (New York: McGraw-Hill, 1957), 129.

7. *O.R.*, series 1, vol. 2, 817, 865. Robert S. Henry, *The Story of the Confederacy* (New York: Bobbs-Merrill, 1936), 181. Marcus J. Wright, *General Officers of the Confederate Army* (New York: Neale Publishing Co., 1911), 23, 53.

8. J. B. Magruder to W. B. Blair, 23 May 1861, Beverly R. Welford Papers, Virginia Historical Society Library, Richmond. *O.R.*, series 1, vol. 2, 37. Stephen W. Sears, *To the Gates of Richmond: The Peninsula Campaign* (New York: Ticknor and Fields, 1992), 25–27.

9. Benjamin S. Ewell, "To Magruder-Ewell Camp," typescript, n.d., Richard Stoddert Ewell Papers, Library of Congress, Washington, D.C., 6. Lyon G. Tyler, ed., *Encyclopedia of Virginia Biography*, vol. 3 (New York: Lewis Publishing Co., 1915), 197. A. L. Long, *Memoirs of Robert E. Lee: His Military and Personal History* (reprint, Secaucus, N.J.: Blue and Grey Press, 1983), 146. Baker P. Lee, "Magruder's Peninsula Campaign in 1862," *Southern Historical Society Papers* 19 (1891), 64.

10. Robert M. Hughes, *General Johnston* (New York: D. Appleton and Co., 1893), 112. Baker P. Lee, "Magruder's Peninsula Campaign," 61. Jefferson Davis, *The Rise and Fall of the Confederate Government*, vol. 1 (New York: D. Appleton and Co., 1881), I, 340.

11. Undated newspaper clipping, in M. J. Solomons Papers, William R. Perkins Library, Duke University.

12. Hal Bridges, *Lee's Maverick General: Daniel Harvey Hill* (reprint, Lincoln: University of Nebraska Press, 1991), 28. Douglas Southall Freeman, *Lee's Lieutenants: A Study in Command*, vol. 1 (New York: Charles Scribner's Sons, 1942), I, 152. *O.R.*, series 1, vol. 2, 917–918.

13. *O.R.*, series 1, vol. 2, 883. John Bell Hood, *Advance and Retreat: Personal Experiences in the United States and Confederate Armies* (New Orleans: G. T. Beauregard, 1880), 17–18. Robert M. McMurry, *John Bell Hood and the War for Southern Independence* (Lexington: University Press of Kentucky, 1982), 25–26.

14. *O.R.*, series 1, vol. 2, 876 ff. Freeman, *Lee's Lieutenants*, vol. 1, 21.

15. *O.R.*, series 1, vol. 2, 871, 888, 891. Undated newspaper clipping, M. J. Solomons Papers. Ervin L. Jordan, Jr., *Black Confederates and Afro-Yankees in Civil War Virginia* (Charlottesville: University Press of Virginia, 1995), 58. Benjamin F. Butler, *Butler's Book: A Review of His Legal, Political, and Military Career* (Boston: A. M. Thayer and Co., 1892), 258–259.

16. Ewell, "To Magruder-Ewell Camp," 6. Stephen Z. Starr, *The Union Cavalry in the Civil War*, vol. 1 (Baton Rouge: Louisiana State University Press, 1979), 264–265. Sears, *To the Gates of Richmond*, 53.

17. H. T. Douglas to S. T. C. Bryan, Bryan Papers, 25 February 1909 (see this source for a detailed account of Magruder's staff). Wright, *General Officers of the Confederate Army*, 129, 134. Gary W. Gallagher, ed., *Fighting for the Confederacy: Personal Recollections of General Edward Porter Alexander* (Chapel Hill: University of North Carolina Press, 1989), 604. Alexander Watkins Terrell, *From Texas to Mexico and the Court of Maximilian* (reprint, Dallas: The Book Club of Texas, 1933), 18.

18. Baker P. Lee, "Magruder's Peninsula Campaign," 62–63. G. Moxley Sorrel, *Reflections of a Confederate Staff Officer* (New York: Neale Publishing Co., 1905), 63. Butler, *Butler's Book*, 267.

19. *O.R.*, series 1, vol. 2, 93–94, 213, 913. Bridges, *Lee's Maverick General*, 28. Henry, *Story of the Confederacy*, 50.

20. *O.R.*, series 1, vol. 2, 93–95. Butler, *Butler's Book*, 269. B. M. Hord, "The Battle of Big Bethel, Va.," *Confederate Veteran* 26 (1918), 419.

21. *O.R.*, series 1, vol. 2, 95. Butler, *Butler's Book*, 268–269. *New York Times*, 14 June 1861; *Baltimore American*, 12 June 1861.

22. *New York Times*, 14 June 1861. Hord, "Battle of Big Bethel," 419. James Dinkins, "The Battle of Big Bethel, Va.," *Confederate Veteran* 26 (1918), 291.

23. *O.R.*, series 1, vol. 2, 91–93. Freeman, *Lee's Lieutenants*, vol. 1, 18. Gallagher, ed., *Fighting for the Confederacy*, 44, 562.

24. Joseph B. Carr, "Operations of 1861 about Fort Monroe," in *Battles and Leaders of the Civil War*, vol. 2 (New York: The Century Co., 1887), 151. C. Vann Woodward and Elisabeth Muhlenfeld, eds., *The Private Mary Chesnut: The Unpublished Civil War Diaries* (New York: Oxford University Press, 1984), 82. *O.R.*, series 1, vol. 2, 925. Crist and Dix, eds., *Papers of Jefferson Davis*, vol. 7, 420.

25. Freeman, *Lee's Lieutenants*, vol. 1, 19. *New York Times*, 12 June 1861. *Baltimore Republican*, 11 June 1861.

26. Carr, "Operations about Fort Monroe," 148. Magruder's Special Order 732, 14 April 1862, J. B. Magruder Papers, Brockenbrough Library, Museum of the Confederacy, Richmond. Wise, *Military History of VMI*, 121–122. Baker P. Lee, "Magruder's Peninsula Campaign," 62: Magruder's order of 14 April says, "Rifled guns and Parrot [*sic*] Guns will only be fired at long range, smooth fire guns are more effective at short distances."

27. *O.R.*, series 1, vol. 2, 682–686. Two undated newspaper clippings, M. J. Solomons Papers, Duke University.

28. Wright, *General Officers of the Confederate Army*, 23, 53. Gary W. Gallagher, "The Fall of 'Prince John' Magruder," *The Civil War* 19 (August 1989), 10. Ebbitt, "John Magruder," *Army and Navy Journal*, 25 September 1880, 149. *O.R.*, series 1, vol. 2, 930. Jed Hotchkiss, *Virginia*, in *Confederate Military History*, vol. 3 (Atlanta: Confederate Publishing Company, 1899), 3, 145.

29. Davis, *Rise and Fall of the Confederate Government*, vol. 2, 94. Magruder's Special Order 30, 9 September 1861, William T. Dean Papers, Howard-Tilton Library, Tulane University, New Orleans. *O.R.*, series 1. vol. 4, 648–650. Clifford Dowdey, *The Seven Days: The Emergence of Lee* (Boston: Little, Brown, 1964), 48.

30. McMurry, *Hood and the War for Southern Independence*, 26. Hood, *Advance and Retreat*, 18. *O.R.*, series 1, vol. 2, 297.

31. Hotchkiss, *Virginia*, 148–150. *O.R.*, series 1, vol. 4, 568–570. *New York Times*, 10 August 1861.

32. *O.R.*, series 1, vol. 2, 938, 951; vol. 4, 598. Magruder's Order 105, 10 November 1861, J. B. Magruder's Order Book, Army of the Peninsula, War Department Collection of Confederate Records (Record Group 109), National Archives, Washington, D.C. J. B. Magruder to Lafayette McLaws, 23 December 1861, Lafayette McLaws Papers, Southern Historical Collection, University of North Carolina Library

at Chapel Hill. Hugh Thomas Douglas, "A Famous Army and Its Commander: Sketch of the Army of the Peninsula and General Magruder . . . ,"*Southern Historical Society Papers* 42 (1917), 189–191.

33. J. B. Magruder to John Letcher, 26 October 1861, Magruder Papers, Museum of the Confederacy. J. B. Magruder to C. St. John Nolan, 17 November 1861, Nolan Family Papers, Alderman Library, University of Virginia, Charlottesville. J. B. Magruder to John Letcher, undated, Cabell Family Papers, Virginia Historical Society Library, Richmond. R. G. Lowe, "Magruder's Defense of the Peninsula," *Confederate Veteran* 8 (1900), 105.

___ 6. Up the Peninsula ___

1. Secretary of War, *The War of the Rebellion: A Compilation of the Offical Records of the Union and Confederate Armies* (Washington, D.C.: Government Printing Office, 1880 ff), series 1, vol. 9, 32–33, 34, 36, 38–43 (hereafter cited as *O.R.*). Forrest Conner, ed., "Letters of Lieutenant Robert H. Miller to His Family, 1861–1862," *Virginia Magazine of History and Biography* 70 (January 1962), 64. Joseph E. Johnston, *Narrative of Military Operations* (reprint, Bloomington: Indiana University Press, 1959), 111. Emory M. Thomas, *The Confederate Nation, 1861–1865* (New York: Harper & Row, 1979), 120–123.

2. *O.R.*, series 1, vol. 9, 53, 69. Charles F. Bryan, Jr., "The Siege of Yorktown: Part I," *Civil War Times Illustrated* 21 (1982), 11. Charles W. Trueheart to Dear Mother (Ann Thompkins Minor Trueheart), 21 February 1862, Charles W. Trueheart Papers, Alderman Library, University of Virginia, Charlottesville. (This letter is plainly misdated; references to subsequent events in Texas and Virginia would suggest February 21, 1863, as the proper date.)

3. J. Thomas Scharf, *History of the Confederate Navy: From Its Organization to the Surrender of Its Last Vessel* (New York: Rogers and Sherwood, 1887), 221ff. Mark M. Boatner, *The Civil War Dictionary* (New York: David M. McKay Co., 1959), 560. Joseph P. Cullen, *The Peninsula Campaign, 1862: McClellan and Lee Struggle for Richmond* (Harrisburg, Pa.: The Stackpole Co., 1973), 30.

4. *O.R.*, series 1, vol. 9, 44. A. A. Hoehling, *Thunder at Hampton Roads* (Englewood Cliffs, N.J.: Prentice-Hall, 1976), 179. Boatner, *Civil War Dictionary*, 560.

5. William C. Davis, *Duel Between the First Ironclads* (New York: Doubleday, 1975), 17–20. Boatner, *Civil War Dictionary*, 561. William Champan White and Ruth White, *Tin Can on a Shingle* (New York: E. P. Dutton, 1957), 48–51.

6. Boatner, *Civil War Dictionary*, 651. *O.R.*, series 1, vol. 9, 14. Emory M. Thomas, *Richmond: The Peninsula Campaign* (Harrisburg, Pa.: Eastern Alcorn Press, 1985), 13.

7. Stephen W. Sears, *George B. McClellan: The Young Napoleon* (New York: Ticknor and Fields, 1988), 125–167. Alexander S. Webb, *The Peninsula: McClellan's Campaign of 1862* (reprint, New York: Jack Brussell, Publisher, 1959), 10 ff. George B. McClellan, *Report on the Organization and Campaigns of the Army of the Potomac* (reprint, Freeport, N.Y.: Books for Libraries Press, 1970), 155–158.

8. George B. McClellan, "The Peninsula Campaign," in *Battles and Leaders of the Civil War,* vol. 2 (New York: The Century Co., 1888), vol. 2, 168–169. Stephen W.

Sears, *To the Gates of Richmond: The Peninsula Campaign* (New York: Ticknor and Fields, 1992), 34–36. A. L. Long, "Memoir of General John Bankhead Magruder," *Southern Historical Society Papers* 12 (1884): 108–109.

9. Roy P. Basler, ed., *The Collected Works of Abraham Lincoln*, vol. 5 (New Brunswick, N.J.: Rutgers University Press, 1953), 123. *O.R.*, series 1, vol. 11, 264. Mark Grimsley, "Inside a Beleaguered City: A Commander and Actor, Prince John Magruder," *Civil War Times Illustrated* 21 (September 1982), 16. Edward P. Alexander, *Military Memoirs of a Confederate* (New York: Charles Scribner's Sons, 1908), 63.

10. *O.R.*, series 1, vol. 9, 66–68.

11. Magruder's Special Order 198, 25 March 1862, Magruder's Special Order 704, 30 March 1862, J. B. Magruder Papers, Brockenbrough Library, Museum of the Confederacy, Richmond. Hal Bridges, *Lee's Maverick General: Daniel Harvey Hill* (reprint, Lincoln: University of Nebraska Press, 1991), 35. William Garrett Piston, *Lee's Tarnished Lieutenant: James Longstreet and His Place in Southern History* (Athens: University of Georgia Press, 1987), 18.

12. J. B. Magruder to A. Cumming, 13 March 1862, J. B. Magruder Papers, Museum of the Confederacy, Richmond. J. B. Magruder to A. Cumming, 14 March 1862, A. Cumming to Lafayette McLaws, 14 March 1862; Lafayette McLaws Papers, Southern Historical Collection, University of North Carolina, Chapel Hill. Thomas, *Richmond: The Peninsula Campaign*, 5.

13. McClellan, "The Peninsula Campaign," 171. Boatner, *Civil War Dictionary*, 952–953. Sears, *McClellan: The Young Napoleon*, 174–177. Robert S. Henry, *The Story of the Confederacy* (New York: Bobbs-Merrill, 1936), 138–139.

14. Boatner, *Civil War Dictionary*, 736. Charles F. Bryan, "The Siege of Yorktown: Part 2," *Civil War Times Illustrated* (1982), 19. *O.R.*, series 1, vol. 11, 302.

15. Bryan, "Siege of Yorktown: Part 2," 19. Joseph E. Johnston, "Manassas to Seven Pines," in *Battles and Leaders of the Civil War*, vol. 2, 202. *O.R.*, series 1, vol. 11, 406.

16. Paul D. Casdorph, *Lee and Jackson: Confederate Chieftains* (New York: Paragon House, 1992), 143–145. Thomas, *Richmond: The Peninsula Campaign*, 8. T. Harry Williams, *P. G. T. Beauregard: Napoleon in Grey* (Baton Rouge: Louisiana State University Press, 1954), 66–80. Robert M. Hughes, *General Johnston* (New York: D. Appleton and Company, 1893), 116–118.

17. Gilbert E. Govan and James W. Lovingood, *A Different Valor: The Story of General Joseph E. Johnston, C.S.A.* (Indianapolis: Bobbs-Merrill, 1956), 110–113. R. E. Lee to Joseph E. Johnston, 3 April 1867, Lee Family Papers, Virginia Historical Society Library, Richmond. Hughes, *General Johnston*, 118–119.

18. James Longstreet, *From Manassas to Appomattox: Memoirs of the Civil War in America* (Philadelphia: J. B. Lippincott, 1903), 66. Craig L. Symonds, *Joseph E. Johnston: A Civil War Biography* (New York: W. W. Norton, 1992), 148–150. William C. Davis, *Jefferson Davis: The Man and His Hour* (reprint, New York: HarperCollins, 1992), 415. Johnston, *Narrative of Military Operations*, 114–116.

19. Magruder's Special Order 733, 15 April 1862, Magruder to S. D. Ramseur, 16 April 1862, J. B. Magruder Papers, Museum of the Confederacy, Richmond. Gary W. Gallagher, *Stephen Dodson Ramseur: Lee's Gallant General* (Chapel Hill: University of North Carolina Press, 1985), 36–37. Sears, *To the Gates of Richmond*, 55–56. *O.R.*, series 1, vol. 11, 406–408.

20. Hughes, *General Johnston*, 119–121. J. E. Johnston to J. B. Magruder, 18 April 1862, J. B. Magruder Papers, Museum of the Confederacy, Richmond. Bryan, "Siege of Yorktown: Part 2," 21. Gary W. Gallagher, ed., *Fighting for the Confederacy: The Personal Recollections of General Edward Porter Alexander* (Chapel Hill: University of North Carolina Press, 1989), 77.

21. Clifford Dowdey, *The Seven Days: The Emergence of Lee* (Boston: Little, Brown, 1964), 57. Hughes, *General Johnston*, 120. *O.R.*, series 1, vol. 11, 275.

22. Grimsley, "Inside a Beleagured City," 17. H. T. Douglas to S. T. C. Bryan, 29 February 1909, St. George T. C. Bryan Papers, Brockenbrough Library, Museum of the Confederacy, Richmond. *O.R.*, series 1, vol. 11, 275. James I. Robertson, *General A. P. Hill: The Story of a Confederate Warrior* (New York: Random House, 1987), 50–51.

23. Bryan, "Siege of Yorktown: Part 2," 25. Sears, *To the Gates of Richmond*, 66. Clement Eaton, *Jefferson Davis* (New York: Free Press, 1977), 157–158.

24. Longstreet, *From Manassas to Appomattox*, 72. H. T. Douglas to S. T. C. Bryan, 29 February 1909, Bryan Papers. *O.R.*, series 1, vol. 11, 403–406. See also John Bankhead Magruder, *Major General Magruder's Report of His Operations on the Peninsula, and of the Battles of Savage Station and Malvern Hill* (Richmond: C. H. Wynne, Printer, 1862).

25. *O.R.*, series 1, vol. 11, 275. John Bratton, "The Battle of Williamsburg," *Southern Historical Society Papers* 7 (1879), 301–302. Richard L. Maury, "The Battle of Williamsburg and the Charge of the Twenty-fourth Virginia of Early's Brigade," *Southern Historical Society Papers* 8 (1880), 285–287.

26. *O.R.*, series 1, vol. 11, 275. Johnston, *Narrative of Military Operations*, 119. Marcus J. Wright, *General Officers of the Confederate Army* (New York: Neale Publishing Co., 1911), 30. John Bankhead Magruder, "Official Report of Gen. J. B. Magruder" (handwritten manuscript, bound by Charles C. Jones Jr., 1941), passim, copy in Perkins Library, Duke University.

27. Longstreet, *From Manassas to Appomattox*, 81. *O.R.*, series 1, vol. 11, 697. Dowdey, *The Seven Days*, 66. John F. Lee to Unknown, 1871?, Lee Family Papers, Virginia Historical Society Library, Richmond. Grimsley, "Inside a Beleaguered City," 33.

28. Longstreet, *From Manassas to Appomattox*, 78–79 (D. H. Hill quote). Warren Lee Goss, "Yorktown and Williamsburg: Reflections of a Private," in *Battles and Leaders of the Civil War*, vol. 2, 179. William Swinton, *Campaigns of the Army of the Potomac* (New York: Charles Scribner's Sons, 1882), 116–117. Kenneth P. Williams, *Lincoln Finds a General: A Military Study of the Civil War*, vol. 1 (New York: Macmillan, 1964), 156–168.

29. Scharf, *History of the Confederate Navy*, 223. Cullen, *The Peninsula Campaign*, 48. R. W. Daly, *How the Merrimac Won: The Strategic Story of the C.S.S. Virginia* (New York: Thomas Y. Crowell, 1957), 183–186.

30. J. B. Magruder to G. W. Randolph, 18 May 1862, Rebel Archives, War Department, National Archives (M-474), Washington, D.C. J. B. Magruder to W. N. Pendleton, 21, 29 May 1862, William Nelson Pendleton Papers, Southern Historical Collection, University of North Carolina, Chapel Hill.

31. J. B. Magruder to G. W. Smith, May 22, 1862, Maury J. Smith Papers, U.S. Army Military History Institute, Carlisle Barracks, Pennsylvania. Davis, *Jefferson*

Davis, 461. Gary W. Gallagher, "The Fall of 'Prince John Magruder.' " *Civil War* 19 (August 1989), 10. Walter P. Webb, ed., *The Handbook of Texas,* vol. 1 (Austin: Texas State Historical Association, 1952), 792.

32. *O.R.,* series 1, vol. 11, part 3, 551.

33. Ibid., 557. Vincent J. Esposito, *West Point Atlas of American Wars,* vol. 2 (New York: Frederick A. Praeger, 1960), 43. Robertson, *General A. P. Hill,* 63. Gustavus W. Smith, *The Battle of Seven Pines* (New York: C. G. Crawford, Printer and Stationer, 1891), 95.

34. Jefferson Davis, *The Rise and Fall of the Confederate Government,* vol. 2 (New York: D. Appleton and Co., 1881), 123. Symonds, *Joseph E. Johnston,* 172. Casdorph, *Lee and Jackson,* 253–255.

35. Davis, *Rise and Fall of the Confederate Government,* vol. 2, 123. Smith, *Seven Pines,* 101.

36. G. J. Fiebeger, *Campaigns of the American Civil War* (West Point: USMA Printing Office, 1914), 39. Thomas L. Livermore, *Numbers and Losses in the American Civil War, 1861–1865* (Boston: Houghton Mifflin, 1900), 81. John Coxe, "In the Battle of Seven Pines," *Confederate Veteran* 30 (1922), 25. Longstreet, *From Manassas to Appomattox,* 86.

— 7. The Seven Days —

1. Joseph P. Cullen, *The Peninsula Campaign of 1862: McClellan and Lee Struggle for Richmond* (Harrisburg, Pa.: Stackpole Books, 1973), 52. Clifford Dowdey, *Lee* (Boston: Little, Brown, 1965), 214–220. Margaret Sanborn, *Robert E. Lee: The Complete Man* (Philadelphia: J. P. Lippincott, 1967), 57. Secretary of War, *The War of the Rebellion: A Compilation of the Official Records of the Union and Confederate Armies,* series 1, vol. 11, part 3 (Washington, D.C.: Government Printing Office, 1880), 569–612 (cited hereafter as *O.R.*).

2. Paul D. Casdorph, *Lee and Jackson: Confederate Chieftains* (New York: Paragon House, 1992), 253. Vincent J. Esposito, *The West Point Atlas of American Wars,* vol. 2 (New York: Praeger and Co., 1960), 43. John Bankhead Magruder, "Offical Report of Gen. J. B. Magruder" (handwritten manuscript, bound by Charles C. Jones, Jr., 1941, copy in Perkins Library, Duke University), passim.

3. James Longstreet, *From Manassas to Appomattox: Memoirs of the Civil War in America* (Philadelphia: J. P. Lippincott, 1903), 112–113. *O.R.,* series 1, vol. 11, part 3, 569. Clifford Dowdey, *The Seven Days: The Emergence of Lee* (Boston: Little, Brown, 1960), 130–131. Jefferson Davis, *The Rise and Fall of the Confederate Government,* vol. 2 (New York: D. Appleton and Co., 1881), 130–131.

4. Edward Porter Alexander, *Military Memoirs of a Confederate* (New York: Charles Scribner's Sons, 1908), 112. *O.R.,* series 1, vol. 11, part 3, 569–578. Dowdey, *The Seven Days,* 140. Joseph L. Brent, *Memoirs of the War Between the States* (New Orleans: Fontana Printing Co., 1940), 169.

5. A. L. Long, *The Memoirs of Robert E. Lee: His Military and Personal History* (reprint, Secaucus, N.J.: Blue and Grey Press, 1983), 164. George Cary Eggleston, *The History of the Confederate War: Its Causes and Conduct,* vol. 1 (New York: Sturgis and Walton, 1910), 397. Robert Lewis Dabney, *Life and Campaigns of Lieut.-Gen. Thomas*

Jonathan Jackson (New York: Blelock and Co., 1866), 431. *O.R.*, series 1, vol. 11, part 3, 586–589.

6. *O.R.*, series 1, vol. 11, part 3, 590. William P. Snow, *Lee and His Generals* (reprint, New York: Fairfax Press, 1982), 380–382. John W. Thomason, *JEB Stuart* (reprint, New York: Charles Scribner's Sons, 1959), 144 ff. Emory M. Thomas, *Richmond: The Peninsula Campaign* (reprint, Harrisburg, Pa.: Eastern Alcorn Press, 1985), 28.

7. Thomas, *Richmond: The Peninsula Campaign*, 28. Thomason, *Stuart*, 151. Stephen W. Sears, *George B. McClellan: The Young Napoleon* (New York: Ticknor and Fields, 1988), 202.

8. Longstreet, *Manassas to Appomattox*, 120. Esposito, *West Point Atlas of American Wars*, vol. 2, 44. *O.R.*, series 1, vol. 11, part 3, 612.

9. Robert E. Lee's General Order No. 75, 14 June 1862, J. B. Magruder Papers, Brockenbrough Library, Museum of the Confederacy, Richmond. *O.R.*, series 1, vol. 11, part 2, 499. Charles Royster, *The Destructive War: William Tecumseh Sherman, Stonewall Jackson and the American Civil War* (New York: Alfred A. Knopf, 1991), 42–43.

10. Percy Gatling Hamlin, *"Old Bald Head": General R. S. Ewell* (Richmond: Whittet and Shepperson, 1955), 108. Alexander S. Webb, *The Peninsula: McClellan's Campaign of 1862* (reprint, New York: Jack Brussell, Publisher, 1959), 114–116. *O.R.*, series 1, vol. 11, part 2, 19–20. Stephen W. Sears, *To the Gates of Richmond: The Peninsula Campaign* (New York: Ticknor and Fields, 1992), 189.

11. James I. Robertson, *General A. P. Hill: The Story of a Confederate Warrior* (New York: Random House, 1987), 74–75. William Swinton, *Campaigns of the Army of the Potomac* (New York: Charles Scribner's Sons, 1882), 151. Webb, *The Peninsula*, 126–127.

12. R. E. Lee to J. B. Magruder, 26 June 1862, William Norris Papers, Alderman Library, University of Virginia, Charlottesville. *O.R.*, series 1, vol. 11, 746. Dowdey, *The Seven Days*, 173–174. Sears, *To the Gates of Richmond*, 200; see also Herman Hattaway, *General Stephen D. Lee* (Oxford: University Press of Mississippi, 1976), passim.

13. *O.R.*, series 1, vol. 11, part 2, 20–21, 715. Esposito, *West Point Atlas of American Wars*, vol. 1, 45. Sears, *George B. McClellan*, 209–210.

14. Magruder, "Official Report of Gen. J. B. Magruder," 2. Jed Hotchkiss, *Virginia*, in *Confederate Military History*, vol. 3 (Atlanta: Confederate Publishing Company, 1899), 290. Hal Bridges, *Lee's Maverick General: Daniel Harvey Hill* (reprint, Lincoln: University of Nebraska Press, 1985), 69–70. *O.R.*, series 1, vol. 11, part 2, 491–492.

15. Hotchkiss, *Virginia*, 286–287. Henry Kyd Douglas, *I Rode With Stonewall* (Chapel Hill: University of North Carolina Press, reprint, 1984), 103. John Esten Cooke, *A Life of General Robert E. Lee* (New York: D. Appleton and Co., 1871), 84.

16. Richard M. McMurry, *John Bell Hood and the War for Southern Independence* (Lexington: University Press of Kentucky, 1982), 49–50. Hotchkiss, *Virginia*, 287. Thomas, *Richmond: The Peninsula Campaign*, 36–37. Casdorph, *Lee and Jackson*, 270. John Selby, *Stonewall Jackson as Military Commander* (London: B. T. Batsford, 1968), 111–113.

17. An English Combatant, *Battle-Fields of the South: From Bull Run to Fredericksburg* (New York: John Bradburn, 1864), 333–341. Magruder, "Report of Gen. J. B. Magruder," 2. *O.R.*, series 1, vol. 11, part 2, 579.

18. Magruder, "Official Report of Gen. J. B. Magruder," 5. Gary W. Gallagher, *Stephen Dodson Ramseur: Lee's Gallant General* (Chapel Hill: University of North Carolina Press, 1988), 41. Brent, *Memoirs of the War Between the States*, 175–176.

19. Brent, *Memoirs of the War Between the States*, 176–177. Sears, *To the Gates of Richmond*, 217. Webb, *The Peninsula*, 122–124.

20. Magruder, "Official Report of Gen. J. B. Magruder," 5–6. Hamlin, *"Old Bald Head,"* 113–115; Long, *Memoirs of Lee*, 175.

21. Douglas Southall Freeman and Grady McWhiney, eds., *Lee's Dispatches: Letters of Robert E. Lee, C.S.A., to Jefferson Davis and the War Department of the Confederate States of America, 1861–1862* (New York: G. P. Putnam's Sons, 1957); 21. Brent, *Memoirs of the War Between the States*, 182.

22. Magruder, "Official Report of Gen. J. B. Magruder," 11–12. Long, *Memoirs of Lee*, 175. Walter H. Taylor, *Four Years with General Lee* (New York: D. Appleton and Co., 1877), 49. Brent, *Memoirs of the War Between the States*, 182.

23. Magruder, "Official Report of Gen. J. B. Magruder," 12–15. Mark M. Boatner, *The Civil War Dictionary* (New York: David M. McKay, 1959), 721–722. D. Augustus Dickert, *History of Kershaw's Brigade* (reprint, Dayton, Ohio: Morningside Book Shop, 1973), 129. Longstreet, *Manassas to Appomattox*, 134–136. Kenneth P. Williams, *Lincoln Finds a General: A Military Study of the Civil War*, vol. 1 (New York: Macmillan, 1964), 235–236.

24. *O.R.*, series 1, vol. 11, part 2, 543, 551. Burke Davis, *They Called Him Stonewall: The Life of Lt. General T. J. Jackson, C.S.A.* (reprint, New York: Fairfax Press, 1988), 231–233. William Fox, *Regimental Losses in the American Civil War* (Albany, N.Y.: Albany Publishing Company, 1893), 543, 541.

25. Orlando T. Hanks, "History of Captain B. F. Benton's Company, 1861–1865," typescript, Stephen F. Austin State University Archives, Nacogdoches, Texas, 14. Madeline Martin, *More Early Southeast Texas Families* (Quanah, Texas: Nortex Press, 1978), 59. Robertson, *General A. P. Hill*, 87–89. Esposito, *West Point Atlas of American Wars*, vol. 2, 47. Magruder, "Official Report of Gen. J. B. Magruder," 15.

26. Mark Grimsley, "Inside a Beleaguered City: A Commander and Actor, Prince John Magruder," *Civil War Times Illustrated* 21 (September 1982), 33. Brent, *Memoirs of the War Between the States*, 191–192. Snow, *Lee and His Generals*, 64–65.

27. Magruder, "Official Report of Gen. J. B. Magruder," 20–22. Longstreet, *Manassas to Appomattox*, 139–141.

28. *O.R.*, series 1, vol. 11, part 2, 495, 665, 680. Webb, *The Peninsula*, 148–151. John Bell Hood, *Advance and Retreat: Personal Experiences in the United States and Confederate Armies* (New Orleans, G. T. Beauregard, 1880), 29–30.

29. Jennings C. Wise, *The Long Arm of Lee: The History of the Artillery in the Army of Northern Virginia* (reprint, New York: Oxford University Press, 1959), 56. Eggleston, *The Confederate War*, 412. James M. McPherson, *Battle Cry of Freedom: The Civil War Era* (New York: Ballantine Books, 1988), 470.

30. Magruder, "Official Report of Gen. J. B. Magruder," 22–23. Brent, *Memoirs of the War Between the States*, 203–204.

31. Jed Hotchkiss, *Virginia*, 297–300. *O.R.*, series 1, vol. 11, part 2, 676. Brent, *Memoirs of the War Between the States*, 205–207. Esposito, *West Point Atlas of American Wars*, vol. 2, 47. J. L. Brent to Mrs. Leeds, 17 June 1902, Rosella Kenner Brent Pa-

pers, Louisiana and Lower Mississippi Valley Collections, Louisiana State University Libraries, Baton Rouge.

32. Brent, *Memoirs of the War Between the States*, 231. *O.R.*, series 1, vol. 11, part 2, 670, 801.

33. Boatner, *Civil War Dictionary*, 507. Emory M. Thomas, *The Confederate Nation, 1861–1865* (New York: Harper & Row, 1979), 162. Long, *Memoirs of Lee*, 183. Fitzhugh Lee, *General Lee* (New York: D. Appleton and Co., 1894), 164–166. Freeman and McWhiney, eds., *Lee's Dispatches*, 25.

34. *O.R.*, series 1, vol. 11, part 3, 630. Albert Castel, *General Sterling Price and the Civil War in the West* (Baton Rouge: Louisiana State University Press, 1993), 87–89. William C. Davis, *Jefferson Davis: The Man and His Hour* (reprint, New York: Harper-Collins, 1992), 461–462.

35. *O.R.*, series 1, vol. 11, part 2, 683; part 3, 641. Letter fragment, 17 July 1862, Hinsdale Family Papers, Perkins Library, Duke University. Charlotte Wickham Lee to "Dear Girls," Lee Family Papers, Virginia Historical Society Library, Richmond.

⸺ 8. Galveston ⸺

1. J. B. Magruder to Jefferson Davis, 13 August 1862, J. B. Magruder Papers, Chicago Historical Society Library, Chicago. Secretary of War, *The War of the Rebellion: A Compilation of the Official Records of the Union and Confederate Armies* (Washington, D.C.: Government Printing Office, 1880), series 1, vol. 11, part 2, 660–683 (cited hereafter as *O.R.*). John Bankhead Magruder, *Major General Magruder's Report of His Operations on the Peninsula, and of the Battles of Savage Station and Malvern Hill* (Richmond: C. H. Wynne, Printer, 1862), passim. J. B. Magruder, "Official Report of Gen. J. B. Magruder" (handwritten manuscript, bound by Charles C. Jones, 1941), 1–40, copy in Perkins Library, Duke University, Durham, North Carolina. Gary W. Gallagher, "The Fall of 'Prince John' Magruder," *Civil War 19* (August 1989), 12–15. Stephen B. Oates, "Texas Under the Secessionists," *Southwestern Historical Quarterly* 47 (October 1963), 200–202.

2. *O.R.*, series 1, vol. 14, 560–570. Mark M. Boatner, *The Civil War Dictionary* (New York: David M. McKay, 1959), 631.

3. *O.R.*, series 1, vol. 13, 832, 855. Oates, "Texas Under the Secessionists," 184. William C. Davis, *Jefferson Davis: The Man and His Hour, A Biography* (reprint, New York: HarperCollins, 1991), 461. Harry N. Scheiber, "The Pay of Troops and Confederate Morale in the Trans-Mississippi," *Arkansas Historical Quarterly* 18 (1959), 351–352.

4. *O.R.*, series 1, vol. 15, 826. Oates, "Texas under the Secessionists," 195. Francis R. Lubbock, *Six Decades in Texas: Or Personal Memoirs of Francis Richard Lubbock* (Austin: Ben C. Jones and Company, Printers, 1900), 424.

5. *Dallas Herald*, 15 July 1862. Claude Elliot, "Union Sentiment in Texas, 1861–1865," *Southwestern Historical Quarterly* 50 (April 1947), 456, *passim*. Harold B. Simpson, *Hood's Texas Brigade: Lee's Grenadier Guard* (Waco: Texian Press, 1970). *O.R.*, series 1, vol. 14, 921.

6. Frank H. Smyrl, "Unionism in Texas," *Southwestern Historical Quarterly* 68 (October 1964), 185. Llerena Friend, *Sam Houston: The Great Designer* (Austin: Uni-

versity of Texas Press, 1954), 336–339; see also Ralph A. Wooster, *The Secession Conventions of the South* (Princeton: Princeton University Press, 1962).

7. Friend, *Sam Houston,* 388. Floyd E. Ewing, "Unionist Sentiment on the Northwest Texas Frontier," *West Texas Historical Association Yearbook* 33 (1957), 63–69.

8. Frank H. Smyrl, "Texans in the Union Army, 1861–1865," *Southwestern Historical Quarterly* 65 (October 1861), 233–236. O. M. Roberts, *Texas in Confederate Military History,* vol. 11 (Atlanta: Confederate Publishing Company, 1899), 92. Paul D. Casdorph, *A History of the Republican Party in Texas, 1865–1965* (Austin: Pemberton Press, 1965), 17–33.

9. Robert W. Shook, "The Battle of the Nueces, August 10, 1862," *Southwestern Historical Quarterly* 66 (July 1962), 32–34, *passim.* Walter P. Webb, ed., *The Handbook of Texas,* vol. 1 (Austin: Texas State Historical Association, 1952), 683, vol. 2, 291. Elliott, "Union Sentiment in Texas," 472–473; see also Rudolph L. Biesele, *The History of the German Settlements in Texas* (Austin: Texas, Von Boeckmann-Jones Co., 1930), and Terry L. Jordan, *German Seed in Texas Soil* (Austin: University of Texas Press, 1966).

10. Eldon S. Branda, ed., *The Handbook of Texas: A Supplement* (Austin: Texas State Historical Association, 1976), 321. Thomas Barrett, *The Great Hanging at Gainesville, Cooke County, Texas, October, A.D. 1862* (reprint, Austin: Texas State Historical Association, 1961), 21. Ewing, "Unionist Sentiment on the Northwest Texas Frontier," 64–65; see also Richard B. McCaslin, *Tainted Breeze: The Great Hanging at Gainesville, Texas, 1862* (Baton Rouge: Louisiana State University Press, 1994).

11. William Norris to J. B. Magruder, 17 October 1862, William Norris Papers, Alderman Library, University of Virginia, Charlottesville. Joseph L. Brent, *Memoirs of the War Between the States* (New Orleans: Fontana Printing Company, 1940), 238.

12. J. B. Magruder to Smith P. Bankhead, 30 October 1862, Ada Bankhead Collection, Alderman Library, University of Virginia, Charlottesville. *Dallas Herald,* 15 November 1862. *O.R.,* series 1, vol. 15, 1066, vol. 26, part 2, 25.

13. *Dallas Herald,* 29 November 1862.

14. Thomas North, *Five Years in Texas; Or, What You Did Not Hear During the War, January 1861 to January 1865* (Cincinnati: Elm Street Printing Company, 1871), 107. Lota M. Spell, "Music in Texas," *Civil War History* 4 (September 1958), 304. Stephen B. Oates, ed., *Rip Ford's Texas* (Austin: University of Texas Press, 1963), 343. Unidentified newspaper clipping, 7 December 1862, M. J. Solomons Papers, Perkins Library, Duke University, Durham, North Carolina.

15. A. L. Long, "Memoir of General John Bankhead Magruder," *Southern Historical Society Papers* 12 (1884), 110. *O.R.,* series 1, vol. 15, 932. *Dallas Herald,* 7 January 1863. "Mother" to John A. Wharton, 18 November 1862, Edward C. Wharton and Family Papers, Louisiana and Lower Mississippi Valley Collections, Louisiana State University Libraries, Baton Rouge.

16. *O.R.,* series 1, vol. 14, 880–881. Frank H. Smyrl, *Texas in Gray: The Civil War Years, 1861–1865* (Boston: American Press, 1983), 12–15. Oates, "Texas Under the Secessionists," 178–181. Lubbock, *Six Decades in Texas,* 428; see also J. B. Magruder, Printed Broadside, Rosenberg Library, Galveston, Texas.

17. *O.R.,* series 1, vol. 14, 882. Fred Harvey Harrington, *Fighting Politician: Major General N. P. Banks* (Philadelphia: University of Pennsylvania Press, 1948),

128–130. Roy P. Basler, ed., *The Collected Works of Abraham Lincoln*, vol. 4 (New Brunswick: Rutgers University Press, 1953), 286, vol. 6, 39–43. John L. Waller, *Colossal Hamilton of Texas: A Biography of Andrew Jackson Hamilton* (El Paso: University of Texas at El Paso Press, 1968), 39–43.

18. Paeder Joel Hoovestol, "Galveston in the Civil War" (M.A. thesis, University of Houston, 1950), 26–27. North, *Five Years in Texas*, 106–107.

19. Hoovestol, "Galveston in the Civil War," 27–33. Philip C. Tucker, "The United States Gunboat *Harriet Lane*," *Southwestern Historical Quarterly* 21 (April 1918), 361–362. X. B. DeBray, "A Sketch of DeBray's Twenty-Sixth Regiment of Texas Cavalry: Paper No. 1," *Southern Historical Society Papers* 12 (1884), 551. *O.R.*, series 1, vol. 14, 204.

20. *Dallas Herald*, 22 November 1862; Lubbock, *Six Decades in Texas*, 430 ff. *O.R.*, series 1, vol. 15, 900–901, 909.

21. North, *Five Years in Texas*, 108. Lubbock, *Six Decades in Texas*, 428. Alwyn Barr, "Texas Coastal Defense, 1861–1865," *Southwestern Historical Quarterly* 65 (July 1961), 14.

22. Timothy Dale Spell, "John Bankhead Magruder: Defender of the Texas Coast, 1863" (M.A. thesis, Lamar University, 1981), 33 ff. DeBray, "Sketch of DeBray's Regiment," 551. Barr, "Texas Coastal Defense," 15. *O.R.*, series 1, vol. 15, 210–214.

23. *O.R.*, series 1, vol. 15, 221. Barr, "Texas Coastal Defense," 15. Harry M. Henderson, *Texas in the Confederacy* (San Antonio: The Naylor Company, 1955), 84 and passim.

24. L. J. Storey to Augustus M. Hill, 21 February 1908, Augustus M. Hill Papers, Center for the Study of American History, University of Texas, Austin. J. B. Magruder to Isaac S. Burrell, 24 October 1869, Massachusetts MOLLUS Collection, U.S. Army Military History Institute, Carlisle Barracks, Pennsylvania.

25. *O.R.*, series 1, vol. 15, 214–215. Howard C. Westwood, "The Battle of Galveston," *U.S. Naval Institute Proceedings* 109 (1983), 52. Eber Worthington Cave, *Official Report of the Battles of Galveston and Sabine . . . with Sketch of the Life and Public Services of Maj. Gen. J. Bankhead Magruder* (Houston: Texas Printing Co., 1866). *Dallas Herald*, 7 January 1863.

26. J. Thomas Scharf, *History of the Confederate Navy from Its Organization to the Surrender of Its Last Vessel* (New York: Rogers and Sherwood, 1887), 507. Spell, "Magruder: Defender of the Texas Coast," 41–46. Barr, "Texas Coastal Defense," 16–18.

27. Tucker, "U.S. Gunboat *Harriet Lane*," 367–368. Scharf, *History of the Confederate Navy*, 511.

28. Tucker, "U.S. Gunboat *Harriet Lane*," 368–369. Scharf, *History of the Confederate Navy*, 508. *O.R.*, series 1, vol. 15, 216.

29. *O.R.*, series 1, vol. 15, 226. J. B. Magruder to Isaac S. Burrell, 24 October 1869, MOLLUS Collection. *Dallas Herald*, 3 January 1874. Alvin M. Josephy, *The Civil War in the American West* (New York: Alfred A. Knopf, 1991), 167.

30. *O.R.*, series 1, vol. 15, 219. North, *Five Years in Texas*, 116–117. Lubbock, *Six Decades in Texas*, 446–449.

31. *O.R.*, series 1, vol. 15, 931, 659. Stephen R. Wise, *Lifeline of the Confederacy: Blockade Running During the Civil War* (Columbia: University of South Carolina Press, 1988), 168 ff.

32. Spell, "Magruder: Defender of the Texas Coast," 56. Barr, "Texas Coastal Defense," 19–21. Arthur F. L. Fremantle, *Three Months in the Southern States, April–June 1863* (New York: John Bradburn, 1864), 72–73. Lubbock, *Six Decades in Texas*, 456–458; see also William Armstrong to Thaddeus Armstrong, 12 January 1863, Thaddeus Armstrong Papers, Rosenberg Library, Galveston, for a description of the random shelling after the battle.

33. *Galveston News*, 3 January 1863. Hoovestol, "Galveston in the Civil War," 43. Mark Grimsley, "Inside a Beleaguered City: A Commander and Actor, Prince John Magruder," *Civil War Times Illustrated* 21 (September 1982), 35. Roberts, *Texas*, in *Confederate Military History*, 78. DeBray, "Sketch of DeBray's Regiment," 553.

34. Spell, "Magruder: Defender of the Texas Coast," 49. Fremantle, *Three Months in the Southern States*, 35. *O.R.*, series 1, vol. 15, 211. Jefferson Davis, *The Rise and Fall of the Confederate Government*, vol. 2 (New York: D. Appleton and Co., 1881), 235. Emory Thomas, *The Confederate Nation, 1861–1865* (New York: Harper & Row, 1979). 128–130.

35. Amelia W. Williams and Eugene C. Barker, eds., *The Writings of Sam Houston, 1823–1863*, vol. 8 (Austin: University of Texas Press, 1945), 324. Randolph B. Campbell, *Sam Houston and the Southwest* (New York: HarperCollins, 1993), 159. *O.R.*, series 1, vol. 15, 221. S. G. S. Lee to J. B. Magruder, January 1863, S. G. S. Lee Papers, Rosenberg Library, Galveston, Texas.

9. "The People of Texas
— Have Made a Demi-god of Him" —

1. O. M. Roberts, *Texas*, in *Confederate Military History*, vol. 9 (Atlanta: Confederate Publishing Company, 1899), 9, 97–101. Alwyn Barr, "Texas Coastal Defense, 1861–1865," *Southwestern Historical Quarterly* 65 (July 1861), 18–19. Secretary of War, *The War of the Rebellion: A Compilation of the Official Records of the Union and Confederate Armies* (Washington, D.C.: Government Printing Office, 1880), series 1, vol. 15, 237–238 (cited hereafter as *O.R.*).

2. O. M. Roberts, *Texas*, 95–96. Paeder Joel Hoovestol, "Galveston in the Civil War" (M.A. thesis, University of Houston, 1950), 47. *O.R.*, series 1, vol. 15, 237, 936.

3. William R. Geise, "General Holmes Fails to Create a Department, August, 1862–February, 1863," *Military History of Texas and the Southwest* 14 (1978), 117.

4. *Houston Tri-Weekly News*, 3 December 1862. Timothy Dale Spell, "John Bankhead Magruder: Defender of the Texas Coast, 1863" (M.A. thesis, Lamar University, 1981), 79. J. S. Richardson to Mrs. E. C. Wharton, 14 April 1863, Edward C. Wharton and Family Papers, Louisiana and Lower Mississippi Valley Collections, Louisiana State University Libraries, Baton Rouge. Francis Richard Lubbock, *Six Decades in Texas: Or Memoirs of Francis Richard Lubbock* (Austin: Ben C. Jones and Co., Printers, 1900), 425.

5. Alexander Watkins Terrell, *From Texas to Mexico and the Court of Maximilian 1865* (reprint, Dallas: Book Club of Texas, 1933), 48–49. Walter P. Webb, ed., *The Handbook of Texas*, vol. 2 (Austin: Texas State Historical Association, 1952), 665–667, 725.

6. Ada Bankhead to Julia Nutt, 5 April 1863, Nutt Family Papers, Huntington Library, San Marino, California. Sarah Elizabeth Walker, "San Antonio During the Civil War" (M.A. thesis, Sam Houston State Teachers College, 1942), 60–62.

7. *O.R.*, series 1, vol. 15, 914–915, 1036.

8. Robert L. Kerby, *Kirby Smith's Confederacy: The Trans-Mississippi South, 1863–1865* (reprint, Tuscaloosa: University of Alabama Press, 1990), 13–14. Thomas W. Cutrer, *Ben McCulloch and the Frontier Military Tradition* (Chapel Hill and London: University of North Carolina Press, 1993), 176 ff. B. P. Gallaway, ed., *Texas: The Dark Corner of the Confederacy* (reprint, Lincoln and London: University of Nebraska, 1994), 55–56.

9. J. B. Magruder to F. R. Lubbock, 7 April 1863, Francis R. Lubbock Records, Record Group 301, Archives Division, Texas State Library, Austin. Katherine Elliott, "The Frontier Regiment," typescript, 39–45, Katherine Elliott Essay, The Center for the Study of American History, University of Texas, Austin. David Paul Smith, *Frontier Defense in the Civil War: Texas' Rangers and Rebels* (College Station: Texas A&M University Press, 1992), 48–55. Webb, ed., *Handbook of Texas*, vol. 1, 651–652.

10. Charles W. Ramsdell, "The Texas State Military Board, 1862–1865," *Southwestern Historical Quarterly* 27 (April 1924), 261–266. Arthur F. L. Fremantle, *Three Months in the Southern States: April–June, 1863* (New York: John Bradburn, 1864), 35–37. Callaway, ed., *Dark Corner of the Confederacy*, 166–169.

11. F. R. Lubbock to J. B. Magruder, 3 January, 7 March 1863, Lubbock Records. Fredericka Meiners, "The Texas Border Cotton Trade, 1862–1863," *Civil War History* 33 (December 1977), 294–298. Althea Wanda Shaver, "The Cotton Bureau in the Trans-Mississippi Department," typescript, 4–7, Althea W. Shaver Narrative, Center for the Study of American History, University of Texas, Austin. *O.R.*, series 1, vol. 15, 1030–1031.

12. E. Merton Coulter, *The Confederate States of America, 1861–1865* (Baton Rouge: Louisiana State University Press, 1950), 251. Frank E. Vandiver, *Their Tattered Flags: The Epic of the Confederacy* (New York: Harper's Magazine Press, 1970), 178. Printed Broadside, General Orders No. 65, John Bankhead Magruder Papers, Rosenberg Library, Galveston, Texas. J. B. Magruder to H. P. Bee, 19 June 1863, James W. Eldridge Papers, Huntington Library, San Marino, California.

13. *O.R.*, series 1, vol. 26, 86, 95, 125–126. Guy M. Bryan to J. B. Magruder, 15 August 1863, Guy Morrison Bryan Papers, Center for the Study of American History, University of Texas, Austin (copy also in F. R. Lubbock Records).

14. *O.R.*, series 1, vol. 26, part 1, 112–113. Meiners, "Texas Border Cotton Trade," 303–304. J. B. Magruder to H. P. Bee, 15 October, 16 November 1863, Eldridge Papers. T. G. Rhett to G. M. Bryan, 20 November 1863, Bryan Papers. Harold B. Simpson and Marcus J. Wright, *Texas in the War, 1861–1865* (Hillsboro: Hill County Junior College Press, 1965), 202–204.

15. Ludwell H. Johnson, *Red River Campaign: Politics and Cotton in the Civil War* (Baltimore: Johns Hopkins University Press, 1958), 28–31. Mark M. Boatner, *The Civil War Dictionary* (New York: David M. McKay, 1958), 426–427. *O.R.*, series 1, vol. 15, 1043.

16. J. B. Magruder to H. P. Bee, 14 May 1863, Eldridge Papers. Elijah S. C. Robertson to J. B. Magruder, 2 August 1863, Sterling Clack Robertson Papers, Center

for the Study of American History, University of Texas, Austin. F. R. Lubbock to J. B. Magruder, 19 June 1863, Lubbock Records. Kerby, *Kirby Smith's Confederacy*, 274. W. Buck Yearns, *The Confederate Governors* (Athens: University of Georgia Press, 1985), 205–206.

17. Roberts, *Texas*, 102. Barr, "Texas Coastal Defense," 21; *O.R.*, series 1, vol. 15, 402–403.

18. *O.R.*, series 1, vol. 15, 404–405. Webb, ed., *Handbook of Texas*, vol. 2, 818–819. Gallaway, ed., *Dark Corner of the Confederacy*, 250.

19. Lubbock, *Six Decades in Texas*, 485–487; J. B. Magruder, printed broadside, 4 June 1863, Lubbock Records.

20. *O.R.*, series 1, vol. 26, part 1, 241–247, part 2, 132, 159, 170. Spell, "Magruder: Defender of the Texas Coast," 62–63. Barr, "Texas Coastal Defense," 23.

21. *O.R.*, series 1, vol. 22, part 2, 982. F. R. Lubbock to J. B. Magruder, 11 July, 29 August 1863, J. B. Magruder to F. R. Lubbock, 20 June 1863, Lubbock Records. Ella Lonn, *Foreigners in the Confederacy* (reprint, Gloucester, Mass.: Peter Smith, 1979), 223–224. Emory M. Thomas, *The Confederate Nation, 1861–1865* (New York: Harper & Row, 1979), 261–264. J. B. Magruder, printed broadside, 15 June 1863, Magruder Papers, Rosenberg Library.

22. Fred Harvey Harrington, *Fighting Politician: Major General N. P. Banks* (Philadelphia: University of Pennsylvania Press, 1948), 128. Roy P. Basler, ed., *The Collected Works of Abraham Lincoln*, vol. 6 (New Brunswick: Rutgers University Press, 1953), 6, 346. *O.R.*, series 1, vol. 26, part 2, 187–189, 196.

23. *O.R.*, series 1, vol. 26, part 2, 203. P. W. Gray to G. M. Bryan, 28 September 1863, Bryan Papers. Webb, ed., *Handbook of Texas*, vol. 1, 723.

24. *O.R.*, series 1, vol. 26, part 2, 196, 204. Lester N. Fitzhugh, "Saluria, Fort Esperanza, and Military Operations on the Texas Coast, 1861–1864," *Southwestern Historical Quarterly* 61 (July 1957): 87–89. Webb, ed., *Handbook of Texas*, vol. 1, 289, 625, vol. 2, 537.

25. Washington J. Smith, "Battle of Sabine Pass," *Confederate Veteran* 27 (1919), 461–462. Jo Young, "The Battle of Sabine Pass," *Southwestern Historical Quarterly* 52 (January 1949), 400–401. Frank X. Tolbert, *Dick Dowling at Sabine Pass* (New York: McGraw-Hill, 1962), 7–10. Webb, ed., *Handbook of Texas*, vol. 1, 517.

26. Young, "Battle of Sabine Pass," 404–406. Tolbert, *Dick Dowling at Sabine Pass,* 110–114. Alvin M. Josephy, *The Civil War in the American West* (New York: Alfred A. Knopf, 1991), 181–185. Sid S. Johnson, *Texans Who Wore the Gray* (Tyler, Texas, n.p.: 1907), 307–309 (this source has a complete listing of all participants in the Battle of Sabine Pass); see also Frances Robertson Sackett, *Dick Dowling* (Houston: Gulf Publishing Co., 1937).

27. *O.R.*, series 1, vol. 26, part 1, 307–312, part 2, 242–244. Tolbert, *Dick Dowling,* 127. J. B. Magruder to H. P. Bee, 16 September 1863, Eldridge Papers.

28. F. R. Lubbock to J. B. Magruder, 2, 8, 14 October 1863, Lubbock Records, Texas State Archives.

29. Kerby, *Kirby Smith's Confederacy*, 292. Robert W. Glover and Linda Brown Cross, *Tyler and Smith County, Texas: A Historical Survey* (Tyler: American Bicentennial Committee, 1976), 46. Webb, ed., *Handbook of Texas*, vol. 1, 281. *O.R.*, series 1, part

1, 850–851; see also F. Lee Lawrence and Robert W. Glover, *Camp Ford, CSA: The Story of Union Prisoners in Texas* (Austin: Texas Civil War Centennial Advisory Committee, 1964).

30. *O.R.*, series 1, vol. 26, part 1, 301. Charles L. Robards and A. M. Jackson, *Reports of Cases Argued and Decided in the Supreme Court of Texas . . . 1863–1865* (St. Louis: Gilbert Book Co., 1903), 564–571. Kerby, *Kirby Smith's Confederacy*, 271–274. Nancy Head Bowen, "A Political Labyrinth: Texas in the Civil War—Questions in Continuity" (Ph.D. diss., Rice University, 1974), 172.

31. Simpson and Wright, *Texas in the War*, 202. Edward Beaumont to A. Aiken, 23 November 1863, J. B. Magruder, Special Order No. 349, 21 December 1863, John Bankhead Magruder Collection, Archives of the Big Bend, Sul Ross State University, Alpine, Texas. *O.R.*, series 1, vol. 26, part 2, 432, part 1, 383–384.

32. *O.R.*, series 1, vol. 26, part 1, 433–437. James A. Irby, *Backdoor at Bagdad: The Civil War on the Rio Grande* (El Paso: Texas Western Press, 1977), 29.

33. Harrington, *Fighting Politician*, 132–133. F. R. Lubbock to J. B. Magruder, 30 March, 22 October 1863, Lubbock Records. John L. Waller, *Colossal Hamilton of Texas* (El Paso: Texas Western Press, 1968), 57.

34. Jerry Don Thompson, *Vaqueros in Blue and Gray* (Austin: Presidial Press, 1976), 97–98. Jerry Don Thompson, Mexican-Texans in the Union Army (El Paso: Texas Western Press, 1986), 15 ff. Daisey B. Tanner, "J. L. Haynes," typescript, John L. Haynes Vertical File, Center for the Study of American History, University of Texas, Austin. *O.R.*, series 1, vol. 26, part 1, 830–831. Spell, "Magruder: Defender of the Coast," 106.

35. Alwyn Barr, "Confederate Artillery in the Trans-Mississippi" (M.A. thesis, University of Texas, Austin, 1961), 136. Fitzhugh, "Saluria and Military Operations," 95–96. *O.R.*, series 1, vol. 26, part 1, 436, part 2, 433–434.

36. Fitzhugh, "Saluria and Military Operations," 96–98. Barr, "Texas Coastal Defense," 28–29. *O.R.*, series 1, vol. 26, part 2, 458.

37. Joseph H. Parks, *General Edmund Kirby Smith, C.S.A.* (Baton Rouge: Louisiana State University Press, 1954), 341. *O.R.*, series 1, vol. 26, part 2, 467, 485, 515, 529.

38. Paul D. Escott, *After Secession: Jefferson Davis and the Failure of Confederate Nationalism* (reprint, Baton Rouge and London: Louisiana State University Press, 1992), 133–134 (Barringer quote). J. B. Magruder to W. P. Barringer, 24 May 1865, William Pitt Barringer Papers, Center for the Study of American History, University of Texas, Austin. Guy M. Bryan to F. R. Lubbock, 1 September 1863, Francis Richard Lubbock Papers, Center for the Study of American History, University of Texas, Austin. Ralph A. Wooster, "With the Confederate Cavalry in the West: The Civil War Experience of Isaac Dunbar Affleck," *Southwestern Historical Quarterly* 80 (July 1979), 1, 11–12, 22. Spell, "Magruder: Defender of the Texas Coast," 79. Webb, ed., *Handbook of Texas*, vol. 1, 739, vol. 2, 76.

39. *O.R.*, series 1, vol. 26, part 2, 536. Harrington, *Fighting Politician*, 133. William S. McFeely, *Grant: A Biography* (New York and London, W. W. Norton, 1982), 157. Rebecca W. Smith and Marion Mullins, eds., "The Diary of H. C. Medford: Confederate Soldier," *Southwestern Historical Quarterly* 34 (October 1930), 118.

___ 10. "You May Fully Depend on Me" ___

1. Robert S. Henry, *The Story of the Confederacy* (New York: Bobbs-Merrill, 1936), 260–265. J. B. Magruder to Pendleton Murrah, 9 November 1863, 9 January 1864, Pendleton Murrah Records, Record Group 301, Archives Division, Texas State Library, Austin. J. B. Magruder to Thomas Green, 1 February 1864, J. B. Magruder Papers, Chicago Historical Society Library. Secretary of War, *The War of the Rebellion: A Compilation of the Official Records of the Union and Confederate Armies* (Washington, D.C.: Government Printing Office, 1880; hereafter cited as *O.R.*), vol. 34, part 2, 1029–1030.

2. Walter P. Webb, ed., *The Handbook of Texas,* vol. 2 (Austin: State Historical Association 1952), 251. Robert L. Kerby, *Kirby Smith's Confederacy: The Trans-Mississippi South, 1863–1865* (reprint, Tuscaloosa and London: University of Alabama Press, 1991), 277. J. B. Magruder to Pendleton Murrah, 22 November 1863, 28 January 1864, Murrah Records.

3. J. B. Magruder to Pendleton Murrah, 16 March 1864, Pendleton Murrah to J. B. Magruder, 19 March 1864, Murrah Records. Harold B. Simpson and Marcus J. Wright, *Texas in the War, 1861–1865* (Hillsboro, Texas: Hill Junior College Press, 1965), 203. David Paul Smith, *Frontier Defense in the Civil War: Texas' Rangers and Rebels* (College Station: Texas A&M University Press, 1992), 49 ff. Joseph H. Parks, *General Edmund Kirby Smith, C.S.A. 1829–1893* (Baton Rouge: Louisiana State University Press, 1954), 347. Francis R. Lubbock, *Six Decades in Texas: Or Memoirs of Francis Richard Lubbock* (Austin: Ben C. Jones and Co., Printers, 1900), 534.

4. Parks, *General Edmund Kirby Smith,* 347. *O.R.*, vol. 34, part 2, 870. H. P. Dance to Guy M. Bryan, 28 December 1864, Guy Morrison Bryan Papers, Center for the Study of American History, University of Texas, Austin. W. W. Morris to M. G. Howe, 30 January 1864, Milton G. Howe Papers, Center for the Study of American History, University of Texas, Austin.

5. William R. Boggs, *Military Reminiscences* (Durham, N.C.: Seeman Printery, 1913), 60–61. Simpson and Wright, *Texas in the War,* 143. *O.R.*, vol. 34, part 2, 1081.

6. *O.R.*, vol. 34, part 2, 1107. Typescript, John Villasana Haggard Papers, Center for the Study of American History, University of Texas, Austin, 32–33. J. B. Magruder to A. W. Spaight, 13 April 1864, Ashley Wood Spaight Papers, Center for the Study of American History, University of Texas, Austin. E. Kirby Smith to U. S. Grant, 15 March 1866, E. Kirby Smith Papers, Southern Historical Collection, University of North Carolina, Chapel Hill. Lubbock, *Six Decades in Texas,* 532–535.

7. Henry, *Story of the Confederacy,* 431. Fred Harvey Harrington, *Fighting Politician: Major General N. P. Banks* (Philadelphia: University of Pennsylvania Press, 1948), 151. Benjamin P. Thomas and Harold M. Hyman, *Stanton: The Life and Times of Lincoln's Secretary of War* (New York: Alfred A. Knopf, 1962), 306–307.

8. Norman D. Brown, ed., *Journey to Pleasant Hill: The Civil War Letters of Captain Elijah P. Petty, Walker's Texas Division, CSA* (San Antonio: University of Texas Institute of Texan Cultures, 1982), 171. Harrington, *Fighting Politician,* 152–153. T. Michael Parrish, *Richard Taylor: Soldier Prince of Dixie* (Chapel Hill, University of North Carolina Press, 1992), 320–324.

9. J. B. Magruder to Pendleton Murrah, 22 November 1863, Murrah Records; *O.R.*, vol. 43, part 2, 904. Sid S. Johnson, *Texans Who Wore the Gray*, vol. 1 (Tyler, Texas: n.p., 1907), 31–33.

10. Kerby, *Kirby Smith's Confederacy*, 283–284. *O.R.*, vol. 34, part 2, 709, 906. J. B. Magruder, General Orders No. 110, 19 April 1864, Spaight Papers. (Significant differences exist between Magruder's orders in broadside form and those in the *O.R.*)

11. *O.R.*, vol. 34, part 1, 1027. J. B. Magruder to Thomas Green, 6 March 1864, Magruder Papers, Chicago Historical Society. Lubbock, *Six Decades in Texas*, 536.

12. *O.R.*, vol. 34, part 1, 494–496. Ludwell H. Johnson, *Red River Campaign: Politics and Cotton in the Civil War* (Baltimore: Johns Hopkins University Press, 1958), 92–94. Lester N. Fitzhugh, "Texas Forces in the Red River Campaign," *Texas Military History* 3 (Spring 1963), 15–16.

13. Odie Faulk, *Tom Green: Fightin' Texan* (Waco: Texian Press, 1963), 50–62. Webb, ed., *Handbook of Texas*, vol. 1, 727–728. Alwyn Barr, *Polignac's Texas Brigade* (Houston: Texas Gulf Coast Historical Association, 1964), 38 and passim. Fredericka Meiners, "Hamilton P. Bee in the Red River Campaign of 1864," *Southwestern Historical Quarterly* 78 (July 1974), 22–24. Parrish, *Richard Taylor*, 364.

14. J. B. Magruder to Pendleton Murrah, 31 March, 4, 5, 28 April 1864, Pendleton Murrah to J. B. Magruder, 5 April 1864, Murrah Records. *O.R.*, vol. 34, part 3, 802. Kerby, *Kirby Smith's Confederacy*, 278–279.

15. Parks, *General Edmund Kirby Smith*, 394 ff. Brown, ed., *Journey to Pleasant Hill*, 345–346. Michael B. Dougan, *Confederate Arkansas: The People and Policies of a Frontier State in Wartime* (Tuscaloosa: University of Alabama Press, 1976), 121–122. Stephen B. Oates, *Confederate Cavalry West of the River* (Austin: University of Texas Press, 1961), 141.

16. *O.R.*, vol. 34, part 1, 476, part 3, 768–769. Parrish, *Richard Taylor*, 380. Kerby, *Kirby Smith's Confederacy*, 277 ff.

17. Faulk, *Tom Green*, 72. Harrington, *Fighting Politician*, 158–159. Meiners, "Bee and the Red River Campaign," 39–40. Alwyn Barr, "Texan Losses in the Red River Campaign," *Texas Military History* 3 (Summer 1963), 110.

18. *O.R.*, vol. 34, part 3, 779–780. Howell Cobb to J. B. Magruder, 4 March 1864, Edward C. Wharton and Family Papers, Louisiana and Lower Mississippi Valley Collections, Louisiana State University Libraries, Baton Rouge. J. B. Magruder to A. C. Jones, 2 February 1864, Alexander C. Jones Papers, Virginia Historical Society Library, Richmond.

19. Santiago Vidaurri to A. C. Jones, 14 June 1864, Jones Papers. *O.R.*, vol. 34, part 4, 651. Parks, *General Edmund Kirby Smith*, 362–364.

20. Alwyn Barr, "Texas Coastal Defense, 1861–1865," *Southwestern Historical Quarterly* 65 (July 1961), 29. *O.R.*, vol. 34, part 3, 779, 833–834. Simpson and Wright, *Texas in the War*, 203. Stephen B. Oates, "Texas Under the Secessionists," *Southwestern Historical Quarterly* 67 (October 1963), 206.

21. Simpson and Wright, *Texas in the War*, 203. Paeder Joel Hoovestol, "Galveston in the Civil War" (M.A. thesis, University of Houston, 1950), 60–63. *O.R.*, vol. 34, part 2, 944, 1035, 1043. William R. Geise, "Kirby Smith's War Department, 1864:

A Study of Organization and Command in the Trans-Mississippi West," *Military History of Texas and the Southwest* 15 (1979), 56–59.

22. Stephen B. Oates, ed., *Rip Ford's Texas* (Austin: University of Texas Press, 1963), 353–363. James I. Irby, *Backdoor at Bagdad: The Civil War on the Rio Grande* (El Paso: Texas Western Press, 1977), 31–37. *O.R.*, vol. 34, part 4, 669, 684, 695, vol. 41, part 1, 211.

23. Oates, "Texas under the Secessionists," 208. Kerby, *Kirby Smith's Confederacy*, 334. *O.R.*, vol. 41, part 2, 1068.

24. Pendleton Murrah to Guy M. Bryan, 21 June 1864, Guy Morrison Byran Papers, Center for the Study of American History, University of Texas, Austin. Robert E. Waterman and Thomas Rothrock, eds., "The Earle-Buchanan Letters of 1861–1876," *Arkansas Historical Quarterly* 23 (Summer 1974), 156. Carl H. Moneyhon, *The Impact of Civil War and Reconstruction on Arkansas* (Baton Rouge: Louisiana State University Press, 1994), 129–130.

25. Parks, *General Edmund Kirby Smith*, 399–430. Parrish, *Richard Taylor*, 398–401. *O.R.*, vol. 41, part 2, 1091 ff.

26. *O.R.*, vol. 41, part 2, 1081, 1087. Parks, *General Edmund Kirby Smith*, 436–438. Albert Castel, *Sterling Price and the Civil War in the West* (Baton Rouge: Louisiana State University Press, 1993), 197 ff.

27. Harold L. McDonald, "The Battle of Jenkin's Ferry," *Arkansas Historical Quarterly* 7 (Spring 1948), 60 ff. Dougan, *Confederate Arkansas*, 121. John M. Harrell, *Arkansas* in *Confederate Military History* (Atlanta: Confederate Publishing Company, 1899), 10, 252.

28. Rebecca W. Smith and Marion Mullins, eds., "The Diary of H. C. Medford, Confederate Soldier, 1864," *Southwestern Historical Quarterly* 34 (October 1930), 128. Harrell, *Arkansas*, 80. Boggs, *Reminiscences*, 80–81. Brown, ed., *March to Pleasant Hill*, 442.

29. *O.R.*, vol. 41, part 3, 917–918.

30. Dougan, *Confederate Arkansas*, 121. Moneyhon, *Impact of the Civil War*, 129–134. *O.R.*, vol. 41, part 3, 917–918, 950.

31. John L. Ferguson, ed., *Arkansas and the Civil War* (Little Rock: Pioneer Press, 1965), 64–67. W. Buck Yearns, ed., *The Confederate Governors* (Athens: University of Georgia Press, 1985), 53–56. *O.R.*, vol. 41, part 4, 1066, 1073–1075, 1077. James L. Nichols, *The Confederate Quartermaster in the Trans-Mississippi* (Austin: University of Texas Press, 1964), 45.

32. *O.R.*, vol. 41, part 4, 1029, 1140, vol. 48, part 1, 16–17. Edwin C. Bearss, "The Confederate Attempt to Regain Fort Smith, 1863," *Arkansas Historical Quarterly* 28 (Winter 1969), 358–362, Ed Bearss and Arrell M. Gibson, *Fort Smith: Little Gibraltar on the Arkansas* (Norman: University of Oklahoma Press, 1969), 267–269. Parks, *General Edmund Kirby Smith*, 437–438.

33. *O.R.*, vol. 46, part 1, 1317, 1333–1334. James M. McPherson, *Battle Cry of Freedom: The Civil War Era* (New York: Ballantine Books, 1989), 821–822. J. B. Magruder to Jefferson Davis, 12 February 1865, Civil War Collection, Huntington Library, San Marino, California. Eli N. Evans, *Judah P. Benjamin: The Jewish Confederate* (New York: Free Press, 1988), 277–279.

34. *O.R.*, vol. 48, part 1, 1416, 1453–1454. Kerby, *Kirby Smith's Confederacy*, 405–408. Castel, *Sterling Price*, 271–273.

— 11. Last Things —

1. *Dallas Herald*, 20 April 1865. Douglas Southall Freeman, *Lee's Lieutenants: A Study in Command*, vol. 3 (New York: Charles Scribner's Sons, 1944), 644–651. Brooks D. Simpson, ed., *With Grant and Meade: From the Wilderness to Appomattox by Theodore Lyman* (reprint, Lincoln and London: University of Nebraska Press, 1994), 303. O. M. Roberts, *Texas*, in *Confederate Military History*, vol. 11 (Atlanta: Confederate Publishing Company, 1899), 137–138.

2. *Dallas Herald*, 20 April 1865. Mrs. John A. Wharton to William P. Barringer, 13 May 1865, William Pitt Barringer Papers, Center for the Study of American History, University of Texas, Austin. Walter P. Webb, ed., vol. 1, *The Handbook of Texas* (Austin: Texas State Historical Association, 1952), 123.

3. Secretary of War, *The War of the Rebellion: A Compilation of the Official Records of the Union and Confederate Armies* (Washington, D.C.: Government Printing Office, 1880), vol. 48, part 2, 1284, 1289 (cited hereafter as *O.R.*).

4. *O.R.*, vol. 48, part 2, 1288–1289, 1291. Clement Eaton, *Jefferson Davis* (New York: Free Press, 1977), 260. William C. Davis, *Jefferson Davis: The Man and His Hour* (reprint, New York: HarperCollins, 1992), 617–628. Ben H. Proctor, *Not Without Honor: The Life of John H. Reagan* (Austin: University of Texas Press, 1962), 159. Jefferson Davis, *The Rise and Fall of the Confederate Government*, vol. 2 (New York: D. Appleton and Co., 1881), 696–697.

5. J. B. Magruder to Pendleton Murrah, 26, 29 May 1865, Pendleton Murrah Records, Record Group 301, Archives Division, Texas State Library, Austin. J. P. Jones to A. C. Jones, 1 June 1865, Alexander C. Jones Papers, Virginia Historical Society Library, Richmond. Robert L. Kerby, *Kirby Smith's Confederacy: The Trans-Mississippi South, 1863–1865* (reprint, Tuscaloosa and London: University of Alabama Press, 1991), 426.

6. J. H. Reagan to F. R. Lubbock, 4 January 1882, Jefferson Davis to F. R. Lubbock, 29 February 1886, Francis R. Lubbock Papers, Center for the Study of American History, University of Texas, Austin. Charles R. Benton to E. C. Wharton, 29 May 1886, Edward C. Wharton and Family Papers, Louisiana and Lower Mississippi Valley Collections, Louisiana State University Libraries, Baton Rouge.

7. *O.R.*, vol. 48, part 1, 189 ff., vol. 48, part 2, 1293. J. B. Magruder to Pendleton Murrah, 25 April 1865, Pendleton Murrah Records.

8. J. B. Magruder to E. K. Smith, 16 May 1865, E. Kirby Smith Papers, Southern Historical Collection, University of North Carolina, Chapel Hill. Sid S. Johnson, *Texans Who Wore the Gray* (Tyler, Texas: n.p., 1907), 240. J. B. Magruder to E. K. Smith, telegram, 26 May 1865, John Bankhead Magruder Papers, Chicago Historical Society Library; see also A. W. Sparks, *Recollections of the Great War* (Tyler, Texas: Lee and Burnett, 1901). Magruder's communiqué to Smith in the Southern Historical Collection at Chapel Hill, North Carolina, is merely dated May 1865, without day. In the *O.R.* (vol. 48, part 2, 1308), the same missive is dated May 16.

9. *O.R.*, vol. 48, part 2, 1313–1314. E. K. Smith to S. B. Buckner, Simon Bolivar Buckner Papers, Huntington Library, San Marino, California. J. B. Magruder to E. K. Smith, 24 May 1865, Magruder Papers, Chicago Historical Society Library.

10. Kerby, *Kirby Smith's Confederacy*, 417–418. Max L. Heyman, Jr., *Prudent Soldier: A Biography of Major General E. R. S. Canby* (Glendale, Calif.: Arthur H. Clark Company, 1959), 235. J. B. Magruder to Ashbel Smith and W. P. Barringer, 24 May 1865, Barringer Papers. Johnston, *Texans Who Wore the Gray*, 61–62. A copy of the Magruder letter to Smith and Barringer can also be found in the Magruder Papers, Rosenberg Library, Galveston.

11. E. K. Smith to Pendleton Murrah, 30 May 1865, E. K. Smith to J. B. Magruder, 2 June 1865, E. Kirby Smith Papers. *O.R.*, vol. 48, part 1, 193–194.

12. David W. Yandell to "My Dear Sir," 24 April 1868, James W. Eldridge Papers, Huntington Library, San Marino, Calif. C. R. Benton to E. C. Wharton, Edward C. Wharton and Family Papers. J. B. Magruder to E. K. Smith, 4 June 1865, E. Kirby Smith Papers. *New York Times*, 20 August 1867.

13. W. S. Oldham, Diary, 421, handwritten copy in Williamson Simpson Oldham Papers, Center for the Study of American History, University of Texas, Austin. Callie Wright Clapp to Miss J. W. [?] Heighty, 11 June 1865, Josepha "Jodie" Wright Papers, Center for the Study of American History, University of Texas, Austin. *New York Times*, 20 August 1867.

14. *New York Times*, 2 April 1916. Egbert Watson Magruder, ed., *Year Book of the American Clan Gregor Society, 1916* (Richmond: Appeals Press, 1916), 61–72. Alexander W. Terrell, *From Texas to Mexico and the Court of Maximilian in 1865* (reprint, Dallas: Book Club of Texas, 1933), 68–70. James A. Padgett, "Life of Alfred Mordecia in Mexico in 1865–1866, As Told in His Letters to his Family," *North Carolina Historical Review* 22 (April 1945), 198–227 (the name of Maximilian's wife has been spelled, in various sources, as either *Carlota* or *Carlotta;* the present writer has adopted the former).

15. Daniel O'Flaherty, *General Jo Shelby: Undefeated Rebel* (Chapel Hill: University of North Carolina Press, 1954), 243–245. Magruder, ed., *1916 Year Book*, 62–63; Terrell, *From Texas to Mexico*, 18.

16. Terrell, *From Texas to Mexico*, 18–27. *Mexican Times*, 16 December 1865, 2 June 1866.

17. Robert H. Murray, ed., *Maximilian: Emperor of Mexico, Memoirs of His Private Secretary, José Luís Blasio* (New Haven: Yale University Press, 1934), 6. Ramón Eduardo Ruiz, *An American in Maximilian's Mexico, 1865–1866: Diaries of William Marshall Anderson* (San Marino, Calif.: Huntington Library, 1959), xxii. Magruder, ed., *1916 Year Book*, 65.

18. Richard O'Connor, *The Cactus Throne: The Tragedy of Maximilian and Carlotta* (New York: G. P. Putnam's Sons, 1971), 74–75. Robert Ryal Miller, *Mexico: A History* (Norman: University of Oklahoma Press, 1985), 321 ff. Berita Harding, *Phantom Crown: The Story of Maximilian and Carlota of Mexico* (New York: Halcyon House, 1934), 148.

19. Terrell, *From Texas to Mexico*, 43–45. Ida Pendleton to J. R. Landis, 13 July 1925, John Bankhead Magruder File, Aztec Club Archives, U.S. Army Military History Institute, Carlisle Barracks, Pa. (this letter contains a well-crafted Magruder family tree). Andrew F. Rolle, *The Lost Cause: The Confederate Exodus to Mexico* (Norman: University of Oklahoma Press, 1965), 21–23.

20. Magruder, ed., *1916 Year Book*, 65–66. Frances Leigh Williams, *Matthew Fontaine Maury: Scientist of the Sea* (New Brunswick, N.J.: Rutgers University Press,

1963), 434, 635. John N. Edwards, *Shelby's Expedition to Mexico: An Unwritten Leaf in the War* (reprint, Austin, Texas: Steck Co., 1964), 79.

21. *Mexican Times*, 14 October 1865. George D. Harmon, "Confederate Migrations to Mexico," *Hispanic American Historical Review* 17 (November 1937), 461. Edwards, *Shelby's Expedition to Mexico*, 20.

22. Edwards, *Shelby's Expedition to Mexico*, 20. Ida Pendleton to J. R. Landis, 13 July 1925, Aztec Club Archives. James A. Padgett, "Life of Alfred Mordecia in Mexico, 1865–1866, As Told to His Wife in His Letters—Part IV," *North Carolina Historical Review* 23 (January 1964), 85, 94–96.

23. Edwards, *Shelby's Expedition to Mexico*, 79. Albert Castel, *General Sterling Price and the Civil War in the West* (reprint, Baton Rouge: Louisiana State University Press, 1993), 273–275. Harmon, "Confederate Migrations to Mexico," 474–475; see also Carl Coke Rister, "Carlota: A Confederate Colony in Mexico," *Journal of Southern History* 10 (February 1945), 33 ff.

24. Rolle, *The Lost Cause*, 36–37. Roy P. Basler, ed., *The Collected Works of Abraham Lincoln*, vol. 8 (New Brunswick, N.J.: Rutgers University Press, 1953), 137. Carl Sandburg, *Abraham Lincoln: The War Years*, vol. 4 (New York: Harcourt, Brace and Co., 1947), 264. Ulysses S. Grant, *Personal Memoirs of U. S. Grant* (reprint, New York: Da Capo Press, 1982), 585–586.

25. Ruiz, *An American in Maximilian's Mexico*, xxiv. John F. Marszalek, *Sherman: A Soldier's Passion for Order* (New York: Free Press, 1993), 370–371. Joan Haslip, *The Crown of Mexico: Maximilian and Carlota* (New York: Holt, Rinehart and Winston, 1971), 350, 456–458. Magruder, ed., *1916 Year Book*, 68.

26. Haslip, *The Crown of Mexico*, 400, 457. John Bierman, *Napoleon III and His Carnival Empire* (New York: St. Martin's Press, 1988), 302.

27. *Mexican Times*, 19 May, 19 November 1866. Magruder, ed., *1916 Year Book*, 68–69. Castel, *Sterling Price and the West*, 247.

28. Magruder, ed., *1916 Year Book*, 70. Haslip, *The Crown of Mexico*, 429. Henry B. Parkes, *A History of Mexico* (Boston: Houghton Mifflin, 1960), 272. Bierman, *Napoleon III*, 293–303.

29. *Dallas Herald*, 8 December 1866. *Mexican Times*, 11 December 1866. U.S. Congress, "Correspondence with Ministers to Mexico," House Executive Document, 40th Congress, 1st Session, 1867, 11–12.

30. J. B. Magruder to Reverdy Johnson, 17 November 1866, Samuel L. M. Barlow Papers, Huntington Library, San Marino, California.

31. Robert E. Lee Jr., *Recollections and Letters of General Robert E. Lee* (Garden City, N.Y.: Garden City Publishing Company, 1903), 26–28. Bernard C. Steiner, *Life of Reverdy Johnson* (Baltimore: Norman, Remington Co., 1914), 225–233. U. S. Grant to E. K. Smith, 16 October 1865, E. Kirby Smith Papers. *New York Herald*, 13 December 1866. Thomas M. Settles, "The Military Career of John Bankhead Magruder" (Ph.D. diss., Texas Christian University, 1972), 308.

32. *New York Herald*, 13 December 1866. Webb, ed., *Handbook of Texas*, vol. 1, 773. Philip C. Tucker, "The United States Gunboat *Harriet Lane*," *Southwestern Historical Quarterly* 21 (April 1918), 375.

33. J. B. Magruder to S. B. Buckner, 29 April 1867, Simon Bolivar Buckner Papers, Huntington Library, San Marino, Calif., *New York Times*, 20 August 1867.

34. E. Merton Coulter, *The South During Reconstruction, 1865–1877* (reprint, Baton Rouge: Louisiana State University Press, 1962), 306. *New York Herald*, 5 September 1868. *New York Times*, 5 September 1868. Emory M. Thomas, *Robert E. Lee: A Biography* (New York: W. W. Norton, 1995), 390–391.

35. *New York Herald*, 25 October 1868. Mark M. Boatner, *The Civil War Dictionary* (New York: David M. McKay, 1959), 399.

36. J. B. Magruder to Mrs. ———, 10 July 1869, Edward C. Wharton and Family Papers. Baltimore *American and Commerical Advertiser*, 23 July, 2 August 1869. Boatner, *Civil War Dictionary*, 437. J. B. Magruder to I. S. Burrell, 24 October 1869, Massachusetts MOLLUS Collection, U.S. Army Military History Institute, Carlisle Barracks, Pennsylvania.

37. J. B. Magruder to E. C. Wharton, 20 February 1870, Edward C. Wharton and Family Papers. *Mobile Register*, 25 February 1870. Robert S. Sobel and John Raimo, *Biographical Directory of the Governors of the United States, 1787–1978* (Westport, Conn.: Meckler Books, 1978), 14–15. Magruder's Order No. 105, 10 November 1862, J. B. Magruder's Order Book, Army of the Peninsula, War Department Collection of Confederate Records (Record Group 109), National Archives, Washington. *New York Times*, 7 March 1871, 2 April 1916.

38. J. B. Magruder to E. C. Wharton, 8, 10 February 1870, Edward C. Wharton and Family Papers. *New Orleans Picayune*, 8, 10 March 1870.

39. *New York Times*, 23 May 1870. Houston City Directory, 1877–1878 (n.p., 1878), 196. *Houston Post*, 15 May 1949.

40. *Galveston Daily News*, 21 February 1871. *Dallas Herald*, 25 February 1871. *New York Times*, 20 February 1871. *New York Herald*, 21 February 1871.

41. John F. Lee to Unknown, 1871, Lee Family Papers, Virginia Historical Society Library, Richmond. *New York Herald*, 20 February 1871. B. G. Wood, "Monument to General Magruder," *Confederate Veteran* 5 (1897), 171.

Bibliography

⎯⎯ Manuscripts ⎯⎯

Thaddeus Armstrong Papers, Rosenberg Library, Galveston, Texas.

Samuel L. M. Barlow Papers, Huntington Library, San Marino, Calif.

Ada Bankhead Collection, Alderman Library, University of Virginia, Charlottesville.

William Pitt Barringer Papers, Center for the Study of American History, University of Texas, Austin.

James Breckenridge Papers, Alderman Library, University of Virginia, Charlottesville.

Rosella Kenner Brent Papers, Louisiana and Lower Mississippi Valley Collections, Louisiana State University Libraries, Baton Rouge.

Guy Morrison Bryan Papers, Center for the Study of American History, University of Texas, Austin.

St. George T. C. Bryan Papers, Brockenbrough Library, Museum of the Confederacy, Richmond.

Simon Bolivar Buckner Papers, Huntington Library, San Marino, Calif.

Cabell Family Papers, Virginia Historical Society Library, Richmond.

Civil War Collection, Huntington Library, San Marino, Calif.

Cave Johnson Couts Papers, Huntington Library, San Marino, California.

William T. Dean Papers, Howard-Tilton Memorial Library, Tulane University, New Orleans.

James Duncan Papers, United States Military Academy Archives, West Point.

James W. Eldridge Papers, Huntington Library, San Marino, Calif.

Richard Stoddert Ewell Papers, Library of Congress, Washington.

Fort Clark Records, Center for the Study of American History, University of Texas, Austin.

John Villasana Haggard Papers, Center for the Study of American History, University of Texas, Austin.

John L. Haynes Vertical File, Center for the Study of American History, University of Texas, Austin.

Augustus M. Hill Papers, Center for the Study of American History, University of Texas, Austin.

Hinsdale Family Papers, Perkins Library, Duke University, Durham, North Carolina.

Milton G. Howe Papers, Center for the Study of American History, University of Texas, Austin.

Alexander C. Jones Papers, Virginia Historical Society Library, Richmond.

Lee Family Papers, Virginia Historical Society Library, Richmond.

S. G. S. Lee Papers, Rosenberg Library, Galveston, Texas.

Francis Richard Lubbock Papers, Center for the Study of American History, University of Texas, Austin.

Francis Richard Lubbock Records, Record Group 301, Archives Division, Texas State Library, Austin.

Lafayette McLaws Papers, Southern Historical Collection, University of North Carolina, Chapel Hill.

George A. Magruder Papers, Department of the Navy Library, Washington Navy Yard, Washington, D.C.

John Bankhead Magruder Papers, Archives of the Big Bend, Sul Ross State University, Alpine, Texas.

John Bankhead Magruder Papers, Aztec Club Archives, U.S. Military History Institute, Carlisle Barracks, Pennsylvania.

John Bankhead Magruder Papers, Brockenbrough Library, Museum of the Confederacy, Richmond.

John Bankhead Magruder Papers, Chicago Historical Society Library, Chicago.

John Bankhead Magruder Papers, Perkins Library, Duke University, Durham, North Carolina.

John Bankhead Magruder Papers, Rosenberg Library, Galveston, Texas.

John Bankhead Magruder, Vertical File, Center for the Study of American History, University of Texas, Austin.

Massachusetts MOLLUS Collection, U.S. Army Military History Institute, Carlisle Barracks, Pennsylvania.

Pendleton Murrah Records, Record Group 301, Archives Division, Texas State Library, Austin.

Nolan Family Papers, Alderman Library, University of Virginia, Charlottesville.

William Norris Papers, Alderman Library, University of Virginia, Charlottesville.

Nutt Family Papers, Huntington Library, San Marino, Calif.

Williamson Simpson Oldham Papers, Center for the Study of American History, University of Texas, Austin.

William Nelson Pendleton Papers, Southern Historical Collection, University of North Carolina, Chapel Hill.

William Mumford Ellis Rachal Papers, Virginia Historical Society Library, Richmond.

Records of the Adjutant General's Office, National Archives, Record Group 94, Washington.

Sterling Clack Robertson Papers, Center for the Study of American History, University of Texas, Austin.

E. Kirby Smith Papers, Southern Historical Collection, University of North Carolina, Chapel Hill.

Maury J. Smith Papers, U.S. Army Military History Institute, Carlisle Barracks, Pennsylvania.

Smith-Kirby-Webster-Black-Danner Papers, U.S. Army Military History Institute, Carlisle Barracks, Pennsylvania.

M. J. Solomons Papers, Perkins Library, Duke University, Durham, North Carolina.

Ashley Wood Spaight Papers, Center for the Study of American History, University of Texas, Austin.

Charles W. Trueheart Papers, Alderman Library, University of Virginia, Charlottesville.

Virginia Miscellaneous Letters, Alderman Library, University of Virginia, Charlottesville.

War Department Collection of Confederate Records, National Archives, Record Group 109, Washington.

Beverly R. Welford Papers, Virginia Historical Society Library, Richmond.

Edward Clifton Wharton and Family Papers, Louisiana and Lower Mississippi Valley Collections, Louisiana State University Libraries, Baton Rouge.

Josepha "Jodie" Wright Papers, Center for the Study of American History, University of Texas, Austin.

⸺ Newspapers ⸺

Baltimore American and Commercial Advertiser, 1831, 1861, 1869.

Baltimore Republican, 1861.

Baltimore Sun, 1855, 1950.

Dallas Herald, 1862, 1863, 1865, 1866, 1871.

Houston Post, 1949.

Houston Tri-Weekly News, 1862.

Galveston Daily News, 1863, 1871.

Mexican Times, 1865–1866.

Mobile (Alabama) *Register,* 1870.

Newport (Rhode Island) *Mercury,* 1858, 1859.

New York Herald, 1853, 1866, 1868, 1871.

New York Times, 1853, 1861, 1867, 1870, 1871, 1916.

Raleigh Weekly Register and North Carolina Gazette, 1835.

San Diego Herald, 1853.

⸺ Government Publications ⸺

Delafield, Richard, "Report . . . on the Art of War in Europe, 1854, 1855, and 1856," Senate Executive Document, 35th Congress, 1st Session, 1857.

"Letters Received by the Office of the Adjutant General, 1822–1860," National Archives Publication M-567.

"Letters Received by the Office of the Secretary of War, 1801–1870," National Archives Publication M-221.

"Letters Sent by the Office of the Adjutant General, 1800–1890," National Archives Publication M-565.

"Orders and Endorsements Sent by the Secretary of War, 1846–1870," National Archives Publication M-444.

"Orders of General Zachary Taylor to the Army of Occupation in the Mexican War, 1845–1847," National Archives Publication M-29.

Register of Officers and Cadets of the U.S. Military Academy, June 1827. West Point, N.Y.: USMA, 1884.

Register of Officers and Cadets of the U.S. Military Academy, June 1829. West Point, N.Y.: USMA, 1884.

Register of Officers and Cadets of the U.S. Military Academy, June 1830. West Point, N.Y.: USMA, 1887.

"Returns from U.S. Military Posts, 1800–1916." National Archives Publication M-91.

"U.S. Military Academy Cadet Application Papers, 1805–1866." National Archives Publication M-688.

U.S. Congress. *Biographical Directory of the American Congress, 1774–1961.* Washington, D.C.: Government Printing Office, 1961.

U.S. Congress. "Correspondence with Ministers to Mexico." House Executive Document, 40th Congress, 1st Session, 1867.

U.S. Congress. House Executive Document 60, 30th Congress, 1st Session, 1848.

U.S. Congress. Senate Executive Document 1, 30th Congress, 1st Session, 1848.

——— Secondary Works ———

A Brief History of Fort Adams, Newport, R.I. N.p., n.d. Copy in U.S. Naval War College Library, Newport, R.I.

Alexander, Edward P. *Memoirs of a Confederate.* New York: Charles Scribner's Sons, 1908.

Ambler, Charles H., and Festus P. Summers. *West Virginia: The Mountain State.* Englewood Cliffs, N.J.: Prentice-Hall, 1957.

Ambrose, Stephen B. *Duty, Honor, Country: A History of West Point.* Baltimore: Johns Hopkins University Press, 1962.

Aptheker, Herbert. *Nat Turner's Slave Rebellion.* New York: Humanities Press, 1966.

Arnold, Thomas Jackson. *Early Life and Letters of General Jackson.* New York: Fleming H. Revell Co., 1916.

Association of the Graduates of the Unites States Military Academy: Annual Reunion, June 17, 1871. West Point, N.Y.: USMA, 1871.

Ballentine, George. *Autobiography of an English Soldier in the United States Army Comprising Observations and Adventures in the United States and Mexico.* New York: Stringer and Townsend, 1853.

Barker, A. J. *The War Against Russia.* New York: Holt, Rinehart and Winston, 1970.

Barr, Alwyn. *Polignac's Brigade.* Houston: Gulf Coast Historical Association, 1964.

Barrett, Thomas. *The Great Hanging at Gainesville, Cooke County, Texas, October, A.D. 1862.* Reprint, Austin: Texas State Historical Association, 1966.

Barringer, Paul Brandon. *The University of Virginia.* New York: Lewis Publishing Company, 1904.

Bartlett, John Russell. *Personal Narrative of Explorations and Incidents in Texas, New Mexico, California, Sonora, and Chihuahua.* New York: D. Appleton and Co., 1854.

Basler, Roy P., ed. *The Collected Works of Abraham Lincoln.* New Brunswick, N.J.: Rutgers University Press, 1953.

Bauer, Jack. *Zachary Taylor: Soldier, Planter, Statesman of the Old South.* Baton Rouge: Louisiana State University Press, 1985.

Bearss, Edwin C., and Arrell M. Gibson. *Fort Smith: Gibraltar on the Arkansas.* Norman: University of Oklahoma Press, 1969.

Bell, Horace. *Reminiscences of a Ranger: Or Early Times in Southern California.* Los Angeles: Yandell, Caystile and Mathes, Printers, 1881.

Bierman, John. *Napoleon III and His Carnival Empire.* New York: St. Martin's Press, 1988.

Biesele, Rudolph. *The History of the German Settlements in Texas.* Austin: Von Boeckmann-Jones Co., 1930.

Bill, Alfred Hoyt. *Rehearsal for Conflict: The War With Mexico, 1846–1848.* New York: Alfred A. Knopf, 1947.

Blackwood, Emma J., ed. *To Mexico with Scott: Letters of E. Kirby Smith to His Wife.* Cambridge: Harvard University Press, 1917.

Blake, R. L. V. French. *The Crimean War.* Reprint, Hamden, Conn.: Archon Books, 1971.

Boatner, Mark M. *The Civil War Dictionary.* New York: David M. McKay, 1959.

Boggs, William R. *Military Reminiscences.* Durham, N.C.: Seeman Printing, 1913.

Branda, Eldon S. *The Handbook of Texas: A Supplement.* Austin: Texas State Historical Association, 1976.

Brent, Joseph L. *Memoir of the War Between the States.* New Orleans: Fontana Printing Co., 1949.

Bridges, Hal. *Lee's Maverick General: Daniel Harvey Hill.* Reprint, Lincoln: University of Nebraska Press, 1991.

Brown, Norman D. *Journey to Pleasant Hill: The Civil War Letters of Captain Elijah P Petty, Walker's Texas Division, C.S.A.* San Antonio: University of Texas Institute of Texan Cultures, 1982.

Bruce, Philip Alexander. *History of the University of Virginia.* New York: Macmillan, 1921.

Buchan, John. *Oliver Cromwell.* London: The Reprint Society, 1941.

Butler, Benjamin F. *Butler's Book: A Review of His Legal, Political and Military Career.* Boston: A. M. Thayer and Co., 1892.

Burrage, Henry S. *Maine and the Northeastern Boundary Controversy.* Portland, Maine: Marks Printing House, 1919.

Callahan, Edward W. *List of Officers of the Navy of the United States and of the Marine Corps, from 1775 to 1900.* New York: Haskell House Publishers, reprint, 1969.

Campbell, Randolph B. *Sam Houston and the Southwest.* New York: HarperCollins, 1993.

Canton Days: The First Hundred Years or So. Baltimore: Canton Company of Baltimore, 1928.

Casdorph, Paul D. *History of the Republican Party in Texas, 1865–1965.* Austin, Texas: Pemberton Press, 1965.

—. *Lee and Jackson: Confederate Chieftains.* New York: Paragon House, 1992.

Castel, Albert. *General Sterling Price and the War in the West.* Baton Rouge: Louisiana State University Press, 1993.

Cave, Eber Worthington. *Official Report of the Battles of Galveston and Sabine . . . With Sketch of the Life and Public Services of Maj. Gen. J. Bankhead Magruder.* Houston: Texas Printing Co., 1866.

Chitwood, Oliver P. *John Tyler: Champion of the Old South.* Reprint, New York: Russell and Russell, 1964.

Cochran, Hamilton. *Noted American Duels and Hostile Encounters.* Philadelphia and New York: Chilton Books, 1963.

Cometti, Elizabeth, and Festus P. Summers. *The Thirty-Fifth State: A Documentary History of West Virginia.* Morgantown: West Virginia University Library, 1966.

Connor, Seymour V., and Odie B. Faulk. *North America Divided: The Mexican War, 1846–1848.* New York: Oxford University Press, 1971.

Constitution of the Aztec Club of 1847 and Its Members, 1893. Reprint, Louisville, Ky.: Lost Cause Press, 1980.

Cook, Roy B. *The Family and Early Life of Stonewall Jackson.* Reprint, Charleston, W.V.: Education Foundation, 1967.

Cooke, John Esten. *A Life of General Robert E. Lee.* New York: D. Appleton and Co., 1871.

———. *Stonewall Jackson: A Military Biography.* New York: D. Appleton and Co., 1866.

Coulter, E. Merton. *The Confederate States of America, 1861–1865.* Baton Rouge: Louisiana State University Press, 1950.

———. *The South During Reconstruction.* Baton Rouge: Louisiana State University Press, 1962.

Crist, Lynda Laswell, ed., *The Papers of Jefferson Davis, 1853–1855.* Baton Rouge: Louisiana State University Press, 1985.

———, and Mary Seaton Dix, eds. *The Papers of Jefferson Davis, 1861.* Baton Rouge: Louisiana State University Press, 1992.

Croffut, W. A., ed. *Fifty Years in Camp and Field: Diary of Major General Ethan Allen Hitchcock, USA.* New York: G. P. Putnam's Sons, 1901.

Cullen, Joseph P. *The Peninsula Campaign of 1862: McClellan and Lee Struggle for Richmond.* Harrisburg, Pa.: Stackpole Books, 1973.

Cullum, George W. *Biographical Register of the U.S. Military Academy at West Point, From Its Establishment, March 16, 1802, to the Army Reorganization of 1867.* New York: D. Van Nostrand, 1868.

Cutrer, Thomas W. *Ben McCulloch and the Frontier Military Tradition.* Chapel Hill and London: University of North Carolina Press, 1994.

Dabney, Robert L. *Life and Campaigns of Lieut.-Gen. Thomas J. Jackson.* New York: Blelock and Company, 1866.

Daly, R.W. *How the Merrimac Won! The Strategic Story of the CSS Virginia.* New York: Thomas Crowell, 1957.

Davis, Burke. *They Called Him Stonewall: The Life of Lieutenant General T. J. Jackson.* Reprint, New York: Fairfax Press, 1988.

Davis, Jefferson. *The Rise and Fall of the Confederate Government.* New York: D. Appleton and Co., 1881.

Davis, William C. *"A Government of Their Own": The Making of the Confederacy.* New York: Free Press, 1994.

———. *Duel Between the First Ironclads.* New York: Doubleday, 1975.

———. *Jefferson Davis: The Man and His Hour.* Reprint, New York: HarperCollins, 1992.

Derr, Mark. *Some Kind of Paradise: A Chronicle of Man and the Land in Florida.* New York: William Morrow, 1987.

de Vere, Maximilian Schele. *Students at the University of Virginia.* Charlottesville: University of Virginia, 1878.

Dickert, D. Augustus. *History of Kershaw's Brigade.* Reprint, Dayton, Ohio: Morningside Book Co., 1973.

Dilts, James D. *The Great Road: The Building of the Baltimore & Ohio, the Nation's First Railroad, 1828–1853.* Stanford: Stanford University Press, 1993.

Doubleday, Rhoda Van Bibber, ed., *Journal of the Late Brevet Major Philip Norbourne Barbour, Captain in the 3rd Regiment, United States Infantry.* New York: G. P. Putnam's Sons, 1936.

Dougan, Michael B. *Confederate Arkansas: The People and Politics of a Frontier State in Wartime.* Tuscaloosa: University of Alabama Press, 1976.

Douglas, Henry Kyd. *I Rode with Stonewall.* Reprint, Chapel Hill: University of North Carolina Press, 1984.

Dowdey, Clifford. *Lee.* Boston: Little, Brown, 1965.

———. *The Seven Days: The Emergence of Lee.* Boston: Little, Brown, 1964.

Eaton, Clement. *Jefferson Davis.* New York: Free Press, 1977.

Edwards, John N. *Shelby's Expedition to Mexico: An Unwritten Leaf in the War.* Reprint, Austin, Texas: Steck Company, 1964.

Eggleston, George Cary. *The History of the Confederate War: Its Causes and Conduct.* New York: Sturgis and Walton, 1910.

Eisenhower, John S. D. *So Far from God: The U.S. War with Mexico, 1846–1848.* New York: Random House, 1989.

Eliot, Ellsworth. *West Point and the Confederacy.* New York: G. A. Baker, 1941.

Englehardt, Fr. Zephyrin. *San Diego Mission.* San Francisco: James H. Barry, 1920.

English Combatant. *Battle-Fields of the South: From Bull Run to Fredericksburg.* New York: John Bradburn, 1864.

Escott, Paul D. *After Secession: Jefferson Davis and the Failure of Confederate Nationalism.* Reprint, Baton Rouge and London: Louisiana State University Press, 1992.

Esposito, Vincent J. *West Point Atlas of American Wars, 1689–1900.* New York: Frederick A. Praeger, 1960.

Evans, Eli N. *Judah P. Benjamin: The Jewish Confederate.* New York: Free Press, 1988.

Ex-Cadet (James Dabney McCabe). *The Life of Thomas J. Jackson.* Richmond: James E. Goode, 1864.

Falkus, Christopher. *The Life and Times of Charles II.* Garden City, N.Y.: Doubleday, 1972.

Faulk, Odie B. *Tom Green: Fightin' Texan.* Waco: Texian Press, 1963.

Ferguson, John L., ed. *Arkansas and the Civil War.* Little Rock: Pioneer Press, 1965.

Fiebeger, G. J. *Campaigns of the American Civil War.* West Point: USMA Printing Office, 1914.

Fleming, Thomas J. *West Point: The Men and Times of the United States Military Academy.* New York: William Morrow, 1969.

Fox, William. *Regimental Losses in the American Civil War.* Albany, N.Y.: Albany Publishing Co., 1893.

Freeman, Douglas Southall. *Lee's Lieutenants: A Study in Command.* New York: Charles Scribner's Sons, 1942.

————. *Robert E. Lee: A Biography.* New York: Charles Scribner's Sons, 1934.

Freeman, Douglas Southall, and Grady McWhiney, eds. *Lee's Dispatches: Letters of Robert E. Lee to Jefferson Davis and the War Department of the Confederate States of America, 1861–1865.* New York: G. P. Putnam's Sons, 1957.

Fremantle, Arthur Lyon. *Three Months in the Southern States, April–June 1863.* New York: John Bradburn, 1864.

Friend, Llerena. *Sam Houston: The Great Designer.* Austin: University of Texas Press, 1954.

Gallagher, Gary W., ed. *Fighting for the Confederacy: Personal Recollections of General Edward Porter Alexander.* Chapel Hill and London: University of North Carolina Press, 1989.

Gallagher, Gary W. *Stephen Dodson Ramseur: Lee's Gallant General.* Chapel Hill and London: University of North Carolina Press, 1988.

Gallaway, B. P., ed. *Texas: The Dark Corner of the Confederacy.* Reprint, Lincoln and London: University of Nebraska Press, 1994.

Genealogy and Biography of Leading Families of the City of Baltimore County, Maryland. Chicago and New York: Chapman Printing Company, 1897.

Glover, Robert W., and Linda Cross. *Tyler and Smith County, Texas: A Historical Survey.* Tyler: American Bicentennial Committee, 1976.

Govan, Gilbert E., and James W. Lovingood. *A Different Valor: The Story of General Joseph E. Johnston.* Indianapolis: Bobbs-Merrill, 1956.

Grant, Ulysses S. *Personal Memoirs.* Reprint, New York: Da Capo Press, 1982.

Gwathmey, John H. *Twelve Virginia Counties: Where the Western Migration Began.* Richmond: Dietz Press, 1937.

Hamilton, Holman. *Zachary Taylor: Soldier of the Republic.* Reprint, Hamden, Conn.: Archon Books, 1966.

Hamley, Edward. *The War in the Crimea.* Reprint, Westport, Conn.: Greenwood Press, 1971.

Hamlin, Percy Gatling. *"Old Baldhead": General R. S. Ewell.* Richmond: Whittet and Shepperson, 1955.

Harding, John M. *Phantom Crown: The Story of Maximilian and Carlota.* New York: Halcyon House, 1934.

Harrell, John M. *Arkansas.* In *Confederate Military History.* Atlanta: Confederate Publishing Co., 1899.

Harrington, Fred Harvey. *Fighting Politician: Major General N. P. Banks.* Philadelphia: University of Pennsylvania Press, 1948.

Haskin, William L. *A History of the First Regiment of Artillery from Its Organization in 1821, to January 1st 1876.* Portland, Maine: B. Thurston and Co., 1879.

Haslip, Joan. *The Crown of Mexico: Maximilian and Carlota.* New York: Holt, Rinehart and Winston, 1971.

Hattaway, Herman. *General Stephen D. Lee.* Oxford: University Press of Mississippi, 1976.

Heitman, Francis B. *Historical Register and Directory of the United States Army, 1789–1903.* Washington, D.C.: Government Printing Office, 1903.

Henderson, Harry M. *Texas in the Confederacy.* San Antonio: Naylor Co., 1955.

Henry, Robert S. *The Story of the Confederacy.* New York: Bobbs-Merrill, 1936.

———. *The Story of the Mexican War.* New York: Bobbs-Merrill, 1950.

Heyman, Max L. *Prudent Soldier: A Biography of Major General E. R. S. Canby, 1817–1873.* Glendale, Calif.: Arthur H. Clarke Co., 1959.

History of the State of Kansas. Chicago: A. T. Andreas, 1883.

Hoehling, A. A. *Thunder at Hampton Roads.* Englewood Cliffs, N.J.: Prentice Hall, 1976.

Hood, John Bell. *Advance and Retreat: Personal Experiences in the United States and Confederate Armies.* New Orleans: G. T. Beauregard, 1880.

Hotchkiss, Jed. *Virginia,* in *Confederate Military History.* Atlanta: Confederate Publishing Company, 1899.

Hughes, Robert M. *General Johnston.* New York: D. Appleton and Co., 1893.

Hutton, Ronald. *Charles The Second: King of England, Scotland, and Ireland.* Oxford: Clarendon Press, 1988.

Irby, James A. *A Backdoor at Bagdad: The Civil War on the Rio Grande.* El Paso: Texas Western Press, 1977.

Jackson, Mary Anna. *Memoirs of Stonewall Jackson by His Widow.* Louisville: Prentice Press, 1895.

Jacobs, Timothy. *The History of the Baltimore & Ohio: America's First Railroad.* New York: Crescent Books, 1989.

James, Marquis. *Andrew Jackson: Portrait of a President.* Reprint, New York: Grosset & Dunlap, n.d.

Johannsen, Robert W. *To the Halls of Montezuma: The Mexican War in the American Imagination.* New York: Oxford University Press, 1985.

Johnson, Ludwell H. *The Red River Campaign: Politics and Cotton in the Civil War.* Baltimore: Johns Hopkins University Press, 1958.

Johnson, Sid S. *Texans Who Wore the Gray.* Tyler, Texas: n.p., 1907.

Johnston, Joseph E. *Narrative of Military Operations.* Reprint, Bloomington: Indiana University Press, 1959.

Jones, J. William. *Life and Letters of Robert Edward Lee: Soldier and Man.* New York: Neale Publishing Co., 1906.

Jordan, Ervin L. *Black Confederates and Afro-Yankees in Civil War Virginia.* Charlottesville: University of Virginia Press, 1995.

Jordan, Terry L. *German Seed in Texas Soil.* Austin: University of Texas Press, 1966.

Josephy, Alvin M. *The Civil War in the American West.* New York: Alfred A. Knopf, 1991.

Kerby, Robert L. *Kirby Smith's Confederacy: The Trans-Mississippi South, 1863–1865.* Reprint, Tuscaloosa: University of Alabama Press, 1991.

Klein, Philip S. *President James Buchanan: A Biography.* University Park: Pennsylvania State University Press, 1962.

Kneitel, Tom. *Directory of U.S. Army Forts, Camps, and Airfields, 1789–1945.* Commack, N.Y.: CRB Research Books, 1947.

Lane, Lydia Spencer. *I Married a Soldier: Or Old Days in the Old Army.* Philadelphia: J. B. Lippincott, 1893.

Lawrence, F. Lee, and Robert W. Glover. *Camp Ford, CSA: The Story of Union Prisoners in Texas.* Austin: Texas Civil War Centennial Advisory Committee, 1964.

Lawton, Eba Anderson, ed. *An Artillery Officer in the Mexican War, 1846–7: Letters of Robert Anderson.* New York: G. P. Putnam's Sons, 1911.

Lee, Edmund Jennings. *Lee of Virginia, 1642–1892.* Philadelphia: Franklin Publishing Co., 1894.

Lee, Fitzhugh. *General Lee.* New York: D. Appleton and Co., 1894.

Lee, Lawrence. *The History of Brunswick County, North Carolina.* N.p., 1978.

Lee, Robert E., Jr. *Recollections and Letters of General Robert E. Lee.* Garden City, N.Y.: Garden City Publishing Co., 1903.

Lee, Sarah P., ed. *Memoirs of William Nelson Pendleton, D.D.* Philadelphia: J. B. Lippincott, 1893.

Leech, Margaret. *Reveille in Washington, 1860–1865.* Reprint, New York: Time Incorporated, 1962.

Lewis, George Washington. *Address Delivered Before the Literary Society and Students of the Rappahannock Academy and Military Institute, July 30, 1851.* Washington, D.C.: Gideon and Co., 1852.

Lewis, Lloyd. *Captain Sam Grant.* Reprint, Boston: Little, Brown, 1991.

Linquist, G. E. E. *The Red Man in the United States.* Reprint, Clifton, New Jersey: Augustus M. Kelley Publishers, 1973.

Livermore, Thomas L. *Numbers and Losses in the American Civil War.* Boston: Houghton Mifflin, 1900.

Long, A. L. *Memoirs of Robert E. Lee: His Military and Personal History.* Reprint, Secaucus, N.J.: Blue and Gray Press, 1983.

Longstreet, James. *From Manassas to Appomattox: Memoirs of the Civil War in America.* Philadelphia: J. B. Lippincott, 1903.

Lonn, Ella. *Foreigners in the Confederacy.* Reprint, Gloucester, Mass.: Peter Smith, 1979.

Lubbock, Francis R. *Six Decades in Texas: Or Personal Memoirs of Francis Richard Lubbock.* Austin, Texas: Ben C. Jones and Co., Printers, 1900.

Magruder, Egbert Watson, ed. *Yearbook of the American Clan Gregor Society, 1913.* Richmond: Ware and Duke Printers, 1914.

———. *Yearbook of the American Clan Gregor Society, 1916.* Richmond: Appeals Press, 1916.

Magruder, John Bankhead. *Major General Magruder's Report of His Operations on the Peninsula and the Battles of Savage Station and Malvern Hill.* Richmond: C. H. Wynne Printers, 1862.

———. *Presidential Contest of 1856 in Three Letters.* San Antonio: Book and Job Office of the San Antonio Texan, 1856.

Mahon, James K. *History of the Second Seminole War, 1835–1845.* Gainesville: University of Florida Press, 1967.

Malone, Dumas, ed. *Dictionary of American Biography.* New York: Charles Scribner's Sons, 1928.

Mansfield, Edward D. *The Mexican War: A History of Its Origin.* New York: A. S. Barnes and Co., 1849.

Martin, Madeline. *More Early Northeast Texas Families.* Quanah, Texas: Nortex Press, 1978.

Marvel, William. *Andersonville: The Last Depot.* Chapel Hill and London: University of North Carolina Press, 1994.

Marszalek, John F. *Sherman: A Soldier's Passion for Order.* New York: Free Press, 1993.

McCaslin, Richard B. *Tainted Breeze: The Great Hanging at Gainesville, Texas, 1862.* Baton Rouge: Louisiana State University Press, 1994.

McClellan, George B. *Report on the Organization and Campaigns of the Army of the Potomac.* Reprint, Freeport, N.Y.: Books for Libraries Press, 1970.

McComb, David G. *Houston: A History.* Austin: University of Texas Press, 1981.

McCoy, Charles A. *Polk and the Presidency.* Austin: University of Texas Press, 1960.

McFeely, William S. *Grant: A Biography.* Reprint, New York and London: W. W. Norton, 1982.

McGregor, James C. *The Disruption of Virginia.* New York: Macmillan, 1922.

McMurry, Richard M. *John Bell Hood and the War for Southern Independence.* Lexington: University Press of Kentucky, 1982.

McPherson, James M. *Battle Cry of Freedom: The Civil War Era.* New York: Ballantine Books, 1988.

Meade, George. *The Life and Letters of George Gordon Meade.* New York: Charles Scribner's Sons, 1913.

Miller, Robert Ryal. *Mexico: A History.* Norman: University of Oklahoma Press, 1985.

Mitchison, Rosalind. *A History of Scotland.* London: Methuen and Co., 1970.

Moneyhon, Carl H. *The Impact of the Civil War and Reconstruction on Arkansas.* Baton Rouge: Louisiana State University Press, 1994.

Monroe, Haskell M., and James T. McIntosh, eds. *The Papers of Jefferson Davis, 1808–1840.* Baton Rouge: Louisiana State University Press, 1971.

Moore, Jerold N. *Confederate Commissary: Lucius Bellinger Northrop.* Shippensburg, Pa.: White Mane Publishing Co., 1995.

Morris, Jerome E. *The Brief Belligerence of Fort Macon.* Raleigh: North Carolina Confederate Centennial Commission, n.d.

Morrison, James L. *"The Best School in the World": West Point, the Pre–Civil War Years, 1833–1866.* Kent, Ohio: Kent State University Press, 1986.

Murray, Robert H., ed. *Maximilian: Emperor of Mexico, Memoirs of His Private Secretary, José Luís Blasio.* New Haven: Yale University Press, 1934.

Myres, William Starr, ed. *The Mexican War Diary of George B. McClellan.* Princeton: Princeton University Press, 1917.

Nadeau, Remi. *Los Angeles: From Mission to Modern City.* New York: Longmans, Green and Co., 1960.

Nance, John M. *After San Jacinto: The Texas–Mexican Frontier, 1836–1841.* Austin: University of Texas Press, 1963.

Nichols, James L. *The Confederate Quartermaster in the Trans-Mississippi.* Austin: University of Texas Press, 1964.

Nichols, Roy F. *Franklin Pierce: Young Hickory of the Granite Hills.* Philadelphia: University of Pennsylvania Press, 1931.

North, Thomas. *Five Years in Texas: Or What You Did Not Hear During the War.* Cincinnati: Elm Street Printing Company, 1871.

Nunn, W. C., ed. *Ten Texans in Gray*. Hillsboro, Texas: Hillsboro Junior College Press, 1968.

O'Connor, Richard. *The Cactus Throne: The Tragedy of Maximilian and Carlotta*. New York: G. P. Putnam's Sons, 1971.

O'Connor, Richard. *The Golden Summers: An Antic History of Newport*. New York: G. P. Putnam's Sons, 1974.

O'Flaherty, Daniel. *General Jo Shelby: Undefeated Rebel*. Chapel Hill: University of North Carolina Press, 1954.

Oates, Stephen B. *Confederate Cavalry West of the River*. Austin: University of Texas Press, 1961.

Oates, Stephen B., ed. *Rip Ford's Texas*. Austin: University of Texas Press, 1963.

Parkes, Henry B. *A History of Mexico*. Boston: Houghton Mifflin, 1960.

Parks, Joseph H. *General Edmund Kirby Smith, C.S.A.* Baton Rouge: Louisiana State University Press, 1954.

Parrish, T. Michael. *Richard Taylor: Soldier Prince of Dixie*. Chapel Hill: University of North Carolina Press, 1992.

Patterson, Gerard. *Rebels from West Point*. New York: Doubleday, 1987.

Pessen, Edward. *Jacksonian America: Society, Personality, and Politics*. Reprint, Homewood, Ill.: Dorsey Press, 1969.

Phillips, George H. *Chiefs and Challengers: Indian Resistance and Cooperation in Southern California*. Berkeley: University of California Press, 1975.

Piston, Walter Garrett. *James Longstreet and His Place in Southern History*. Athens: University of Georgia Press, 1987.

Polk, William M. *Leonidas Polk: Bishop and General*. New York: Longmans, Green and Co., 1915.

Pope-Hennessy, Una. *Edgar Allan Poe: A Critical Biography*. New York: Haskell House, 1971.

Potter, David M. *The Impending Crisis, 1848–1861*. New York: Harper & Row, 1976.

Powell, Henry. *List of Officers of the United States Army from 1799 to 1900*. New York: L. R. Hamersby and Company, 1900.

Proceedings of the Special Meeting of the Medical and Chirurgical Faculty of Maryland in Relation to the Death of Dr. Riggin Buckler, Held September 5, 1884. Baltimore: Journal Publishing Co., 1884.

Proctor, Ben H. *Not Without Honor: The Life of John H. Reagan*. Austin: University of Texas Press, 1962.

Putnam, Cora. *The Story of Houlton*. Portland, Maine: House of Falmouth, 1958.

Radolf, Morris L. *The Old Line State: A History of Maryland*. Annapolis: Hall of Records Commission, 1971.

Rawlings, Mary, ed. *Early Charlottesville: Recollections of James Alexander, 1828–1874*. Charlottesville: Mitchie Company, 1942.

Remini, Robert V. *Henry Clay: Statesman for the Union*. New York: W. W. Norton, 1991.

Revised Statutes of the State of North Carolina . . . 1836–1837. Raleigh: Turner and Hughes, 1837.

Rhodes, Charles Dudley. *Robert E. Lee: West Pointer*. Richmond: Garrett and Massie, 1932.

Robards, Charles L., and A. M. Jackson. *Reports of Cases Argued and Decided in the Supreme Court of Texas . . . 1863–1865*. St. Louis: Gilbert Book Co., 1903.

Roberts, O. M. *Texas*, in *Confederate Military History*. Atlanta: Confederate Publishing Co., 1899.

Roberts, Robert B. *Encyclopedia of Historic Forts: The Military, Pioneer, and Trading Posts of the United States*. New York: Macmillan, 1988.

Robertson, James I. *General A. P. Hill: The Story of a Confederate Warrior*. New York: Random House, 1987.

Rolle, Andrew F. *The Lost Cause: The Confederate Exodus to Mexico*. Norman: University of Oklahoma Press, 1965.

Roseboom, Eugene H. *A History of Presidential Elections*. New York: Macmillan, 1959.

Royster, Charles. *The Destructive War: William Tecumseh Sherman, Stonewall Jackson and the Americans*. New York: Alfred A. Knopf, 1991.

Ruckert, Norman G. *Fort McHenry: Home of the Brave*. Baltimore: Bodine and Associates, 1983.

Ruiz, Ramon Eduards. *An American in Maximilian's Mexico, 1865–1866: Diaries of William Marshall Anderson*. San Marino, Calif.: Huntington Library, 1959.

Sackett, Frances Robertson. *Dick Dowling*. Houston: Gulf Publishing Co., 1937.

Sanborn, Margaret. *Robert E. Lee: The Complete Man*. Philadelphia: J. B. Lippincott, 1967.

Sandburg, Carl. *Abraham Lincoln: The War Years*. New York: Harcourt, Brace, 1947.

Scharf, J. Thomas. *The Chronicles of Baltimore: Being a Complete History of "Baltimore Town" and Baltimore City*. Reprint, New York: Kennikat Press, 1972.

———. *History of the Confederate Navy from Its Organization to the Surrender of Its Last Vessel*. New York: Rogers and Sherwood, 1887.

Scott, Ed. *San Diego County Soldiers-Pioneers, 1846–1866*. National City, Calif.: Crest Publishing Co., 1976.

Scott, Winfield. *Memoirs: By Himself*. New York: Sheldon and Co., 1867.

Sears, Stephen W. *George B. McClellan: The Young Napoleon*. New York: Ticknor and Fields, 1988.

———. *To the Gates of Richmond: The Peninsula Campaign*. New York: Ticknor and Fields, 1992.

Secretary of War. *The War of the Rebellion: A Compilation of the Official Records of the Union and Confederate Armies*. Washington, D.C.: Government Printing Office, 1880 ff.

Secretary of the Society for the History of the Germans in Maryland, *Sixth Annual Report*. Baltimore: n.p., n.d.

Selby, John. *Stonewall Jackson as Military Commander*. London: B. T. Batsford, 1968.

Short History of General J. B. Magruder (packed in Duke's Cigarettes). New York: Knapp and Co., Lithographers, 1888.

Simpson, Brooks D., ed. *With Grant and Meade: From the Wilderness to Appomattox*. Lincoln and London: University of Nebraska Press, 1994.

Simpson, Harold B. *Hood's Texas Brigade: Lee's Grenadier Guard*. Waco: Texian Press, 1970.

Simpson, Harold B., and Marcus J. Wright. *Texas in the War, 1861–1865.* Hillsboro, Texas: Hill County Junior College Press, 1965.

Smith, Arthur D. S. *Old Fuss and Feathers: The Life and Exploits of Lt. General Winfield Scott.* New York: Greystone Press, 1937.

Smith, David Paul. *Frontier Defense in the Civil War: Texas' Rangers and Rebels.* College Station: Texas A&M University Press, 1992.

Smith, George W., and Charles Judah. *Chronicles of the Gringoes: The U.S. Army in Mexico, 1846–1848.* Albuquerque: University of New Mexico Press, 1968.

Smith, Gustavus W. *The Battle of Seven Pines.* New York: C. G. Crawford, Printer and Stationer, 1918.

Smith, Justin H. *The War with Mexico.* New York: Macmillan, 1917.

Smyrl, Frank H. *Texas in Gray: The Civil War Years, 1861–1865.* Boston: American Press, 1983.

Smythe, William E. *History of San Diego.* San Diego: The History Company, 1907.

Snow, William P. *Lee and His Generals.* Reprint, New York: Fairfax Press, 1982.

Sobel, Robert S., and John Raimo. *Biographical Directory of the Governors of the United States, 1787–1978.* Westport, Conn.: Meckler Books, 1978.

Sorrel, G. Moxley. *Reflections of a Confederate Staff Officer.* New York: Neale Publishing Co., 1905.

Sparks, A. W. *Recollections of the Great War.* Tyler, Texas: Lee and Burnett, 1901.

Starr, Stephen Z. *The Union Cavalry in the Civil War.* Baton Rouge: Louisiana State University Press, 1979.

Steiner, Bernard C. *Life of Reverdy Johnson.* Baltimore: Norman, Remington Co., 1914.

Stewart, George R., *John Phoenix, Esq., The Veritable Squibob: A Life of Captain George H. Derby, U.S.A.* Reprint, New York: Da Capo Press, 1969.

Sunderman, James F., ed. *Journey into the Wilderness: An Army Surgeon's Account of Life in Camp and Field During the Creek and Seminole Wars, 1836–1838, by Jacob Rhett Motte.* Gainesville: University of Florida Press, 1953.

Swanberg, W. A. *First Blood: The Story of Fort Sumter.* New York: Charles Scribner's Sons, 1882.

Swinton, William. *Campaigns of the Army of the Potomac.* New York: Charles Scribner's Sons, 1882.

Symonds, Craig L. *Joseph E. Johnston: A Civil War Biography.* New York: W. W. Norton, 1992.

Taylor, Richard. *Deconstruction and Reconstruction: Personal Experiences of the Late War.* New York: D. Appleton and Co., 1879.

Taylor, Walter, H. *Four Years with General Lee.* New York: D. Appleton and Co., 1877.

Taylor, Zachary. *Letters of Zachary Taylor from the Battle Fields of Mexico.* Reprint, New York: Kraus, 1970.

Tebeau, Charlton. *A History of Florida.* Coral Gables, Fla.: University of Miami Press, 1971.

Terrell, Alexander Watkins. *From Texas to Mexico and the Court of Maximilian.* Reprint, Dallas: The Book Club of Texas, 1933.

Thomas, Benjamin P., and Harold M. Hyman. *Stanton: The Life and Times of Lincoln's Secretary of War.* New York: Alfred A. Knopf, 1962.

Thomas, Emory M. *The Confederate Nation, 1861–1865*. New York: Harper & Row, 1977.

———. *Richmond: The Peninsula Campaign*. Harrisburg, Pa.: Eastern Alcorn Press, 1985.

———. *Robert E. Lee: A Biography*. New York: W. W. Norton, 1995.

Thomason, John W. *JEB Stuart*. Reprint, New York: Charles Scribner's Sons, 1959.

Thompson, Jerry Don. *Mexican-Texans in the Union Army*. El Paso: Texas Western Press, 1986.

———. *Vaqueros in Blue and Gray*. Austin: Presidial Press, 1976.

Thorpe, Thomas Bangs. *Our Army on the Rio Grande*. Philadelphia: Cary and Hart, 1848.

Tolbert, Frank X. *Dick Dowling at Sabine Pass*. New York: McGraw-Hill, 1962.

Turner, Frederick Jackson. *The United States, 1830–1850: The Nation and Its Sections*. New York: Henry Holt and Co., 1935.

Tyler, Lyon G., ed. *Encyclopedia of Virginia Biography*. New York: Lewis Publishing Co., 1915.

Utley, Robert M. *Frontiersmen in Blue: The United States Army and the Indian, 1848–1865*. New York: Macmillan, 1967.

University of Virginia. *Catalogue of Students, 1826*. Charlottesville: University of Virginia, 1826.

Van Deusen, Glyndon. *The Jacksonian Era, 1828–1848*. Reprint, New York: Harper & Row, 1963.

Vandiver, Frank E. *Mighty Stonewall*. New York: McGraw-Hill, 1957.

———. *Their Tattered Flags: The Epic of the Confederacy*. New York: Harper's Magazine Press, 1970.

Wakelyn, Jon L. *Biographical Directory of the Confederacy*. Westport, Conn.: Greenwood Press, 1977.

Waller, John L. *Colossal Hamilton of Texas*. El Paso: Texas Western Press, 1968.

Walton, George. *Sentinel of the Plains: Fort Leavenworth*. Englewood Cliffs, N.J.: Prentice-Hall, 1973.

Watson, Alan D. *A History of New Bern and Craven County*. New Bern, N.C.: Tyron Palace Commission, 1987.

Wayland, Francis Key. *Andrew Stevenson: Democrat and Diplomat*. Philadelphia: University of Pennsylvania Press, 1949.

Webb, Alexander S. *The Peninsula: McClellan's Campaign of 1862*. Reprint, New York: John Brussell Publishers, 1959.

Weems, John Edward. *To Conquer a Peace: The War Between the United States and Mexico*. Garden City, N.Y.: Doubleday, 1947.

White, Henry Alexander. *Robert E. Lee and the Southern Confederacy*. New York: G. P. Putnam's Sons, 1910.

White, Jon M. *Everyday Life of the American Indians*. New York: Dorsey Press, 1979.

White, William Chapman. *Adirondack Country*. New York: Alfred A. Knopf, 1968.

White, William Chapman, and Ruth White. *Tin Can on a Shingle*. New York: E. P. Dutton, 1957.

Wilcox, Cadmus. *History of the Mexican War*. Washington, D.C.: Church News Publishing Co., 1892.

Williams, Amelia, and Eugene C. Barker, eds. *The Writings of Sam Houston, 1823–1863.* Austin: University of Texas Press, 1945.

Williams, Frances Leigh. *Matthew Fontaine Maury: Scientist of the Sea.* New Brunswick, N.J.: Rutgers University Press, 1963.

Williams, Kenneth P. *Lincoln Finds a General: A Military Study of the Civil War.* New York: Macmillan, 1964.

Williams, T. Harry. *P. G. T. Beauregard: Napoleon in Gray.* Baton Rouge: Louisiana State University Press, 1954.

Wilson, Major L. *The Presidency of Martin Van Buren.* Lawrence: University Press of Kansas, 1984.

Wingfield, Marshall. *A History of Caroline County, Virginia: From Its Formation in 1727 to 1924.* Richmond: Trevvet Christian Co., 1924.

Wise, Jennings C. *The Long Arm of Lee: The History of the Artillery in the Army of Northern Virginia.* Reprint, New York: Oxford University Press, 1959.

———. *The Military History of the Virginia Military Institute, 1831–1865.* Lynchburg, Va.: J. B. Bell Co., 1915.

Wise, Stephen R. *Lifeline of the Confederacy: Blockade Running During the Civil War.* Columbia: University of South Carolina Press, 1988.

Woodward, Arthur. *Feud on the Colorado.* Los Angeles: Westernlore Press, 1955.

Wooster, Ralph A. *The Secession Conventions of the South.* Princeton: Princeton University Press, 1962.

Wright, Marcus J. *General Officers of the Confederate Army.* New York: Neale Publishing Co., 1911.

Yearns, W. Buck. *The Confederate Governors.* Athens: University of Georgia Press, 1985.

——— Articles ———

Baker, B. G. "Monument to General Magruder." *Confederate Veteran* 5 (1897).

Barr, Alwyn. "Texas Coastal Defense, 1861–1865." *Southwestern Historical Quarterly* 65 (July 1961).

———. "Texan Losses in the Red River Campaign." *Texas Military History* 3 (Summer 1963).

Barry, Richard S. "Fort Macon: Its History." *North Carolina Historical Review* 27 (April 1950).

Bearss, Edwin C. "The Confederate Attempt to Regain Fort Smith." *Arkansas Historical Quarterly* 28 (Winter 1969).

Bratton, John. "The Battle of Williamsburg." *Southern Historical Society Papers* 8 (1879).

Bryan, Charles F. "The Siege of Yorktown." *Civil War Times Illustrated* 21 (1982).

Carr, Joseph B. "Operations of 1861 about Fort Monroe." In *Battles and Leaders of the Civil War.* New York: Century Co., 1887.

Clinton, Amy Cheney. "Historic Fort Washington." *Maryland Historical Magazine* 32 (September 1937).

Conner, Forrest, ed. "Letters of Lieutenant Robert H. Miller to His Family, 1861–1862." *Virginia Magazine of History and Biography* 70 (January 1962).

Coxe, John. "In the Battle of Seven Pines." *Confederate Veteran* 30 (1922).

Cridlin, William. "Caroline County Marriage Records." *Virginia Magazine of History and Biography* 38 (October 1929).

Dabney, Robert L. "Memoir of a Narrative Received from Colonel John B. Baldwin of Staunton Touching on the Origins of the War." *Southern Historical Society Papers* 1 (January–June 1876).

DeBray, X. B. "A Sketch of DeBray's Twenty-Sixth Regiment of Texas Cavalry." *Southern Historical Society Papers* 12 (1884).

Dinkins, James. "The Battle of Big Bethel, Va." *Confederate Veteran* 26 (1918).

Douglas, Hugh Thomas. "A Famous Army and Its Commander: Sketch of the Army of the Peninsula and General Magruder." *Southern Historical Society Papers* 42 (1917).

"Ebbitt." "John Magruder." *Army and Navy Journal* 19 (25 September 1880).

Elliott, Claude. "Union Sentiment in Texas, 1861–1865." *Southwestern Historical Quarterly* 50 (April 1947).

Ewing, Floyd E. "Unionist Sentiment on the Northwest Texas Frontier." *West Texas Historical Association Yearbook* 33 (1957).

Fitzhugh, Lester N. "Saluria, Fort Esperanza, and Military Operations on the Texas Coast, 1861–1864." *Southwestern Historical Quarterly* 61 (July 1957).

———. "Texas Forces in the Red River Campaign." *Texas Military History* 3 (Spring 1953).

Gallagher, Gary W. "The Fall of Prince John Magruder." *Civil War* 19 (August 1989).

Geise, William R. "General Holmes Fails to Create a Department, August, 1862–February, 1863." *Military History of Texas and the Southwest* 14 (1978).

———. "Kirby Smith's War Department, 1864: A Study of Organization and Command in the Trans-Mississippi West." *Military History of Texas and the Southwest* 15 (1979).

Goss, Warren Lee. "Yorktown and Williamsburg: Reflections of a Private." In *Battles and Leaders of the Civil War.* New York: Century Co., 1887.

Grimsley, Mark. "Inside a Beleaguered City: A Commander and Actor, Prince John Magruder." *Civil War Times Illustrated* 21 (September 1982).

Harmon, George D. "Confederate Migrations to Mexico." *Hispanic American Historical Review* 17 (November 1937).

Hill, Daniel H. "The Real Stonewall Jackson." *Century Magazine* 25 (February 1884).

Hord, B. M. "The Battle of Big Bethel, Va." *Confederate Veteran* 26 (1918).

James, Joseph B. "West Point One Hundred Years Ago." *Mississippi Valley Historical Review* 31 (December 1944).

Johnston, Joseph E. "Manassas to Seven Pines." In *Battles and Leaders of the Civil War.* New York: Century Co., 1888.

Lee, Baker P. "Magruder's Peninsula Campaign in 1862." *Southern Historical Society Papers* 19 (1891).

Long, A. L. "Memoir of General John Bankhead Magruder." *Southern Historical Society Papers* 12 (1884).

Lowe, R. G. "Magruder's Defense of the Peninsula." *Confederate Veteran* 8 (1900).

Magruder, Allan B. "A Piece of Secret History: President Lincoln and the Virginia Convention of 1861." *Atlantic Monthly* 35 (April 1870).

Maury, Richard L. "The Battle of Williamsburg and the Charge of the Twenty-Fourth Virginia of Early's Brigade." *Southern Historical Society Papers* 8 (1880).

McClellan, George B. "The Peninsula Campaign." In *Battles and Leaders of the Civil War.* New York: Century Co., 1888.

McDonald, Harold L. "The Battle of Jenkins Ferry." *Arkansas Historical Quarterly* 7 (Spring 1948).

Meiners, Fredericka. "Hamilton P. Bee in the Red River Campaign of 1864." *Southwestern Historical Quarterly* 78 (July 1974).

———. "The Texas Border Cotton Trade, 1862–1863." *Civil War History* 33 (December 1977).

Oates, Stephen B. "Texas Under the Secessionists." *Southwestern Historical Quarterly* 47 (October 1963).

Padgett, James A. "Life of Alfred Mordecia in Mexico, 1865–1866, as Told in His Letters to His Family." *North Carolina Historical Review* 22 (April 1945).

———. "Life of Alfred Mordecia in Mexico, 1865–1866, as Told to His Wife in His Letters—Part 4." *North Carolina Historical Review* 23 (January 1946).

Pohl, James W. "The Influence of Henri de Jomini on Winfield Scott's Campaign in Mexico." *Southwestern Historical Quarterly* 77 (July 1873).

Rainwater, Percy L., ed. "The Autobiography of Benjamin Grubb Humphreys, August 26, 1808–December 20, 1882." *Mississippi Valley Historical Review* 21 (June 1934).

Ramsdell, Charles W. "The Texas Military Board, 1862–1865." *Southwestern Historical Quarterly* 27 (April 1924).

"A Regular." "The Soldiers' Temperance Movement." *Army and Navy Journal* 21 (20 October 1883).

Rister, Carl Coke. "Carlota: A Confederate Colony in Mexico." *Journal of Southern History* 10 (February 1945).

Scheiber, Harry N. "The Pay of Troops and Confederate Morale in the Trans-Mississippi." *Arkansas Historical Quarterly* 18 (Summer 1959).

Scott, Geraldine Tidd. "Fortifications on Maine's Boundary, 1828–1845." *Maine Historical Quarterly* 29 (Winter/Spring 1990).

Smith, Rebecca W., and Marion Mullins, eds. "The Diary of H. C. Medford: Confederate Soldier." *Southwestern Historical Quarterly* 34 (October 1930).

Smith, Washington J. "Battle of Sabine Pass." *Confederate Veteran* 27 (1919).

Smyrl, Frank H. "Texans in the Union Army, 1861–1865." *Southwestern Historical Quarterly* 65 (October 1961).

———. "Unionism in Texas." *Southwestern Historical Quarterly* 68 (October 1964).

Spell, Lota M. "Music in Texas." *Civil War History* 4 (September 1958).

Stark, Burwell. "Reminiscences." *Alumni Bulletin of the University of Virginia* 1 (1894).

Swift, Eben. "The Military Education of Robert E. Lee." *Virginia Magazine of History and Biography* 35 (August 1927).

Tucker, Philip C. "The United States Gunboat *Harriet Lane.*" *Southwestern Historical Quarterly* 21 (April 1918).

Waterman, Robert E., and Thomas Rothrock, eds. "The Earle-Buchanan Letters of 1861–1876." *Arkansas Historical Quarterly* 23 (Summer 1974).

Westwood, Howard C. "The Battle of Galveston." *U.S. Naval Institute Proceedings* 109 (1983).

Wooster, Ralph A. "With the Confederate Cavalry in the West: The Civil War Experience of Isaac Dunbar Affleck." *Southwestern Historical Quarterly* 80 (July 1979).

Wynne, Mae Samuella Magruder. "General John Bankhead Magruder." In *Year Book of the American Clan Gregor Society, 1913*. (Richmond: Ware and Duke, Printers, 1914.)

Young, Jo. "The Battle of Sabine Pass." *Southwestern Historical Quarterly* 52 (January 1949).

—— Theses and Dissertations ——

Barr, Alwyn. "Confederate Artillery in the Trans-Mississippi." M.A. thesis, University of Texas, Austin, 1961.

Barry, Richard S. "The History of Fort Macon." M.A. thesis, Duke University, 1950.

Bowen, Nancy Head. "A Political Labyrinth: Texas in the Civil War—Questions in Continuity." Ph.D. diss., Rice University, 1974.

Hoovestol, Paeder Joel. "Galveston in the Civil War." M.A. thesis, University of Houston, 1950.

Milota, Robert Stephen. "John Bankhead Magruder: The California Years." M.A. thesis, University of San Diego, 1990.

Settles, Thomas M. "The Military Career of John Bankhead Magruder." Ph.D. diss., Texas Christian University, 1972.

Spell, Timothy D. "John Bankhead Magruder: Defender of the Texas Coast, 1863." M.A. thesis, Lamar University, 1981.

Walker, Sarah Elizabeth. "San Antonio During the Civil War." M.A. thesis, Sam Houston State Teachers College, 1942.

White, John L. "Founder of Fort Yuma: Excerpts from the Diary of Major Samuel Heintzelman, U.S.A., 1849–1853." M.A. thesis, University of San Diego, 1975.

—— Miscellaneous Sources ——

Class Rolls (Fourth Class Rolls, 1827, Third Class Rolls, 1828, and First Class Rolls, 1830), vol. 1, Register of Merit, Personal Records—Records Relating to Cadets, Records of the United States Military Academy, Record Group 404, National Archives, records on deposit at U.S. Military Academy, West Point.

Delinquency Record of J. B. Magruder, Record of Delinquencies, 1822–1828, p. 544, Department of Tactics, 1813–1875, Records of the United States Military Academy, Record Group 404, National Archives, records on deposit at U.S. Military Academy, West Point.

Katherine Elliott Essay. Typescript. Center for the Study of American History, University of Texas, Austin.

Hamilton, S. G. DeR. "The Site of Fort Johnston." Copy of 1911 address in North Carolina State Library, Raleigh.

Hanks, Orlando, T. "History of Captain B. F. Benton's Company, 1861–1865." Typescript. Stephen F. Austin State University Library, Nacogdoches, Texas.

Houston City Directory, 1877–1878.

Magruder, J. B., Matriculation Records, Alderman Library, University of Virginia Archives, Charlottesville.

Magruder, J. B. "Official Record of Gen. J. B. Magruder." Handwritten manuscript, bound by Charles C. Jones, 1941. Perkins Library, Duke University.

Muster Roll for 1828, 1829, 1830, Muster Rolls, Corps of Cadets, vol. 3, 1825–1830. Records of the Department of Tactics, Records of the United States Military Academy, Record Group 404, National Archives, records on deposit at U.S. Military Academy, West Point.

"Roll of Attorneys." Handwritten ledger, California State Archives, Sacramento.

Althea Wanda Shaver Narrative. Center for the Study of American History, University of Texas, Austin.

Index